THE
Catholic Faith Handbook
FOR YOUTH

THE
Catholic
Faith
Handbook
FOR YOUTH

Brian Singer-Towns
with
Janet Claussen
Clare vanBrandwijk
and other contributors

Genuine recycled paper with 10% post-consumer waste.
Printed with soy-based ink. 50534

The Ad Hoc Committee to Oversee the Use of the Catechism, United States Conference of Catholic Bishops, has found this catechetical text, copyright 2003, to be in conformity with the *Catechism of the Catholic Church.*

Nihil Obstat: Rev. William M. Becker, STD
   Censor Librorum
   August 1, 2003
Imprimatur: † Most Rev. Bernard J. Harrington, DD
   Bishop of Winona
   August 1, 2003

The nihil obstat and imprimatur are official declarations that a book or pamphlet is free of doctrinal or moral error. No implication is contained therein that those who have granted the nihil obstat or imprimatur agree with the contents, opinions, or statements expressed.

Janet Claussen, Brian Singer-Towns, and Clare vanBrandwijk were the principal authors. Nora Bradbury-Haehl, Ellen Cavanaugh, Maura Hagarty, Barbara Murray, Betty Singer-Towns, and Fred Thelen authored the supplemental articles. Eileen Daily, Laurie Delgatto, Marilyn Kielbasa, Lorraine Kilmartin, and Thomas Zanzig were the principal consultants and reviewers.

The publishing team for this book included Brian Singer-Towns, general editor; Mary Koehler, permissions editor; Laurie Berg-Shaner, copy editor; James H. Gurley, production editor; settingPace, LLC, Cincinnati, typesetter; Andy Palmer, designer; Alan S. Hanson, pre-press specialist; Genevieve Nagel, image researcher; Margaret Hentz, indexer; manufacturing coordinated by the production services department of Saint Mary's Press.

The acknowledgments continue on page 445.

Printed in the United States of America

Printing: 9 8 7 6 5 4 3 2 1

Year: 2012 11 10 09 08 07 06 05 04

ISBN 0-88489-759-1, paper
ISBN 0-88489-767-2, hardcover

Library of Congress Cataloging-in-Publication Data

Singer-Towns, Brian.
  The Catholic faith handbook for youth / by Brian Singer-Towns, Janet Claussen, Clare vanBrandwijk, and contributing authors.
  p. cm.
Summary: Introduces teens to Catholic beliefs, art, culture, and history as expressed in the Catechism of the Catholic Church, discussing Church teachings on social issues of today and providing ideas for putting faith into action.
ISBN 0-88489-759-1 (pbk.)
  1. Catechisms, English. 2. Catholic Church—Catechisms—English. 3. Christian education—Textbooks for youth—Catholic. [1. Catholic Church—Catechisms. 2. Catechisms. 3. Christian life.] I. Claussen, Janet. II. VanBrandwijk, Clare. III. Title.
BX1961 .S56 2003
268'.82—dc21

               2002156174

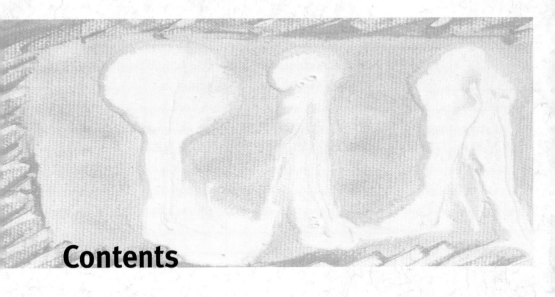

Contents

Part B: Liturgy and Sacraments

Part C: Christian Morality

Part D: Christian Prayer

Catholic Quick Facts

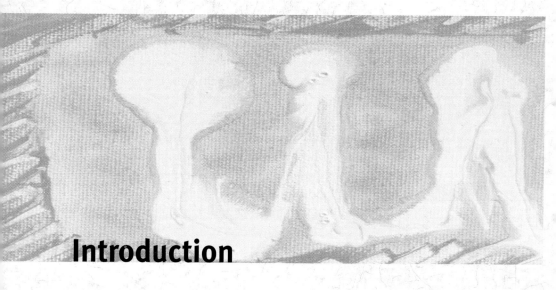

Introduction

"My Dear Young Friends"

Pope John Paul II begins many of his talks to youth with these words. It is also a fitting welcome to this handbook about Catholic beliefs and practices. It may seem presumptuous to address you as a friend when we haven't personally met. But it is symbolic of a truth that the Holy Father (another name for the Pope) is constantly living out, the belief that we are all one family. Every member of the human race is a member of that family, united by the one God who created us all, which is why we should be able to call one another friends, despite differences in nationality or religious beliefs.

Within the human family is another large family, the family of those who are members of the Catholic Church. This handbook is a guide to that family, an overview of the important teachings and beliefs of the Catholic Church. You may be a member of that family, and as a baptized Catholic, you are using this handbook as a textbook or reference book in a religion class. Or you may be using this handbook as part of a program preparing you to become a member of the Catholic family. Or perhaps you are reading this handbook simply because you are curious about what Catholics believe and do.

This handbook has been created for all these purposes. Its uniqueness is that it was created especially for teens and young adults. It is not a child's book. You will not find any cartoon

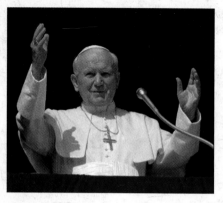

characters or cute talking vegetables—which have their place, but not here! We have created it to respect your curiosity and provide you with honest, to-the-point answers. Every word and image has been carefully chosen to show you something about Catholic beliefs, art, culture, and history.

We who created this handbook care deeply about young people, and about the Catholic Church, so we dare to call you our dear young friends. We hope and pray that you enjoy using this handbook as much as we enjoyed creating it.

Pope John Paul II is an enthusiastic supporter of young people.

This Handbook and the *Catechism of the Catholic Church*

You may have heard of a book called the *Catechism of the Catholic Church* (referred to from here on as the *Catechism* or *CCC*). Perhaps you have seen a copy at home or at school. It is a book of the most important teachings of the Catholic Church. The Pope himself approved the *Catechism*. Bishops, priests, youth ministers, teachers, and other adult Catholics use it as a reference book for authentic Catholic teaching. This handbook reflects the *Catechism* in its content and structure.

For example, the *Catechism* is divided into four major sections. Each section reflects an important aspect of Catholic teaching. This book follows the same structure. After a couple of introductory chapters, you will find the following sections:

- **Part A.** This section is an overview of what Catholics believe about God, Jesus Christ, the Holy Spirit, and the Church. It is based on the Apostles' Creed.
- **Part B.** This section is an overview of how Catholics worship God and encounter Jesus Christ through the seven sacraments of the Church.

○ **Part C.** This section is about Catholic moral decision-making, sin, and conscience. The Ten Commandments are used as the basis for exploring and understanding what the Church teaches about specific moral issues.

○ **Part D.** This section is about the Church's teaching on prayer. It talks about types of prayer, ways of praying, and what we pray for when we pray the Lord's Prayer.

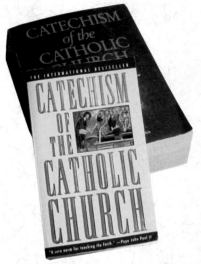

In a way this book is like a *Catechism* for teens. It contains the essential teachings of the *Catechism of the Catholic Church* but is presented using language and examples that will be easier for you to understand. Each chapter also contains additional short articles to help you further understand and live these teachings. The boxes on this page will explain the purpose of the five types of articles you will find in most chapters.

Did You Know?

The chapters do not explain everything there is to know about the Catholic faith. They cover the essentials, the basics. The Did You Know? articles give additional information that a well-informed Catholic should be aware of. They provide you with the answers to questions like, "Why are the priest's vestments (special clothing worn during Mass) different colors at different times of the year?" or "How many Catholics are there in the world?" If you familiarize yourself with the Did You Know? articles, you can amaze your family and friends with your knowledge of Catholic trivia!

The *Catechism of the Catholic Church* is the authoritative source for Catholic beliefs. This handbook reflects its content and structure.

LIVE it!

The Live It articles contain ideas and advice for putting your faith into action. A faith that isn't lived out isn't true faith. The Letter of James says:

> What good is it, my brothers and sisters, if you say you have faith but do not have works? Can faith save you? If a brother or sister is naked and lacks daily food, and one of you says to them, "Go in peace; keep warm and eat your fill," and yet you do not supply their bodily needs, what is the good of that? So faith by itself, if it has no works, is dead. (2:14–17)

In the Live It articles, you will find advice on setting up a prayer time, suggestions for keeping control of your tongue, ideas on how to respond when someone questions your faith, and a description of how to go to confession. You will find that the Live It articles contain lots of solid, practical advice.

Looking Back

The Catholic Church has a long and rich history, and most of us are familiar with only a little piece of it. The Looking Back articles will help you understand and appreciate more of our history. They describe historical events, present the teaching of saints and Church leaders, and explain why certain Church councils were called. Through the Looking Back articles, you will gain a better appreciation of the wisdom of two thousand years of Church history.

Saintly Profiles

The Catholic Church has an important tradition of honoring women and men whose holy life is an inspiration to others. These are the official saints of the Catholic Church, and there are hundreds of them. The Saintly Profile articles give you short biographies of thirty-seven of these saints. These saints were chosen to represent the wide variety of people that have become official saints in the Catholic Church. Most of them are famous names that you will hear if you hang around involved Catholics for very long. We hope their stories will inspire you to learn more about these great people and to explore your own call to holiness. The date of each saint's feast day is also given, which is the day the Church designates for remembering and celebrating the saint's life.

Prayer is a rich part of the Catholic tradition. As a young person, you may not yet have experienced all the ways in which Catholics pray. These articles will expose you to lots of different ways to expand your prayer life. They will teach you the Jesus prayer, how to create your own blessing prayer, and how to say traditional prayers like the rosary. Many of the articles explain different aspects of the liturgy, the public worship of the Church. They include quotes from the prayers used in the Mass and the sacraments so you can reflect on the meaning of these prayers more deeply.

Catholic Quick Facts

In addition to the material in the chapters, you will find a treasury of easy-to-access information at the end of the book. We call this information Catholic Quick Facts, and in it you will find the following sections:

- lists of Catholic beliefs and practices
- a collection of traditional Catholic prayers and devotions
- timeline with important dates and events from the history of the Catholic Church
- a list of patron saints and their causes
- a glossary of Catholic terms and their definitions

Turn to Catholic Quick Facts when you want to find a prayer for a special need, find a list with the gifts of the Holy Spirit, or look up the meaning of a word you are not familiar with. You may find it interesting just to browse through these lists from time to time.

How to Use This Handbook

You can make use of this handbook in many ways. You may be using it as a textbook for your parish religious education program or Confirmation preparation program. But this handbook isn't meant to be used just as a textbook. It's a guide you can use in many different ways.

For example, you and your Confirmation sponsor or mentor could read it together. When you meet, use the reflection questions at the end of each chapter to discuss how you feel about what you have learned and read. A parent might be interested in doing this with you as a way to brush up on his or her Catholic faith.

Maybe you want to use this book just for private reading, and go through it in your own time. The chapters are short, so it won't take you long to read through one. If you do read the handbook this way, we suggest that you keep a Bible close at hand. The handbook contains many references to Bible stories and passages that you will want to look up.

Or maybe you just want to keep this book handy as a reference when you have a question about the Catholic faith. The index in the back will help you quickly find a specific teaching or topic. The handbook was designed to make it quick and easy for you to find the information you need. Take it with you on retreats and conferences so that if questions come up, you have a resource handy with answers you can trust.

The people at Saint Mary's Press believe in you. We want you to experience the deep peace, joy, and love that come through faith in Jesus Christ and membership in his Church. We hope this handbook will help you to better understand what faith in Jesus and membership in the Church truly mean. With Saint Paul we pray, "that the one who began a good work among you will bring it to completion by the day of Jesus Christ" (Philippians 1:6). God bless you!

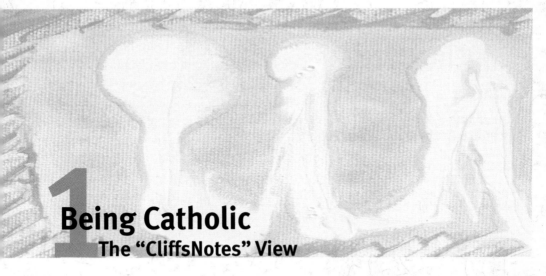

Being Catholic
The "CliffsNotes" View

Being Catholic means many different things to people. For some people it means a whole culture or way of being in the world. It means Friday fish fries, Advent wreaths and crucifixes, having priests and sisters as friends, and saying rosaries, among many other things. For these folks, being Catholic is a wonderful way of experiencing God in the world and following Jesus Christ. We hope you know some Catholics like this.

On the other hand, many people's only understanding of Catholicism comes from what they see and hear in the popular media. They see the priest or bishop involved in a scandal, the Catholic social activist, and the nuns from *Sister Act*. The media also present us with the travels of Pope John Paul II and the heroic service of Mother Teresa and her sisters. The popular image of Catholicism formed by the media is filled with stereotypes and misinformation, and is an inadequate source for truly understanding what Catholics are all about.

This book will help you understand what motivates the devoted Catholic, and how to figure out what is true and what isn't true in what you see and hear in the popular media. This chapter begins with some basic facts about Catholics and a brief overview about what we believe as Catholics. But don't settle for this "CliffsNotes" view of Catholicism. Let it whet your appetite for exploring the rest of the book!

Why Are All These People Catholic?

It is estimated that there are just over one billion Catholics living in the world. That is about 17 percent of the world's population. There are more Catholics than there are people in any other Christian denomination. There are also more Catholics than there are Jews, Hindus, or Buddhists—only Muslims have more members. Catholics and Catholic Churches can be found almost anywhere in the world.

So what do these numbers mean? Let's be honest. On the one hand, they do not necessarily mean anything at all. A religion isn't necessarily good or true simply because lots of people belong. The truth of Catholicism cannot be determined by how many people are Catholic.

On the other hand, the great number of Catholics in the world testifies to Catholicism's universal appeal and to the power that the Catholic faith has in people's lives. Since the Catholic Church's humble beginnings following the death and Resurrection of Jesus Christ, it has truly become a worldwide religion. People of every nationality and cultural background embrace it. Surely such a religious tradition must have something compelling to offer.

If you ask a dozen different Catholics what is compelling about their faith, you will probably get a dozen different answers. This is one of the wonderful things about the Catholic faith! Its rich tradition provides something for all people, no matter what their particular personality or spiritual need may be. The Catholic Church includes people who desire quiet, meditative prayer as well as those who enjoy communal prayer filled with sound and action. The Catholic Church embraces people who desire a clear and unchanging set of beliefs, as well as those who want to explore how those beliefs are applied to different cultures and a changing world. The Catholic Church is made

Did You Know?

How Many Catholics Are There?

Catholics in North America
Canada: 12.6 million Catholics (44 percent of the population)
Mexico: 125.8 million Catholics (90 percent of the population)
United States: 63.7 million Catholics (23 percent of the population)

Catholics in the World
Africa: 124.2 million (15.5 percent of the population)
North America: 219.1 million (46 percent of the population)
South America: 293 million (87.3 percent of the population)
Asia: 107 million (2.9 percent of the population)
Europe: 281.7 million (41.3 percent of the population)
Oceania: 8 million (27.5 percent of the population)

(Source: 2002 *Catholic Almanac*)

up of people who provide direct service to those in need as well as people who want to change structures in society to create a more just world.

But if you listen carefully, you will hear some common threads when Catholics talk about what is important to them about the Catholic faith. They often will talk about the beliefs of the Catholic faith that are rooted in the revelation of the Scriptures and Tradition (more on that in the next chapter). They also talk about the practices of the Catholic faith, the ways in which Catholics pray and make moral decisions. And they talk about the worldview of Catholicism, that is, the attitudes that Catholics display as they live out their faith in the world. Let's look briefly at these three areas: beliefs, practices, and attitudes.

Some Core Catholic Beliefs

The following list is meant to give you a quick glimpse of the core beliefs of Catholic Christians. These statements may leave you with many questions. In fact, we hope they raise questions for you, which is why you will find them explained in greater depth in later chapters.

- ○ God created human beings to be in perfect union with God and one another. However, the sin of our first parents—called original sin—deprived the human race of our original holiness and justice.
- ○ Throughout human history God worked to restore the relationship of love and trust that was lost through original sin. He did this by entering into covenants—special relationships based on mutual promises—with Noah, Abraham and Sarah, and the people of Israel. But the people often broke their covenant promises.

Young People's Testimony

My first thought is that I am Catholic because I was raised Catholic. But that is not the only reason I am Catholic. Being Catholic is also feeling like I am part of God's family when I am in my church. It is also important to me that the Catholic faith is the only faith that believes that Christ is in the Eucharist and that the bread and wine are really the body and blood of Jesus Christ. These are the greatest reasons that I am a Catholic.

(Tara, age 17)

Catholicism means knowing you're never alone and never being left alone. It means knowing that someone is always there, even in spirit. Sometimes at night I like to lie in bed and wonder, "What place do I have in the Lord's plan?" Without my faith and love in our religion, I would be lost. Catholicism is more than the light in the dark; it's the light of the world. It's impossible to conceal because it's in the hearts of millions. We are all a part of Catholicism's great mysteries because we are its home—every one of us living and working and praying together.

(Laura, age 15)

- Ultimately God sent his only begotten son, Jesus Christ, as savior for the human race. Christ was both fully God and fully man. He became the perfect sacrifice for the forgiveness of sins and the restoration of the relationship of love and trust between God and humankind.
  - Following his death Jesus was brought back to life in the Resurrection! Christ overcame death and opened heaven's gates for all the just.
  - The Holy Spirit has been at work in the world from the beginning of creation to the present day. The Holy Spirit is one with the Father and the Son, and is also called the Advocate (Paraclete) and the Spirit of Truth.

In this painting Mary and the Apostles are receiving the Holy Spirit at Pentecost. Do you think the artist conveyed the importance of Mary? How?

- God has revealed himself to be Trinity, that is, the mystery of one God in three divine persons: Father, Son, and Holy Spirit. This mystery cannot be arrived at by reason but was revealed by Jesus Christ.
- Christ established the Catholic Church on the foundation of the Apostles. Christ and the Holy Spirit revealed the fullness of religious truth to the Apostles. The fullness of God's revealed truth is called Sacred Tradition, and is entrusted to the Apostles' successors, the bishops of the Church.
- The Bible, or the Sacred Scriptures, is another source of God's revealed truth for Catholics. The Bible is closely connected to Sacred Tradition. The Holy Spirit inspired the authors of the Bible to write what God wants us to know for our salvation.
- All people are destined for eternal life after death. The baptized who have put their faith in Jesus Christ as their savior will find their eternal reward in heaven. Those who have rejected Christ will find their eternal punishment in hell.

Some Core Catholic Practices

Catholic practices are closely related to Catholic beliefs. Some important Catholic practices in worship and morality could also have been listed as beliefs in the previous section. As in the belief section, the practices listed here are not complete and should raise some questions that will be answered in later chapters.

- Catholics celebrate seven sacraments that form the basis of their worship, or communal prayer, together. The seven sacraments were instituted by Christ and entrusted to the Church to make the love of God real and present in the world.
- The sacrament of the Eucharist is the heart of the Church's life. We believe that in the sacrament we literally receive the body and blood of Christ in the appearance of bread and wine.
- Sunday, or the "Lord's Day," is the principal day for the celebration of the Eucharist. Catholics keep the day holy by attending Mass and resting from work, in honor of Christ's Resurrection.
- Catholics follow a special calendar with all the feasts and holy days of the liturgical year. The special seasons of Advent and Lent prepare us to understand God's great love, which we celebrate at Christmas and Easter.
- Catholics place a strong emphasis on living morally because we believe we are called to new life in the Holy Spirit. The moral code for this new life is based on the Ten Commandments and the Beatitudes.
- Catholics defend the dignity of human life, and Catholic morality is often described as pro-life. Catholics are opposed to anything that threatens the sanctity of human life, including abortion, euthanasia, capital punishment, and human cloning.
- Serving people in need and working to transform society are essential elements of Catholic life. We believe that the Church is called to be a sign of God's perfect Kingdom yet to come, by working for justice and human rights in this life.

Saintly Profiles

Mary, the First Disciple

Catholics have a special devotion to Mary, the mother of Jesus Christ. We do not worship her or pray to her as God, as some people mistakenly believe. But we do honor her as the mother of God, and at times we ask her to approach Jesus with a special need or concern. She is the only person besides Jesus who was born without original sin, and at her death we believe she was taken up directly to heaven.

But Catholics wouldn't believe any of these things about Mary if we did not first believe that she was the first follower, the first disciple, of Jesus. Her yes to the angel Gabriel in the Gospel of Luke (1:26–38) made it possible for Jesus to come into the world. In the Gospel of John, Mary is the first person to believe that Jesus can work miracles, at the wedding feast of Cana (2:1–11). At the cross Jesus tells the beloved disciple, "Here is your mother" (John 19:27), which the Church teaches has the symbolic meaning that Mary is the mother of all believers. And Mary was present at Pentecost (Acts 1:14), receiving the gift of the Holy Spirit, and without a doubt she was very active in spreading the Gospel message about her son.

What an amazing woman! What trust she had in God, what heartache she suffered on account of her son, and what faith she had in Jesus and his message. Mary is a model for all who wish to follow Jesus more closely. She is our loving and patient mother, and we do well to honor her and ask for her prayers on our behalf—she will never turn a deaf ear to our requests.

○ Catholics honor the great people of faith who have preceded them, the saints, and in a dear and special way, Mary, the mother of Jesus.

Looking Back

The Mystery of the Church

On special occasions the Pope calls all the bishops of the world together to address important issues in the Church. These gatherings are called ecumenical councils, and the last one, held from 1962 to 1965, was called the Second Vatican Council. Here is part of a statement on the Church from that council:

[God] planned to assemble in the holy Church all those who would believe in Christ. Already from the beginning of the world, the foreshadowing of the Church took place. She was prepared for in a remarkable way throughout the history of the people of Israel and by means of the Old Covenant. Established in the present era of time, the church was made manifest by the outpouring of the Spirit. At the end of time she will achieve her glorious fulfillment. Then, as may be read in the holy Fathers, all just men from the time of Adam, "from Abel, the just one, to the last of the elect" will be gathered together with the Father in the universal Church. (*Dogmatic Constitution on the Church*, number 2)

Catholic Attitudes

Because of what we believe and how we live, Catholics see the world in a unique way. Many Catholics don't even realize that they have this unique perspective until they spend time with people with other religious or nonreligious backgrounds. See how many of the following attitudes describe your own perspectives:

○ Catholics recognize that God is present to, in, and through all creation—including the natural world, persons, communities, and historical events. For us all creation is sacred and has the potential to be a source of God's grace.

○ Catholics place their trust in the essential goodness of the human person, who is made in the image of God, even though we are flawed by the effect of original sin.

○ Catholics appreciate both faith and reason, both religion and science. Reason can lead us to faith. When we experience conflict between religion and science, it is because we have an inadequate understanding of one or the other.

○ Although the fullness of truth resides in the Catholic Church, Catholics seek to recognize and affirm the aspects of God's revealed truth that we share with other religions and all people of good will.

○ Because we are saved by participating in the community of faith—that is, the Church— rather than as isolated individuals, Catholics emphasize community life and communal worship. Though we value and nurture our personal relationship with God, we distrust any spirituality that reflects a primary attitude of "me and God."

- Catholicism respects the great diversity of cultures in the world, and is committed to proclaiming the message of Jesus to all people in all cultures at all times.
- Catholics respect and embrace a wide variety of spiritualities and prayer forms.

For Further Reflection

- What attracts you to the Catholic faith? If someone asked, "Why are you Catholic?" how would you answer?
- Do you know a faithful and committed Catholic? Consider asking the person about what she or he finds motivating about the Catholic faith.

Pray It!

Act of Faith

The Act of Faith is an old and traditional prayer of the Catholic Church. People prayed it as a sign of commitment to the core truths of the faith. Can you pray it as a sign of your desire to believe?

My God, I firmly believe you are one God in three Divine Persons, Father, Son, and Holy Spirit.
I believe in Jesus Christ, your son, who became man and died for our sins, and who will come to judge the living and the dead.
I believe these and all the truths which the Holy Catholic Church teaches, because you have revealed them, who can neither deceive nor be deceived. Amen.

2 Knowing God
Reason and Revelation

Do you remember pestering your parents to let you do something you really wanted to do but they didn't want you to?
Even after they said no and explained their reasons, you kept
asking: "Why? Why not? Come on, why?" If your parents are
like most parents, at some point their patience wore out and
they simply answered, "Because I said so, that's why!"

Would you believe that there is a parallel to this common
relationship between parent and child in the truths held by the
Catholic Church? The Church makes frequent appeal to
human reason in teaching us about the religious truths God
has revealed. But reason can take us only so far in explaining
the great mysteries of life and of religious truth. Ultimately
we must trust that God has revealed to the Church what he
wants us to know for our salvation. In this chapter we explore

Words to Look For

- canon
- reason
- Revelation
- covenant
- Apostolic Tradition
- Scriptures
- Gospels
- Magisterium
- salvation history
- Israelites
- Law
- Old Testament
- New Testament
- inspiration

our need for God and how we can come to know the truth about God.

Our Need for God

When you take a moment to look at what you really want from life, what do you think about? Most people name things like a happy family, success in work, a comfortable life, good health, and so on. Now look a little deeper and ask, "What do these things symbolize for us?" Don't they really symbolize our need to be loved and accepted for who we really are—and our need to return love, to make a difference in the world and in people's lives?

Consider one more thing. Literature and movies are full of stories about people who have everything that one could desire—and yet they are still unsatisfied, they still seek something more. Could it be that our need to be loved and to return love, and the emptiness we feel even when we have everything the world tells us we need, are signs of our need for God? The simple truth is that we are by nature religious beings, and each of us has an empty place—a God-shaped hole—that can never be filled by anything less than God. We are made to live in spiritual union with him, in whom we can find true happiness. Perhaps Saint Augustine said it best when he said, "For you have made us for yourself, [God], and our hearts are restless until they rest in you."

The Canon of the Bible

In the first centuries of the Church, quite a few letters and gospels existed that Christians used for information and inspiration. It was the responsibility of the early popes and bishops, guided by the Holy Spirit, to determine which of these books were truly inspired. Pope Damascus, at the Council of Rome in 382, determined the official list of books, sometimes called the **canon,** that make up the Catholic Bible. At that time the list was considered complete, so no more books can ever be added or taken away.

Catholic Bibles have seven more books in the Old Testament than do most Protestant Bibles. This goes back to a disagreement over whether to use the original Greek or the Hebrew version of the Old Testament. The Catholic Church used the Greek version, which contained the additional books of Tobit, Judith, 1 and 2 Maccabees, Wisdom, Sirach, and Baruch. These books are sometimes called the Apocrypha (Greek for "hidden") or the deuterocanonical (Greek for "second canon") books.

Reason and Revelation

Well, if we all have God-shaped holes, how do we discover the God who can fill them? One way people have been doing it for all human history is to use our natural gifts of observation and **reason.** When confronted by an awesome display of a star-filled night or by the overpowering experience of being truly loved by another person, we know that we are in touch with something far greater than just what we can see and touch. Reason tells us that something had to create such order and possibility. Or when you experience the voice directing you to act lovingly and generously instead of selfishly— reason tells us that something greater than us is responsible for placing that voice within us.

For these reasons the Church teaches that when we listen to the message of creation and to the voice of conscience, every person can come to certainty about the existence of God. Through the natural light of human reason, we can know the one true God from his works, that is, from the world and from the human person. This is one reason why the Church teaches that salvation is possible for every person, even those who have never heard of Jesus Christ.

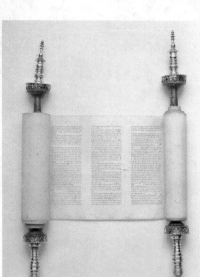

The original books of the Old Testament were written in Hebrew on scrolls, usually one book on one scroll. In Jewish worship services, the Scriptures are still read from scrolls like the one pictured here.

Yet human reason rarely seems like it is enough by itself to come to know God. Pope Pius XII put it like this:

> The human mind, in its turn, is hampered in the attaining of such truths, not only by the impact of the senses and the imagination, but also by disordered appetites which are the consequences of original sin. So it happens that men in such matters easily persuade themselves that what they would not like to be true is false or at least doubtful.[1] (*CCC,* number 37)

So how do we overcome this gap created by the limits of human reason? Well, we cannot overcome it, but God can! In his great love, he has revealed himself to us in order to restore the communion that human beings were created to have with him, before the relationship was broken by original sin.

Revelation in this sense is God making himself and his divine plan known to the human race through words and deeds in human history. This Revelation is communicated to us in the Bible's stories of how God made himself known to the chosen people by acting throughout their history. But when those attempts met with failure, God took a radical step.

He sent his son, Jesus Christ, into the world to be our savior. While remaining fully God, Jesus Christ took on a human nature, that is, he is both true God and true man. Thus Jesus Christ is the fullest and complete Revelation of who God is, and through Christ, God established his **covenant** with the human race forever (more on this later). As the Bible tells us, "[Christ] is the image of the invisible God" (Colossians 1:15).

The Church teaches everything that we need to know about God; everything we need to know for our eternal union with him has been revealed in Christ. Nothing more needs to be added or taken away—although we keep coming to new and deeper insights by reflecting on everything Jesus did and taught. But how do we, who live so many centuries after Christ, know who he is and what he revealed about God? God has provided for this by giving us two sources for coming to know Jesus Christ: **Apostolic Tradition** and the Sacred **Scriptures.**

The Scriptures and Tradition

Christ promised to send the Holy Spirit to his closest followers, the Apostles, after he physically left them to ascend into heaven: "When the Spirit of truth comes, he will guide you into all the truth" (John 16:13). The Holy Spirit helped the Apostles remember and understand all that Jesus did and taught. These truths about Jesus and his teaching are therefore called the Apostolic Tradition, or sometimes just the Tradition. Under the inspiration of the Holy Spirit, the Apostles handed on everything they knew about Jesus to the first Christians and to the generation of leaders who followed them.

As the years passed, the Holy Spirit inspired people in the early Church to create

Reading the Bible: The PRIMA Process

Having an effective strategy for reading the Bible can make the difference between giving up and staying on course. We call one such method the PRIMA process. *Prima* is the Latin word for "first." In the PRIMA process, each letter of the word stands for a step in studying the Bible, either individually or with a group:

- *Pray.* Begin with a prayer that your time with the Bible will draw you closer to God.
- *Read* attentively, trying to hear the words as if for the first time. Reading the passage aloud, even if you are alone, can help with this.
- *Imagine* being part of the story you just read. What would you feel, how would you react? Do you know anything about the background of the story that can help you understand what the author is trying to get across?
- *Meditate* on what you have read. How does the message of the story fit in with the rest of the Bible's teaching? with the Church's teaching? What do you think God is teaching you?
- *Apply* what you have read to your life. God may be calling you to make a change in your life. Or you may find encouragement that you need during a difficult time. Carry God's word into the rest of your day!

written documents explaining what the Apostles had handed down about Jesus. The **Gospels** were written, and each Gospel gives a slightly different faith perspective on the meaning of Jesus Christ's life and teaching. The Gospels of Matthew, Mark, Luke, and John were collected with some letters written by Paul and other early Church leaders and the Book of Revelation to form the New Testament of the Bible.

This is the opening page from a fifteenth-century Bible. Before the printing press was invented, Bibles were copied and illustrated by hand. How long do you think it would take you to copy an entire Bible by hand?

As you follow this explanation, it is hoped you will see that the Bible, particularly the New Testament, is really a written portion of the Apostolic Tradition. We speak of the Scriptures and Tradition as two sources of Revelation, but they are closely connected, and together form a single sacred deposit of truth under the guidance of the Holy Spirit. They can never be in conflict, and each one helps us to understand the other.

The Church looks to God's Revelation in the Scriptures and Tradition as the only authentic and complete source for our knowledge about God and God's will for the whole human race. It is the responsibility of the Church, through her teaching, her worship, and her ministries, to transmit to every new generation all that God has revealed. As the successors of the Apostles, it is the particular and exclusive responsibility of the bishops in union with the Pope—who are also called the **Magisterium**—to faithfully teach, interpret, and preserve the Scriptures and Tradition for all believers until Christ returns in glory.

The Big Picture of the Sacred Scriptures

Most of this book will be devoted to helping you understand the Tradition of the Catholic Church. It is not intended to be a Bible study resource. For that we suggest you find a book like *The Catholic Youth Bible,* also published by Saint Mary's Press. That Bible, together with this handbook, are in a sense a matched set—*The Catholic Youth Bible* helping you understand the Scriptures, and this book helping you understand Tradition.

However, you will better appreciate the Apostolic Tradition if you understand some of the "big picture" of God's relationship with the human race, as told in the Bible. This big picture is sometimes called **salvation history,** because it shows how God has worked within the people and events of human history to restore our lost union with him.

The story of salvation history begins with Creation. In the beginning of the Bible, we learn that God created the world and all that is in it, and everything was good. The story of Adam and Eve tells us that God intended us to be in direct communion with him. But the sin of our first parents disrupted that perfect communion. But despite their sin, God continued to care for them and promised them salvation.

We then go on to read how the world fell under the domination of sin. In the story of the great flood, God attempted to wipe out sin. Afterward, he made an everlasting covenant with Noah and the whole human race to never destroy the world by flood again. Later he made another covenant with Abraham, promising that Abraham's descendants would be as numerous as the stars, and that through them "all the families of the earth shall be blessed" (Genesis 12:3).

Abraham's descendants ended up living for a time in Egypt, where they eventually became slaves. God sent Moses to free the people and lead them to a Promised Land. God entered into yet another covenant with these **Israelites,** promising that they would be his chosen people. A special **Law,** summed up by the Ten Commandments, marked this covenant.

After a period marked by hardship and wandering, the Israelites eventually entered and settled in the Promised Land. At first they were only a loosely organized association of twelve tribes, but eventually God appointed kings to rule over them. The greatest king was David, who was a brave warrior and charismatic leader. David established Jerusalem as the capital

Looking Back

Sola Scriptura!

Sola Scriptura means "Scripture alone," and it was a rallying cry for some of the Protestant reformers who broke away from the Catholic Church in the 1500s. They felt that by appealing to Tradition, Catholic religious leaders were exercising a biased control over the Church, and the only truly objective source for God's Revelation was the Bible. So they rejected Tradition as a source of Revelation and tried to make their case for the Scriptures alone. This disagreement over the source of Revelation continues to be a major difference between Catholic Christians and many Protestant Christians yet today. But through patient dialogue, the different Christian churches are more tolerant and appreciative of one another than they have been in centuries.

city. After David's death, his son Solomon ruled. Solomon made Jerusalem a mighty city, and he also built an impressive Temple in which to worship God.

Unfortunately after Solomon's death the kingdom split into two parts, a northern kingdom and a southern kingdom. Two royal lines ruled over these kingdoms for several hundred years. Many of the royalty, the religious leaders, and even the people strayed from their covenant with God, falling into idolatry (worshiping false Gods) and greed. God raised up prophets to call the people to reform their lives and warn them that if they didn't, bad things would happen. And bad things did happen: Assyrians conquered the northern kingdom in 721 B.C., and the southern kingdom was conquered by the Babylonians in 587 B.C. The Babylonians destroyed Jerusalem and the Temple and led the leaders into exile.

Saint Thomas Aquinas is a doctor of the Church, an official title given to only a few wise and holy men and women whose teachings are especially worthy of study.

During the exile in Babylon, the prophets' message became a prophecy of hope. They told the people that even though their kingdom had been destroyed, God would not abandon them. They foretold the coming of a savior who would lead the people to peace. After nearly fifty years in exile, a sympathetic Persian king let the people return to rebuild Jerusalem and the Temple. Now known as the Jews, they would never again be an independent nation until modern times. Persian, Greek, and Roman governors would rule them until the time of Jesus.

It was into this world that Jesus was born. He was a Jew, a member of the chosen people, and a descendant of King David. He became known as the Messiah, meaning "the anointed one." His followers grew to understand that he was the savior the prophets had predicted. God established his new and final covenant with the human race through Christ Jesus' sacrifice: "This cup that is poured out for you is the new covenant in my blood" (Luke 22:20).

The Church was founded after Jesus' Resurrection and Ascension, when the Holy Spirit descended on the Apostles at Pentecost. The Acts of the Apostles and the letters of the New Testament show us how from the beginning the Apostles spread the message of God's love by preaching about Jesus

Christ and encouraging people to believe in him as Lord and Savior. Through their work the Church grew rapidly, becoming the worldwide body it is today.

The Organization of the Bible

The books of the Bible are actually organized into sections, and if you are familiar with these sections, it makes it easier to find your way around in the Bible. The **Old Testament** has forty-six books divided into the following sections:

○ **The Pentateuch** (Genesis through Deuteronomy). These five books are the core of the Old Testament. They tell the stories of Creation, sin, and the origin of God's chosen people.

○ **The Historical Books** (Joshua through 2 Maccabees). These books tell how the Israelites settled in the Promised Land. They also tell the stories of their great—and not-so-great—kings.

○ **The Wisdom Books** (Job through Sirach). These are books of poetry and the collected wisdom of the Israelites.

○ **The Prophets** (Isaiah through Malachi). These books are the collected speeches and biographies of the Israelite prophets. The prophets spoke for God against idolatry and injustice.

The **New Testament** has twenty-seven books divided into the following sections:

○ **The Gospels** (Matthew, Mark, Luke, and John). These four books are the most important books for Christians since they convey the meaning of Christ Jesus' life and teaching as their central message.

○ **The Acts of the Apostles.** This book is a continuation of the Gospel of Luke and tells the stories of how the early Church was spread.

○ **The Epistles** (Romans through Jude). These are twenty-one letters, written by Paul and other early Church leaders, that give teachings and guidance to individuals and the first Christian churches.

○ **The Book of Revelation.** This book records the visions of an early Christian named John.

This is a sixth-century mosaic of Saint Matthew, the Gospel writer. Notice his tools: pen, ink, and scrolls. What might the angel in the upper corner symbolize?

Biblical Inspiration and Interpretation

Something that has been a source of conflict between Catholics and some other Christians is the way Catholics interpret the Bible. This conflict has its roots over different understandings of biblical **inspiration.** All Christians believe that God is the ultimate author of the Bible because the Holy Spirit inspired the human authors in their writing. But some Christians—sometimes called fundamentalists or literalists—believe that every part of the Bible must be absolutely true in every way: historically true, geographically true, and scientifically true. Thus, for example, they believe that God created the world in six twenty-four hour days.

The Catholic Church teaches that the Holy Spirit inspired the biblical authors to write what God wanted us to know for our salvation. The Holy Spirit did not take over the biblical authors' humanity when they wrote. Thus the authors were subject to natural human limitations, and they also used their human creativity in their writing. To continue the example above, Catholics believe in the religious truth that God created the world and everything in it, without having to believe that the world was literally created in six twenty-four-hour days. Catholics understand that the Bible is without error in communicating what God wants us to know for salvation without having to be historically and scientifically correct in every detail.

For Further Reflection

○ Take a moment to meditate on the idea that God was willing to take the radical step of becoming fully human in order to communicate with us. What a tremendous sign of his love! What are some signs of God's love in your life?

○ How familiar are you with the Bible? Find a Bible and open it up to the table of contents. Scan the list of books for any that look familiar. Pick one of the Gospels (Matthew, Mark, Luke, or John) and make a commitment to read a chapter a day.

Pray It

Story of the Man and the Birds

Now the man to whom I'm going to introduce you was not a scrooge, he was a kind, decent, mostly good man. But he just didn't believe the Jesus story, about God coming to Earth as a man. "I'm truly sorry to distress you," he told his wife, "but I'm not going with you to church this Christmas Eve." He said he'd feel like a hypocrite.

Shortly after the family drove away in the car, snow began to fall. Minutes later he was startled by a thudding sound. When he went to the front door to investigate, he found a flock of birds that had been caught in the storm and, in a desperate search for shelter, had tried to fly through his large landscape window. Well, he couldn't let the poor creatures lie there and freeze, so he hoped to direct the birds to his barn for shelter.

Quickly he tried shooing them into the barn by walking around them waving his arms. Instead they scattered in every direction, except into the warm, lighted barn. And then he realized that they were afraid of him. If only I could think of some way to let them know that they can trust me.

"If only I could be a bird," he thought to himself, "and mingle with them and speak their language. Then I could tell them not to be afraid. Then I could show them the way to the safe, warm barn. But I would have to be one of them so they could see and hear and understand." At that moment the church bells began to ring, pealing the glad tidings of Christmas. The sound reached his ears above the sounds of the wind. And he sank to his knees in the snow. (Author unknown)

believe in God, the Father almighty, creator of
  heaven and earth.
believe in Jesus Christ, his only Son, our Lord.
e was conceived by the power of the Holy
  Spirit and born of the Virgin Mary.
e suffered under Pontius Pilate, was crucified,
  died, and was buried. He descended into hell.
n the third day he rose again.
e ascended into heaven and is seated at the
  right hand of the Father. He will come again to
  judge the living and the dead.
believe in the Holy Spirit, the holy catholic
  Church, the communion of saints, the forgiveness of sins, the resurrection of the body, and
  life everlasting,
men.

Part A

The
Creed

3

Faith

Jesus once told his disciples, "If you have faith the size of a mustard seed, you will say to this mountain, 'Move from here to there,' and it will move; and nothing will be impossible for you" (Matthew 17:20). Did Jesus mean that if we can't work spectacular miracles, we do not have faith? Of course he didn't. Jesus was using a figure of speech, an exaggeration, to make a point. In Jesus' time a person who could "move mountains" was a person who could make difficult things easy to understand. Jesus seemed to be telling us that all difficulties can be overcome if you have true faith in him.

Stories like these illustrate that having **faith** is extremely important to Jesus. He talks about it numerous times in the Gospels. So it is no surprise that faith is a central part of the Catholic Church's teaching. But what does it mean to have faith? Why is it so important?

This might be easier to think about if we put it in another context. Consider that faith and trust are closely related. Some-

Words to Look For

- *faith*
- *religion*
- *denominations*
- *ecumenism*
- *Catholic Church*
- *salvation*
- *creed*

times the two words are used interchangeably. When you say to your parents, "Just trust me!" what you are probably saying is, "Have faith in me, believe in me!" We all want other people to believe in us, to approve of who we are and what we do. Why? Because when we know that people we care for approve of us, we also feel their love.

Following this line of thought, you can see how closely related faith, trust, and love really are. If a person trusts us, it is easier to believe that he or she really loves us. And if we trust in another person it makes it easier to love him or her without holding back. What happens if we take this concept and apply it to God?

Faith Is Our Response to God's Love

It all comes down to this: "We love because [God] first loved us" (1 John 4:19). The Bible teaches us that God formed the universe as a joyful, free, creative expression of his love. As the crowning act of Creation, God made human beings, creatures that are more like him than any other created thing. Because of this we have greater free will than any other part of creation. We can consciously choose good or evil; we can even choose to believe in God or not believe in God. He did not create us as robots who have to be good, or who even have to believe in him. So when you struggle to believe in God, or struggle in making a moral choice, you are being exactly what God created you to be—a creature who must make choices.

In giving us freedom, God also gave us the ability to give and receive love. Any being that cannot make its own decisions about what to believe in or how to act is not capable of self-giving love. Unfortunately the effects of original sin confuse our ability to make totally free choices. We are too easily fooled into believing sinful choices are good choices. This limits our ability to love.

Did You Know?

Those Who Do Not Know Christ

What about a person who has never heard of Jesus? It's not their fault! Would God condemn that person for not believing in something they'd never heard of? The Church teaches that "in ways known to himself"[2] (*CCC,* number 848) God can lead people to faith who have not had the opportunity to know Christ and the Church. And those who "seek God with a sincere heart, and, moved by grace, try in their actions to do his will"[3] (*CCC,* number 847) may receive eternal life. In other words, we know that faith in Jesus has been revealed as the way to heaven, but we also believe that God's love and mercy is not limited by our understanding!

But God never gives up on us. Throughout human history God has revealed himself so that we might see him more clearly and exercise our freedom to choose good, to choose him. As his final Revelation, God sent his only Son, Jesus Christ, into the world. Christ is the ultimate sign of God's love for us and of how we are to love God and one another. In a very real sense, if you fully understand Christ and his message and you still reject him, then you are rejecting God's efforts to be in a loving relationship with you.

God's Revelation of himself, particularly in the person of Jesus Christ, is his loving invitation to us to be in a relationship. We respond to that invitation with trust, with faith in all that God has revealed, particularly through Jesus Christ. With our hearts we give ourselves in complete love to God. With our intellect we believe what he has revealed in the Scriptures and in Tradition. And with our wills we act on what we believe by choosing to do good and avoid sin. This sounds a lot simpler than it really is—all the great saints tell us that it takes a lifetime, and then only with God's help!

Saint Peter walking on the water is a classic biblical story about having faith in Jesus.

Faith and the Catholic Church

Faith is a personal act. Each person is free to believe or not to believe in what God has revealed. But belief is not an isolated act. No one can believe alone. For one thing, other people pass on God's Revelation to us. Parents, teachers, and clergy teach us about the Scriptures and Tradition. They witness to us how their faith in God has made a difference in their life. Through their words and actions, they support and nourish our faith. This is the way the Catholic faith has been spread for two thousand years. These faithful believers have passed faith on from generation to generation by their word and example.

Some people make a distinction between faith and **religion.** They claim that they can have faith, that they can be spiritual, without belonging to the Catholic Church or any other organized religion. But this is a difficult theory to support. True, every person is spiritual and can perform spiritual practices like prayer without belonging to a church. But having true faith means believing everything that God reveals; it doesn't mean picking and choosing the things we want to believe. And the Scriptures and Tradition teach that he wants us to be part of a church, a community of believers. Here are some reasons why:

- Christ promised that the Holy Spirit would guide the Church in a special way, revealing the full truth of the Gospel message.
- The Church provides the human mechanism through which God's Revelation—the Scriptures and Tradition—are passed on and safeguarded.
- The sacraments that Jesus instituted are celebrated in Christian community so that the people receiving the sacraments are more closely united with the community.
- We need the support and encouragement of other believers to live the Gospel message even when it is difficult and challenging. (Remember what Jesus said about faith and moving mountains?)
- Throughout the New Testament, the followers of Christ are commanded to "love one another" as an example to the rest of the world. Only as part of a Christian community can we give effective witness to the love of God.

For all these reasons and more, it is clear that faith in Christ means being a baptized and active member of the Catholic Church. Although Catholics recognize that they are not the only Christian community with gifts to offer the world, the Catholic Church is the original church founded by Christ after his Resurrection. Only the Catholic Church has the unbroken connection with the original Apostles. Only the Catholic Church passes on God's Revelation complete and unchanging.

Believe!

Belief is a popular theme in stories and movies. Think of the belief that children have in the stories of Peter Pan or Santa Claus. There is something powerful and compelling in the idea of having faith in something or someone. In most of these stories, belief makes all the difference. It makes something crucial happen or fail to happen. For Catholics, having faith does make all the difference. Even though we struggle with the particulars, having faith is like saying: "Yes, God! I believe in your love for me!" When we can say that, a road of adventure and promise opens up before us, a journey beyond our imagination.

Think about Jesus' mother, Mary, or the Apostles, or any of the saints. How different would their lives have been without faith? What work was God able to accomplish through them because they said "Yes, I believe!"? What work might God accomplish through you because you say "Yes, I believe!"? Many of the great saints had their doubts and questions and spoke about them quite freely. It is through the struggle with our doubts that we come to deeper faith. If we never ask the questions, how can we get to the answers?

The Catholic Church has a special unity with other Christian churches. All Christians share "one Lord, one faith, one baptism" (Ephesians 4:5). All Christians are brothers and sisters to one another. By our Baptism we all share a sacramental bond of unity and a common life in Christ, even though significant differences exist between different Christian Churches, or **denominations.** Catholics are encouraged to practice **ecumenism,** that is, to work toward overcoming those differences and to build unity with other Christians. We do this by praying together, serving the community together, and honestly searching for God's truth together.

The Characteristics of Faith

Let's summarize: Christian faith is the human person's response to God's loving invitation to believe in him. Faith means giving yourself completely—heart, mind, and will—to a loving relationship with God. Faith also means believing in and being part of the Church, which is the Body of Christ here on earth. The **Catholic Church** also teaches some other things about faith, which are summarized here:

- **Faith is a grace, a supernatural gift of God.** This is a fancy way of saying that we don't initiate our relationship with God, that he is the one who initiates it. In fact, without the Holy Spirit's help, we wouldn't be able to recognize God's invitation or respond to it.
- **Faith is certain.** God is trustworthy, and everything he reveals is trustworthy, even when it does not make complete sense to our human reason. The teachings of our faith are more trustworthy than any human knowledge.
- **Faith seeks understanding.** True faith means having a passion for always wanting a deeper and clearer understanding of God. It is an ongoing process: the more we understand

Looking Back

Other Religions

What can we learn from other religions? How do they understand God? If we believe differently, does that mean they're wrong? In the Second Vatican Council (1961–1965), the bishops of the world defined the Catholic Church's positive understanding of other faiths and our relationship to them: "The Catholic Church rejects nothing which is true and holy in these religions. She looks with sincere respect upon those ways of conduct and of life, those rules and teachings which, differing in many particulars from what she holds and sets forth, nevertheless often reflect a ray of that Truth which enlightens all [people]" (*Declaration on the Relationship of the Church to Non-Christian Religions,* number 2).

When we talk with friends about our faith and listen to them talk about their faith, we often come away with a deeper understanding of that person, of God, and of our own experience. In a similar way, the Pope and the bishops want the Catholic Church to be in dialogue with other religions. We will know God and the Catholic faith more deeply as we seek to understand the beliefs of other religions.

God, the deeper our faith will be. And as our faith deepens, we become more committed followers of Jesus Christ.

○ **Faith is not opposed to science.** God created both physical reality and spiritual reality, and the two can never truly conflict. The humble and honest seeker will see the hand of God in both the world of science and the world of religion.

○ **Faith is necessary for salvation.** By definition **salvation** means having our relationship with God restored to what he intended it to be from the beginning. But as was said earlier, faith in God is a necessary part of having a truly loving relationship with him. Thus without faith we have cut ourselves off from God, and that means no salvation. Without faith in God, even if a person had all the exterior signs of a good and upright life, she or he will not be saved. (Just remember that God is always there to take us back!)

○ **Faith is the beginning of eternal life.** Through faith we deepen our relationship with God. Through faith we experience the joy and love that comes with being part of a community of believers. Through faith we get a preview of what heaven is like.

Creeds Are Statements of Faith

The chapters in this section are based on the statements of the Apostles' Creed, found on the first page of this section. A **creed** is a brief summary of the things you believe in. Christians use creeds as a type of prayer that summarizes the beliefs of our faith, a summary of the things that God has revealed. One of the very first creeds we have is in Paul's First Letter to the Corinthians:

Pray It!

Prayer of Unknowing

Thomas Merton, born in France in 1915, eventually became an American citizen, a scholar, a Catholic, and in 1941 a Cistercian monk at the Abbey of Gethsemani, in Kentucky. Merton is considered one of the most influential spiritual writers of modern times, and his autobiographical book *The Seven Storey Mountain* is a spiritual classic. He wrote the following famous prayer, which shows he had learned that his doubts could still lead to faith:

My Lord God, I have no idea where I am going. I do not see the road ahead of me. I cannot know for certain where it will end. Nor do I really know myself, and the fact that I think I am following your will does not mean that I am actually doing so. But I believe that the desire to please you does in fact please you. And I hope I have that desire in all that I am doing. I hope that I will never do anything apart from that desire. And I know that if I do this you will lead me by the right road, though I may know nothing about it. Therefore I will trust you always though I may seem to be lost and in the shadow of death. I will not fear, for you are ever with me, and you will never leave me to face my perils alone. (Thomas Merton, *Thoughts in Solitude*, page 83)

For I handed on to you as of first importance what I in turn had received: that Christ died for our sins in accordance with the scriptures, and that he was buried, and that he was raised on the third day in accordance with the scriptures, and that he appeared to Cephas, then to the twelve. (15:3–5)

Notice how simple this formula is. The focus is primarily on the death and Resurrection of Jesus.

The Apostles' Creed isn't found in the Bible, but it is very old, dating back to the early Church in Rome, the city in which Peter settled to become the first pope. It contains belief statements about all three persons of the Trinity as well as a statement about the Church. It reflects the early Christians' growing understanding of the doctrine of the Trinity and the importance of the Church in God's plan. Because of this it is one of the most important statements of faith in the Catholic Church.

Saint Helen is pictured with her son, Saint Constantine. How have your parents and your extended family passed their faith on to you?

The church has other important creeds. The one you are probably most familiar with is the Nicene Creed. Catholics around the world recite the Nicene Creed every Sunday at Mass. It is also an old creed, dating back to the end of the fourth century A.D. It is longer than the Apostles' Creed and contains more statements about Jesus Christ and the Holy Spirit. This is because in the fourth century, some significant conflicts arose in the Church about Jesus' identity and the role of the Holy Spirit (see "Mistaken Identity: Heresies About Christ," on page 63). The Nicene Creed affirms the beliefs that were clarified as a result of those conflicts.

As a young person, you are growing in your faith and learning more about the Catholic faith. Using the Apostles' Creed or the Nicene Creed as an outline is an excellent way to explore those beliefs. This is why the first sections of the *Catechism* and this handbook are based on those creeds. Please use the chapters in this section to explore your questions and deepen your understanding of Catholic beliefs. God has given you the gift of faith, but only you can decide to accept that gift and act on it.

For Further Reflection

○ This chapter began with the claim that Jesus said all difficulties can be overcome if we have true faith in him. What are some difficulties you need to overcome in your life? What gifts, skills, or insights could you ask Jesus for, so he could help you overcome these difficulties?

○ This chapter mentions that faith seeks understanding, which means that it is okay to have questions and doubts about God and the Church! What are some things about God and the Catholic Church that you would like to better understand? See if you can find them in the index of this handbook.

Saintly Profiles

Saint Helen (ca. 250–330)

Saint Helen was the mother of the first Christian emperor, Constantine. She married the Roman general Constantius Chlorus. In 292 he divorced her to marry the emperor's stepdaughter. Helen's ex-husband and eventually her son each became emperor. Her son, Constantine, is known as the patron saint of the church. After his conversion to Christianity in 312, Constantine legalized Christianity, made generous donations to the Church, erected numerous basilicas (churches), and even called the bishops together for the first ecumenical (worldwide) council in Nicaea in 325.

Helen, who also became a Christian in 312, is the patron saint of converts. She was over sixty at the time of her conversion, and was attentive to the needs of poor people, orphans, and those in prison. As an old woman, Helen visited the Holy Land and founded many churches on sacred sites, including the Mount of Olives and Bethlehem. Saint Helen is often pictured with the cross, both because she did much to spread the Christian faith and because tradition connects her with the discovery of the cross of Christ. Her feast day is August 18.

4 God Our Father

The Apostles' Creed starts out with a very simple statement: "I believe in God, the Father almighty, creator of heaven and earth." This statement is at the foundation of everything that Christians believe. But how many Catholics have really stopped to analyze this statement? How many of us could really give a reasonable explanation of who God is and what God wants from us?

Some people—called **atheists**—claim there is no God. They point out that scientists cannot prove God's existence. And they point out all the evil in the world and ask, "So how can there be a God?" If we are honest, it isn't just atheists who have these questions. To varying degrees, seeking Christians at some point in their life also ask themselves, "How do we know there is a God?"

The Church's answer is both simple and complex. We know that human beings cannot discover God purely on their own power. We can make a case that it is reasonable to believe

Words to Look For

- atheists
- Trinity
- monotheism
- Creator
- original sin
- angels

40

in God (see the article "Proofs for the Existence of God," on page 44), but we cannot prove God's existence in a scientific way. So the Church's simple answer is that we know about God because God has chosen to reveal himself to us.

But as we try to understand what God has revealed to us, the answer becomes complex. So much of what we know is in the negative. We know things such as God *is not* a creature like us, God *has no* beginning or no end, and God *is not* subject to the limitations of space and time. Even when God reveals himself, God remains a mystery beyond words. To help us understand the mystery of God, we use images of and stories about things that we can see, hear, and touch in order to understand God, whom we cannot directly see, hear, or touch. This chapter looks at some of those images and stories to deepen our understanding of God.

The Trinity: One God, Three Persons

Let's start with the foundational image that God has revealed to us, the **Trinity.** The Trinity is the mystery of one God in three persons. It is the central mystery of the Christian faith, and we call it a mystery because it cannot be understood only by reason—God alone can make it known to us. Belief in one God is called **monotheism.** But the belief in the Trinity distinguishes Christians from other monotheistic religions (like Judaism and Islam), because these religions do not believe there are three persons in one God.

The belief in one God comes to us through our Jewish ancestry. One of the primary prayers in the Jewish faith is taken from the Book of Deuteronomy: "Hear, O Israel: The LORD is our God, the LORD alone. You shall love the LORD your God with all your heart, and with all your soul, and with all your might" (6:4–5). This was truly a unique revelation. Other ancient peoples—the Egyptians, the Greeks, and the

---

Pray It!

Trinity Sunday

On the Sunday after Pentecost, the Church celebrates Trinity Sunday. This prayer from the liturgy for this feast day speaks about the mystery of the Trinity:

God, we praise you:
Father all-powerful, Christ Lord and Savior, Spirit of love.
You reveal yourself in the depths of our being,
drawing us to share in your life and your love.
One God, three Persons,
be near to the people formed in your image,
close to the world your love brings to life.
We ask you this, Father, Son, and Holy Spirit,
one God, true and living, for ever and ever. Amen.
(*The Sacramentary,* page 346)

Romans, for example—believed in and worshiped a collection of gods and goddesses. God revealed himself to the Chosen People as the one and only God.

In this famous image, painted by Michelangelo on the ceiling of the Sistine Chapel, God passes the spark of life to Adam.

But how did we come to believe that there were three persons in the one God? This belief came later, and was revealed by the life and words of Jesus Christ. First the Apostles came to understand that Christ was God. The Gospel of John says, "No one has ever seen God. It is God the only Son, who is close to the Father's heart, who has made him known" (1:18). A little later the Apostles came to know and understand that the Holy Spirit was also God. In the Gospel of John, Jesus says, "When the Advocate comes, whom I will send to you from the Father, the Spirit of truth who comes from the Father, he will testify on my behalf" (15:26).

The Father, Son, and Holy Spirit are not three Gods, but one God. To use philosophical terms, they share the same "substance" or "essence." Yet we believe that the three are also distinct from one another. They are really three different "persons," not just three ways of describing how God works.

On the other hand, when we describe their roles, we do think of the Father primarily as Creator, the Son as Savior, and the Holy Spirit as the Sanctifier (the one who helps us become holy). Yet we must remember that the Father, Son, and Holy Spirit are inseparable from one another and they all share in the "work." For example, both Christ and the Holy Spirit, as well as the Father, were present at and part of the creation of the world.

Are you confused yet? Don't be alarmed if you are; great minds have been struggling to understand the mystery of the Trinity for almost two thousand years! Just remember this: The central thing that the Trinity teaches us is that God is not solitary. God exists as a communion of persons who perfectly communicate with one another and perfectly support one another. If this is true for God, it is also true for us, who are made in God's image and likeness. We are made for community; acknowledging our need for other people is honoring the Trinity! Striving to be in good, honest, supportive relationships isn't just a nice thing to do, it is part of what we must do if we are to truly become the image of God we were created to be.

The Father Almighty

Let us now turn our attention to the first person of the Trinity, God the Father. Have you ever wondered why we call God "Father"? It is an old and honored title that many religions use for God. But Christians claim it in a special way because Jesus used it frequently to describe his own unique relationship with God: "No one knows the Son except the Father, and no one knows the Father except the Son and anyone to whom the Son chooses to reveal him" (Matthew 11:27). Jesus is God the Father's divine Son, who has existed with the Father for all eternity. When Jesus Christ took on human nature, he was able to reveal his Father to us in the way that only a child can speak about a parent.

Further, in the Bible accounts, Jesus called God "Abba," an Aramaic word for father that was used in families (see 14:36 and Galatians 4:6). It was sort of like calling God "Dad" or "Papa." It implied an intimate and loving relationship with God. To think about God this way was a challenge for many of the Jews of Jesus' time because they thought about God primarily as a judge or king. Many Christians today take for granted the image of God as a loving Father, but if it hadn't been for Jesus, we might never have had this understanding.

But let's not forget the adjective that describes God the Father in the creed: almighty. There is no creature, no power, and no force anywhere in creation that is more powerful than God is. In describing this we

Looking Back

The Problem of Evil

If God is all good, why did he create a world in which there is so much pain and suffering caused by natural disasters and by the evil choices that human beings make? The *Catechism* has an excellent response to this question that can only be summarized here. If you want to read the entire answer, check out paragraph numbers 309 through 314 of the *Catechism*.

- The problem of evil is pressing and unavoidable, and no quick answer will suffice for those who have experienced pain and suffering. Only the Christian faith as a whole provides the answer to the question.
- God could have chosen to create a world so perfect that physical evil did not exist, but in his wisdom and goodness he created a world that is still journeying to its ultimate perfection. This means that physical evil will exist alongside of physical good until creation reaches its ultimate perfection.
- God also chose to give men and angels free will so that we could journey freely to our ultimate destiny. Besides making good choices that bring greater love into the world, we can also make sinful choices that bring evil into the world. God does not in any way cause moral evil, but he respects our freedom by allowing us to choose it.
- Finally, and this is the cause of our hope, nothing is so evil that God cannot cause a good to come from it: "We know that all things work together for good for those who love God" (Romans 8:28). All the saints affirm this truth.

43

Proofs for the Existence of God

Saint Thomas Aquinas (1225–1274), known as a doctor of the Church, developed the following five proofs *(quinque viae)* for the existence of God:

1. Life is in motion. For life to be in motion, there must have been a "first mover" to get everything going. That mover is God.
2. An egg cannot just cause itself to be an egg. There must be a cause outside of the egg (in other words, a rooster and a hen!) that causes it to be an egg. Likewise there must be a first cause outside of all creation that caused creation to come into existence, and that first cause is God.
3. For the possibility of everything else to exist, by necessity there had to be something in existence first. This something we call God.
4. There is something we call truest and best against which we measure everything else that is true and good. This something isn't just an abstract concept but is God.
5. The order in nature isn't just a happy accident. An intelligent being exists to direct all things to their natural end, and this being we call God.

These are not scientific proofs, but they are arguments based on philosophical reason. Saint Thomas Aquinas is trying to let us know that something greater than humankind must have set creation in motion. This something we call God, because by definition God is greater than anything else we can imagine.

sometimes say that God is omnipotent (all-powerful), omnipresent (God is everywhere), and omniscient (all-knowing). Yes, God is our Father, but he is also an awesome, powerful force worthy of our praise and worship: "Who can utter the mighty doings of the LORD, / or declare all his praise?" (Psalm 106:2).

You might be asking yourself, "If we call God Father, does this mean the Catholic Church teaches that God is male?" Absolutely not. In fact, the *Catechism* says, "God's parental tenderness can also be expressed by the image of motherhood,[1] which emphasizes God's immanence, the intimacy between Creator and creature" (number 239). The Bible also contains many feminine images of God. However, God transcends, or is bigger than, the distinction we make between the sexes. Although Catholics honor in a special way the image of God as loving Father, we recognize that any human image we have of God is incomplete.

Creator of Heaven and Earth

Another reason Christians call God Father is that it acknowledges God as the **Creator**—the Father—of everything that is. Though science seeks to explain the how and why of the physical processes of creation, science cannot explain the why of creation. The why is revealed to us by God himself. God did not need to create the world but freely chose to do so. Nor did God start with anything or have any help in forming the world; he created it out of nothing. By creating the world and all that is in it, God wishes to share his love and goodness with every creature—but especially with us, the people he created in his image. God's plan for all creatures to live in loving union with their creator is what the Garden of Eden represents. And for those who see the world with the eyes of faith, creation itself gives witness to God's love and wisdom.

For love to be truly love, though, it must be freely given and freely received. So God created human beings with the freedom to choose love and goodness. The dark side of that freedom is that we can also choose hate and evil. Our original parents, Adam and Eve, made a choice to reject God's love, and their **original sin** disrupted God's plan for creation. But God never abandoned us. He continued to work in the created world to restore his loving union with the human race. Through God's "new creation" in Jesus Christ, this restoration will be fulfilled.

The Catholic teachings about creation answer the two most fundamental questions we have as human beings: "Why am I here?" and "What is my ultimate destiny?" Knowing that God created the universe out of love and to communicate his glory, we know that we are here because of God's love and to share in God's truth, goodness, and beauty. God's plan is that we should spend eternity joyfully in perfect union with him. A later chapter will explore this more thoroughly.

Another important thing that we believe about creation is that a reality exists that lies beyond our senses. In the Nicene Creed, we say that we believe in God, "maker of all that is, seen and unseen." Knowing of an unseen part of reality opens us up to the miraculous, to understanding that God is at work even when we may not see any evidence at the moment. Although we should be very careful about making claims about what belongs to the unseen order of creation, we know about one thing for sure: the existence of **angels.**

Angels are every bit as real as you and me, but they are beings of spirit, not matter. They have intelligence and will, they have individuality, and they are immortal. The word *angel*

Does God Make a Difference?

Think about the events of September 11, 2001. One of the stories of that day tells about the group of people on the flight that crashed in Pennsylvania. These people prayed Psalm 23 before taking action against the terrorists who hijacked the plane. This plane was probably headed for Washington. Think of the greater destruction that would have occurred if this plane had hit the White House.

Their faith gave the group of people on this airplane the courage to act. And their act—even though it cost them their lives—probably saved countless numbers of people, possibly including many of the nation's leaders. If we have faith, God gives us the courage and strength to do things that normally would be beyond our capability. Read Psalm 23 and try to discover why they might have chosen this psalm. How does your faith in God make a difference in your life?

comes from the Greek *aggelos,* meaning "messenger." Angels' sole purpose is to be God's servants and messengers and to glorify God without ceasing. The Bible tells of angels in both the Old and the New Testaments, and even gives three of their names: Michael, Gabriel, and Raphael. We believe that angels unite with us in praising God when we celebrate the Eucharist, and that angels watch over each of us, from conception to death. Most Catholics find it very comforting to know that we are united with these unseen servants of God.

JULIAN OF NORWICH

Saint Julian spent many hours at the window of her small room, compassionately listening to those who came to her for spiritual advice and hope.

God Is Truth and Love

In the famous story of Moses and the burning bush (Exodus, chapter 3), God reveals his name to Moses: "I AM WHO I AM." This name for God means that God alone IS, that he is perfection of all that is and needs nothing else to be. Everything else in creation is dependent on something else for its existence, but not so with God. In fact, God keeps the entire universe in existence at every moment. Without the Trinity to sustain and uphold creation, it would simply cease to exist.

Taken by itself, "I AM WHO I AM" does not describe a personal and loving God. But many other references in the Bible describe God as faithful and loving. For example, God tells Moses that he is "merciful and gracious, / slow to anger, / and abounding in steadfast love and faithfulness" (Exodus 34:6). God tells the prophet Hosea to marry a prostitute and remain faithful to her, "just as the LORD loves the people of Israel, though they turn to other gods" (Hosea 3:1). And the First Letter of John tells us that "God is light and in him there is no darkness at all" (1:5) and "Whoever does not love does not know God, for God is love" (4:8).

God is truth. God is love. In the end these two statements probably say more about God than anything else we could say. Our God will never deceive us or lie to us. And most important, God loves us more than we could possibly imagine. The love of the people in our life is often imperfect and limited; even mothers and fathers can hurt us cruelly. But the love of our divine parent can never fail us. "O give thanks to the God of heaven, / for his steadfast love endures forever" (Psalm 136:26).

For Further Reflection

- Consider the questions posed at the beginning of this chapter. What reasons do you have for believing in God? How would you describe God to a friend?
- If God is the creator of everything that is, how do you explain the existence of evil?
- After reading this chapter, what do you think God might want from us?

Saintly Profiles

Blessed Julian of Norwich (ca. 1342–1420)

Julian of Norwich was an anchoress (from the Greek word for recluse) who lived a life of solitude and contemplation. Julian stepped away from worldly activity to spend her days contemplating God. As part of her daily life, she lived only on prayer and the essentials of food and shelter. Julian lived in a cell attached to the church of Saint Edmund and Saint Julian in Norwich, and was visited by pilgrims from all over England. She was famous for her compassion and optimism. She is said to have received sixteen visions on the Passion of Christ, on the Trinity and other mysteries of faith. These visions are described in her *Book of Showings*, also known as the *Revelations of Divine Love*.

Julian used images familiar to the people of her time to describe the tremendous love of God. Many of her descriptions were feminine, such as her image of God as a wise and nurturing mother who protects us from harm. For Julian everything was about God's love, which she believed was best expressed in the Passion of Jesus. Despite the fact that she lived during the horrible plague, which killed millions in Europe, one of her most famous prayers speaks of her complete faith and trust in God and ends with the comforting words, "All shall be well, and all shall be well, and all manner of thing shall be well." Her feast day is May 8.

5

The Human Person

If you are like most people, you probably have good days and bad days. On the good days, you feel connected and at peace. You are aware that life is good, and you know that the Almighty has blessed you. Your own life has purpose and meaning, and you know that you are loved and cared for.

The bad days are a little different. On the bad days, you feel anything but peace. You feel used and abused and misunderstood. You aren't sure that anyone really cares; you might even feel that your life has little meaning or purpose. Sometimes it doesn't take much to move us from a good day to a bad day. It might just be someone's barbed comment or a disappointing grade on a test that makes us start to feel bad about ourselves.

God has something to say to us about those bad days. The Scriptures and Tradition are very clear about this: God loves every person—without exception—and every human person has infinite value in God's plan. God's love doesn't

Words to Look For

- ○ soul
- ○ stewardship
- ○ the fall
- ○ concupiscence

depend on what you've done or how you feel. As we grow in faith, we understand this more and more. And though we remember that God's love may not stop those bad days from happening, it can help make them easier to get through!

Made in the Image of God

At times in life, most people ask the same fundamental questions: "Who am I?" and "Why am I here?" Sadly some people do not accept the existence of God as a starting point in trying to answer these questions. They reject the answers provided by the Christian faith. The Christian faith starts from the simple premise that we are creatures and that God is our creator. So if you want to know who you are and why you are here, start by looking at the Creator's Revelation in the Scriptures and in Tradition.

Contemporary Haitian artist Gabriel Alix painted his vision of the Garden of Eden. What do you think the Garden of Eden might have looked like?

For the Catholic faith, an important starting point in answering these questions is the beginning of the Bible, the Book of Genesis. The Book of Genesis actually has two different Creation stories in its first chapters. Each story has something unique to tell us about God's plan for human beings.

The first story is from a hymn that tells how God created the whole world in seven days (Genesis 1:1—2:4). Well, actually six days, because the story says God rested on the seventh day. You've probably heard or read this story many times. The important thing isn't really about what God created when, as some Christians want to emphasize. They take the story too literally, and try to read scientific meaning into it. For example, they want to use it to prove that evolution never occurred. But because it is pretty obvious that the biblical author didn't write this as a science lesson, it is misleading to read the story in this way.

The key event happens on the sixth day of creation. On that day God created man and woman. But they weren't created like the other animals. No, instead the Bible tells us, "God created humankind in his image, / in the image of God he created them; / male and female he created them" (1:27). Human beings are the crown of God's creation. Made in the

Satan

What do you believe about Satan? Is he just a mythical creature used as a plot device in horror movies? Christians believe he is a very real force of evil who was once a good angel, also called Lucifer, meaning "being of light." Satan pitted his will against the will of God, and as punishment was cast from heaven. He seeks to draw us into his rebellion against God, which is why we make promises to reject Satan and all his empty promises.

It might surprise you to learn that the earliest stories about Satan did not portray him to be fighting against God (Job 1:6 and Zechariah 3:1). Rather he worked in God's heavenly court as a sort of prosecutor, testing human virtue by afflicting misfortune, in order to gauge the virtuousness of human reaction. The word *Satan* comes from a root word meaning "accuser."

Over time Satan's work of testing virtue becomes active involvement in doing evil. Satan becomes a powerful controller of the forces of evil, acting out of hatred for God and humankind. He tempts people (2 Corinthians 2:11), he has the power to kill (Hebrews 2:14), and he has influence in the evil that leads to Jesus' death (John 13:2). But Satan is only a creature, and as such is subject to the power of God. In the death and Resurrection of Jesus, God overcomes the evil of Satan, now and forever. Whenever you find yourself tempted to cooperate with evil, ask the Holy Spirit to give you strength to resist Satan's influence—God will give it to you!

image of God, we have capabilities that go beyond all other creatures. We have self-awareness and self-knowledge. We alone are capable of knowing God and freely returning God's love. It was for this that God created us, that there would be creatures who could freely know and love him.

God is our parent every bit as much as our physical parents. How can this be? We are both physical and spiritual beings. At the moment of our conception, the combined DNA from our human parents created our physical body. But at the same time, God created the spiritual principle that animates our spiritual life and makes us truly human. We call this spiritual aspect of human beings the **soul.** The soul is immortal, and it is not separated from the body—our body and our soul are completely united. Just as we carry the genetic imprint of our physical parents, we carry the spiritual imprint of our spiritual parent.

The first Creation story also teaches us that human beings are not meant to be alone (this is also taught in the second Creation story). God did not create just one person but two: "In the image of God he created them; / male and female he created them." In the original Hebrew language, the poetic structure of this phrase suggests that it is only when men and women are together that we are most fully in the divine image. Just as the three persons of the Trinity live in perfect community, so we also must live in loving community with others to be all that God created us to be. And the partnership of men and women is the primary form of human community.

Finally, the first Creation story teaches us that God gives human beings a special responsibility for caring for Creation: "Be fruitful and multiply, and fill the earth and subdue it; and have dominion over the fish of the sea and over the birds of the air and over every living thing that moves upon the earth" (Genesis 1:28). God created a huge diversity of creatures, each with their own goodness. We are only now learning just how many different species of life there are! All plants and animals live together in a complex and orderly web of life. At the center of this web stands the human race, and we are beginning to understand how our choices either help preserve this web of life or destroy it.

Even though the Bible uses verbs like *subdue* and *have dominion,* that doesn't mean God wants us to use nature and other creatures selfishly and destructively. It really means the opposite, that we have a special responsibility, called **stewardship,** to honor and preserve creation. God is counting on us to make wise use of the earth's resources and creatures, and to protect them from destruction.

The Fall from Grace

The second Creation story is in Genesis 2:4—3:24. This is the story of Adam and Eve and the Garden of Eden. Unlike the first Creation story, in the second story, man is created first, then all the animals, and finally woman. Like the first Creation story, it teaches that God gave us a spiritual soul by the symbolic action of breathing life into Adam (2:7). It also teaches that man and woman need each other to be complete (2:23), and that human beings are to cultivate and care for creation (2:15). But then it goes even further.

In the second Creation story, God places Adam and Eve in the Garden of Eden. The Garden of Eden symbolizes the ideal relationship that God intended to have with human beings. In the garden there is no pain, no death, and no shame. Adam and Eve see God face-to-face. They are in a perfect state

Overcoming Temptation

Why are cartoon superheroes often pitted against a villainous master of disguise? Such plots point to the fact that evil often masquerades as something else. How true when it comes to temptation! Gossip presents itself as a way to appear popular, sexual activity outside of marriage pretends to be true love, and drinking alcohol appears to be a way to have fun or fit in. With all these clever disguises and more, how can you see temptation for what it really is and avoid it?

Saint Augustine would tell us that the root of most temptations is a hunger or a need that only God can fill. He said, "Our hearts are restless until they rest in you, [God]." If you want to stand up to temptation, get to know the hungers in your heart, such as a need for being in control, for attention, or for fitting in. Then follow Jesus' lead, and put trust in God's care to fill your hungers (Matthew 4:1–11).

of holiness and justice. They are friends with God, and from that friendship flows their happiness.

But then something terrible happened. Eve was tempted by a serpent to eat some fruit from the tree of knowledge of good and evil (3:1–6). God's only command to Adam and Eve was to not eat from this tree (2:16–17). Eve gave the fruit to Adam, and he also ate it. They had disobeyed God and committed the first sin. They had lost their trust in God and his goodness. The tree of the knowledge of good and evil symbolized the limits that human beings have as creatures. We must recognize those limits and accept them with trust. If we try to exceed those limits, we are in a sense setting ourselves against God, or at least we aren't believing God's word about what our limits are. This was Adam and Eve's sin, which is sometimes simply called **the fall.**

Adam and Eve's sin had immediate consequences. They knew the shame of having disobeyed God and tried to cover it up with makeshift clothing and by hiding from God in the garden. They start the blame game: Adam blames Eve and Eve blames the serpent. God announces further consequences. Childbirth will be a painful experience. The relationship between men and women will be filled with tension and marked by domination (3:16). The earth will no longer freely give its bounty, so human beings will have to work hard at tilling the soil for their food (3:17–19). And finally, Adam and Eve and all their descendants will experience death, for "you are dust, / and to dust you shall return" (3:19).

Thus Adam and Eve's sin has consequences, not just for themselves but for all their descendants, which means all of us! The harmony that should exist between people, the harmony that should exist between human beings and nature, and the harmony that should exist between people and God has been wounded. The Catholic Church explains the impact of Adam and Eve's sin in its teaching on original sin. Much of the Old

Pray It!

Prayer for Accepting Our Humanity

I am a person like no one else in the world.
I am the people I have met.
I am the experiences I have had.

I am the mistakes I have made and the wisdom I have gained from them.
I am the lessons I have learned and the ones I have given.
I am the good times in my life and the bad ones too.
I am the emotions I have felt And the thoughts I have thought.

God, I am the life I have lived.
Although it's not a perfect one, understand that I'm doing the best I can
with what you have given me.
Because all that I have to work with . . . is me.

(Tom Moore, in *Dreams Alive,* page 24)

Testament shows the continuing influence of sin, starting with the story of Cain killing Abel.

Original Sin

Original sin is the name for the fact that "Adam and Eve transmitted to their descendants human nature wounded by their own first sin and hence deprived of original holiness and justice" (*CCC*, number 417). The Church doesn't attempt to explain how this happens. We accept it as a mystery that we cannot fully understand. What we know is that Adam and Eve did not receive their state of original holiness for themselves alone but for all human nature. Thus when they sinned their sin didn't affect just themselves but affected their human nature, which was passed on to all their descendants.

Perhaps this analogy will help you understand. If for some reason a genetic abnormality develops in a person's DNA—such as nearsightedness—it may get passed on to the person's children. The children didn't do anything to deserve this physical defect, but they still receive it. In a similar way, a spiritual defect was created in Adam and Eve's spiritual nature that now gets passed on to every human being (with two exceptions: Jesus and his mother, Mary). We didn't do anything to be in this state—we were born into the state of original sin before we ever had a chance to commit a personal sin ourselves!

Original sin does not cause us to lose our goodness or make us completely spiritually corrupt. Some of the Protestant reformers did teach that original sin had completely perverted human nature and destroyed our freedom to choose right and wrong, and some Protestant Christians today still hold that belief. In response the Catholic Church more clearly articulated its teaching on God's

Looking Back

Limbo

Limbo comes from a Latin word meaning "border" or "edge." Because Baptism is necessary for salvation (see John 3:5) but Church leaders knew that God would not condemn an infant to hell just because it died before being baptized, it was theorized that there might be another place those infants would go. Thus, from about the Middle Ages to the twentieth century, some theologians used the word *limbo* to name the destiny of good but unbaptized infants and children. Limbo was described as a state or place of natural happiness without the enjoyment of God's presence.

Limbo was never officially a part of the Church's Tradition, and in recent times we have quit referring to it. The *Catechism* contains no mention of it at all. Rather the Church focuses on the simple truth that Christ died for all, and that those who do not know the Gospel but who honestly seek God and his truth can be saved. So the funeral rites for an unbaptized child entrust the child to God's mercy and ask that God "grant him/her a place in your kingdom of peace." For the child's parents, we pray: "Give them courage and help them in their pain and grief. May they all meet one day in the joy and peace of your kingdom" (*The Rites of the Catholic Church*, volume 1, pages 1037 and 1040).

Revelation. Original sin does not completely pervert human goodness, but it does weaken our natural powers for relating to God and for choosing to do good. The effect of original sin is that we are more influenced by ignorance, suffering, and the knowledge of our own death. We are more inclined to sin, an inclination that in the history of the Church is called **concupiscence.**

With the support of his mother, Saint Monica, Saint Augustine overcame the temptations of sin to become one of the great leaders of the Church.

The doctrine of original sin is behind another important concept in the Scriptures and Tradition. The concept is this: that since the fall of Adam and Eve, the human race has been involved in a spiritual battle between good and evil. On one side of this battle, the evil one, Satan, continues to tempt human beings to reject God and God's laws. Because of original sin, we often give in to this temptation, leading to all kinds of evil, sin, and suffering. On the other side of the battle is the Father, Son, and Holy Spirit. God has promised to help us win this battle against evil. In fact, Jesus Christ's life, death, and Resurrection have already won the battle, and we just have to decide whose side we are going to be on!

Destined for Glory

The story of Adam and Eve raises some difficult questions. Why didn't God keep Adam and Eve from temptation? Why did one single act have such tremendous consequences? Why did God give us such power in the first place?

There are no easy answers to these questions. Sometimes the truth is hard. The truth in this story is that God gave the human race a tremendous gift, the freedom to choose our own destiny. It was only in giving us this gift that God could create beings in his own likeness who could freely choose to receive love and to give love in return. When this gift is used as God hoped it would be, it makes for harmony, joy, creativity, and deep, abiding love relationships. When this gift is used selfishly, it causes disharmony, despair, rigidity, and hate.

But the wonderful news is that God's love is so much greater than our weakness! God has destined us for glory, and his will cannot be stopped by our sin. The great saints understood that God permits sin, but then he brings forth an even greater good from the results of the sin. Nowhere is this more apparent than in the gift of his son, Jesus Christ. Through the horrible sin that resulted in Christ's suffering and death, God turned Adam and Eve's sin into a glorious victory. Jesus Christ has become the new Adam, who rose above temptation to conquer the effects of original sin once and for all. And we are invited to join him in his glory.

> Who will separate us from the love of Christ? Will hardship, or distress, or persecution, or famine, or nakedness, or peril, or sword? . . . No, in all these things we are more than conquerors through him who loved us. For I am convinced that neither death, nor life, nor angels, nor rulers, nor things present, nor things to come, nor powers, nor height, nor depth, nor anything else in all creation, will be able to separate us from the love of God in Christ Jesus our Lord. (Romans 8:35–39)

For Further Reflection

○ Think about times when you have felt worthless or unloved or unsure about what your purpose in life should be. How could reminding yourself that God created you in his image and likeness—that in God's eyes you have infinite value—make a difference?

○ How are you tempted to make bad choices? When do you feel like Saint Paul: "I can will what is right, but I cannot do it. For I do not do the good I want, but the evil I do not want is what I do" (Romans 7:18–19)?

Saintly Profiles

Augustine of Hippo (354–430)

Saint Augustine of Hippo is one of the most significant figures in the history of Western Christianity. The influence of his many books, sermons, and letters can be found on virtually every Christian doctrine, particularly the theology of original sin. But Augustine was not a plaster saint who wrote from an ivory tower.

Saint Augustine was born in Tagaste, North Africa, the son of a successful businessman and an ardent Christian mother, Monica. As a youth he was a brilliant student who found the Bible dull, and preferred the pursuit of other philosophies. Augustine had an appetite for pleasure, pride, sensuality, and wisdom that led him to Rome in 383. He was followed by his widowed mother, who never tired of praying over his many sins—including living for many years with his mistress.

In Rome, despite his fame as a teacher and speaker, Augustine was tormented by depression. At his mother's advice, he sought the counsel of Bishop Ambrose. Through the bishop's teaching, Augustine began to realize that his anxious pursuit of pleasure and quest for wisdom were at their root a disordered quest for God.

After a long delay, Augustine was baptized by Ambrose in 387. He quickly became a priest, a bishop, and a defender of the faith. His classic autobiography, *Confessions,* is an account of his struggle with good and evil, his conversion, and his testimony to the power of grace. Saint Augustine's feast day is August 28.

6 Jesus Christ
True God and True Man

Consider these song titles from both Christian and secular music: "What a Friend We Have in Jesus," "The Wind Beneath My Wings," "Jesus Is the Rock and He Rolled My Sins Away!" and "One of Us." Two of these songs are obviously about Jesus, but the other two could also describe him. Taken together these songs describe several things about Jesus: he is our friend, he encourages us to be our best, he saves us from our sins, and he is God who took on human nature for our sake. From song titles alone, it is clear that Jesus means many things to many people.

The Catholic faith is centered on Jesus Christ. Everything we believe has been revealed in him or through him. You will find that every chapter in this handbook mentions him. Many people have devoted their entire life to studying Jesus and all he means. The Gospel of John puts it this way: "But there are also many other things that Jesus did; if every one of them were written down, I suppose that the world itself could not

Words to Look For

- Gospels
- canon
- Incarnation
- Theotokos
- Immaculate Conception

contain the books that would be written"
(21:25).

In this chapter we look at some basic
things the Catholic Church teaches about
Jesus. We investigate what kind of literature
the Gospels are, and why we have four
Gospels instead of just one. We look at some
of the titles used to describe Jesus, to see what
they can teach us about him. And we learn
about the Incarnation, the belief that Jesus is
both fully God and fully man.

The Gospels:
Faith Portraits of Jesus

Let's be perfectly clear; the best way to learn
about Jesus is to spend time reading the
Gospels yourself. The Catholic Church
strongly encourages its members to read the
Bible—particularly the Gospels. The **Gospels**
are the written accounts of Jesus' life that
were inspired by the Holy Spirit. Reading
them is an important way for us to personally
meet Jesus and to understand his message and
his life. This section explains what the
Gospels are and what to look for when you
read them.

People have some common misperceptions about the four Gospels. Some people
think they were written soon after Jesus' life,
death, and Resurrection. They were not.
The first Gospel, the Gospel of Mark, was
probably written thirty to forty years after
Jesus Christ's death and Resurrection. The
last Gospel to be written, the Gospel of John,
was probably written sixty or seventy years
after Jesus' death and Resurrection.

Some people think the Gospels are
simple biographies of Jesus' life and are
historically accurate in every detail. But by
comparing the same stories in different

The Development of the Gospels

The Gospels are the inspired word
of God, but they did not fall from
the sky in their current form. A
process of development took place
in four stages among the followers
of Jesus:

1. **Appearing in person.** During the
   earthly life and ministry of Jesus,
   people experienced the message
   of the Kingdom of God in his
   words and actions.
2. **Proclaiming the Good News.**
   With the Resurrection came en-
   lightened understanding of what
   Jesus has said and done. The disciples told the stories of the life
   and teachings of Jesus Christ.
   They followed his command to
   "make disciples of all nations"
   (Matthew 28:19). As they did this,
   collections of stories and sayings
   of Jesus' began to take shape.
3. **Writing it down.** The collections
   were edited and shaped by the
   writers we know as Matthew,
   Mark, Luke, and John. Each one
   was inspired to organize the
   Good News (Gospel) in a form
   that best spoke to their different
   communities.
4. **Authorizing the list.** Some
   writings, such as the Gospel of
   Thomas and the Gospel of Peter,
   were not accepted into the canon
   of the New Testament. The **canon**
   is the official list of books of the
   Bible accepted by the Church.
   These other writings were not
   accepted because they did not
   accurately represent the life of
   Jesus according to the Tradition of
   the Church. The canon of twenty-
   seven books in the New Testament that Catholics use today
   was established by the end of
   the fourth century.

Gospels, we can see that this is also a mistaken belief. For example, Jesus' cleansing of the Temple takes place toward the end of the Gospel of Matthew (21:12–17), but it happens at the beginning of the Gospel of John (2:13–16). Here's another famous example: in Matthew Jesus delivers his first great speech from a mountain (5:1), but in Luke Jesus delivers the same speech from a level place or plain (6:17).

These differences may surprise you. But remember that God reveals in the Bible what we need to know for our salvation. Historical, geographical, or even scientific accuracy isn't necessary for our salvation. Let's examine this from another perspective. Have you ever wondered why there are four Gospels instead of just one? It isn't because each Gospel covers a different aspect of Jesus' life. In fact, almost all the Gospel of Mark is repeated in Matthew and Luke.

This painting is titled *The Penitent Saint Peter*. If the image were larger, you could see the tear coming down his cheek. Why is it important for all of us, great and small, to be sorry for our sins and the harm we have caused?

Simone Cantarini © Smith College Museum of Art

The reason we have four Gospels is because the four authors were members of different communities, facing different concerns and challenges. The Holy Spirit guided these communities in understanding and applying the stories and teachings about Jesus to their situations. So sometimes they used the same stories, but told them in slightly different ways to emphasize a religious truth needed for their community.

For example, Matthew's Gospel was probably written for a community with a lot of Jewish converts to Christianity. So the author emphasizes how Jesus was the fulfillment of the expectations and prophecies of the Jewish Scriptures (which Christians call the Old Testament). Thus in Matthew Jesus delivers his first great speech—the message of the New Covenant—from a mountain. Because in Exodus 19:16–25, God communicated the Old Covenant from a mountain, the Jewish people Matthew was addressing would immediately understand that Jesus was much like Moses, offering a new covenant to them.

The Gospels are faith portraits of Jesus, not historical biographies. When they created the Gospels, the authors wrote their stories about Jesus in a way that emphasized the religious truths their communities had learned through the Holy Spirit.

Because of this, we need all four Gospels to understand the whole truth about Jesus. But don't worry about getting confused about the essentials. The religious truths found in the four Gospels never contradict one another—even if the historical details don't always match.

Titles of Jesus in the Bible

In the beginning of the Gospel of Luke, the angel Gabriel tells Mary, "You will conceive in your womb and bear a son, and you will name him Jesus" (1:31). *Jesus* means "God saves" in Hebrew. Jesus' very name reflects his identity and his mission as savior of the world. It is through Jesus, and Jesus alone, that we are saved from our sins, which is why God "gave him the name that is above every name, so that at the name of Jesus every knee should bend, in heaven and on earth and under the earth" (adapted from Philippians 2:9–10).

"Christ" is not Jesus' last name, even though it sounds like we use it that way. It is a formal title for Jesus that is used over four hundred times in the New Testament. *Christ* is the Greek translation of the Hebrew word *messiah,* which means "anointed." To be anointed in the religious sense is to have oil placed on you in preparation for a special mission. In the Old Testament, kings and sometimes prophets were anointed in God's name. After their kingdom collapsed, many Jews believed that God would send a new anointed one, the Messiah (or Christ), who would fulfill all God's promises for salvation. Peter was the first to proclaim about Jesus, "You are the Messiah" (Mark 8:29), announcing that Jesus was the savior the Jews had been hoping for. So when you say, "Jesus Christ," what you are really saying is "Jesus, the anointed one sent by God to be the savior of the world."

Saintly Profiles

Peter

Simon Peter came from obscurity to become one of our greatest saints and our first pope. He came from the village of Bethsaida, in the outback region of Galilee. He and his brother Andrew were humble fishermen when Jesus called them. We know Peter was married because of the miracle in which Jesus healed Peter's mother-in-law (Matthew 8:14, 1 Corinthians 9:5).

Because Peter is an Apostle, it is surprising to discover that he often just doesn't get it. He and the other disciples misunderstand things, forcing Jesus to explain them (Mark 4:10). He objects to Jesus going to Jerusalem to die, and Jesus sharply rebukes him saying, "Get behind me, Satan!" (Matthew 16:23). To his shame Peter denies Jesus three times after Jesus' arrest (Luke 22:54–62).

But Peter's weaknesses are transformed through his faith in Christ. Peter was the first to recognize Jesus as the Messiah, and receives "the keys of the kingdom of heaven" (Matthew 16:16–19). After the Resurrection Jesus commissions Peter to shepherd his flock of believers (John 21:15–17). The Book of Acts shows us Peter as the Church's first dynamic leader. Saint Peter shows that if we are open to the Holy Spirit, we will do great things—despite our weaknesses and mistakes! Saint Peter and Saint Paul share the same feast day, June 29.

Another title frequently used for Jesus is Son of God. In the Old Testament, the title "son of God" is sometimes used for angels, for the people of Israel, and for Israel's kings. The title signifies their special relationship with God. But when it is applied to Jesus in the New Testament, it takes on additional meaning. We are all children of God, but Jesus has a unique relationship with God the Father. At both Jesus' Baptism and his Transfiguration, the Father's voice announces, "This is my Son, the Beloved" (Matthew 3:17, 17:5). Jesus is the only true, eternal Son of the Father, and he is part of the Trinity, fully God himself.

This painting from India of the Nativity does not contain images of angels or the star of Bethlehem. Why do some paintings emphasize the human nature of Jesus' birth and other paintings emphasize his divine nature?

Finally, Jesus is frequently referred to as Lord in the New Testament. *Lord* was a title of respect in Jesus' time, and frequently people who were approaching Jesus called him Lord. But the word had another, unique meaning. *Lord* is the Greek word they used instead of *Yahweh,* the Hebrew name often used for God in the Old Testament. *Yahweh* was considered too sacred to be pronounced out loud, so the Jews came to use the name *Lord* to refer to God. When Thomas calls Jesus "My Lord and my God!" (John 20:28), he is calling Jesus by a title the Jews used for God. Today, whenever we call Jesus Lord, we recognize his divinity and acknowledge that he alone is worthy of our worship and our complete obedience.

The Incarnation: True God and True Man

When we consider the titles used for Jesus in the Bible, we are led to an inescapable conclusion: that the authors of the Gospels came to the conclusion that Jesus Christ was fully God. But does that mean that he wasn't fully human? Absolutely not! Jesus had a human nature just as we do. He laughed, he wept, he felt joy, he experienced temptation, and he felt pain. He had a human body and human will and intellect, thus he could grow "in wisdom and in years" (Luke 2:52). But he also had a divine intellect and will. "He is truly the Son of God who, without ceasing to be God and Lord, became a man and our brother" (*CCC*, number 469).

The mystery of the union of Jesus' divine and human natures in one person is called the **Incarnation.** Like the Trinity, the Incarnation is a mystery that we will never be able to fully understand. But we do know that at the time appointed by God, Jesus Christ, the Word of God, became incarnate. That is, without losing his divine nature, he became fully human. This is expressed in the Nicene Creed when we say, "For us men and for our salvation he was born of the Virgin Mary, and became man."

The common phrase used in Catholic teaching is that Jesus Christ is both "true God and true man." This may sound a little odd to our gender-sensitive modern ears, but the Church uses this phrasing to emphasize that the Word of God became fully human, and human beings are always male or female. The phrase "true man" isn't meant to make us focus on Jesus' masculinity as much as his humanity.

Because in Jesus Christ the human and the divine are perfectly united, he is the perfect and only mediator between God and humanity. God is able to fully reveal his loving plan for us through Jesus. And in learning about Jesus, we understand more fully what God requires of us. In fact, God wants us to share in Christ's divinity! That doesn't mean that he wants to make us gods, but that he wants us to become the image of God we were created to be. By believing in Jesus and in giving ourselves to him with all our whole heart, mind, and soul, the Holy Spirit will help us become more fully the image of God, which is our ultimate destiny.

Who Is Jesus for You?

What kind of a relationship do you have with Jesus? Even if you do not have an answer right away, the question can take you on a journey of discovery. Here are some suggestions:

1. Be patient. Just walk with the question for a while.
2. Make it personal. Think of it as getting to know a new friend. Talk to Jesus. Introduce yourself—he wants to hear from you! Let him know your questions about him. Tell him your doubts and dreams, your fears, and what you are thankful for in life.
3. Investigate. Read Bible stories about Jesus. Imagine yourself there with Jesus and what he says to you. Ask a grandparent, an uncle or an aunt, a parent or a friend about how they have gotten to know Jesus better in their life. Join in Church youth activities and retreats.
4. Reach out and see the face of Jesus in someone in need (Matthew 25:31–46).

Mary, Mother of God

As the Church explored the mystery and meaning of Jesus' life, the Holy Spirit also revealed a deeper understanding of the role played by his mother, Mary. An earlier chapter discussed her position as the first disciple. Now let's explore the meaning of another title given to Mary, ***Theotokos,*** a Greek word that literally means "Mother of God."

The Old Testament contains many stories of holy women who, though society considered them to be weak and powerless, were chosen by God to be his instruments in fulfilling his covenant promises. Some of these women were Miriam, Sarah, Hannah, Ruth, Judith, and Esther. These holy women of Israel paved the way for the plan God had from eternity, that a woman from his chosen people would be the mother of his Son. That plan was fulfilled in Mary, a simple young woman from the little known village of Nazareth. When she said yes to the angel Gabriel, Mary freely gave herself to God's plan to become the mother of the eternal Son of God made man. Because Jesus is God himself, Mary is truly the mother of God.

When Gabriel visited Mary to announce that she was chosen to bear God's Son, the angel said to her, "Greetings, favored one!" (Luke 1:28). God truly favored Mary. This special favor is expressed in two important Catholic beliefs about Mary, her perpetual virginity and her Immaculate Conception.

In God's plan Jesus Christ was born of a virgin as a sign of Christ's divine nature. When Mary asked how she would give birth because she was a virgin, Gabriel answered her, "The Holy Spirit will come upon you, and the power of the Most High will overshadow you" (Luke 1:35). Jesus' birth is a result of God's initiative. As a result Jesus has only God as Father. The virgin birth also symbolizes that Jesus is the new Adam (who also didn't have an earthly father), and will usher in the new heaven and earth that is our ultimate destiny.

Mary remained a virgin throughout her life. Although the Bible mentions Jesus' brothers and sisters, it was common at the time for any close relative, such as a cousin, to be referred to in this way. Because Mary has no physical children other than Jesus, her spiritual motherhood extends to all of us who call Jesus brother.

Pray It!

The Jesus Prayer

The Jesus prayer is an ancient and still popular way to open yourself to a deeper relationship with Jesus. You simply pray these words: **Lord Jesus Christ, Son of God, have mercy on me, a sinner.** The biblical roots of this prayer are in the story of Bartimaeus, the blind beggar who cries out to Jesus from the roadside, "Jesus, Son of David, have mercy on me!" (Mark 10: 46–52), as well as the story of the tax collector who utters very similar words (Luke 18:13).

Pray the Jesus prayer by sitting in a relaxing place, breathing in deeply, and as you slowly exhale, letting go of distractions and worries. Imagine yourself as Bartimaeus before Jesus. What do you ask of Jesus? Then slowly say the prayer over and over to the rhythm of your breathing. Pray the first phrase as you breathe in, the second as you exhale, and so on. Repeat the prayer throughout the day, and be aware of Jesus' presence in everything you do. Try it!

God's special plan for Mary also meant that she was conceived without original sin. The formal name for this belief is called the **Immaculate Conception.** We say that Mary was in a perfect state of grace—that is, her relationship with God was not marred by sin from the first moment she came into being (her conception). Because she was without sin, she had perfect freedom to cooperate with God's plan for our salvation. And Mary remained without sin her entire life. The Catholic Church celebrates Mary's sinless life on the feast of the Immaculate Conception (December 8).

For Further Reflection

○ When you hear the phrase "Jesus saves," what does it mean to you? How would you describe what it means, to someone who isn't a believer?

○ Other titles have been used for Jesus besides those mentioned in this chapter. Some of these titles are Emmanuel (Matthew 1:23), Suffering Servant (Isaiah 53:11), the Alpha and the Omega (Revelation 1:8), and the good shepherd (John 10:11). You may wish to look up the Bible passages associated with these titles to learn more about Jesus.

Looking Back

Mistaken Identity: Heresies About Christ

In the first five centuries of the Church, major controversies arose about whether Jesus was both fully human and fully divine (true God and true man.) Following are some of the false teachings, called heresies, that were condemned:

Docetism claimed that Jesus is truly God but only appears in disguise as human. This teaching denied the full humanity of Jesus.

Arianism, on the other hand, denied that Jesus is fully God. Arius lived around the years 250–336, and taught that Jesus was a creature like we are, and did not exist before he was conceived. Arius saw Jesus as greater than other humans but less than God.

Nestorianism held that the two natures of Jesus (his divinity and his humanity) were like two separate persons and were not fully united in the one person of Jesus Christ. For Nestorius and his followers, this also meant that Mary was the mother of the human Jesus, but not the Mother of God.

Monophysitism said that Jesus had only one divine nature, because after the Incarnation, his human nature was absorbed into his divine nature.

Several important Church councils of bishops were called to correct these heresies. This resulted in some of the carefully defined language about Jesus Christ in the Nicene Creed.

7

Jesus' Message and Mission

Have you ever thought about what your mission in life might be—not just what profession you might like to work in but what your real purpose in life is? Maybe you haven't given it a lot of thought, but as you look toward graduation from high school and move on to work or more school or even volunteer service, it is something to which you will want to give some thought. Jesus had a clear understanding of his mission from an early age. And his mission will give you some clear direction about your purpose in life.

Jesus' Mission: Proclaim the Kingdom of God

Luke has a story about Jesus when he was twelve years old and became separated from his parents for three days (Luke 2:41–52). Mary and his foster father, Joseph, finally find him talking with the teachers in the Temple in Jerusalem. When Mary begins to scold Jesus, he answers, "Did you not know that I must be in my Father's house?" (2:49). Then he returns

Words to Look For

- Kingdom of God
- parables
- miracles
- disciples
- Apostles

with Mary and Joseph and is obedient to them. Luke implies that even as a youngster, Jesus was aware of his special relationship to God and his religious mission.

Outside of this one story, we know very little about Jesus Christ's life as a child, teenager, and young adult. The Church calls these years the hidden life of Jesus. Yet what we do know about these years—that Jesus was obedient to his parents, that he participated in humble but honest work, that he grew in the knowledge of his religion—gives us an example of holiness lived out in daily life. Born without original sin and never committing a sin his entire life, Jesus was preparing for his mission even in these hidden years.

Jesus' public life begins with his Baptism by John the Baptist. Although Jesus had no need to be baptized because he was without sin (and John's Baptism was about turning away from sin), he still asked John to baptize him. In doing so Jesus identified himself with sinners and anticipated the moment when he would take upon himself the sin of all humankind. After his Baptism Jesus immediately went out into the desert to fast and pray in preparation for his mission. During that time he rejected the devil's temptations to achieve his mission through fame, comfort, or political power.

When Jesus returned from the desert, he was truly ready to begin his mission. Each Gospel has its own variation on how he announces his mission. In Matthew and Mark, Jesus begins by proclaiming the Good News of God: "The time is fulfilled, and the kingdom of God has come near; repent" (Mark 1:15). In Luke Jesus reads a prophecy from Isaiah and says that he will fulfill the prophecy (4:16–21). And in John Jesus begins by recruiting disciples who immediately recognize him as the Messiah and Son of God (1:35–51). All these accounts point to one thing: that as the savior of all humanity, an important part of Jesus' mission is to proclaim the **Kingdom of God** and

---

Pray It!

Making the Kingdom Real

Here's a prayer to begin each day, asking for God's help in participating in the mission of Christ:

> As I begin this day become flesh
>   again in me, Father.
> Let your timeless and everlasting
>   love
> live out this sunrise to sunset
> within the possibilities, and
>   impossibilities
> of my own, very human life.
>
> Help me to become Christ to my
>   neighbour,
> food to the hungry, health to the
>   sick,
> friend to the lonely, freedom to
>   the enslaved,
> in all my daily living.
>
> (J. Barrie Shepherd,
> *Diary of Daily Prayer*)

to be a sign of the Kingdom. [*Note:* The word *kingdom* might be misleading because it sounds like we are talking about a particular place, or even about heaven. As will become clear, the Kingdom of God isn't limited to a particular place or time. This is why people sometimes use the phrase "Reign of God," which doesn't imply a particular time or place.]

Jesus' Teaches About the Kingdom

You might be asking, what is the Kingdom of God? We need to start by understanding a little bit about Jesus and the culture he lived in. Jesus was a Jew, and grew up learning the Jewish way of life and practicing the Jewish faith. The Jews understood that God was king over all creation. They believed that the Law given to them at Mount Sinai was God's instrument for ruling people. Some Jews, particularly the Pharisees, believed that anyone who disobeyed even a single law would not be welcome in God's Kingdom. Some Jews also believed that because they were God's Chosen People, anyone who wasn't a Jew could not be part of the Kingdom of God. Another commonly held belief was that God would send a new king, the Messiah, who would use political and military force to make Israel independent again.

Jesus used the parable of the sower to explain how people react to the word of God (Mark 4:1–20). He used parables to make people think differently about God and the world. What parable challenges you to think differently?

Jesus' teaching affirmed the Jewish people's core beliefs that God was Lord of creation, that he had called the Jews to be his special people, and that he had given them the Law. But Jesus also challenged misinterpretations of these core beliefs. A look at the Sermon on the Mount and Jesus' parables will help make this clear. The Sermon on the Mount, found in Matthew, chapters 5–7, is probably the best summary of Jesus' teachings in the Gospels. You may want to take time to read these three chapters if you have not done so before. In the Sermon on the Mount, Jesus assures his listeners, "I have come not to abolish [the Law] but to fulfill [it]" (5:17). Jesus then goes on to quote some of the common religious laws and make their true meaning clear.

For example, the old Law says you should not murder, but Jesus tells us not even to hold onto anger toward another person (5:21–26). The old Law says not to commit adultery, but Jesus tells us not even to lust after someone who is not your spouse (5:27–30). The old Law says love your neighbor and hate your enemy, but Jesus tells us to love our enemies and pray for them (5:43–48). In the Sermon on the Mount, Jesus teaches that in the Kingdom of God, people will grow to reflect God's perfect love (5:48).

Now you might be thinking—just as the people who first heard Jesus—"Who can be this perfect?" That is where the parables come in. They offer a balance to the challenging teachings of the Sermon on the Mount. The **parables** are stories Jesus told that often had a surprising twist, to shock the people who were hearing them into a new way of seeing things.

For example, some Jewish religious leaders taught that sinners (people who break God's Law) are not part of the Kingdom of God, and that good people should not associate with them. In response to this, Jesus told the parable of the prodigal son (Luke 15:11–32). The surprising twist is that the father in the story was totally unconcerned about what his neighbors would think of him welcoming home his errant son. The shock is lost on us because we don't understand that in Jesus' time a father was supposed to disown a sinful son—not welcome him back with robe, ring, sandals, and a dinner in his honor! In contrast to what the religious leaders of Jesus' time taught, the parable teaches that any sinner who repents is welcome in the Kingdom of God.

Holiness in Daily Life

"Don't let what you can't do interfere with what you can." These words of former UCLA basketball coach John Wooden became one young person's motto and helped her face challenges and live a truly holy life. At the age of nine, Carrie Mach was diagnosed with cancer. In the years that followed, up until her death at age seventeen, she underwent twelve major surgeries and several rounds of radiation and chemotherapy.

Though sad and angry at first, Carrie embraced her struggle, and through her faith in Christ, found her purpose in life: reaching out to others who had cancer, telling her story to people her age, and writing poetry. Her message: never allow adversity to rob you of your spirit, but see each day as a precious gift and an opportunity to be who God made you to be. Carrie's life teaches that holiness begins by looking at life with gratitude. In her words, "You will be amazed at how many good things you can find."

Although her life was relatively short, because of her faith Carrie inspired thousands of people in her hometown, in her diocese, and in her state. A special diocesan award was created in her honor to inspire other young people to live with the same faith, hope, and love that Carrie so fully lived. (Quoted in Laurie Delgatto with Marilyn Kielbasa, *Church Women*, page 121)

Jesus taught so much more about the Kingdom by using parables. In the parable of the rich man and Lazarus (Luke 16:19–31), Jesus taught that a rich person who ignores the needs of poor people is not part of the Kingdom of God. In the parable of the good Samaritan (Luke 10:30–37), he taught that even those people who aren't Jews can be members of the Kingdom of God. And in the parable of the unforgiving servant (Matthew 18:23–35), Jesus taught that even though God is quick and generous to forgive us, we cannot be part of God's Kingdom if we do not practice forgiveness ourselves. Thus in the Sermon on the Mount, Jesus reveals the ultimate meaning of the Jewish Law, and in the parables he reveals how God wants to save us, despite the fact that no one has ever kept the Law perfectly.

Although the road traveled by the good Samaritan would have been rugged and mountainous, this portrayal sets it in the lush landscape of the Nicaraguan countryside. By imagining Jesus' stories in settings we are familiar with, artists help the stories come alive for us.

So to summarize, Jesus taught that the Kingdom of God is wherever people are trying to live out God's call to love and forgiveness in a way that goes beyond the "minimum requirements." Anyone can be in the Kingdom, and sometimes the people you least expect are already part of it. You don't have to be perfect to be in the Kingdom, but you do have to be willing to let the Holy Spirit help you grow more perfect in your love and forgiveness.

Jesus Lives the Kingdom of God

If someone advises you to be honest, and a week later you see the person cheating on a test, you probably wouldn't believe much else the person said. The same was true for Jesus: people wouldn't have believed him just because he had an inspiring vision of the Kingdom of God—they believed him because he actually lived the Reign of God. People who were around Jesus experienced God's love and power in a profound way. His whole life, his love for people, his care for the poor and unnoticed, his miracles, his acceptance of his suffering and death made his words real and revealed the nature of the Kingdom of God.

Jesus' miracles are a powerful sign that he made the Kingdom of God present. But before we talk about his miracles, let us look at some other ways people experienced the Kingdom of God when they were around Jesus Christ. One way that is easy to overlook is that Jesus welcomed everybody. Jesus spent time with the rich and the poor, the young and the old, saintly people and known sinners. He was always eating with people; he loved a good meal and conversation. He even invited himself to people's homes to stay (see the story of Zacchaeus, in Luke 19:1–10). In Jesus' acceptance of every person, many people saw a sign of the Kingdom of God.

In fact, Jesus made a special effort to reach out to individuals that "respectable" people shunned. The story of the woman at the well (John 4:1–42) is a wonderful example. In the story Jesus starts a conversation with a woman he doesn't know, something a proper Jewish man would never do. Even worse, she was a Samaritan woman, and at the time Jews despised Samaritans. Finally, she was a known sinner, living with a man who wasn't her husband. The fact that Jesus reached out to sinners and non-Jews scandalized many of the religious leaders of his time. But many people realized that his inclusion of the poor, the sinners, and the outcast was another sign that the Kingdom of God was near.

Another way that Jesus made the Kingdom of God real was through the forgiveness of sins. The Jews believed that only God could forgive sins, which was accomplished by asking the Temple priests to offer animal sacrifices on their behalf. But Jesus claimed the power to forgive sins directly, equating himself with God (Mark 2:1–12, Luke 7:36–50). Today we take the forgiveness of sins almost for granted, but the people in Jesus' time did not do so. For them,

Did You Know?

Four Portraits of Jesus

"Should I use an AGD?" Jamie asked. Baffled, his teacher responded, "What's an AGD?" "An attention-grabbing device," said Jamie, explaining that he learned to start his papers with something to immediately draw readers into the theme of his work. The Gospel writers used this technique.

Mark, addressing persecuted Christians, opens with words that summarize his whole Gospel and alert disciples that they must follow Jesus even unto death: "The beginning of the good news of Jesus Christ, the Son of God" (1:1). To know Jesus as the Son of God is to believe that he is the suffering Messiah who died on the cross and who now lives as their risen Lord.

Matthew grabs the attention of his Jewish Christian audience with a genealogy that connects Jesus to Abraham and David. Accordingly, Jesus becomes the authoritative interpreter of Jewish Law, who brings all that has gone before to fulfillment.

Luke packs tandem accounts of the births of John the Baptist and Jesus with hints of what he will develop in his Gospel: women and poor people are models of faith, Jesus is the savior of all, and salvation is cause for great joy.

In a short but symbolic prologue, John spells out the themes of his Gospel: Jesus is the pre-existent Word of God, the fullest Revelation of God. Those who walk in his light come to know God.

How would you introduce the Good News to people of this century?

to have their sins forgiven by God was just as miraculous as a physical healing. Because the forgiveness of sins is necessary for eternal life with God, it is actually a more important sign of the Kingdom of God than a physical healing.

In the miracle of the loaves and fishes, Jesus provides an abundance of food for hungry people. This miracle is meant to point us to the Eucharist, the nourishment God provides to satisfy our spiritual hunger.

Jesus' Miracles: Making the Kingdom Real

This brings us to miracles. You are probably aware that in the Gospels there are many stories of Jesus performing miracles. Jesus' miracles are often grouped into four categories: physical healings (curing people of paralysis, blindness, leprosy, and so on); exorcisms (driving out demons); bringing the dead back to life (Mark 5:1–23, Luke 7:11–17, John 11:1–44); and nature miracles (feeding five thousand people with a few fish, walking on water, calming storms, and so on). *The Catholic Youth Bible* has an index that lists all Jesus' miracles and parables.

The **miracles** show that Jesus had power over all creation—even demons—and that in the Kingdom of God, we are rescued from evil, suffering, pain, and death. No wonder those who walked with Jesus, who watched him perform these mighty works, were convinced that he was the Messiah, the Son of God. They realized that Jesus Christ and the Kingdom of God are linked together—you cannot have one without the other. Jesus says, "even though you do not believe me, believe the works, so that you may know and understand that the Father is in me and I am in the Father" (John 10:38).

The miracles in the Scriptures—whether performed by or through God the Father, Jesus Christ, or the Holy Spirit—are all signs of God's power and loving presence. Many people continue to experience miracles, often in response to prayer. Because our modern minds want scientific proof, some people have a hard time accepting the reality of miracles. But just because some people do not believe in them does not mean that miracles aren't real! And believing in miracles doesn't mean that you have to believe that God suspends the laws of nature on a regular basis. For people who believe in the Kingdom of God, a starfilled sky, the recovery of a loved one who was seriously ill, and the birth of each new baby can all be experienced as miraculous events.

Jesus' Disciples Share the Mission

Jesus did one more important thing in his public life. At the beginning of his ministry (Matthew 4:18–22, Mark 1:16–20, Luke 5:1–11, John 1:35–51), Jesus gathered a group of women and men whom he taught by his word and example. We call them **disciples**—which means students or followers—and Jesus was preparing them to share in his mission to proclaim the Kingdom of God. The Gospels speak about twelve special disciples who were Jesus' inner circle: Simon Peter, Andrew, James, John, Philip, Bartholomew, Thomas, Matthew, James son of Alphaeus, Thaddaeus, Simon the Cananaean, and Judas Iscariot (Matthew 10:2–4). They are sometimes called the Twelve, or the twelve **Apostles.** The number calls to mind the twelve tribes of ancient Israel—another sign of the continuity between the Old and New Covenants. The bishops of the Catholic Church are the direct successors of the Apostles.

Jesus had many other disciples besides the Apostles. These disciples were married and unmarried, poor and wealthy, young and old, women and men. In fact, the Gospels tell about a group of women who were among Jesus' closest followers. Luke names some of them: Mary Magdalene, Joanna, Susanna, "and many others, who provided for them out of their resources" (Luke 8:3). These women not only financed Jesus' ministry but also traveled with him throughout his ministry, and became witnesses to his death and Resurrection. Because many rabbis from Jesus' time

Looking Back

A Modern Miracle

Every evening the cook at the Catholic parish in Ribera del Fresno, Spain, began to prepare dinner for the town's poor people and the children of the nearby orphanage. This night, January 25, 1949, the cook could see there was not enough rice and meat to feed everyone. She prayed to Blessed John Macías, the town's patron, and shortly thereafter noticed the rice pot was overflowing. She filled additional pots, but when the overflow continued, she called in witnesses. At evening's end everyone had been fed and there were leftovers.

Vatican experts and theologians examined the leftover rice and interviewed twenty-two witnesses, but found no natural explanation. The multiplication of rice at Ribera del Fresno is considered a modern miracle.

In the process of naming saints, the church has approved hundreds of miracles during the last century alone. The Catholic Church has a scrupulous process for approving miracles, and many more possible miracles are rejected than accepted. Miracles like the one at Ribera del Fresno remind us that God's grace continues to overflow in the modern world. (Based on Kenneth L. Woodward, *Making Saints*, pages 209–210) warned against even speaking with women in public, Jesus' close association with these women seems to be another way he challenged commonly held beliefs of his time in order to make the Kingdom of God present.

The relationship between Jesus and his disciples teaches us several things about the Kingdom of God. If you've been following closely, you may be able to guess what they are. First, it teaches us that the Kingdom of God isn't about just the relationship between you and Jesus but the relationship between you, other believers, and Jesus. We need the love and support of other Christians to be true disciples of Jesus Christ. Second, the relationship between Jesus and his disciples teaches us that God wants us to take part in proclaiming the Gospel message. Jesus sent the Twelve out on their own (Matthew 10:1–7), and another time he sent out seventy disciples to be his messengers (Luke 10:1–20). Even though as God, Jesus could have accomplished everything needed without human help, he honors our freedom by giving us the responsibility of being partners in his mission.

In this image of Saint Francis, notice the wounds on his hands, called stigmata. Stigmata appear mysteriously on the hands and feet of people of great holiness, uniting them with the suffering of Christ on the cross. Saint Francis is the first person reported to have experienced stigmata.

Everything that we have just said about the disciples is also true for the Catholic Church today. Under the guidance of the Holy Spirit, the Church has the responsibility for continuing Jesus' mission of proclaiming and making real the Kingdom of God. Jesus Christ has given the Church permission to act in his name. Despite this some people still ask, "If I believe in Jesus and live a good life, why do I need to belong to a church?" The answer is simple: to be a disciple of Jesus means you must belong to a community committed to continuing his mission together.

Even though the answer is simple, it doesn't mean that living it out is always easy. The Church has never been a perfect example of the Kingdom of God and does not claim to be. Conflict, sin, and scandal can be found in both the local churches and the universal Church. The Church can only claim to be made up of sinful but redeemed (saved) people, relying on the power of the Holy Spirit to be a sign of the

Reign of God in the world. Fortunately we have Jesus' promise that God's love will always prevail.

For Further Reflection

○ What is your favorite story about Jesus from the Gospels? Why is this story meaningful to you? What message does this story have about how we should live our lives?

○ What do you believe about miracles? Have you ever witnessed an event you consider to be a miracle?

○ The chapter started by asking what is your mission in life. How does the idea of sharing in Jesus' mission help you clarify your purpose in life?

Saintly Profiles

Saint Francis of Assisi (1182–1226)

Fame. Comfort. Power. Like Jesus in the desert, Saint Francis faced down these temptations to find his purpose in life. He was the son of a wealthy twelfth-century Italian merchant, and early in his life was devoted to partying and his social status.

Then his life changed. He became seriously ill after a soldiering experience, and he began to rethink his values. Encountering a begging leper, he embraced the man, gave him money, and began to spend more time with the poor and outcasts. His father was furious for what he saw as a waste of time, and dragged him before the local bishop to set Francis straight. Instead, Francis stripped out of his fine clothes, gave them to his father, and renounced all worldly wealth and possessions.

At first Francis's former partymates looked at his new way of life and scoffed. However, there was something remarkably appealing about the way that Francis loved the poor and the sick, prayed, preached the Good News, and went about rebuilding the Church one stone at a time. Francis is known for his prayer life, particularly the way that his prayers reflect the joy and awe of God that he experienced in nature. Wild animals were known to flock to him and even obey him!

The joy and freedom with which Francis lived as a follower of Christ soon attracted so many followers that he had to establish an order and write a rule for them. Today Franciscans are fond of summarizing the rule with Francis's words: "Preach the gospel. If necessary, use words." Saint Francis's feast day is October 4.

8

Jesus' Death

Around A.D. 30 a traveling Jewish rabbi made a decision that would change the world forever. For several years he had been traveling in Galilee and Samaria, teaching, healing, and forming a band of disciples to continue his mission after his departure. Now his disciples were ready for the final challenge that lay ahead. One of them just announced that he believed the rabbi was the Messiah, the Son of the Living God. Then the rabbi—known as Jesus, son of Joseph the carpenter—made the decision to travel to Jerusalem, where he knew that he would meet his death.

The **Passion** (the word we use to describe Jesus' suffering) and death of Jesus is a visible part of Catholic life. Catholic crucifixes have the dead body of Christ—called the corpus—on them, even though most other Christians remember Jesus with empty crosses. We have special prayer forms—the stations of the cross and the mysteries of the rosary—to help us reflect on the meaning of Jesus' death. On Good Friday we strip our churches bare to emphasize the emptiness and sorrow that

Words to Look For

- Passion
- scribes
- chief priests
- Pharisees

Jesus and his disciples felt on that fateful day long ago. Why does Jesus' death have such importance for Catholics? Maybe your question is even more basic: Why did Jesus have to die at all?

The Jewish and Roman Leaders Wanted Jesus Dead

The mystery of the Incarnation tells us that Jesus was both true God and true man. So it is no surprise that we believe in both natural and supernatural reasons behind the death of Jesus. To fully understand the importance of Jesus' death, we need to understand both sets of reasons. Let's start with the natural—the human—reasons.

The Nicene Creed states, "Jesus Christ suffered under Pontius Pilate, was crucified, died, and was buried." This statement tells us that a Roman governor—Pontius Pilate— was involved in Jesus' death, but it doesn't mention the Jewish religious leaders. The Gospels are clear that both Jewish and Roman leaders wanted Jesus dead. But why?

For the religious leaders, the answer is fairly clear: Jesus challenged their authority to such an extent that they believed Jesus would lead the common people to rebel against their teaching. The previous chapter mentioned how Jesus' mission confronted some of the teachings of the Pharisees and priests. These are some specific examples:

Christians and Jews

During the earliest years of the church, when most Christians were also Jews, animosity sprang up. Some Jews persecuted the Jews who believed in Christ. The language of John's Gospel reflects this discord. The Gospel according to John refers to those responsible for Jesus death as "the Jews," even though it was a relatively small group of Jewish leaders. Through the ages it became a mispercep- tion that the whole Jewish race is responsible for Jesus' death, and has been used to justify everything from discrimination to genocide.

Even today anti-Semitism (the sentiment of hatred against Jews) is seen in many parts of the world. This is a gross misunderstanding. Christianity has no room in it for hatred and intolerance. Contem- porary Church teaching tells us that not only are the Jews *not* to blame for Jesus' death but that we are spiritual descendants of Judaism, and that Christians and Jews have much to learn from each other.

- **Mark 2:23—3:6.** The **Pharisees** and **scribes** taught that you could do absolutely no work on the Sabbath. Jesus' disciples plucked grain on the Sabbath, and Jesus healed on the Sabbath. Jesus challenged the Pharisees' and scribes' teaching by saying, "The sabbath was made for humankind, and not humankind for the sabbath" (2:27).
- **Mark 2:1–12.** Jesus claimed to have the power to forgive sins, which the Jewish religious leaders believed was a power that belonged to God alone.

- **Luke 16:19–31.** Many of the religious leaders believed that having material wealth was a sign of being right with God. Jesus claimed that God also blessed the poor. He even taught that being rich while ignoring the poor was a sin.
- **Luke 15:1–10.** The religious leaders avoided having anything to do with common sinners such as prostitutes and tax collectors. Yet Jesus freely associated with these people, and chided the Pharisees for avoiding them.

By showing the violence associated with the Passion and death of Jesus, artists remind us that he really suffered for us. Do the depictions of violence in today's popular media have any positive value?

When Jesus decided to bring his mission to Jerusalem, things came to a head. Jesus' presence in the city that was the center of Jewish faith was too direct a challenge to ignore. First of all, when Jesus arrives crowds welcome him as a triumphant king (Matthew 21:1–11)! Next Jesus goes to the Temple, the very seat of the priests' and scribes' authority, and casts out the moneychangers (Matthew 21:12–13). He did this to protest how the chief priests and scribes had let commerce and profit become intertwined with the practice of the Jewish faith. Mark and Luke indicate that it was after this act that the religious leaders began looking for a way to kill Jesus (Mark 11:18).

However, the Jewish leaders could not put Jesus to death simply because he challenged their authority. No, the crime they charged him with was blasphemy, the crime of speaking irreverently about God. The **chief priests** and scribes claimed that Jesus committed blasphemy when he claimed powers for himself that belonged to God alone. According to the Law of the Old Covenant, a person could be stoned to death for this. The irony is that as the Son of God, Jesus was not committing blasphemy but simply speaking the truth—a truth that the religious leaders of his time could not accept.

The Romans' reasons for wanting the death of Jesus are a little harder to figure out from the Gospel stories. Because Israel was part of the Roman Empire at the time, we know that the Jewish religious leaders needed the backing of Pilate to have someone executed. As the Roman governor of the region, Pilate ordered all public executions. Most likely the chief priests convinced Pilate that Jesus was the potential leader of a rebellion (Luke 23:5)—which the Romans were quick to squash.

The Gospel stories give indications that Pilate did not want to execute Jesus. In Luke Pilate even publicly declares Jesus innocent three times. But facing an angry mob, he ultimately gives his permission for Jesus' death. Were the Gospel authors downplaying Pilate's responsibility for Jesus' death to make the Christian faith more appealing to Roman citizens? Or did the otherwise ruthless Pilate (we know this from other writings of the time) have a soft spot in his heart for Jesus?

Jesus' Death Is the Real Thing

Some people think that because Jesus was God, his death was no big deal for him. After all, didn't he know how it would all turn out? But the Gospel stories take great care to show that Jesus experienced doubt, pain, and fear, as he was betrayed, put through a mock trial, tortured, and crucified. He was fully human, and was not saved from these human feelings because of his divine nature. Before his arrest he prayed in the garden at Gethsemane, "Father, if you are willing, remove this cup from me; yet, not my will but yours be done" (Luke 22:42). Jesus knew that the end was near, and like any of us, did not want to experience the pain of a torturous death.

Jesus' execution was especially brutal. A Roman execution was meant to be as horrible as possible to frighten people into obedience. First, Jesus was scourged (whipped) with a whip that had pieces of bone and metal embedded in the leather. It

One Solitary Life

He was born in an obscure village, the child of a peasant. He grew up in another village, where he worked in a carpenter shop until he was thirty. Then, for three years, he was an itinerant preacher.

He never wrote a book. He never held an office. He never had a family or owned a home. He didn't go to college. He never lived in a big city. He never traveled more than two hundred miles from the place where he was born. He did none of the things that usually accompany greatness. He had no credentials but himself.

He was only thirty-three when the tide of public opinion turned against him. His friends ran away. One of them denied him. He was turned over to his enemies and went through the mockery of a trial. He was nailed to a cross between two thieves. While he was dying, his executioners gambled for his garments, the only property he had on earth. When he was dead, he was laid in a borrowed grave, through the pity of a friend.

Twenty centuries have come and gone, and today he is the central figure of the human race. I am well within the mark when I say that all the armies that ever marched, all the navies that ever sailed, all the parliaments that ever sat, all the kings that ever reigned—put together—have not affected the life of man on this earth as much as that one solitary life.

(Attributed to James Allen Francis)

was meant to tear the skin from a person's back. Many people died from this alone. Then, he had to carry on his bloody back the crossbeam on which he would be crucified. Finally, he was

stripped of his clothes to completely humiliate him and nailed through his wrists to a crossbeam, which was lifted into place on a permanent post. His arms and feet would have been tied to the cross to keep his body from tearing free of the nails. People who were crucified often lived for days before dying from blood loss, exposure, or from the inability to breathe. According to the Gospel accounts, Jesus died in six hours or less, no doubt in part due to the blood he lost from the scourging.

"And being found in human form, he humbled himself and became obedient to the point of death— even death on a cross" (Philippians 2:7–8).

It is reassuring for us to know that Jesus Christ shared our humanity in his fear of pain and death. It isn't wrong to want to avoid pain and death. But Christ's commitment to following the will of God was stronger than his fear. He could have stayed away from Jerusalem or he could have slipped out of town when things started to heat up. But he didn't. He willingly accepted one of the most painful and humiliating ways to die that human beings have ever devised. His final words on the cross, "Father, into your hands I commend my spirit" (Luke 23:46), signify the complete trust he ultimately had in his Father.

The Religious Meaning of the Cross

Jesus Christ's death was not merely a chance event or an unfortunate set of circumstances. His death was part of the mystery of God's plan for the salvation of the human race. Saint Peter, in talking about the death of Jesus, said, "This man [was] handed over to you according to the definite plan and foreknowledge of God" (Acts 2:23). This doesn't mean that Pilate, the soldiers, the chief priests and scribes, or anyone else responsible for Jesus' death was just a puppet, acting without free will. God is master of time and history, and can accomplish his purposes through freely made human decisions, even sinful decisions.

And what was God's purpose in the death of Christ? Ever since the sin of Adam and Eve, the human race has been under the curse of death as the penalty for their sin. Listen to the words of Saint Paul: "Therefore, just as sin came into the world through one man, and death came through sin, and so death spread to all because all have sinned" (Romans 5:12). But God would not abandon his beloved creatures to death. He planned that his Son, God himself, would take on the burden of sin for all humanity, dying so that we might be free from the sentence of death. "[Christ] himself bore our sins in his body on the cross, so that, free from sins, we might live for righteousness; by his wounds you have been healed" (1 Peter 2:24). Salvation from sin and death for every person in every age comes through the death and Resurrection of Jesus Christ.

Does all this sound too fantastic to believe? Evidently many people living at the time of Jesus thought so. Many of the speeches in the Acts of the Apostles and much of the teaching in the letters of the New Testament are devoted to explaining how Jesus' death frees us from sin. Their teaching tended to fall into three metaphors, or symbolic explanations: Jesus, the suffering servant; Jesus, the Paschal lamb; and Jesus, the ransom for many. Because the symbols and the Scriptures associated with these metaphors are important in Catholic liturgy and theology, let's look at each one of them.

Looking Back

Christ's Suffering

Julian of Norwich, a medieval mystic, was born around 1342. You can find her Saintly Profile in the God the Father chapter. Julian's visions connected the sufferings of Christ with God's tender and infinite love. To Julian, Jesus' willingness to suffer is a sign of his deep compassion and intimate care for us.

At the same time as I saw this sight of the head bleeding, our good Lord showed a spiritual sight of his familiar love. I saw that he is to us everything which is good and comforting for our help. He is our clothing, who wraps and enfolds us for love, embraces us and shelters us, surrounds us for his love, which is so tender that he may never desert us. (*Julian of Norwich: Showings*, long text, chapter 5)

Jesus, the Suffering Servant

It is important to remember that the first Christians, like Jesus himself, were Jews. So when they looked for explanations of Jesus' death, it is natural that they looked to their sacred writings, the Jewish Scriptures (which are some of the books in the Christian Old Testament). No doubt they immediately thought of the "suffering servant" passages in Isaiah. You can find these in Isaiah 42:1–4, 49:1–6, 50:4–9, and 52:13—53:12. These passages describe an unnamed servant of the Lord who suffers greatly—not as punishment for his own sins but to save the people from theirs. "He [the suffering servant] was wounded for our transgressions, / crushed for our iniquities; / upon him was the punishment that made us whole, / and by his bruises we are healed" (Isaiah 53:5).

It is easy to see how these passages apply to the suffering and death of Jesus. In making this connection, the early Christians began to understand how Jesus' freely given obedience to the Father's will (or plan) was part of the explanation for how we have been freed from our sins. "For just as by the one man's disobedience the many were made sinners, so by the one man's obedience the many will be made righteous" (Romans 5:19).

Jesus, the Paschal Lamb

Another story in the Jewish Scriptures that connects to Jesus' suffering and death is the story of the Paschal, or Passover, lamb. This story goes all the way back to the time when the Israelites were slaves in Egypt. To convince the Pharaoh to let the people go, God sent a series of ten plagues upon the Egyptian people. The last and most horrible plague was an angel of death that killed the firstborn son of every family in the land. Moses instructed the Israelites to kill a lamb and put its blood on their doorpost so the angel of death would pass over their home without killing the firstborn son. After this Pharaoh let the people go, and they began their journey to the Promised Land.

In the Gospel of John and in the Book of Revelation, Jesus is referred to as "the Lamb of God who takes away the sin of the world" (John 1:29). To make it perfectly clear, in the Gospel of John, Jesus is crucified on the feast of the Passover, the same day that the Paschal lambs were being slaughtered in the Temple. Just as the blood of the Paschal lambs liberated the Israelites from death and slavery, so too does Jesus' death and Resurrection save all humanity from death and from slavery to sin. You will sometimes hear Christians expressing this idea with phrases such as, "I've been washed in the blood of the lamb."

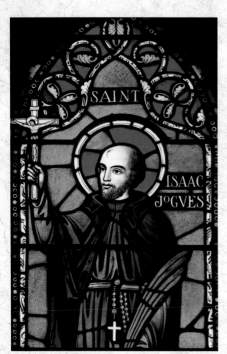

Stained-glass windows in churches often portray saints. This image of Saint Isaac Jogues shows him with a palm branch, which symbolizes his martyrdom. What saints are pictured in your church, and do you know their stories?

Jesus, the Ransom for Many

In the Roman world, a ransom was the price paid to release a slave. The payment was made in front of a shrine to a local god, to indicate the slave was becoming the property of that god and could no longer be owned by another person. Because they wanted to reach Gentiles (non-Jews) as well as Jews, the early Christians adapted this concept to help explain the saving nature of Jesus' death to Roman citizens. We see this particularly in the Gospel of Mark, where Jesus says, "For the Son of Man came not to be served but to serve, and to give his life a ransom for many" (10:45). The idea of ransom helps us understand that Jesus paid to God the price of our freedom, so that we are no longer "owned" by sin and death.

All these explanations are important for understanding what Catholics mean when we say that Jesus died for our sins. We must be careful, though, not to interpret them too literally. If you take any of these metaphors to the extreme, God comes off as an angry and cold-hearted accountant, demanding exact payment in blood before setting us free. This is the exact opposite of Jesus' description of God as a loving and forgiving Father. What these three explanations want us to appreciate is that through the death of Jesus Christ, the separation between God and humanity—which is caused by sin—has been bridged. This is God's great gift of love to us, the freely offered sacrifice of God himself, in the person of Jesus Christ.

What Jesus' Death Means for Us

For Catholics and for all Christians, the death of Jesus Christ is not some abstract teaching or event that happened long ago. It

---

Saintly Profiles

Saint Isaac Jogues

Throughout the history of the Church, Catholics have imitated Jesus' willingness to suffer and die for the sake of the Kingdom of God. This was particularly true for some missionaries who preached the Gospel to people who were hostile to its message. Saint Isaac Jogues was one of those people. Born in Orléans, France, in 1607, Isaac Jogues became a Jesuit and was ordained to the priesthood. He was sent as a missionary to the Hurons in Canada. The Huron tribe was open to the Christian message, and many were baptized into the Catholic faith. But the Huron's enemy, the Mohawk tribe, was not as open. Isaac Jogues and his traveling companions were captured by Mohawks and tortured. His lay assistant was killed. Isaac Jogues was made a slave to the chief, and was later freed by Dutch traders who eventually returned him to France.

In 1644 Isaac Jogues returned to Canada and attended a peace conference between the Iroquois federation and the French. He was chosen as an envoy to the Mohawks to secure their approval of the peace treaty, which he accomplished. On his return to Quebec, he requested and received permission to go back to the Mohawks as a missionary. On the journey there he was captured again by the Mohawks, who thought the gifts he had left for them on his previous visit were responsible for a crop failure and an epidemic. This time he was tortured and killed. Several other Jesuit missionaries were also martyred during those early years, and together with Isaac Jogues, they are known as the North American Martyrs, the patron saints of North America. Their feast day is October 19.

is the ultimate sign of the love of God that is available to each and every person who puts their faith and trust in God. The cross, the symbol of death, has been transformed into the symbol of freedom and life! Why else would we wear and display a symbol of public execution? (Think about it, wearing a cross is kind of like wearing a small model of an electric chair.) Catholics display crucifixes—crosses with the tortured body of Jesus—to remind us visually of the great love God has for us. The words of Saint Paul say it best:

> For while we were still weak, at the right time Christ died for the ungodly. Indeed, rarely will anyone die for a righteous person—though perhaps for a good person someone might actually dare to die. But God proves his love for us in that while we still were sinners Christ died for us. Much more surely then, now that we have been justified by his blood, will we be saved through him from the wrath of God. For if while we were enemies, we were reconciled to God through the death of his Son, much more surely, having been reconciled, will we be saved by his life. But more than that, we even boast in God through our Lord Jesus Christ, through whom we have now received reconciliation. (Romans 5:6–11)

Pray It!

The Triduum

The holiest days of the year for Catholics are the days of the Easter Triduum. Holy Thursday, Good Friday, Holy Saturday, and Easter Day for us are inextricably linked. Jesus' suffering and death does not stand alone but finds the fullness of its meaning when it is placed in the context of the Last Supper and the Resurrection. As early as the fourth century, Christians had an understanding of these days as connected to one another. On Good Friday the celebration of the Lord's Passion—which comprises a liturgy of the word, veneration of the cross, and the distribution of Holy Communion—helps us meditate on Jesus' suffering. We are not meant to meditate in morbid sorrow, but to always remember that Jesus' suffering and death mean love, salvation, and hope.

At the veneration the priest or deacon announces three times: "This is the wood of the cross, on which hung the Savior of the world."

And we respond: "Come, let us worship" (*The Sacramentary*, page 156).

For Further Reflection

- Read one of the Gospel accounts of Jesus' death (Matthew 26:1—27:66, Mark 14:1—15:47, Luke 22:1—23:56, John 18:1—19:42). What thoughts and feelings do you have? What inspires you?
- Catholics remember the sacrifice of Jesus every time we celebrate the Mass. The next time you attend Mass, watch for words or actions that remind you of the three metaphors—the suffering servant, the Paschal lamb, or the ransom for many—used to explain the reason for Jesus' death.

9 Jesus' Resurrection

Would the story of Cinderella be so well known if the prince hadn't noticed Cinderella at the last minute and had her try on the glass slipper? Or would episode IV of *Star Wars* have been much of a movie if Luke Skywalker had missed the tiny, little vent with his final shot and failed to blow up the Death Star? Would you believe that these fictional stories, like so many others, are rooted in the greatest true story of all time: the Resurrection of Jesus Christ?

As human beings we have a deep desire to see the forces of life conquer those of death, especially in the darkest and most hopeless of times. We have this desire in us because in God's plan, we are not destined for death but for eternal life. Through the life, death, and Resurrection of Jesus Christ, all humanity has an opportunity to share in the eternal life God has planned for us from the beginning of time.

This is why Christ's **Resurrection** is the single most important event in all history. Saint Paul says it bluntly, "If Christ has not been raised, then our proclamation has been in vain and your faith has been in vain" (1 Corinthians 15:14).

Words to Look For

- *Resurrection*
- *Paschal mystery*
- *Ascension*

Without the Resurrection of Christ, the Gospels would never have been written and the Catholic Church would never have existed.

Let's bring this to a personal level. The most important question you will ever face is this: "Do I believe that Jesus Christ was raised from the dead?" Why? Because how you answer that question will determine how seriously you live out your belief in Jesus. If you answer, "I believe in the Resurrection!" how can you not make Jesus Christ the center of your life?

The Gospel Accounts

When Jesus appears to two disciples walking to Emmaus, in Luke 24:13–35, they do not recognize him. Then when he blesses and breaks the bread for their meal, as depicted in this painting, they suddenly recognize him as the risen Christ. When have you unexpectedly encountered Jesus?

Each of the four Gospels has a slightly different account of what happened in the days after Jesus' death. The Gospel of Mark offers the fewest clues; it originally ended with several women discovering an empty tomb and an angel telling the women that Jesus had been raised. (A longer ending was later added to the Gospel, in which Jesus appears to Mary Magdalene and the other disciples.) In the Gospel of Matthew, Pilate places a guard at the tomb to keep the disciples from stealing Jesus' body, but an angel rolls away the stone anyway. The resurrected Jesus meets the disciples on a mountain in Galilee, where he gives them a mission to "make disciples of all nations" (Matthew 28:19). The Gospel of John takes the prize for the most Resurrection stories, with four separate accounts of Jesus appearing to different people.

Despite their differences, the Gospel stories have these points in common:

- First the women disciples, and then the men, go to the tomb and discover that the body of Jesus is no longer there.
- The people who go to the tomb find out from angels that Jesus is no longer dead but alive, and will reveal himself to the disciples soon. (Although in the Gospel of John, Jesus reveals himself to Mary Magdalene at the tomb.)
- Later Jesus appears to groups of disciples to wish them peace and charge them with continuing his mission. Often the disciples' initial reaction is shock and fear. But soon they experience Jesus in such striking ways that they cannot

doubt that it is he—alive again, and yet somehow different from the way he was before his death.

The thing that most people want to know is, "What was the resurrected Jesus like?" The fact that the Gospel accounts are purposefully vague gives us one clue: the resurrected Jesus couldn't easily be explained in human terms. He shows up without warning and disappears just as suddenly. The disciples know he's not a ghost because he can be touched and he eats with them. He's different enough that some people do not recognize him immediately, yet when they do recognize him, he's still the same person they knew from before. Being in his risen presence gives them peace and hope.

Because of these things, the Church teaches that a resurrected body is not a reanimated corpse. Jesus was truly transformed by the Resurrection, just as we will be after our death. We will still be the same person, but we will have a resurrected body in an utterly new kind of existence. Beyond that we cannot say much more, but we can trust that it will be truly glorious and wonderful!

Evidence for the Resurrection

But how do we know that the Gospel accounts are all true? What if the Gospel writers simply made it all up? This is a valid question that we must meet head-on if we are to be honest about what we believe. You will find that, just like when trying to prove the existence of God, there are good arguments to show that it is reasonable to believe in the Resurrection of Jesus as an actual historical event. Let's explore some of those arguments.

One argument is that we can trust the historical validity of the New Testament

A Personal Experience of Resurrection

Lisa Boyer is a young adult whose journey to Confirmation was an experience of Resurrection. She tells her story in her own words:

The death of my beloved brother Jason in a car accident so devastated me that for a time I prayed that God would take me too. I saw my parents in agony, and Jason, my best friend, who had always lent me strength, was gone. I felt my soul had been damaged beyond repair. I began to question God. How could God take a man with his whole life ahead of him? How was it possible that my mother's loving God existed when God showed me so little mercy?

In July 2001 I made a pilgrimage to the Basilica of Our Lady of Guadalupe in Mexico City. The tears I had been unable to cry for Jason almost two years before came so easily as I lit a candle for him and first felt the promise of peace. I knew I must heal my relationship with God.

That fall I began the RCIA program so I could receive the sacrament of Confirmation. I found that my anger and pain began to melt away. Then as I knelt during the third scrutiny ceremony in Lent, I felt the power of the Holy Spirit lift me up. At that moment I knew that through all those hard times, the Lord had gotten me through, when I had neither the strength nor desire to go on.

Now it really feels like I am a new person. I feel unbelievable peace and joy and hope for my future.

books and letters. Although we do not have original copies of the New Testament books or letters, we have copies that can be traced back to within a few centuries of Jesus' earthly life. And we have lots of different ancient copies of the New Testament books and letters coming from different locations. When historians take these things into account, we have greater proof for the authenticity of the New Testament books than for any other ancient writing.

This thirteenth-century painting depicts Christ descending into hell to free those righteous people who had died before his Resurrection. Notice the broken door and the devil below Christ's feet—symbols of Christ's power over hell and death.

Another argument is that the Resurrection was a consistent belief in the early Church. You can find it in all four Gospels, in the letters of Saint Paul, and in the speeches contained in the Acts of the Apostles. In fact, experiencing the risen Jesus was considered a key qualification for being accepted as one of the Apostles (Acts 1:15–22). This is clear evidence that the earliest Christians accepted it as a matter of fact.

There is also the argument of the empty tomb. If the tomb was not empty, surely the Romans or the Jewish religious leaders would have produced the corpse to put to rest the rumors of Jesus' Resurrection right away. No evidence has been found that they tried to do this. But you might ask, "Couldn't the disciples have stolen Jesus' corpse and then claimed that he had risen?" The problem with this argument is that several of the disciples died as martyrs rather than deny their faith in the resurrected Jesus. Why would they have chosen to die for a hoax if they knew that Jesus had not really risen?

And we can argue that the Resurrection appearances of Jesus caused a profound change in his followers. This may be the most important evidence of all. After Jesus' death his disciples were beaten, discouraged, and afraid for their lives. Yet somehow they found the courage to go out in public and continue Jesus' mission, facing ridicule, persecution, and even death. They preached with total conviction that Jesus had risen. What other reasonable explanation could there be for this change than their encounter with the risen Christ?

No one can provide you with scientific evidence supporting Jesus' Resurrection. The Resurrection was not a historical event in the same sense that Jesus' death was. Everyone, whether or not they believed that Jesus was the Son of God, could see his dead body. But only those who had faith in Jesus experienced him in his resurrected body (except the Apostle Paul, who was a special case). But these arguments are convincing in showing that it is reasonable for good, intelligent people to believe in the Resurrection of Jesus.

The Religious Meaning of the Resurrection

As was said at the beginning of this chapter, the religious meaning of the Resurrection is huge for Christians. To repeat Saint Paul, "If Christ has not been raised, then our proclamation has been in vain and your faith has been in vain." The following are three important things we know because of the Resurrection.

Jesus Is Confirmed as the Son of God

For the first disciples, seeing the resurrected Jesus was clear proof that Jesus was more than just another human being. The story of doubting Thomas says it most clearly. When Thomas sees the resurrected Jesus for the first time, he declares, "My Lord and my God!" (John 20:28). Belief in Jesus' Resurrection and belief in the Incarnation go hand in hand. Throughout the centuries people have believed in the divinity of Jesus Christ because they first believed in his Resurrection.

All Jesus' Teachings Are True

If the Resurrection reveals the truth of Jesus' divinity, then it also reveals that all his other teachings are true, too. If we believe that Jesus was raised from the dead, how can we not also believe that Jesus spoke the truth

○ in claiming that God's love for us has no limits
○ in claiming that we only find fulfillment first by loving and serving God, and second by loving and serving others

"He Descended into Hell"

The phrase "He descended into hell" first means that Jesus experienced death as completely as we do. He too experienced the complete loss of physical life that comes with death. Second, it means that after his death, Jesus went to the realm of the dead, where the souls of all those who had died before him awaited his judgment. Those who were righteous were brought into heaven, and the unrighteous were condemned to remain in hell, separated from God for all eternity. By descending into hell, Jesus completely established his power over all creation—on earth, in heaven, and in hell.

- in claiming that forgiveness is more powerful and Godlike than revenge
- in teaching that the rich must share with the poor
  - in teaching that we must refuse to accept the human-made prejudices that separate us from one another

The Resurrection is a guarantee that all these things—and many other things Jesus taught that are not on this list—are true beyond a doubt.

In this detail from a larger painting, Mary Magdalene clings to the foot of Jesus' cross. Her presence at the cross when many of the other disciples have already fled is a sign of her courage and her devotion to Christ.

The Paschal Mystery

Finally and wonderfully, the Resurrection teaches us that death is not the end; death is the doorway into new and eternal life. The life that we now live is not all there is, as some people claim. The sufferings and the pain of this life can be endured because we know that something better and glorious is yet to come. When we believe in Jesus Christ and in his Resurrection, our whole way of life is transformed. Who would not want to live this life so that we are ready to enter into the glory of heaven, where:

> He will dwell with them as their God;
> they will be his peoples,
> and God himself will be with them;
> he will wipe every tear from their eyes.
> Death will be no more;
> mourning and crying and pain will be no more.
>
> (Revelation 21:3–4)

The Church calls this—the mystery that Christ had to suffer and die to save us from sin and death and to rise with him to new and glorious life—the **Paschal mystery.** In the Gospel of John and the Book of Revelation, Jesus is compared to the Paschal lamb. Just as the Paschal lamb had to die to save the Israelite people from death in the first Passover, now Jesus saves us all from death in the new Passover.

The Paschal mystery applies to our lives right now. We don't have to wait until our final death to experience new life. Throughout our life we experience big and little "deaths" in a variety of ways. These deaths might be through the suffering caused by illness, the emotional loss of a good friend who moves away, the heartache of failing to make the team, or the anger and hurt caused by divorce. The Paschal mystery promises that if we maintain our faith in God during these times, God can make something life-giving come out of our pain and loss.

If you listen to faithful Christians for a while, you will hear story after story about how God helped them see or experience something good and wonderful during difficult times. Although this life will never be free of suffering and pain, we don't have to wait until heaven to experience the joy God wants us have. Consider these inspiring words from the First Letter of Peter:

> Blessed be the God and Father of our Lord Jesus Christ! By his great mercy he has given us a new birth into a living hope through the resurrection of Jesus Christ from the dead, and into an inheritance that is imperishable, undefiled, and unfading. . . . In this you rejoice, even if now for a little while you have had to suffer various trials, so that the genuineness of your faith—being more precious than gold that, though perishable, is tested by fire—may be found to result in praise and glory and honor when Jesus Christ is revealed. (1:3–7)

Jesus' Ascension

Another dramatic event in the life of Jesus occurs after the Resurrection. It is captured in this phrase of the Nicene Creed: "He ascended into heaven and is seated at the right hand of the Father." The Gospel authors had a hard time putting this event into words. Matthew and John do not mention it at all. In Mark it simply says, "So then the Lord Jesus, after he spoke to them, was taken up

Saintly Profiles

Mary Magdalene

Mary of Magdala (Magdalene indicates she was from the town of Magdala) is among the first and greatest saints who lived in the company of Jesus. Yet she came from a very troubled past. We are told that Jesus cast out seven demons from her (Mark 16:9, Luke 8:2), suggesting she had suffered from severe physical and emotional illnesses. After her healing she became part of the influential group of women disciples who traveled with Jesus (Luke 8:1–2, Mark 15:40–41). She likely had a leadership role among them because her name is first in the lists of women.

Mary Magdalene had courage. She was present at the cross when most of the men who followed Jesus had all run away. In the Resurrection accounts, it is she rather than Peter who is the first to see the empty tomb. Jesus chose to appear to her first, and he sent her to tell the Good News to the others (Matthew 28:1–10, Mark 16:1–10, Luke 24:1–12, John 20:1–18). We see in the Bible how she rose from the shadows of society to great stature in the Christian community.

Unfortunately Mary Magdalene's image has been distorted through the centuries. She has been equated wrongly with the reformed prostitute of Luke, chapter 7. Have you ever felt like you were in the shadows or that people had the wrong image of you? Let Mary Magdalene inspire you to rise above it! Her feast day is July 22.

into heaven and sat down at the right hand of God" (16:19). Luke says, "While he was blessing them, he withdrew from them and was carried up into heaven" (24:51). The author of Luke continues with a slightly longer version of the **Ascension** at the beginning of the Acts of the Apostles (1:6–12).

These Gospel accounts are trying to describe an event that is beyond human comprehension. Many people in the ancient world believed that a layer of water covered the sky and was the physical boundary of the universe. Once you got past those waters, you were in heaven. So it made sense to think that if Jesus were joining his Father in heaven, he would have to rise into the sky and travel past the waters.

Today we know that there is no layer of water over the sky and that heaven doesn't lie just outside our atmosphere. However, that doesn't change the reality the Gospel writers were trying to address: that after spending time with some of his faithful followers after his Resurrection, Jesus left this world to be with his Father in heaven. What does this mean for the human race?

First, it means that all humanity now has the possibility of spending eternity with God in heaven. After his Ascension into heaven, Jesus remains fully God and fully man—he did not give up his human nature even though his mission had been accomplished. By honoring our humanity, Christ has opened the doors to heaven for us all, overcoming the final barriers separating humanity from God. In heaven Jesus' resurrected body assumed its full glory, as will ours.

Second, it means that in a strangely paradoxical way, Jesus can be more present to us now than before his Ascension. Before his final Ascension, Jesus was still somehow limited by time and space. This seems to be indicated by Jesus' mysterious words to Mary Magdalene, "Do not hold on to me, because I have not yet ascended to the Father" (John 20:17). After his

Looking Back

Saint Augustine on Resurrection

Saint Augustine (354–430) was a bishop and a doctor of the Church. You can read more about him in the chapter The Human Person. Here is an excerpt from a homily he directed to those who had been baptized at the Easter Vigil:

You have been buried with Christ by baptism into death in order that, as Christ has risen from the dead, you also may walk in newness of life. . . . When the Lord rose from the dead, he put off the mortality of the flesh; his risen body was still the same body, but it was no longer subject to death. . . .

And so your own hope of resurrection, though not yet realized, is sure and certain, because you have received the sacrament or sign of this reality, and have been given the pledge of the Spirit. . . . When Christ, your life, appears, then you too will appear with him in glory. (*The Liturgy of the Hours*, volume 2, pages 635–637)

Ascension Jesus is no longer limited to being in one place at one particular time. He is free to be everywhere, with everyone, for all time! This is the amazing meaning of the Ascension.

For Further Reflection

○ Read one of the Gospel accounts of Jesus' Resurrection (Matthew 26:1—27:66, Mark 14:1—15:47, Luke 22:1—23:56, John 18:1—19:42). What thoughts and feelings do you have? What inspires you?

○ The Paschal mystery is the reality that for those with faith, God can bring new life from death. How have you experienced something good and positive from a situation that started out as negative and painful?

Pray It

Easter Vigil: Light in the Darkness

The Easter Vigil Mass is the Church's biggest and most important liturgical event. It begins in the darkness of Holy Saturday evening, at the fire where the new Easter candle is lit. During the procession into the dark Church, all the members of the congregation light candles to symbolize the light of Christ that overcomes sin and darkness. Then we hear the Easter proclamation:

> Rejoice, heavenly powers! Sing, choirs of angels! Exult, all creation around God's throne! Jesus Christ, our King is risen! . . . This is the night when Jesus Christ broke the chains of death and rose triumphant from the grave. . . . Therefore, heavenly Father, in the joy of this night, receive our evening sacrifice of praise. . . . Accept this Easter candle, . . . to dispel the darkness of this night! (*The Sacramentary*, pages 182–184)

The Vigil continues with the liturgy of the word, followed by the Baptism and Confirmation of the adults who are being initiated into the Church. Then the whole community joins the newly initiated in the celebration of the Holy Eucharist.

Meditate on the power of this Vigil Mass. Light your own "Easter candle" in a darkened room in your home or with your peers. Pray the words from the Easter proclamation above and let them fill your mind and heart with the joy and power of the Resurrection. Jesus Christ is risen! Alleluia! Amen.

10 The Holy Spirit

Things change; that's simply a fact of life. But not all change is good, which is why the Catholic Church is very careful about changing its language and practices. The Church makes changes not to stay trendy but to better serve the mission of Jesus. And of course the Church cannot change the teachings that have been revealed by God through the Scriptures and Tradition. So the Church makes a change in its language or practice only after a great deal of consideration and prayer.

When the Church changed the English-language name of the third person of the Trinity from Holy Ghost to Holy Spirit (back in the 1960s), people took notice. Your grandparents probably remember this. Why "Spirit" instead of "Ghost"? The answer has to do with the changing meaning of words. In previous centuries *ghost* meant a spirit without a physical body. But in more modern times, due to the influence of books and movies, the word *ghost* came to mean a dead person that frightened you. And the Holy Spirit is nothing

Words to Look For

- Pentecost
- gifts of the Holy Spirit
- fruits of the Holy Spirit

to be frightened of. On the contrary, we have no greater supporter and helper in our life than the Holy Spirit.

The Holy Spirit's Mission

We talk a lot about God the Father and Jesus the Son. But rarely do you hear people talk as much about the third person of the Holy Trinity, the Holy Spirit. Just like God the Father and Jesus Christ, the Holy Spirit is part of everything that God is and does. Starting at the very beginning of creation, we read, "In the beginning when God created the heavens and the earth, the earth was a formless void and darkness covered the face of the deep, while a wind from God swept over the face of the waters" (Genesis 1:1–2). The Hebrew word for wind is *ruah,* which also means "breath" or "spirit." So the verse could also be understood as "the spirit of God swept over the face of the waters." Thus we know that the Holy Spirit was active in the creation of the universe.

Catholics also believe that the Holy Spirit was at work throughout the history of the Jewish people. But you will rarely find the Spirit specifically named in the Old Testament books. You will find, however, a number of references to the "spirit of God" in the Old Testament. The Jewish people closely associated the Spirit of God with prophecy (for example, see 2 Chronicles 15:1 or Ezekiel 11:24), believing that God spoke through the prophets who spoke in his name. The Church believes that these Old Testament passages are early references to the work of the Holy Spirit.

When we move to the New Testament, we find that the Gospels still contain few references to the Holy Spirit—except for the Gospel of Luke, which is sometimes called the Gospel of the Holy Spirit. In Luke the Holy Spirit fills John the Baptist at his birth (1:15), and it is through the power of the Holy Spirit that Jesus is conceived in Mary (1:35). The Holy Spirit fills Elizabeth (1:41) and Simeon (2:25), so that they recognize the specialness of the infant Jesus. The Holy Spirit descends on

This stained-glass window from a Catholic church in California shows the Holy Spirit showering his gifts upon the world. Notice the use of symbolic numbers: three rays of light, seven tongues of fire. In Church teaching, what is special about those numbers?

Jesus at his Baptism (3:22), and fills him after his time in the desert (4:1). And this is just in the first four chapters!

In all four Gospels, John the Baptist prophesies that Jesus will baptize his followers with the Holy Spirit. When Jesus is baptized, the Holy Spirit descends on him in the form of a dove. And in the Gospel of John's account of the Last Supper, Jesus promises to send the Holy Spirit to guide the disciples after he leaves them:

> I will ask the Father, and he will give you another Advocate, to be with you forever. This is the Spirit of truth, whom the world cannot receive, because it neither sees him nor knows him. You know him, because he abides with you, and he will be in you. . . . The Advocate, the Holy Spirit, whom the Father will send in my name, will teach you everything, and remind you of all that I have said to you. (14:16–17,26)

These passages teach us that wherever God sends his Son, he also sends his Spirit. Jesus and the Holy Spirit share the same mission, and their work cannot be separated. However, the Holy Spirit's mission is to never draw attention to himself, but to reveal God the Father and Jesus the Son. For the most part, the significant, ongoing work of the Holy Spirit remained hidden until Jesus ascended into heaven. (*Note:* Although we traditionally use masculine pronouns when referring to the Holy Spirit, the Holy Spirit is neither male nor female.)

The Holy Spirit and Pentecost

The most dramatic manifestation of the Holy Spirit in the Scriptures is recorded at the beginning of the Acts of the Apostles. Jesus had ascended into heaven, and the Apostles, with some of the

---

Looking Back

Catholic Charismatics

A number of Catholics throughout the world participate in a movement called the Catholic Charismatic Renewal. This movement, which began in 1967 at Duquesne University, in Pittsburgh, takes its name from the word *charism,* meaning "gift." Charismatics speak of being "baptized in the Holy Spirit," which is an experience of being reawakened to the activity of the Spirit in their life. This awakening helps them to become more open to receiving the gifts of the Spirit. The primary activity of charismatic groups is prayer, which takes many forms, including praying in tongues.

On the occasion of the thirtieth anniversary of the Catholic Charismatic Renewal, the United States Conference of Catholic Bishops affirmed the contribution of this movement to the Church:

The Catholic Charismatic Renewal has brought personal spiritual renewal to the lives of millions of priests, deacons, religious, and lay Catholics. It has called countless alienated Catholics to reconciliation with the Lord and with the Church. It has deepened a love for Jesus and the Church among young people as well as so many others, including the unchurched. (*Grace for the New Springtime,* 1997)

---

women disciples, were waiting for the Spirit that Jesus had promised. Here's how the story continues:

> And suddenly from heaven there came a sound like the rush of a violent wind, and it filled the entire house where they were sitting. Divided tongues, as of fire, appeared among them, and a tongue rested on each of them. All of them were filled with the Holy Spirit and began to speak in other languages, as the Spirit gave them ability.
>
> Now there were devout Jews from every nation under heaven living in Jerusalem. And at this sound the crowd gathered and was bewildered, because each one heard them speaking in the native language of each. Amazed and astonished, they asked, "Are not all these who are speaking Galileans? And how is it that we hear, each of us, in our own native language?" (2:2–8)

This event is called **Pentecost,** and the name is taken from a Jewish feast with the same title. The Catholic Church celebrates the feast of Pentecost approximately fifty days after Easter. You may hear people call it the birthday of the Catholic Church, for it was on this day that the Holy Spirit gave the Apostles the courage to preach the message of Jesus Christ and to baptize those who believed. Those who were baptized created communities, to share their new faith in Christ with one another. At the end of Acts, chapter 2, we read: "So those who welcomed [Peter's] message were baptized, and that day about three thousand persons were added. They devoted themselves to the apostles' teaching and fellowship, to the breaking of bread and the prayers" (2:41–42).

Led by the Spirit

In talking to Nicodemus about the necessity of being born of the Spirit, Jesus said, "The wind blows where it chooses, and you hear the sound of it, but you do not know where it comes from or where it goes. So it is with everyone who is born of the Spirit" (John 3:8). Think about ways we encounter wind: gentle breezes that bring coolness, steady winds and gusts that make sailboats move and generate power, violent winds that are capable of reshaping the earth. We cannot see the wind, only its effects. Can the Holy Spirit's action in your life be likened to the power and movement of wind? Have you been inspired by the Spirit to do things without knowing what would result?

We often make decisions by listening to a gut instinct or inner voice. However, it is not always easy to tell when the voice prompting us is the Holy Spirit and when it is the voice of selfishness or cultural messages that are at odds with Catholic faith. These influences can have a power that might also be likened to the wind, but they have different effects than the Holy Spirit. One way to figure out if the Holy Spirit is prompting an action is to ask yourself if it is likely to lead to greater joy, peace, patience, kindness, generosity, faithfulness, gentleness, self-control, and most especially, love.

The mission of the Holy Spirit and the work of the Catholic Church are fused together. The Holy Spirit is the primary cause behind the Church's work and directs the Church's mission. The Spirit works through the Church to make the mission of Jesus Christ known. We sometimes call the Catholic Church the Temple of the Holy Spirit. The Holy Spirit is the source of our life together, brings us together in unity despite our diversity, and enriches us with all the gifts needed to be the Body of Christ.

Kateri Tekakwitha is the first Native American to enter the process of becoming an official saint in the Catholic Church. What do you find inspiring about her life (see her Saintly Profile at right)

Titles and Symbols of the Holy Spirit

The *Catechism* describes some of the common titles and names for the Holy Spirit. These can help us understand the work of the Holy Spirit in the Church and in the world. The title that Jesus uses for the Holy Spirit in the Gospel of John is Advocate (14:16, 15:26, 16:7), translated from the Greek word *Paraclete*. (Some Bibles translate it as "helper" or "comforter.") *Advocate* literally means "someone who stands by your side." In a court of law, an advocate is someone who takes your side, who pleads your case. As our Advocate, the Holy Spirit takes our side, helps us defend our belief in Jesus, and supports us in living out our faith in word and deed.

In the letters of Saint Paul, we also find other titles and descriptions for the Holy Spirit: the promise of the Spirit (Galatians 3:14), a spirit of adoption (Romans 1:15), the Spirit of Christ (Romans 8:9), the Spirit of the Lord (2 Corinthians 3:17), and the Spirit of God (Romans 8:14). In First Peter is the title spirit of glory (4:14). All these make it clear that the early Christians clearly identified the Holy Spirit with the work of God the Father and Jesus Christ.

The Catholic Church also uses a number of symbols to identify the work of the Holy Spirit. Some of the following symbols and symbolic actions may be familiar, but others are probably new to you:

○ **Water.** Water signifies the Holy Spirit's action in Baptism. "For in the one Spirit we were all baptized into one body" (1 Corinthians 12:13). And in John 7:37–39, Jesus directly associates the Spirit with the living water that satisfies spiritual thirst.

○ **Fire.** Fire signifies the vibrant and transforming energy of the Holy Spirit. The Holy Spirit appeared as tongues of fire upon the Apostles at Pentecost, and they were transformed into courageous witnesses for Christ.

○ **A cloud and light.** In the Old Testament, God often appeared as a fire or light within a dense cloud (Exodus 40:38, Ezekiel 1:4). These two images together symbolize that the Holy Spirit reveals yet also keeps hidden the glory of God. In the New Testament, clouds play a role in Jesus' Baptism, Transfiguration, and Ascension.

○ **A dove.** In all four Gospels, at Jesus' Baptism the Spirit descends on him in the form of a dove. This is why in Christian art, a dove often symbolizes the Holy Spirit.

○ **Anointing.** As part of our sacramental rites, to be anointed with oil symbolizes that the power of the Holy Spirit is being poured out on the person. The word *Christ* means "the one anointed by God's Spirit." Now Jesus Christ pours his Spirit out on all those who are baptized and confirmed.

○ **Laying on hands.** Jesus healed the sick and blessed children by laying his hands on them (Mark 10:16). People received the Holy Spirit when the Apostles laid hands on them (Acts 8:17).

The Gifts of the Holy Spirit

As a teenager you may hear a lot of references to the Holy Spirit in your preparation for the sacrament of Confirmation. In the sacrament of Confirmation, you receive

Saintly Profiles

Blessed Kateri Tekakwitha (1656–1680)

Kateri, born in present-day Auriesville, New York, to a Christian Algonquin mother and a non-Christian Mohawk chief, was the first Native American to be beatified. When she was four, smallpox killed her parents and younger brother and left her disfigured and partially blind. She met Christian missionaries in later childhood, and through their influence was baptized in 1676. Her new way of life made it difficult to remain in her village, so she walked two hundred miles to live in a Christian village near Montreal. Having made a vow not to marry, she led a life of prayer, fasting, teaching, and service until her death at the age of twenty-four.

Kateri surely had the gifts of wisdom and courage. She once said: "I am not my own; I have given myself to Jesus. He must be my only love. The state of helpless poverty that may befall me if I do not marry does not frighten me. All I need is a little food and a few pieces of clothing. With the work of my hands I shall always earn what is necessary and what is left over I'll give to my relatives and to the poor. If I should become sick and unable to work, then I shall be like the Lord on the cross. He will have mercy on me and help me, I am sure" (*Saint of the Day*, page 154). Her feast day is July 14.

the Holy Spirit into your life in a deeper and more profound way. Just as with the first Christians, the Holy Spirit's gifts help strengthen your bond with the Catholic Church and help you witness to the Christian faith in words and deeds.

We often refer to seven special **gifts of the Holy Spirit.** These seven gifts represent all the gifts God gives us to live a good and holy life (in the Bible, the number 7 often symbolizes fullness or completion). These seven special gifts are rooted in a prophecy from Isaiah about the promised Messiah:

> The spirit of the LORD shall rest on him,
>> the spirit of wisdom and understanding,
>> the spirit of counsel and might,
>> the spirit of knowledge and the fear of
>> the LORD.
> His delight shall be in the fear of the LORD.
> (11:2–3)

Here are some descriptions to help you understand the meaning of these gifts (the names for these gifts come from the prayers used during Confirmation):

- **Wisdom.** With the gift of wisdom, we see God at work in our life and in the world. For the wise person, the wonders of nature, historical events, and the ups and downs of our life take on a deeper meaning and purpose.
- **Understanding.** With the gift of understanding, we comprehend how we need to live as a follower of Jesus Christ. A person with understanding is not confused by all the conflicting messages in our culture about the right way to live.
- **Right judgment.** With the gift of right judgment, we know the difference between right and wrong, and we choose to do what is right. A person with right judgment avoids sin and lives out the values taught by Jesus.
- **Courage.** With the gift of courage, we overcome our fear and are willing to take risks as a follower of Jesus. A person with courage is willing to stand up for what is right in the sight of God, even if it means accepting rejection, verbal abuse, or even physical harm and death.

Fruits of the Holy Spirit

Paul encouraged the people of Galatia to "live by the Spirit" (Galatians 5:16). He proclaimed that everyone who walks with the Spirit can bear much fruit: "love, joy, peace, patience, kindness, generosity, faithfulness, gentleness, and self-control" (5:22–23). This is why these nine things are known as the **fruits of the Holy Spirit.** When you live by the Holy Spirit, do you notice these good things becoming more present in your life?

- **Knowledge.** With the gift of knowledge, we understand the meaning of God's Revelation, especially as expressed in the life and words of Jesus Christ. A person with knowledge is always learning more about the Scriptures and Tradition.
- **Reverence.** With the gift of reverence—sometimes called piety—we have a deep sense of respect for God and the Church. A person with reverence recognizes our total reliance on God and comes before God with humility, trust, and love.
- **Wonder and awe.** With the gift of wonder and awe (fear of the Lord), we are aware of the glory and majesty of God. A person with wonder and awe knows that God is the perfection of all we desire: perfect knowledge, perfect goodness, perfect power, and perfect love.

Of course the Holy Spirit is active in every sacrament. When we freely open our heart and mind to the creative power of the Spirit, we not only deepen the Spirit's activity in our own life but also help increase the Spirit's power within the Church and the world. By accepting the gift of the Holy Spirit, we are empowered to participate in the mission of Jesus and help make the Kingdom of God a reality.

Pray It!

Prayer to the Holy Spirit

The Church invites us to call on the Holy Spirit in prayer every day, especially at important moments. Here is a suggested way to pray from our Tradition:

Come Holy Spirit, fill the hearts of your faithful. Enkindle in them the fire of your love. Send forth your Spirit, and they will be created. And you will renew the face of the earth.

Let us pray:

Lord, by the light of the Holy Spirit, you have taught the hearts of the faithful. In the same Spirit, help us to relish what is right and always rejoice in your consolation. We ask this through Christ our Lord. Amen.

For Further Reflection

- One of the primary roles of the Holy Spirit is to be our Advocate, the one who stands by our side to help us defend our belief in Jesus. When do you feel challenged to defend your Christian beliefs? When are you tempted to compromise the things you believe in? Ask the Holy Spirit for the wisdom and the courage to defend and live out your beliefs.
- Consider one of the seven gifts of the Holy Spirit. How have you already used this gift? How can you continue to grow in making it a part of your life?

11

The Mission
of the Catholic Church

People talk about the Catholic Church in many different ways. When people say, "I'm going to Church," they mean they are going to the Sunday Eucharist (Mass). When people say, "The Church says abortion is wrong," they are often referring to the teaching role of the **Magisterium,** that is, the pope and the bishops who have the responsibility for safeguarding God's revealed truth. Or when people say, "We are the Church," they are referring to the Body of Christ, the scriptural image of all the baptized acting as Jesus' living body in the world.

All these ways of talking about the Church are true. The Catholic Church is too rich in meaning to be captured by any single image. And if we put too much emphasis on any one image, we are in danger of misrepresenting the reality of the Church. For example, if you only emphasize "We are the Church," you may not appreciate the special authority Jesus gave to the Apostles and their descendants to safeguard the

Words to Look For

- Magisterium
- People of God
- Body of Christ
- charisms
- marks of the Church
- canonization
- apostolic succession
- infallible

truths of our faith. Or if you see Church as mainly going to Mass on Sunday, you may be missing the point that being a member of the Church means living as a follower of Jesus twenty-four hours a day, seven days a week.

In this chapter we take a closer look at what it means to be a member of the Church. We learn about the special names and images that have been used to describe the Church over the centuries.

Founded by Christ

Jesus Christ himself laid the spiritual foundation of the Church. A great deal of evidence can be found in the Gospels that Jesus intended for his followers to continue his mission after he was gone. In John's account of the Last Supper, Jesus tells his disciples:

This stained-glass window shows Jesus Christ giving Saint Peter the keys to the Kingdom (Matthew 16:19). What does this story tell us about the role of the pope—the successor of Saint Peter—in the Church?

> I do not call you servants any longer, because the servant does not know what the master is doing; but I have called you friends, because I have made known to you everything that I have heard from my Father. You did not choose me but I chose you. And I appointed you to go and bear fruit, fruit that will last, so that the Father will give you whatever you ask him in my name. (15:15–16)

And after his Resurrection Jesus commands the Apostles:

> All authority in heaven and on earth has been given to me. Go therefore and make disciples of all nations, baptizing them in the name of the Father and of the Son and of the Holy Spirit, and teaching them to obey everything that I have commanded you. And remember, I am with you always, to the end of the age. (Matthew 28:18–20)

Jesus provided a basic structure for the Church by choosing the twelve Apostles and training them for leadership, with Peter as their head. This structure continues today, with the bishops as the successors to the Apostles and the pope as the successor to Saint Peter.

The Mission of the Church

The word *church* means "convocation," which is a gathering of people who have been called together by another person or group. Thus Church designates the people who have been called together by God's Word, Jesus Christ, to continue his mission. The mission of course is to proclaim the Good News that through Christ sin and death have been overcome and humanity's broken relationship with God has been restored.

This photo of thousands of youth and young adults gathered at a World Youth Day candlelight vigil reminds us that the people of God are "as numerous as the stars of heaven" (Genesis 22:17). Have you ever taken the opportunity to attend a large gathering of Catholics?

In church language we sometimes say that the Church is both the means and the goal of God's plan. What do we mean by that? The Church is the means God uses for fulfilling his plan because the people of the Church witness to Jesus Christ and his message. When Christians practice their love for one another and their compassion for those who are suffering and in need, they are doing so in the name of Christ. When they speak out for justice and advocate for moral issues, they are doing so for Jesus Christ. This witness helps others understand what the love of God is all about and draws them to put their faith in Christ.

But the Church is also the goal of God's plan, because with the aid of the Holy Spirit, the people of the Church live together in such a way as to make the Kingdom of God real in the world. By practicing all the things that Jesus command-ed—sacrificial love, forgiveness, prayer, the Eucharist, a just lifestyle, and so on—Christians are already experiencing the Kingdom of God here on earth. Of course sin is still a reality, which means this experience of the Kingdom is only a small taste of the real heaven that awaits us after death.

Another way of saying this is that "the Church in this world is the sacrament of salvation, the sign and instrument of the communion of God and men" (*CCC*, number 780). You might be asking, "How can the Church be a sacrament—aren't there only seven sacraments?" Yes, there are seven official sac-raments of the Church, but the idea of sacrament is bigger than that. A sacrament is both a sign and a cause of God's grace (the undeserved gifts of God's love, salvation, forgiveness, and so on). As the sacrament of salvation, the Church is both a sign of God's saving power and a cause for making God's saving power real in the world.

One more teaching is essential to understanding the Church's mission. This idea is referred to as a mystery, in the same way that doctrines of the Trinity and the Incarnation are talked about as mysteries. The mystery is that the Church is at once both visible and spiritual. Any person—whether they are a believer in the Church or not—can see the visible signs: church buildings; the Pope, bishops, and priests; youth groups doing service projects; families praying together; and so on. But only a person with faith can accept the invisible yet very real spiritual dimension of the Church. In the spiritual dimension, the Holy Trinity is at work to save and sanctify (make holy) the human race. Just as we understand Jesus to be fully divine and fully human, so the Church has two components: the human and the divine.

Scriptural Images of the Church

In the years following Jesus Christ's Resurrection and Ascension, the first Christians reflected on all he had taught in order to understand how the community they were forming in his name should be described. Inspired by the Holy Spirit, they adopted some guiding images that are referred to in the Bible. These images help us to better understand how the Church carries out its mission.

Pray It!

How Does Jesus Send You?

Jesus called the disciples together and then sent them out to further his mission of proclaiming the Kingdom of God, saying, "Take nothing for your journey, no staff, nor bag, nor bread, nor money— not even an extra tunic" (Luke 9:3). And they went and did what Jesus asked.

In your prayer, reflect or journal on Pope John Paul II's question to the youth gathered for World Youth Day 1996:

How does Jesus send you? He promises neither sword, nor money, nor any of the things which the means of social communications make attractive to people today. He gives you instead grace and truth. He sends you out with the powerful message of his paschal mystery, with the truth of the cross and resurrection. That is all he gives you, and that is all you need. (Quoted in *Renewing the Vision*, page 49)

People of God

The people of Israel understood themselves to be the **People of God,** chosen long ago to be the ones through whom God would save the world (Exodus 6:7). The first Christians, who still considered themselves Jews, continued to see themselves as the Chosen People of God because of their faith in Christ and the power they experienced from the Holy Spirit.

Saint Peter put it this way in his first epistle to several Christian communities: "You are a chosen race, a royal priesthood, a holy nation, God's own people" (1 Peter 2:9). As the People of God, the Church is not limited to a particular race, culture, or political perspective. People of all races and cultures are called to be members of this family, recognizing the unity we share as children of God. We are not born into this family through physical birth but enter through faith and Baptism.

The Body of Christ

Saint Paul speaks eloquently about the image of the Church as the **Body of Christ:** "For just as the body is one and has many members, and all the members of the body, though many, are one body, so it is with Christ. . . . Now you are the body of Christ and individually members of it" (1 Corinthians 12:12,27). And Ephesians 4:15 calls Christ the head of the body. Salvation for all people comes through the Church because salvation comes first through Jesus Christ, who is the head of the Church. The image of the Church as the Body of Christ stresses how intimately Jesus Christ and the Church are united.

Saint Paul also uses the Body of Christ to illustrate how the Church finds unity amid diversity. In this passage from the First Letter to the Corinthians, he says:

> If the foot would say, "Because I am not a hand, I do not belong to the body," that would not make it any less a part of the body. And if the ear would say, "Because I am not an eye, I do not belong to the body," that would not make it any less a part of the body. If the whole body were an eye, where would the hearing be? If the whole body were hearing, where would the sense of smell be? (12:15–17)

Defending Your Faith

Q. When someone says that Catholics are wrong to follow the Pope, what should I say?

A. Catholics follow Jesus first and foremost. Together all of us—laity, priests, bishops, cardinals, and the Pope—strive to be the Body of Christ in the world. The ministry of the Pope, called the papacy, plays a central role in this effort. He's like our spiritual quarterback, vital to the Church because he brings unity to the entire community of the faithful and makes us better able to carry out Jesus' mission.

Q. When someone points out that the Church is full of sinners and says that they wouldn't belong to a group of hypocrites, how can I respond?

A. Tell the person that he or she is right; the Church is full of sinners. Making the decision not to belong to the Church because it has sinners is something like not going to the hospital because it has sick people. God calls everyone, and offers us forgiveness for our sins. That is why you belong. The Church gives us the strength and grace to struggle against our sinful and selfish ways.

Remember Peter's words about explaining your faith, "Do it with gentleness and reverence" (1 Peter 3:16).

Saint Paul's point is simply this: every person in the Church is needed; no one is less important than anyone else. Every person brings some gift that is needed by the community. It is in the diversity of these gifts that the Church finds its strength, and it is in using these gifts to fulfill our common mission that the Church has its unity.

The New Testament also compares the relationship between Christ and the Church to the relationship between a husband and wife. A follower of Saint Paul's writes, "Husbands, love your wives, just as Christ loved the church and gave himself up for her" (Ephesians 5:25). Because of this the Church is also called the Bride of Christ, and is sometimes referred to in the feminine form, that is, as "she."

The Temple of the Holy Spirit

In trying to explain to early Christians the mystery of the Church, Saint Paul offers yet another image: "Do you not know that you are God's temple and that God's Spirit dwells in you? . . . God's temple is holy, and you are that temple" (1 Corinthians 3:16–17). In the Old Testament, the Temple was the building in which God was present in a special or unique way. Thus Saint Paul is saying that the Holy Spirit is present in a unique way in the Church. Jesus Christ has poured the Holy Spirit onto all the members of the Church, making the Holy Spirit part of everything that the Church is and does.

The *Catechism* quotes Saint Augustine in explaining how the Church is the Temple of the Holy Spirit: "What the soul is to the human body, the Holy Spirit is to the Body of Christ, which is the Church"[1] (*CCC*, number 797). The Holy Spirit is the source of the Church's life, unity, gifts, and

Did You Know?

Liturgical Rites and Traditions

Did you know that not all Catholics are Roman Catholic? The word *Roman* designates a particular Catholic Church, but there are other Catholic Churches with their own unique traditions: American Ruthenian, Armenian, Bulgarian, Chaldean, Ethiopian, Eparchy Krizevci, Greek, Hungarian, Italo-Albanian, Maronite, Melkite Greek, Rumanian Greek, Slovak, Syriac, Syro-Malabar, Syro-Malankara, and Ukrainian Greek. Most of the non-Roman Catholic Churches reflect the culture of Eastern Europe and the Middle East, and so they are called the Eastern Catholic Churches. The liturgical traditions (or rites) of the Eastern Catholic Churches are different from the Roman Catholic (Latin) liturgical tradition. Like Roman Catholics, Catholics from those Churches acknowledge the Pope as the head of the universal Church.

Of course, not all Eastern Christians are Catholic. The vast majority belong to Eastern Orthodox Churches, which have been separated from the Catholic Church since the East-West schism of the Middle Ages. This fracture was along political boundaries, and involved cultural, political, and theological conflicts that played out across many centuries. Church leaders have been actively working to restore unity through dialogue, though important theological differences remain.

charisms. **Charisms** are the special graces of the Holy Spirit given to the members of the Church for the good of the Church and of the world. The Holy Spirit's charisms can be extraordinary, such as the ability to make prophecies in God's name. Or they can be simple and humble, such as the gift of welcoming new people. They are often given to individuals who fill a special role or office in the Church, such as priest, deacon, minister to the sick, catechist, youth minister, lector, cantor, and so on.

Notice the strong connection with the Holy Trinity in these scriptural images of the Church. The image of the People of God emphasizes the role of God the Father in calling a people to himself. When we speak of the Body of Christ, we emphasize Christ's mission and his role as the mediator between God and humanity. And the image of the Temple of the Holy Spirit emphasizes the important role of the Holy Spirit in leading the Church to holiness. This is another example of how the Church is a sacrament, the sacrament of the Holy Trinity's communion with all people.

Pope John XXIII was pope for only five years, but the renewal in the Church that he started by calling the Second Vatican Council will influence the Church for centuries.

Marks of the Church

In describing the Church, the Nicene Creed states, "We believe in one holy catholic and apostolic Church." The four words used to describe the Church—*one, holy, catholic,* and *apostolic*—were chosen with great care. They are commonly called the **marks of the Church,** and each one describes something essential about the Church and its mission. The Church has these qualities because of Christ, who through the Holy Spirit makes them real in his Church.

One

The Church "acknowledges one Lord, confesses one faith, is born of one Baptism, forms only one Body, is given life by the one Spirit, for the sake of the one hope, at whose fulfillment all divisions will be overcome" (*CCC,* number 866).

With these words the *Catechism* summarizes what it means to say the Church is one. Every Christian shares the beliefs that we are all children of God the Father, that we are saved by Jesus, his Son, and that we are made holy by the Holy Spirit. The very foundation of the Church is the Holy Trinity; thus, the unity of the Church reflects the unity of the Trinity.

The Catholic Church is unified in a special way through the leadership of the Pope. Jesus gave Saint Peter a special role in leading the Church (Matthew 16:18–19). Our union with the Pope is a visible symbol of our unity. However, there is diversity within that unity—with different peoples and cultures, different gifts and roles, different economic conditions and ways of life. All these influence to some degree how the Catholic faith is practiced and celebrated— they enrich the Church and do not take away from its fundamental unity.

Holy

To be holy is to be united with God, to be spiritually perfect, to be free from all sin and evil. With Christ as her head and the Holy Spirit to guide her, the Church strives to be the holy people of God, spiritually perfect and free from all sin and evil. But the holiness of the Church is not yet perfect. The members of the Church are still sinners, whose personal sin affects the holiness of the Church in minor and sometimes major ways. However, even when scandals rock the Church, we have Christ's assurance that "the gates of Hades will not prevail against [the Church]" (Matthew 16:18).

In a special way, the Church encourages all of us to holiness by raising up women and men who have lived especially holy lives as examples. These people have gone through the process of **canonization,** that is,

Saintly Profiles

Blessed John XXIII (1881–1963; Pope 1958–1963)

Pope John XXIII was born Angelo Guiseppe Roncalli to a family of peasant farmers in Italy. He was ordained a priest in 1904 and elected pope in 1958, just shy of his seventy-seventh birthday. Because of his advanced age, many thought his papacy would be short and transitional, in the sense of leading to little change. They were only half right. His papacy lasted less than five years. However, within three months of becoming Pope, he announced a new ecumenical council, the Second Vatican Council, which brought much change to the Church.

Though he lived only long enough to participate in the first of the council's four sessions, held from 1962 through 1965, John XXIII's early leadership set the tone for the whole of the council. He had an optimistic view of the world, and believed that the Church needed updating in light of the signs of the times. His encyclicals (which are letters written by a pope to the whole Church) addressed issues of Church unity, social justice, world peace, and human rights. John XXIII, considered by many to be one of the most beloved popes in modern history, was beatified in September 2000. His feast day is June 3.

the official procedure within the Church for recognizing saints. The heroic example of these people—some of whom are identified in this book—remind us that we are all called to be saints by living holy lives.

Catholic

In an ecumenical council, the bishops from around the world gather to discuss Church beliefs and practices. In this image of the Council of Nicaea (A.D. 325), can you tell which figure is the emperor Constantine, the person who called the Council?

The word *catholic* means "universal" or "comprehensive." The Catholic Church encompasses both these meanings. The Church is comprehensive because she is founded directly on God's Revelation in Jesus Christ, which has been faithfully passed on from the Apostles through the unbroken line of bishops. Thus, more than any other Christian Church, the Catholic Church contains everything human beings need for salvation: the complete Revelation of God, all the sacraments, and the teaching authority of the Magisterium.

The Catholic Church is also universal because she has a mission from Jesus Christ to the whole human race. People of all races, all nationalities, all ages, and all personalities are not only welcome in the Catholic Church, but they enrich the Church with their diversity. "Go therefore and make disciples of all nations, baptizing them in the name of the Father and of the Son and of the Holy Spirit" (Matthew 28:19) was Jesus' final command to the Apostles in the Gospel of Matthew. The Church always seeks in every generation to share the Gospel message with all those who do not yet believe in Jesus Christ. We do not do this out of arrogance, but out of a love for all people and in response to God's desire that people come to know the truth and be saved.

Apostolic

Apostolic means that the Church is founded on the Apostles, those men who were closest to Christ and empowered by the Holy Spirit to pass on the essential truths revealed by God through Christ. The Catholic Church continues to be led by the Apostles through their successors, the Pope and the college of bishops. This is called **apostolic succession,** and this authority is passed on from one bishop to another through the laying on of hands. Further, when speaking definitively on issues of faith and morality, the Pope and the bishops in unison with him are **infallible,** that is, the Holy Spirit guides them to speak the truth without error. Not everything the Pope and the bishops teach is infallible because not everything they say is a definitive statement. But Catholics always take their teachings seriously because of the special gift the Pope and the bishops have received for teaching the truth.

The issues of apostolic succession and infallibility are hard for many non-Catholics to understand. But these beliefs are rooted in the Scriptures and Tradition. Jesus tells the Apostles, "As the Father has sent me, so I send you" (John 20:21) and "Whoever welcomes you welcomes me" (Matthew 10:40)—clearly indicating the special role the Apostles are to play after his Ascension. The Tradition of the Church teaches that the need for this special role, or office, is ongoing and did not end with the Apostles' deaths. In defending the Catholic belief in infallibility, we have Jesus' promise, "When the Spirit of truth comes, he will guide you into all the truth" (John 16:13). The Tradition of the Church takes this promise as a guarantee that the leaders of the Church cannot be led into error when they humbly seek the Spirit's guidance through prayerful discernment.

The marks of the Church bring up a very sensitive issue, the relationship of the Catholic Church with other Christian Churches. More will be said about this in the next chapter. But the bottom line is that the fullness of Christ's Church is found only in the Catholic Church. The Catholic Church is the only Church that fully embodies the four

Looking Back

Ecumenical Councils

An ecumenical council is a gathering of the Church's bishops from around the world. *Ecumenical* means "worldwide." At various times throughout the Church's history, the Pope has called all the bishops together to discuss and make decisions about significant issues. Here are some examples:

- The Councils of Nicaea (325) and Constantinople (381) affirmed that Jesus is human and divine, and they adopted the text of the Nicene Creed, which is recited at Mass by Catholics around the world.
- The Council of Chalcedon (451) reaffirmed Jesus' identity as fully divine and fully human, in response to a claim that Jesus merely took on the outward appearance of a human being while on earth.
- The Council of Trent (1545–1563) responded to the criticisms of the Protestant Reformers by clarifying some important doctrines, especially the teaching that Revelation is found in the Scriptures and Tradition. Trent also reformed some aspects of Church discipline and established seminaries for the education of priests.
- The Second Vatican Council (1962–1965), the most recent ecumenical council, was called for the purpose of renewing the Church. Pope John XXIII, during his opening address to the council, spoke of letting fresh air into the Church. The council examined every aspect of the Church's life, making sure that Catholic Tradition and religious practices were being taught and lived in the way that would be most appropriate in today's world.

marks of one, holy, catholic, and apostolic. But the Catholic Church makes this claim with humility, recognizing that its members have sinned on numerous occasions. We are the Body of Christ, gifted by the Holy Spirit, called to be witnesses and seeds of the Kingdom of God, even as we struggle with our own sin and imperfection.

Looking Back

A Church Sinful and Redeemed

The Second Vatican Council spoke about the ways the Church lives the Kingdom of God. It explained that like Jesus, the Church is both human and divine, communicating divine truth and grace through a visible human structure. But unlike Jesus, who was without sin, the Church sometimes causes conflict, sin, and scandal, leading people to ask, "Why belong to such a Church?"

The Church does not claim to be perfect. Each of us knows personally our own ability to sin. As we come together to make up the Body of Christ that is the Church, we realize that we do not leave our sinful human nature at the door. What belonging to such a Church gives us is the same gift that Jesus gave in his death and Resurrection: the ability to overcome evil and sinfulness. The Second Vatican Council describes this aspect of the Church:

> By the power of the risen Lord, she is given strength to overcome patiently and lovingly the afflictions and hardships which assail her from within and without, and to show forth in the world the mystery of the Lord in a faithful though shadowed way, until . . . it will be revealed in total splendor. (*Dogmatic Constitution on the Church*, number 8)

As the Church, we live the Kingdom when we overcome sin and conflict with patience and with love.

For Further Reflection

- The image of the Church as the Body of Christ teaches us that every member of the Church has a role to play. To paraphrase former President John F. Kennedy, "Ask not what your church can do for you, but what you can do for your church." What role do you play in your church? What roles might you take in the future?
- The four marks of the Church also describe the challenges that each Catholic, as a member of the community, is faced with:
  - *One.* What can you do to break down the walls between groups in your church community that seem to be at odds with one another, or who don't make an effort to reach out to one another?
  - *Holy.* Are you living your life as if you were called to share in Jesus' mission to the world?
  - *Catholic.* What could you do to be more welcoming to those who are different from you?
  - *Apostolic.* Do you make the effort to understand what the church teaches, and wrestle with it if you need to, rather than brushing it aside as old-fashioned or irrational?

12

The Organization of the Catholic Church

Many teens today do not give much thought to what religion their friends practice. You probably care more about whether your friends share your interests in music, sports, and school activities than about whether they are Baptist, Methodist, Catholic, Jewish, or Muslim. This is not to imply that you are totally disinterested in other religions; hopefully you have a healthy interest in what other religions teach. But most teens today are tolerant and accepting of different religious traditions and beliefs.

However, this hasn't always been the case. It wasn't that long ago that there was far more distrust between Catholics and Protestants. Your grandparents might be able to tell you some stories about the relationship between Catholics and

Words to Look For

- doctrine
- dogmas
- encyclicals
- Judaism
- Islam
- ecumenism
- laity

- consecrated life
- religious life
- religious vows
- sisters (nuns)
- brothers (monks, friars)
- religious priests

- diocesan priests
- deacon
- bishops
- Pope
- college of bishops
- hierarchy

111

non-Catholics when they were growing up. Catholic kids were told to stay away from the "bad influence" of those Protestant kids. Some Protestant children were told that Catholics were going to hell and that the Pope was the anti-Christ. Catholic families discouraged their children from dating non-Catholics, and Protestant families discouraged their children from dating and marrying Catholics. Depending on where you live in the United States, some of these things might still be true today.

A Buddhist monk presents Pope John Paul II with a crystal Madonna. The Catholic Church respects the wisdom found in other religious traditions while maintaining that only the Catholic Church contains the fullness of God's Revelation.

Thank God that the Holy Spirit has been active in changing these attitudes. In many ways it has been the Holy Spirit working through young people that has led the way to greater understanding and tolerance among people of different religious beliefs. It is hoped that young people will continue this work. But at the same time, do not fall into the trap of thinking that all religions have basically the same beliefs. Major differences exist between Christianity and other world religions, and even between Catholics and other Christians. This chapter explores some of those differences and the things that make the Catholic faith unique. This section from the *Catechism,* number 870, says it best:

> The sole Church of Christ which in the Creed we profess to be one, holy, catholic, and apostolic, . . . subsists [exists] in the Catholic Church, which is governed by the successor of Peter and by the bishops in communion with him. Nevertheless, many elements of sanctification [practices leading to holiness] and of truth are found outside its visible confines. (*Lumen gentium* 8)

The Catholic Church and Other Religions

The relationship of the Catholic Church with other major non-Christian religions is somewhat complex. A careful balancing act needs to be maintained. On one hand, we know that salvation comes only through belief in Christ as the only Son of God. Because these other religions do not believe in

Christ as the Son of God, they cannot be a true means to salvation. On the other hand, we know that the people in these religions are also children of God. Many of them live their faith with more seriousness than many Christians live the Christian faith. Jews and Muslims even worship the same God, although they do not recognize Jesus as the Son of God.

Unfortunately, at times in the Church's history, the relationship between Catholics and people from non-Christian religions has been characterized by intolerance and even violence on both sides. In some cases Catholics, motivated by a concern for the spiritual welfare of non-Christians, tried to force the conversion of non-Christians by attacking their religions and even their culture. That reasoning was also used by people whose real goal was the accumulation of wealth and political power, and it led to terrible violence against those of other faiths. You may have heard about that violence in studying the Crusades or the treatment of Native Americans during the conquest of the Americas. It is important to remember that those sins were committed by individual Catholics and not by the Church itself.

Things have changed for the better in recent times. The Catholic Church recognizes the authentic search for God in these other religions. In fact, the Catholic Church teaches that those people who through no fault of their own do not know Christ or his Church, but who seek God with a sincere heart and try to do his will—they may also achieve eternal salvation. The Church still has a strong missionary mandate to preach the Gospel of Christ to non-Christian people. Being given the fullness of life in Christ demands that we tell those who do not know

Church Doctrine

Catholic **doctrine** expresses the Church's understanding of God's Revelation through Jesus. The doctrines most fundamental to Catholic belief are authoritatively defined by the Magisterium and are called **dogmas,** and they do not change. The Church's doctrine develops over time in the sense that our understanding of the revealed reality it expresses grows. Although God's Revelation is complete, "it has not been made completely explicit; it remains for Christian faith gradually to grasp its full significance over the course of the centuries" (*CCC*, number 66). "Thanks to the assistance of the Holy Spirit, the understanding of both the realities and the words of the heritage of faith is able to grow in the life of the Church" (*CCC*, number 94).

The Pope contributes to Catholics' understanding of Revelation through pastoral letters and writings that deal with pressing issues in light of Revelation. The Pope's pastoral letters are called **encyclicals** when they are sent to the whole Church. Regional or national groups of bishops also contribute to Church teaching when they issue statements or pastoral letters on matters affecting the Church in their nation or diocese. The documents issued by ecumenical councils and synods of bishops also guide the Church's understanding of Revelation. The papal letters, bishops' statements, and conciliar documents serve the Church by guiding people as they seek to carry out the mission of Jesus in the world today.

Christ about it. Yet we know that faith in Christ must be a free decision, one we cannot force others to make. We pray for the day when every person in the world knows and believes in Jesus Christ.

The Catholic Church has special ties to two religions in particular. The first is **Judaism.** We recognize that the Jewish faith is already a response to God's Revelation in the Old Covenant. The Jews are our spiritual ancestors, whom Catholics hold in special honor as God's Chosen People. In particular, the Catholic Church warns its members not to blame Jewish people for the death of Christ, as has been done by some Christians. According to the Scriptures, only a few Jewish leaders and Romans were responsible for Jesus' death. Blaming them as a group for Jesus' death would be like blaming all Catholics for the atrocities of the Crusades or the Inquisition. The Catholic Church condemns all hatred, persecution, and displays of anti-Semitism directed against the Jewish people.

The other religion we have a special tie to is **Islam,** the faith of Muslims. Like Jews and Christians, Muslims also trace their origins back to Abraham and Sarah. Like us they acknowledge only one God, the creator of us all. They believe that Jesus was a great prophet, but they do not believe that he is the Savior, the Son of God. They place their faith in their founder, Mohammed, whom they believe was the greatest prophet. Mohammed's prophecies are collected in their holy book, the Koran. After the terrorist attack of September 11, 2001, many people became interested in what Muslims believe. What they found out is that most Muslims are a peaceful people, and that those terrible events were the work of radical groups who pervert the true Islamic faith.

Looking Back

The Protestant Reformation

At the start of the sixteenth century, the Catholic Church in the West was badly in need of reform. A variety of reform efforts gave rise to serious conflicts, which eventually led significant numbers of people to break away from the Catholic Church and form new Christian communities. The term *Protestant,* derived from the verb "to protest," describes the denominations that trace their beginnings to these sixteenth-century conflicts.

Martin Luther, the best known of the reformers, was a German monk, priest, and Scripture scholar. With hopes of bringing change rather than division, he wrote a critique of the Church's practice of selling indulgences (something that reduces a person's time in purgatory). Eventually, however, he was excommunicated by the Catholic Church, and after attempts to resolve the conflict failed, the Lutheran Church was born. The reform efforts of Ulrich Zwingli of Switzerland and John Calvin of France followed, and led to further fragmenting of the Church.

The Counter-Reformation refers to the Catholic Church's efforts to address the issues at the heart of the division, most significantly through the Council of Trent (1545–1563). The council brought significant change, but did not restore unity to the Church in the West.

The Catholic Church and Other Christian Churches

The Catholic Church often describes her relationship with other Christian Churches using the image of a family. In this image, members of other Christian Churches are understood to be our brothers and sisters in Christ. But they are our separated brothers and sisters because the Catholic Church is the Church founded by Christ and the Apostles, and the other Churches—Episcopal, Methodist, Lutheran, Baptist, Quakers, Pentecostals, and so on—became separated from full communion with the Catholic Church.

All Christian Churches share the common understanding that salvation comes through Christ, who is the head of the Church. All Christian churches are part of Christ's Body here on earth. Catholics and other Christians who believe in Christ and have been properly baptized share a communion with one another. However, because of some important areas of disagreement, it is not a perfect communion.

You might be wondering, "What are those areas of disagreement?" You should be aware that there are many, some major and some minor. And they can be different depending on which Christian Church you are talking about. But in general these are the most important areas of disagreement:

- disagreement over whether both the Scriptures and Tradition are the sources of God's Revelation
- disagreement over the number of sacraments and whether the seven sacraments are a necessary part of Church life
- disagreement over the centrality of the Eucharist—many non-Catholic Churches do not celebrate the Eucharist or do so only occasionally

Promoting Ecumenism

As Catholics we seek to better understand our faith and the kind of life Jesus' message challenges us to live. Sometimes this exploration focuses on unique aspects of Catholicism, but the ultimate goal is not division or separation from other Christians. And certainly there is no place for a superior attitude. Part of our Catholic faith is the belief that God calls all Christians to unity. Through Baptism all Christians, regardless of denomination, are called to unite in order to be a visible sign of Christ in the world. Jesus prayed to the Father for his disciples "that they may all be one. As you, Father, are in me and I am in you, may they also be in us, so that the world may believe that you have sent me" (John 17:21).

While Church leaders conduct official dialogues, you can foster unity by seeking out relationships with non-Catholics, learning about their faith, and joining with them to pray and to carry out projects that contribute to social justice in the community.

○ disagreement over whether the bread and wine are truly the body and blood of Jesus Christ

○ disagreement over the role of the Pope as the head of the Church—many non-Catholic Churches do not believe in any kind of centralized leadership

At the most recent ecumenical council of the Church, the Second Vatican Council, the bishops called Catholics to accept other Christians as their brothers and sisters in Christ. Since the council was held, the Catholic Church has been working hard to strengthen the communion between the Catholic Church and other churches. This is called **ecumenism.** Theologians have met to try to understand the theological differences that exist among the different Christian churches and to try to bridge those differences if possible. Pope John Paul II has reached out to leaders of other Churches to reconcile past hurts. Individual Catholics are encouraged to pray with other Christians and perform works of service together. In these ways the Catholic Church strives to be a kind and humble mother who works to gather all her children together in full communion with one another.

Roles in the Catholic Church

One of the most significant ways the Catholic Church differs from other Churches is in its structure. The Catholic Church has a well-defined organizational and leadership structure. As the Body of Christ, we have a strong belief that God calls different people to take different roles within the Church. Each role is important and necessary for the Church to function properly. We have already discussed some of these roles, but let's take a closer look at them.

Pray It!

Prayer for Christian Unity

Join with Christians throughout the world in praying for unity, using the following prayer prepared by an international group appointed by the World Council of Churches and the Pontifical Council for Promoting Christian Unity (of the Roman Catholic Church):

God, source of hope,
We praise you.
We thank you for your gift of
    salvation in Christ.
We thank you for all those, our
    brothers and sisters
    through the one baptism into
        Christ,
    who call upon you as the
        source and giver of life.
We thank you for the hope of
    new life in Christ
    for ourselves, our churches,
        and the whole creation.
We thank you that you have
    made us one.
    We long to live as one.
    Forgive our divisions,
    and empower us in our work
        to overcome them.
In the joy of the Resurrection to
    eternal life we pray.
Amen.

The Lay Faithful

The structure of the Catholic Church can be pictured as a series of concentric rings (see diagram below). Each ring represents a special area of responsibility within the Church. The outer circle of our diagram represents the lay faithful, also called the laity. The **laity** are people who are not ordained or in a consecrated state of life. Some would say that this means the role of the laity is less important. But that is not the case at all. The laity are the people whose primary vocation (mission) is to bring Christ to the everyday world. It is the laity who bring Christ into schools, hospitals, factories, and offices.

Through their Baptism laypeople are called to share in the priestly, prophetic, and kingly office of Christ. The laity share in the priesthood of Christ by living a holy life and by raising up their family life, their work, their studies, their relationships with friends, and even their leisure time to God in prayer. Participation in the sacraments, particularly the Eucharist, is also an important way they share in the priesthood of Christ. The laity share in the prophetic office of Christ by proclaiming Christ to others in every situation and every circumstance through their words and deeds. The laity share in the kingly office of Christ by working against immorality in society—by changing sinful institutions, speaking out against sinful situations, and by serving others, particularly those who are poor and suffering. The kingly office also calls laypeople to exercise leadership within the Church wherever it is appropriate.

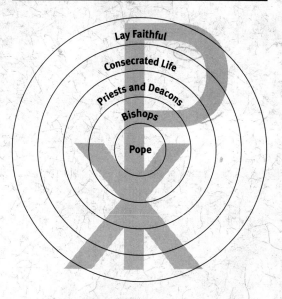

Roles Within the Catholic Church

Lay Faithful
Consecrated Life
Priests and Deacons
Bishops
Pope

☧ is a symbol for Christ. By Baptism, every role is connected to Christ's ministry. As the circles get smaller, the roles are more specific.

Consecrated Life

One role in the structure of Catholic life doesn't fit neatly into our diagram. The people living a **consecrated life** are not necessarily ordained, like deacons, priests, and bishops, but their life and calling is not the same as that of most laypeople. For the purpose of finding a place in our diagram we will place the consecrated life in a circle between the ordained ministers and the laity.

Women and men in religious life can teach us a great deal about following Jesus Christ. Do you know any religious sisters or brothers with whom you can spend time?

To consecrate means to set aside for a holy purpose or to be fully dedicated to pursuing a more intimate relationship with God, and people who choose a consecrated life are doing just that. Many forms of the consecrated life have emerged in the history of the Church, and as people continue exploring creative ways to answer God's call, new forms will emerge. Here are some of the forms that have existed and continue to flourish:

- **Hermits.** In this form of consecrated life, a person devotes herself or himself to the praise of God and the salvation of the world by separating from the world to live in greater solitude and silence. They witness to others that having Christ alone is enough.

- **Consecrated virgins and widows.** In this state a woman commits to lifelong virginity (or perpetual chastity if widowed) in a special ceremony with the bishop. A consecrated widow or virgin devotes herself to Christ through prayer, service to the Church, and service to the world.

- **Religious life.** This is the best-known consecrated state of life. In **religious life,** a person makes a lifelong commitment to belong to a religious community—which is also called a religious order. As part of the commitment, the person makes three **religious vows:** a vow of chastity (not to be sexually active), a vow of poverty (not to own any private property), and a vow of obedience (to the superior of the community). These vows give the person great freedom to be focused on their relationship with God.

Women in religious life are often called nuns or **sisters.** Men in religious life are called monks, friars, or **brothers** unless they are ordained, and then they are called **religious priests.** Literally hundreds of different Catholic religious communities exist across the globe. Each community usually has a unique mission, determined by the person who founded the community.

Priests and Deacons

In the third circle of the Church's structure are religious priests (priests who have made vows to a religious community), diocesan priests and deacons. Through the sacrament of ordination, diocesan priests are called to be coworkers with the bishop of a particular diocese. Usually assigned to a parish community, **diocesan priests** represent the bishop in teaching the faith, celebrating the sacraments—particularly the Eucharist—and providing spiritual leadership. A bishop also ordains deacons, but a **deacon** is not a priest. The deacon's role is more oriented toward service and works of charity. However, they also have a liturgical role, assisting the priest or bishop at the Eucharist, blessing marriages, and presiding over baptisms and funerals. You can read more about priests and deacons in chapter 20, Sacraments at the Service of Communion.

These bishops, attending World Youth Day, represent the cultural diversity of the Church. Why is it important that bishops represent the diversity in the universal Church?

Bishops

In our diagram the bishops occupy the circle surrounding the Pope. The **bishops** are the direct successors of the original Apostles. The have a twofold responsibility. First, they are responsible for the pastoral care of the people within a particular area, called a diocese. Each bishop has the responsibility to see that all the churches in his diocese are working together as a whole. The bishop is a sign of this unity. Within their dioceses bishops are responsible for ordaining priests and deacons, for Confirmations, for assigning priests to parishes and other ministries, for setting policies, and for overseeing the correct teaching and practice of the Catholic faith.

Second, each bishop is responsible for working with other bishops and with the Pope to lead the worldwide Church. Working under the guidance of the Holy Spirit, they address social issues like poverty and war, they make sure the Catholic faith is being correctly taught, and they give guidance to deal with problems and concerns that arise within the Church. In some countries or regions, all the bishops gather for discussion on a regular basis, like the United States bishops do. And once in a great while, the Pope will call all the bishops of the world together in what is called an ecumenical council, to discuss some particular challenge facing the Church.

The Pope

The **Pope**—who is also called the Holy Father—is the center ring. The Pope is the direct successor of Saint Peter, whom Christ made the foundation of the Church and entrusted with the keys of the Kingdom (Matthew 16:18–19). Further, after his Resurrection Christ charged Saint Peter three times to "Feed my sheep" (John 21:15–17). Christ made Peter and all future popes responsible for the care of souls; first for those members of the Church, and second for all people whatever their religious identity might be.

The Pope has a huge job description. To get a picture of all his responsibilities, let's look at some of his many titles:

Saint Gregory the Great was a pope whose leadership helped the Church concentrate on its mission. In this image, what might the dove and the scribes represent in Gregory's life and work?

- **Bishop of the Church of Rome.** To be the Pope, you must first be a bishop. Because the city of Rome became the center of Christianity in the early Church, the diocese of Rome has historically been the Pope's diocese. Like other bishops he celebrates Mass in the cathedral, confirms young people, and ordains priests. (He does have other bishops who help out.)

- **Head of the college of bishops.** All the bishops of the world are united with one another, with the Pope as their head. As a body they are called the **college of bishops,** or sometimes the **hierarchy.** The Pope has the responsibility for providing leadership to the college of bishops.

- **Vicar of Christ.** A vicar is a person who is authorized to act in the place of another person. The Pope is the visible sign of Christ's presence on earth. Catholics all over the world, as well as many world leaders, look to him for guidance and inspiration.

○ **Pastor of the universal Church.** The Pope has the responsibility for the big picture, to minister to Catholics throughout the world. To carry out this tremendous responsibility, Christ gives the Pope full, supreme, and universal power over the entire Church.

Mary, Mother of the Church

In ending these two chapters that describe the Catholic Church, we turn again to Mary. Catholics believe that Mary is not only the mother of Christ but also the mother of the Church. This belief distinguishes Catholics from other Christians. The role of Mary as the mother of the Church is most clearly seen in the Scriptures, in John 19:26–27. In this passage Jesus is dying on the cross, and speaks to his mother and the beloved disciple—who here represents all believers. To Mary Jesus says, "Woman, here is your son"—indicating that the beloved disciple and all believers are her children. To the beloved disciple, Jesus says, "Here is your mother," meaning Mary is the mother of all Christians.

Mary's yes to the angel Gabriel to be the mother of Jesus was not a half-hearted reply. Her yes embraced everything Jesus said and did. With a mother's love she supported him in everything—including his suffering and death. Her role in God's plan did not end with giving birth to Jesus, or even with his death. It continues even after her life here on earth was finished.

The Tradition of the Catholic Church teaches that because of Mary's faithfulness and holiness, God rewarded her in a way that no other human being has ever been rewarded. When Mary's earthly life was at its end, she was taken up body and soul into the glory of heaven. This event is called the Assumption, and the Catholic Church in the United States celebrates it on

Saintly Profiles

Saint Gregory the Great (ca. 540–604; Pope 590–604)

When he was in his thirties, Gregory sold the many properties he owned, established seven monasteries in Italy, and distributed much of his considerable wealth to the poor. The next year he became a monk, and devoted himself to an austere lifestyle of contemplation and pastoral care of the plague-stricken in Rome. Because he was well known for his holiness, in 590 he was elected Pope. Though he did not want the role, he accepted it. As Pope he continued his care of the poor and hungry and challenged other leaders to attend to those in need rather than the worldly interests of the Church.

Gregory also recognized the need for reform in the Church, and imposed important changes in its government. He promoted monasticism, and is credited with writing many of the prayers recited at Mass. Especially noteworthy among his writings is *Pastoral Care,* which describes the ministry of bishops as the shepherding of souls. It became the textbook for medieval bishops. Gregory's way of referring to himself as Pope was as "servant of the servants of God." He is the patron saint of England, musicians, singers, teachers, popes, and victims of plague. His feast day is September 3.

August 15. The Assumption teaches that Mary was the first human being to participate in her son's Resurrection, and that she waits in heaven for us, her spiritual children, to join her in the Resurrection and in life everlasting.

For Further Reflection

° How have you experienced the differences between your religious beliefs and those of your friends? If you hear someone putting down people who practice a particular religion, Catholic or otherwise, how can you respond in a way that promotes tolerance and understanding?

° As a layperson, when are you acting in a priestly way, growing in prayer and in your awareness of God's presence? When are you acting in a prophetic way, proclaiming Christ to others through your words and actions? When are you acting in a kingly way, serving others to ease the suffering and injustice in the world?

13 The Last Things

People in the United States have mixed feelings about death. On one hand, we spend lots of time and money trying to hold off the moment of our death. We add safety features to cars and homes, go on the latest diet or exercise craze, and take life-enhancing herbal supplements—all in the hope of staving off death for a few more years. On the other hand, movies and television often feature violent death to attract viewers. Death seems to fascinate us—as long as it's someone else's death!

Most teens—and most adults—would rather not think too much about their own death. This usually isn't hard to do, because most people in the United States rarely have to address the reality of death. Yet every once in a while, we must face the death of someone we know well. Or maybe we have to face the possibility of our own death because of an accident or a serious illness. In these times the thought that races through most people's minds is, What will happen to me when I die?

Words to Look For

- martyrs
- final judgment
- Parousia (Second Coming)
- heaven
- hell
- purgatory
- communion of saints
- apostolic fathers

Facing our own death isn't easy. It can be sobering, even frightening to face this big unknown. Some people are thrown into despair and even depression thinking about death. The Catholic faith has answers to the question of death, as do most religions. But we have the advantage because the person who supplied those answers has actually died and risen again! Believing in Jesus' promise that we shall rise to new life does not completely take away the sting of death, but our faith does help us understand that death is not a final ending but a new and glorious beginning.

The Resurrection of the Dead

It may surprise you to know that the Old Testament books rarely make any references to an afterlife. The author of the Book of Ecclesiastes expresses what most of Jesus' ancestors felt about death, "The dead know nothing; they have no more reward, and even the memory of them is lost" (9:5). But a couple of centuries before the birth of Jesus Christ, the Jewish people began to believe that there was more than just nothingness after death. We know this because two of the last Old Testament books to be written contain references to life after death (2 Maccabees 7:23, Daniel 12:1–3).

In the New Testament, however, the belief in an afterlife is pervasive. All four Gospels testify to Jesus' own Resurrection from the dead. In particular, the Gospel of John goes further in saying that all people have the possibility of eternal life. John has no less than seventeen references about eternal life. It is instructive to consider the requirements given in the Gospel of John for inheriting eternal life:

- ○ Believe in the Son of Man, God's only son (3:15–16).
- ○ Obey Jesus (3:36).
- ○ Hear Jesus and believe the One who sent him (5:24).

Pray It !

Prayer for the Dead

As Catholics we have the tradition of praying for our deceased brothers and sisters. It is a way of continuing our relationship with them and assisting them on their journey to heaven. We remember them at every Mass. All Souls' Day, on November 2, is a special time set aside to pray for the dead. In Mexico people hold Day of the Dead celebrations in cemeteries, in honor of their loved ones and to mock death with displays of humor. It reminds us not to be so fearful of death, because we believe in the Resurrection.

Remember those who have died with this prayer from the Mass for All Souls' Day:

God, our creator and redeemer, by your power Christ conquered death and returned to you in glory. May all your people who have gone before us in faith share his victory and enjoy the vision of your glory for ever. We ask this through our Lord Jesus Christ, your Son, who lives and reigns with you and the Holy Spirit, one God, for ever and ever. Amen. (*The Sacramentary,* page 734)

○ Eat Jesus' flesh and drink his blood (6:54).

○ "Hate your life in this world," or in other words, do not be attached to the things of this life (12:25).

Saint Paul had such a strong belief in eternal life that he looked forward to death. While he was in prison and awaiting his trial, he wrote to the Philippians: "For to me, living is Christ and dying is gain. . . . I am hard pressed [to choose] between the two: my desire is to depart and be with Christ, for that is far better; but to remain in the flesh is more necessary for you" (Philippians 1:21–24). The only good reason Saint Paul saw for remaining in this present life was to bring Christ to others.

According to the Creation stories in the Bible, death was not part of God's original plan for human beings. Our bodily death is the result of original sin. But God will not let death be our final end. Through an even greater act of love than his original Creation, he allowed his only Son to suffer and die so that every person might have the opportunity for eternal life. Jesus' own Resurrection is the promise of our bodily resurrection after death. At death our souls will be separated from our bodies. But when God raises us from the dead, our souls will be reunited with new, incorruptible bodies, that is, bodies that will never know illness, disease, or death again.

The Final Judgment

No one knows how or when this resurrection of our bodies after death will occur. Time as we know it probably has little meaning after death. But we call the time when all the dead will be raised "the last day" or "the **final judgment**." Saint Paul tries to explain that moment in the First Letter to the Thessalonians:

Martyrdom

Many Christians throughout the centuries have had to decide if their faith was worth dying for. The Roman government outlawed Christianity. Many Christians went to their death rather than deny their faith in Jesus Christ. They are called **martyrs,** and their deaths were compared to the death of Christ on the cross. The Roman leaders thought that they could stamp out Christianity by executing the followers of this "subversive" religion, but instead the bloodshed of these courageous people became the seeds of tremendous growth in the Church.

Let's look at just a few of the many famous martyrs from the Church's history. The first Christian martyr was Stephen. You can read about him in Acts 7:2–60. Felicity and Perpetua were not yet baptized when they were martyred. Perpetua was a nursing mother; Felicity was her African slave, who had given birth just days before. The two women gave each other the kiss of peace before they were executed together in 203. Maximilian was beheaded in 295 for refusing to serve in the Roman army. He said he could only serve the Lord as a soldier of God. Thomas More of England was married and a lawyer. King Henry VIII named him his lord chancellor, but then beheaded him in 1535 when he refused to agree that the king (rather than the Pope) had supreme authority over the Church in England. Archbishop Oscar Romero, of El Salvador, was celebrating Mass on March 24, 1980, when he was shot because of his public opposition to government repression and military violence against the people.

For this we declare to you by the word of the Lord, that we who are alive, who are left until the coming of the Lord, will by no means precede those who have died. For the Lord himself, with a cry of command, with the archangel's call and with the sound of God's trumpet, will descend from heaven, and the dead in Christ will rise first. Then we who are alive, who are left, will be caught up in the clouds together with them to meet the Lord in the air; and so we will be with the Lord forever. (4:15–17)

Saint Paul, along with many of the people who became Christians soon after Jesus' death, thought that Jesus would be returning within their lifetime. Jesus himself foretold of his coming again in Gospel passages such as Mark 13:24–27: "Then they will see 'the Son of Man coming in clouds' with great power and glory" (13:26). This event is called the **Second Coming,** or a more Catholic term, Christ's **Parousia,** a Greek word meaning "arrival." The Parousia will signal a final judgment of all humanity.

Matthew 25:31–46 is the clearest biblical teaching we have about the final judgment. This passage tells how Jesus will gather all humanity together to face a final judgment. Acting as supreme judge, Christ will separate those who have followed his will by caring for others, from those who did not follow his will because they lived only for themselves. Every person will be held accountable for his or her own deeds. Those who followed the will of Christ will be welcomed into God's eternal, heavenly kingdom, prepared for them from the beginning of the world. Those who failed to serve Christ in needy and suffering people will be sent into eternal punishment.

Thus at the end of time, the Kingdom of God will come into its perfection. The Book of Revelation teaches that at that time all creation will be transformed, there will be "a new heaven and a new earth" (21:1). The just will reign with God in heaven for eternity, their souls united with their glorified, resurrected bodies. God will be all in all because the whole of creation will be in perfect and direct relationship with its creator.

This image of the Final Judgment is strongly based on Matthew 25:31–46. Notice the saved at Jesus' right hand and the damned at Jesus' left hand. Notice that Jesus' body is surrounded by an almond shape, which symbolizes his resurrected power and glory.

Jesus Christ did not return for the final judgment during Paul's lifetime. Throughout the centuries that followed, the Church has pondered the question, "When will Christ return again?" And the Catholic Church's answer has always been this: only God knows the time. Human history could well go on for thousands or millions of years. Or Christ could return tomorrow. Some Christian leaders have tried to predict the time of the Second Coming, but Catholics have learned from the first Christians that every effort to do so misses the real point of this teaching—that we should live every day like it could be our last.

Heaven, Hell, and Purgatory

Besides the final judgment, in which every person will take part, there is the personal, particular judgment that every person will undergo immediately after death. The story of the rich man and Lazarus (Luke 16:19–31) and the words of Christ to the repentant thief (Luke 23:43) indicate an immediate judgment that sends our soul on to its ultimate destiny: heaven or hell.

What exactly is **heaven?** Neither the Bible nor the Tradition of the Church have a definitive description of heaven. What we do know is that in heaven the relationship between God and humanity that was broken by original sin will be restored. In heaven we will know the joy of being in perfect relationship with the Holy Trinity, the relationship that God has intended for us from the beginning of time. Think of a moment when you were with a group of good friends and you had just done something really great and exciting—maybe you just won an important game or just finished a retreat or a big service project. Everyone is content and joyful and excited. That experience is a little bit like what heaven will be like, except in heaven it won't be just a moment, it will last for all eternity.

Looking Back

We Share Christ's Death

Leo the Great is a saint who was Pope from 440–461. He is remembered for strengthening papal authority and for resolving difficult conflicts and theological disputes within the Church. He personally persuaded Attila the Hun not to attack Rome. Leo wrote the following words:

> But it is not only the martyrs who share in his passion by their glorious courage; the same is true, by faith, of all who are born again in baptism. . . . As we have died with him, and have been buried and raised to life with him, so we bear him within us . . . in everything we do. (*The Liturgy of the Hours,* volume 2, page 661)

Even though we generally refer to heaven as being up and hell as being down, they are not physical places as we experience time and space. Thus we can only describe them through metaphors and analogies. For example, when speaking of heaven, Jesus used the metaphor of a mansion: "In my Father's house there are many dwelling places. If it were not so, would I have told you that I go to prepare a place for you?" (John 14:2). Some of the most powerful descriptions of heaven come from the Book of Revelation. Consider these examples:

Images of hell tend to be dominated by scenes of torment and suffering. But the hallmark of hell is the eternal separation from the love of God. In this painting, this separation is represented by the distant heavenly figures.

And I heard a loud voice from the throne saying,
"See, the home of God is among mortals.
He will dwell with them as their God;
they will be his peoples,
and God himself will be with them;
he will wipe every tear from their eyes.
Death will be no more;
mourning and crying and pain will be no
    more,
for the first things have passed away."

(21:3–4)

Then the angel showed me the river of the water of life, bright as crystal, flowing from the throne of God and of the Lamb through the middle of the street of the city. On either side of the river is the tree of life with its twelve kinds of fruit, producing its fruit each month; and the leaves of the tree are for the healing of the nations. Nothing accursed will be found there any more. But the throne of God and of the Lamb will be in it, and his servants will worship him; they will see his face, and his name will be on their foreheads. And there will be no more night; they need no light of lamp or sun, for the Lord God will be their light, and they will reign forever and ever. (22:1–5)

Hell will be the opposite of heaven. In describing the final judgment, Jesus says, "You that are accursed, depart from me into the eternal fire prepared for the devil and his angels" (Matthew 25:41). And the Book of Revelation says this: "Then Death and Hades were thrown into the lake of fire. This is the second death, the lake of fire; and anyone whose name was not found written in the book of life was thrown into the lake of fire" (20:14–15). Some scholars think the inspiration for describing hell as a place of fire came from the garbage pit outside of Jerusalem. The pit was often burning, filled with things that no longer filled their purpose.

Popular images of hell are usually of burning pits and of demons with pitchforks torturing the unfortunate souls who end up there for eternity. Hell is indeed a reality. But the principal punishment isn't physical torture; it is the spiritual anguish of being separated from God. Think of hell as the natural and logical consequence for a person who had already decided to separate herself or himself from God here on earth. Once on this journey, a person drifts further and further into sin and away from the One who is the source of all life and happiness—and at death that separation becomes complete.

But the reality is that when most of us die, we are neither perfect saints nor perfect sinners. We believe in God and desire God's grace, yet we have areas of our life that need to be purged of selfishness and sin. Such souls need to undergo a purification in order to achieve the holiness necessary to enter fully into the glory of God in heaven. This purification is also called purgation, and the place in which this purification occurs is called **purgatory.** Souls in purgatory are assured of entering heaven once their purification is complete. This is a belief that is somewhat unique to the Catholic faith and not shared by all Christians. But it is part of the truth God has revealed in Tradition, and it makes perfect sense once you think about it.

Of course the ultimate question is, "How do I get to heaven to share eternal life

Me? A Martyr?

What are you willing to live for? What are you willing to die for? These are questions about what means the most to us in our life. A dramatic example of facing martyrdom took place on April 20, 1999, at Columbine High School, in Littleton, Colorado. Two students with guns and bombs burst into the school, intending to kill. In the library they continued their carnage amid the smoke and fire alarms. Among other things, they apparently had strong negative feelings toward Christian students.

Valeen Schnurr, a student active at Littleton's Saint Francis Cabrini Catholic Church, was there. After being struck by a shotgun blast, she pleaded, "Oh my God, oh my God, don't let me die." A gunman then asked her in a taunting way whether she believed in God, and she said yes. She then crawled away as they reloaded their guns; Valeen survived the attack.

Meanwhile seventeen-year-old Cassie Bernall was under a desk praying out loud when her killer held a gun to her head and taunted her by asking if she believed in God. When she said yes, he asked why—but before she could answer, he pulled the trigger. A book was written about her, titled *She Said Yes: The Unlikely Martyrdom of Cassie Bernall.* She had previously turned her life around from involvement in drugs, alcohol, and the occult to belief in Christ. The story of her life and her courageous witness of faith have inspired thousands, just as the lives of martyrs have inspired the faithful since the earliest days of the Church.

with God?" And the answer is a simple one, already alluded to earlier in this chapter. Believe in Jesus. Believe that he is God's Son, the Savior of the world. Obey his commands. Become baptized into his Body, the Church. This is the only sure path to heaven that God has revealed to us. Of course most of us do not live any of these things perfectly, but that isn't as important as the fact that we are struggling to do so.

Ignatius of Antioch welcomed a martyr's death as a way to witness to his faith in Jesus Christ. What are you willing to sacrifice to witness to your faith?

Does this mean that people from other religions, who have been raised in them all their life and have never heard the truth of Christ presented in a convincing way, will all go to hell? Such a statement would be contrary to God's mercy and love. This is why the Church teaches that good people of all religions, if they seek God with a sincere heart and try to do his will as they understand it, may also achieve eternal salvation.

The Communion of Saints

Right after professing our belief in the Church, the Apostle's Creed continues, "I believe . . . in the communion of saints." The **communion of saints** is really another description of the Church, the gathering of all those who are saints because of their faith in Jesus Christ. But the phrase describes two realities in Catholic life: the spiritual practices that represent and bring about the unity of believers, and the actual communion that ties together all believers, both living and dead.

The spiritual practices that help bring about the communion of saints are many. They include the gifts that each member of the Body of Christ shares in service to the Church and the world, the works of charity to those who are suffering or in spiritual or material need, and the sacraments of the Church, especially the Eucharist. All these practices tie Christ's followers together.

The Catholic Church has consistently taught the revealed truth that the Holy Spirit unites all believers, including those who are alive right now, those who have died and are being purified before entering heaven, and the blessed saints who are in heaven right now. This is the basis for the Catholic practice of praying for and to the dead. Why would we do such a thing? Because people who love one another hold one another up before God in prayer. Just because a person has died, it doesn't mean they no longer need our prayers or they cannot bring our needs before God in heaven.

So we pray for God's mercy on our dead family and friends, asking that their journey to heaven be swift. Remembering them during the celebration of the Mass is an important prayer on their behalf. And we also ask the saints to bring our needs before God. We believe that they hear our prayers and are with God in heaven. This is not limited only to the official saints—you can also ask loved ones who have died to bring you and your needs before God.

You can see that Catholics have an expansive understanding of family. Some Christians like to make sharp distinctions between who is being saved and who is not being saved. At one time Catholics also had that tendency, but at the Second Vatican Council in the 1960s, the bishops of the world made it clear that it is not the Catholic way. God's Revelation about our final destiny only leads us to marvel at the depth of God's love for all people. We want and hope and pray that all people will be saved and that we all will be joined together in the glory that awaits us in heaven.

For Further Reflection

° What have you heard or read about the Parousia, Jesus Christ's Second Coming? Does it scare you or give you hope? Why?

° One of the images that Jesus used to describe heaven was a wedding feast. What can this image tell us about what our future life will be like?

Saintly Profiles

Ignatius of Antioch (ca. 35–107)

Ignatius of Antioch died a martyr's death when he was thrown to the lions in the year 107. He was a Greek Christian who became Bishop of Antioch in 69. Antioch, in Syria, was the most important Christian community outside of Jerusalem. Ignatius is one of the **apostolic fathers,** an early Church leader whose writings have been preserved. He was condemned to death during the persecution of Christians under the Roman emperor Trajan, and taken to Rome as a prisoner to be executed.

During the lengthy journey, he wrote letters to the Churches of Ephesus, Magnesia, Tralles, Rome, Philadelphia, and Smyrna, and the last to Bishop Polycarp of Smyrna. These letters give us important information about the life of the Church community after the first Apostles. Because he had complete confidence that after his death he would be resurrected with Christ, Ignatius fearlessly faced his martyrdom and asked the Christians in Rome not to try to prevent it. His letter to the Church of Rome testifies: "Let me be food for the wild beasts, for they are my way to God. I am God's wheat and shall be ground by their teeth so that I may become Christ's pure bread. . . . No earthly pleasures, no kingdoms of this world can benefit me in any way. I prefer death in Christ Jesus. . . . Do not stand in the way of my birth to real life" (*The Liturgy of the Hours,* volume 4, pages 1490–1491). Saint Ignatius's feast day is October 17.

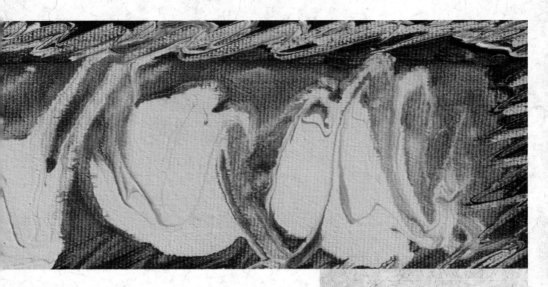

Part B

Liturgy and
Sacraments

14 Introduction to the Liturgy

Perhaps the greatest source of friction that exists between teens and parents when it comes to religion is the argument about going to Sunday Mass. Teens for decades have told their parents, "I'm not going to Church; it's boring and pointless." If you find attending Church boring or without purpose, you are not the first! But instead of trying to wear your parents down, please read these chapters carefully. They will give you an intellectual appreciation of why participating in the liturgy and the sacraments of the Church is so important in God's plan. Then ask the Holy Spirit to help you appreciate the Mass so that it not only makes sense to go but you want to participate.

On the other hand, if you are one of those teens who enjoys going to Mass, you are truly blessed. You have the good fortune to have been graced with an appreciation for God's great gift to the Church, a little taste of heaven on earth. Many people come to truly appreciate the liturgy only as adults,

Words to Look For

- ◦ liturgy
- ◦ liturgical celebration or ritual
- ◦ liturgical year
- ◦ Advent
- ◦ Christmas
- ◦ Ordinary Time
- ◦ Lent
- ◦ Holy Week
- ◦ Triduum
- ◦ Easter

when they find that all the activity, all the gadgets, and all the friends that so occupied their time as teens and young adults does not satisfy their hunger for meaning and connection to God.

Many experts feel that one reason it is harder today to appreciate the meaning of liturgy and the sacraments is because of modern technology and modern media. Before we had movies and television, the Bible stories read at Mass and the priest's homilies were people's "entertainment" and education. Before we had books and magazines, the Church's stained-glass windows and statues were the people's source of visual information and art. Before we had radio and newspapers, talking with your neighbors after Church was your main source of community news.

This doesn't mean that modern technology and media are bad. But it does mean that their flash and instant entertainment can easily distract us from what is really important. You have to look harder today at what God is offering us in the sacred liturgy (the Mass and the sacraments) to discover its true and eternal value. Perhaps this is what the Holy Spirit wants us to do, so this great and wondrous gift from God isn't taken for granted.

What Is Liturgy?

So what is this thing called **liturgy?** Essentially it is the public, communal, and official worship of the Church. It is public, as a sign of our faith to the local community. It is communal, which means it isn't a prayer that you do alone. It is official, which means the Church governs it. The Eucharist (or Mass) is the central liturgy of the Catholic Church and the basis for most other liturgical celebrations. The other six sacraments of the Church,

Looking
Back

Vatican II and Liturgical Reform

The liturgy we experience today is quite different from that of fifty or sixty years ago. Over the ages what began as a gathering of friends and followers of Jesus' sharing a meal and remembering his teachings, became an increasingly elaborate ceremony of sacrifice. The celebrations of the Lord's Supper, held in secret in people's homes during the times of persecution, gave way to highly ritualized ceremonies held in beautiful churches. By the Middle Ages, the priest was saying Mass while the people watched in silence. The focus was primarily on Jesus' sacrifice, which diminished the symbol of a shared meal. Those attending were not participants as much as watchers, separated from the liturgical action by distance, architecture, and language.

In the 1960s the bishops from around the world gathered at the Second Vatican Council. They called for important reforms to renew the liturgy. The language of the liturgy changed from Latin to the vernacular (the local language of the people), so that for the first time in hundreds of years, the people could hear and understand the prayers that were being said. The congregation's participation in song, prayer, and action was encouraged. People were also encouraged to receive Communion, in the hand and from the cup. The idea of a shared meal around a table was reclaimed from the early years of Christianity.

Baptism, Confirmation, Penance and Reconciliation, Anointing of the Sick, Holy Orders, and Matrimony, have their own liturgical rituals. The Liturgy of the Hours (which is explained in the chapter Praying Together) and Catholic funerals are other examples of liturgical celebrations. However, a group prayer service is not liturgy because it is not an official worship service of the Church.

Lectoring, or reading the sacred word during liturgy, is one of the ways in which we are called to participate in the work of God. What liturgical ministries are open to youth in your parish?

The word *liturgy* is taken from the Greek word *liturgia,* which means "a public work" or "service on behalf of the people." In keeping with this definition, for Christians *liturgy* means the participation of the People of God in the work of God. So our liturgies aren't something we do, but something God does and we participate in. "Wait," you say, "it isn't God that's saying the prayers and singing the songs and eating and drinking the bread and the wine. It's us!" Very true, but those words and actions are the physical expression of the spiritual work that God is doing in the liturgy to bring us to eternal salvation.

That's right, in the liturgy God is at work bringing us to our salvation. That is why participation in the liturgy is just as important as having faith in Jesus and avoiding sin and living a moral life. In the liturgy we learn about the great mysteries of our faith by participating in them. We learn about the mystery of the Trinity by experiencing the Trinity in the liturgy. We learn about the Incarnation of Jesus Christ by experiencing him as true God and true man. We learn about the Paschal mystery as we participate in the Passion, death, and Resurrection of Christ through the Eucharist (see chapter 18, The Eucharist).

Before going any further, let's define a few terms. *The* liturgy or *the* sacred liturgy refers to the overall idea of Catholic official worship, but *a* liturgy usually refers to a specific Mass or sacramental celebration. Liturgical describes anything that has to do with the liturgy. A **liturgical celebration or ritual** is another name for a Mass or a Baptism, or any other specific liturgy. A liturgist is a person who plans and coordinates liturgical celebrations. The congregation or assembly is the people who are gathered at a liturgical celebration. The celebrant is the title of the person who leads, or presides at, a liturgical celebration. Only ordained ministers—bishops, priests, and deacons—can preside at sacramental liturgies. The proper celebrant for each sacrament is covered in later chapters.

Liturgy and the Holy Trinity

The Church's sacred liturgy is completely trinitarian (for an explanation of the Holy Trinity, see pages 41–43). In the liturgy we experience the Holy Trinity at work, and through that experience the mystery of the Holy Trinity is more deeply revealed. As a sign of this, we begin the Eucharist with, "In the name of the Father, and of the Son, and of the Holy Spirit." And at the end of the liturgy, the celebrant asks the blessing of the Holy Trinity, "May Almighty God bless you, the Father, and the Son, and the Holy Spirit."

The lighting of the Easter candle marks the beginning of one of the most important liturgies in the Church year, the Easter Vigil.

Each person of the Trinity is involved in the liturgy. We acknowledge the Father as the source of all our blessings. In the Scripture readings and the liturgical prayers, we recall important moments of salvation history in which the Father was at work. We remember and celebrate the Father's greatest gift to us, the gift of his Son, who gave himself up for us so that we might be saved.

Jesus Christ plays a central role in the liturgy because he not only gave us the sacred liturgy, he also makes himself present to us through liturgical celebrations. Something that makes Christ's presence real is called a sacrament, thus we say that liturgy is sacramental. The Church itself is also a sacrament, because it makes Christ' presence real by the power of the Holy Spirit.

We can get more specific and name some of the ways that Christ is in the liturgy. He is present in the assembly, because we are the Body of Christ. He is present in the word of God, the Scriptures. The part of the liturgy in which the Scriptures are proclaimed is called the liturgy of the word, and is an essential part of every liturgical celebration. And in a special way, Christ is present during the Eucharist because his body and blood are present in the bread and the wine (more on this in chapter 18, The Eucharist). Thus liturgy is the work of both Christ, the head, and the Church, his body.

We have already hinted at some of the ways the Holy Spirit is active in the liturgy. The Holy Spirit reveals Christ present in the community, the Scriptures, and the physical signs of liturgical celebrations. But the Holy Spirit is at work even before that, preparing us to receive Christ in the liturgy. And the Holy Spirit does more than just reveal Christ in the liturgy. Through the Holy Spirit, the saving work of Christ is actually made real and present in the liturgy.

It is important that you understand this last point. The liturgy and the sacraments are not just celebrations of past events. They make the saving power of Christ available to us, just as it was available to the original disciples and Apostles. Remember, Christ is alive! After his Resurrection he ascended into heaven so space and time would not limit him and he could be available to everyone everywhere. Of course he is close to us all the time, but we have his promise that his presence and power is available in a special way through the liturgy and the sacraments of the Church. This is discussed more thoroughly in the next chapter.

Pray It!

The Cross

Imagine yourself at Mass. Picture yourself in a particular seat, think of the people who are around you, young and old, rich and poor, happy and sad. Remember that each of these people—the little girl wiggling in the front row, the elderly man in the wheelchair, the young couple holding hands—each of them has been called by God, each of them is related to you. You are a part of the Body of Christ. Think of all the needs of the people in the assembly with you: someone's parent just died, someone just broke up with his girlfriend, someone just had a baby, someone feels far away from God, someone is lonely, someone's parents are getting divorced, someone just got a new job, someone just found out she or he has cancer. Think of all these needs: all the joy and all the pain.

Some people describe liturgy as the two beams of the cross: the vertical beam representing our relationship with God, the horizontal beam representing our relationship with our brothers and sisters in Christ. As you gather with these other Christians, you recognize them as your family members. What comfort can you offer? Hold these people in prayer, offer up their needs to God, and ask for God's direction for yourself.

The Liturgical Year

When you think of a year, probably the calendar year or maybe the academic year pops into your head. But the Church has a special year, called the **liturgical year,** to mark the celebration of her liturgies. The liturgical year celebrates God's time, which is eternal and timeless. We do this by remembering the past, celebrating the present, and looking toward the future.

The liturgical year is built around important historical events—such as Jesus' birth, death, and Resurrection—in

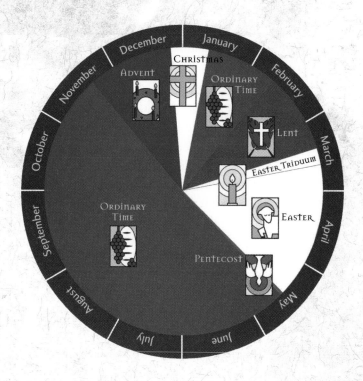

which God's saving power was made real. The liturgies in the liturgical year help us remember God's saving power made real in those historical events. They celebrate that God is saving us in the present moment, and they look forward to the time when God's plan of salvation will reach its ultimate fulfillment in Christ's future Parousia (Second Coming). Let's take a quick tour through the seasons of the liturgical year. The chart above can help you follow along.

Advent

The liturgical year begins in late November or early December, on the fourth Sunday before Christmas. These four weeks are the liturgical season of **Advent.** *Advent* means "coming," and this season is a preparation for the coming of the infant Jesus. The mood is hopeful anticipation, and the Scripture readings focus on God's promise to send a savior to deliver us from sin and death. It is a time to take life a little more slowly, and to focus on what we need to do to allow God to more fully enter our heart. This is a challenge in our culture, with all the shopping, concerts, and parties that happen during this time. Many churches and families mark the passing of the four weeks by lighting the candles of an Advent wreath.

Memorials of the Saints

You will notice that at the end of each Saintly Profiles section, the feast day of that saint is given. Throughout the liturgical year, we celebrate, on particular days, the feast days or memorials of Mary, the Apostles, the martyrs, and other saints. On a saint's feast day, we remember in a special way that person's life and faith in God. In this way we keep in mind what the saints have done. The witness of their faith strengthens us and offers us a model to follow in our own life.

Christmastime

The feast of **Christmas,** on December 25, celebrates the birth of Jesus and the mystery of the Incarnation. God entered the world as an infant, fully human in every way. It is a joyful feast, during which we remember that God is with us, bringing hope and joy to the world by sharing in our humanity.

The feast of Christmas is really the start of the Christmas season, which lasts until the Baptism of the Lord, the third Sunday after Christmas Day. In days past, this was the traditional time that people would exchange gifts, go caroling, and have Christmas parties. In some cultures gifts are still exchanged on the feast of the Epiphany (January 6), which celebrates the Magi from the east visiting Jesus. Many Christians are returning to the practice of having parties, caroling, and gift exchanges during the Christmas season in order to reclaim Advent as a quiet, more reflective time in preparing for the joy of Christmas.

Ordinary Time

We generally have a routine that helps us do the ordinary things that make up daily life. This routine is needed so that we can integrate some of the lessons and experiences we had during times of joy and new life, or sadness and loss. The liturgical year has the same balance. After the high of the Christmas season, we enter a short period of **Ordinary Time.**

During Ordinary Time the Scripture readings focus on the events of Jesus' life between his birth and his death and Resurrection. It is a time when we reflect on the things Jesus lived and taught so that we might make our values and attitudes more like his. Ordinary Time is divided into two periods. The first period is between Christmastime and Lent, and the second period is between the end of the Easter season and the next Advent.

Lent and Holy Week

Lent is a solemn, reflective season of the liturgical year that is the preparation for the mysteries of Easter. It begins on Ash Wednesday, and lasts forty days, until Easter (the forty days do not include the Sundays during Lent). On Ash Wednesday people come to Church to receive ashes on their forehead, a reminder that without God we are simply dust. The forty days of Lent recall the forty days that Jesus spent in the desert before beginning his public ministry. During Lent Christians are called to renew themselves through fasting, prayer, and almsgiving (giving money and service to those in need).

Holy Week begins a week before Easter Day, on Palm Sunday. During Holy Week we remember the events of the final days of Jesus' earthly life, beginning with his triumphal entry into Jerusalem on Palm Sunday. The last three days of Holy Week bring everything to a climax in a series of three special liturgies, called the **Triduum.** Following are very brief descriptions of these important days in the liturgical year:

- **Holy Thursday.** In this liturgy we remember the Last Supper and Jesus' gift of himself in the Eucharist. A foot-washing ritual is part of the liturgy, reminding us that Jesus calls us to serve one another as his followers. On this day we also recall the institution of the priesthood.
- **Good Friday.** In this liturgy we remember Jesus' Passion and death. The liturgy is somber, and starts and ends with a bare altar. During the liturgy we venerate (show love and respect for) the cross in some way, in appreciation of Christ's sacrifice.

Full and Active Participation

The documents of Vatican II called for "full, conscious, and active" participation on the part of the laity (*The Constitution on the Sacred Liturgy,* number 14). That means that we're not supposed to be spectators. We're supposed to be "in the game!" It's a lot easier to be in the game if you know how it is played, if you're in shape, and if you've worked on your skills. Learn about liturgy. These chapters, many other books and online resources, plus the adults in your parish can teach you about the history and meaning of the different parts of the liturgy. Get in spiritual shape. If you are praying and reading the Scriptures, you'll be less likely to be "left behind" at Mass. It's easier to find God when you've gotten yourself into the habit of looking on a regular basis.

Work on your liturgy skills. Spend some time with each week's readings beforehand; get involved in liturgical ministry as a lector, as a Eucharistic minister, or in your parish's music ministry. Finally, get your mind on the game. Too many times we rush into church at the last minute, distracted by other things. Be attentive to all parts of the liturgy—the words of the songs (oh yeah, sing!), the prayers, the actions, the colors of the vestments and banners, the other people, the readings. Come to liturgy *expecting* to encounter Jesus Christ!

○ **Holy Saturday.** The liturgy on Holy Saturday is held at night, and is called the Easter Vigil. It is the greatest celebration of the liturgical year, recalling and reliving the joy of Christ's Resurrection. The celebration incorporates rituals of darkness and light, of water blessing, and lots of Scripture reading. But the highlight is the Baptism, Confirmation, and First Communion of the catechumens, those people who have been preparing to become Catholic.

Saint Cecilia is the patron saint of musicians, singers, and poets. Why are music and poetry such an important part of life?

Easter Season

Easter and the Easter season are the primary focus of the liturgical year. **Easter** celebrates the wonder and joy of Christ's Resurrection, the central mystery of our faith. The Easter Season goes on for fifty days after Easter, until the feast of Pentecost. During this time the Sunday readings focus on the appearances of the risen Christ and on the growth of the early Church (found in the Acts of the Apostles). It is a time of joy and hope, for death has been overcome and Christ has made us all heirs to the Kingdom of God. Because of the events of Easter, we dare to hope for our own Resurrection and eternal life with God.

This season is marked with two special feasts. Forty days after Easter, on the Ascension of the Lord (although this is a Thursday, it is celebrated in many dioceses on the following Sunday), we remember how Jesus said farewell to his disciples in order to live in glory with his heavenly Father and to be present to all his followers without the limitations of time and space. Fifty days after Easter, we remember the coming of the Holy Spirit on the Apostles at Pentecost. After Pentecost the second period of Ordinary Time continues, until another liturgical year begins on the first Sunday of Advent.

Liturgical Rites and Traditions

The article "Liturgical Rites and Traditions," on page 105, talks about the different Catholic Churches that exist within the universal Catholic Church. What does that mean? It means that if you were raised your whole life in a particular Catholic Church tradition, say Roman Catholic (which is true of most Catholics in Western Europe and North and South America), and later you attended Mass at a Greek Catholic church, you might wonder if you were still in a Catholic church. The arrangement of the church might be different (some rites have screens between the people and the altar), the actions might be different (some rites do a lot of kneeling and standing), and the prayers would be different. Yet it is still a legitimate Catholic liturgical tradition.

These different liturgical traditions are called liturgical rites. Although each rite uses symbolic actions and words that originated with the Apostles, the forms of those symbolic actions and words were influenced by local cultures. Yet they are all legitimate expressions of the liturgy, and they all make present the same saving power of God and symbolize the same mysteries of Christ. They also show the catholicity (universality) of the Church that embraces all people and all cultures.

At the same time, all liturgical rites meet certain criteria that assure unity amid the diversity. For example, in all the rites, the Eucharist is still bread and wine becoming Christ's body and blood. Baptism is still new life in Christ, symbolized by immersing someone in water or pouring water over him or her. All the legitimate liturgical rites stay true to the core truths about the sacraments that are revealed in Tradition.

Saintly Profiles

Saint Cecilia

Saint Cecilia is the patron saint of musicians, singers, and poets. She lived in the third century, and died a martyr. Although not much is known about her, a fifth-century legend holds that she had taken a vow of virginity, and refused to consummate her marriage or make sacrifices to the Roman gods. Because of her faith, the Romans condemned her to death during one of the persecutions of Christians. Her death was caused by attempts to suffocate and then behead her, although she survived for three days after these attempts. Her association with music comes from a line in her biography, which said that at her wedding, "Cecilia sung [in her heart] to the Lord, saying: may my heart remain unsullied, so that I be not confounded." She was chosen as the patron saint of the Academy of Music in Rome, at its founding in 1584. Her feast day is November 22.

Celebrating Liturgy

As Catholics we say that we "celebrate" liturgy, implying that liturgy is something joyful. Even during funeral liturgies and on Good Friday, when people may be grieving and the mood may be somber, an underlying current of hope and joy persists because of our belief in the Resurrection.

You might be saying, "Wait a minute, the liturgies at my church are drab and boring." That could mean one of two things. It could mean that you find them drab and boring because you are not actively participating with your whole heart and soul. Other people in your church may be finding meaning in the liturgy, but you may not have truly given yourself to the celebration.

Or the liturgy could be drab and boring because it is being poorly celebrated. The music is mediocre, the priest celebrant speaks in monotone, and the people around you barely sing or respond. Although God is at work even in poorly celebrated liturgies, it can lessen your experience of the celebration.

Celebrating liturgy also implies that liturgies are done in remembrance of something. When we celebrate birthdays or anniversaries, we do so in remembrance of a person's birth or a married couple's wedding day. In a similar way, we remember all the wonderful events in salvation history in the liturgies we celebrate. For example, in Baptism we remember how God saved the Israelites by parting the Red Sea so they could pass through safely, and how Jesus humbly submitted to being baptized by John the Baptist.

Remembering helps us to "re-member," that is, to return things to the way they are supposed to be. Liturgy does that in a special way, by making the saving power of the Holy Trinity directly available to us. Perhaps this helps you understand why the Catholic Church places such a strong emphasis on our obligation to attend Sunday Mass and other liturgical celebrations. To fail to attend Sunday Mass is a sin against the third commandment. The Eucharist is a primary source of spiritual nourishment that enables us to grow as Christ's disciples.

For Further Reflection

○ This chapter introduced a lot of words and phrases you may not be familiar with. How have these words and phrases helped you to better understand liturgy? What do you still have questions about?

○ How would you explain to someone who is not Catholic, the difference between a liturgy and a group prayer service?

15 Introduction to the Sacraments

During the visit of Pope Paul VI to the United States in 1965, thousands of people witnessed a marvelous occurrence. The Pope was addressing a full house in Madison Square Garden, in New York City. Suddenly the electricity failed, causing a blackout. The whole arena was pitch dark; you couldn't see your hand in front of your face.

After a few moments of restless reaction, someone in one corner of the vast arena lit a match. Miraculously it seemed like you could see throughout the whole arena, although dimly. A murmur went through the crowd. The symbolism of the moment was striking: In a time of darkness, even one small flame of hope casts a great light.

The sacraments of the Church incorporate many symbols, like a light in the darkness. They also symbolize the life and work of Jesus Christ. But they do more than just point to something else; they make the thing they symbolize real and

Words to Look For

- symbol
- ritual
- efficacious
- disposition
- sacraments
- grace
- sacramentals

present for those who are participating in the sacrament. They are wonderful gifts from God.

Kinds of Grace

God created human beings for eternal happiness, but we can't get to heaven on our own power. Grace is the free and undeserved help that God gives us to respond to his call to become his "co-heirs" with Christ, destined for eternal life. The sacraments in particular are channels of grace through the power of the Holy Spirit. Here are some of the different types of grace we can receive:

- **Sanctifying grace** is God's free and generous gift, sometimes called the "state of grace." This is a permanent disposition, a change in us that orients us toward God and helps us to live in keeping with God's call. Through Baptism we receive sanctifying grace and a share in the divine life.
- **Actual grace** is God's intervention and support for us in the everyday moments of our life. Actual graces are important for our continuing growth in holiness.
- **Sacramental graces** are gifts specific to each of the seven sacraments.
- **Charisms** are special graces that are associated with one's state in life and are intended to build up the Body of Christ. *Charism* comes from a Greek word meaning "favor" or "gratuitous gift."

Symbols and Rituals

Two important concepts are fundamental to an understanding of the liturgy and the sacraments—symbols and rituals.

The word **symbol** is based on a Greek word meaning "to throw together or compare." So to think symbolically means to take something concrete and throw it together with something else that exists on an invisible or abstract level. Throwing two things together is what symbolic thinking is all about. Fire, for example, may have nothing to do in a literal way with human emotions. But as a symbol, fire is one of the most powerful ways of describing less visible realities such as anger, jealousy, and love. The liturgy and the sacraments are filled with concrete symbols that help us connect with spiritual realities.

Rituals are symbols that include actions and words. In fact, a short definition of a **ritual** is "a symbolic action." Like other symbols, rituals are actions that have a deeper meaning than what immediately meets the eye. Rituals can be as simple as a handshake, a wave, or the sign of the cross; or they can be as complex as the opening ceremonies of the Olympic Games or the inauguration of a president. Because our celebrations of the liturgy and the sacraments all involve symbols and words, we call them rituals.

Signs and symbols are closely related. We sometimes use the two words interchangeably. But understanding the difference between the two can help us understand the richness of the sacraments. A sign refers to an object that represents something else. A simple sign has a direct and unmistakable connection to the reality it represents. An example of a simple sign would be a red light at an intersection. It means, stop here and wait for the light to change. For safety's sake, we don't want that sign to have any other meanings!

Symbols, however, are complex signs. A symbol represents more than just a physical reality, and often has multiple meanings. Symbols are often culturally conditioned, that is, we take their meaning from the history and stories of our culture. A U.S. flag is a good example of a culturally conditioned symbol. For U.S. citizens the flag symbolizes many things: freedom, heroism, sacrifice, prosperity, religious tolerance, and so on. However, for people in other countries, it can symbolize other things: cultural snobbishness, imperialism, hope, or protection. Let's look at two different kinds of symbols that are found in sacramental rituals.

Covenant Symbols

Some of the symbols used in the sacraments receive their meaning from salvation history. Their meaning comes to us through the ways God has worked in our history. They remind us of God's saving action in our life. Some of these symbols include:

- **Consecrating with oil** symbolizes God's blessing and being chosen by God for a special role.
- **Immersion in water** symbolizes turning away from sin, dying, and rising.
- **Laying on of hands** symbolizes receiving the Holy Spirit and being designated for service.

Nature Symbols

Some symbols are universal, that is, they seem to carry the same meaning no matter where or when you live. Usually these are symbols associated with nature. The sacraments make rich use of nature symbols. Here are some of the nature symbols used in the sacraments:

The Sacrament of the Present Moment

It's pretty amazing how Jesus uses the ordinary objects and events of our life and transforms them into occasions of grace. As sacramental people, our awareness of Jesus' presence in the sacraments can expand into every aspect of our life. The welcome we offer to new members of the community in Baptism carries over into how we treat the new kid at school. We relive Baptism's dying and rising every time we sacrifice some of our time and money to help someone who is in need. The gifts of the Spirit that we receive in Confirmation help us to be patient with our parents, to be chaste (sexually pure) in our relationships, and even to make wise decisions about how we drive. Jesus' presence in the Eucharist challenges us to celebrate every meal with gratitude for God's blessings. How are you living out the sacraments in your daily life?

○ **Darkness** symbolizes death, a time of waiting, waiting for rebirth.

○ **Light** symbolizes new life, a new moment, resurrection, Jesus, hope.

○ **Water** symbolizes life and death, cleansing, the womb, rebirth.

○ **Fire** symbolizes action, passion, transformation.

Sacraments: More Than Just Symbols

Being touched—whether it is by the laying on of hands or the anointing with consecrated oil—is an important symbol in almost every sacrament. Why is touch such an important and powerful sign?

Now we are ready to define what a sacrament is. The first and most important thing to understand is that a sacrament is not simply a human-made symbol or ritual. It's true that like a symbol, a sacrament points to something beyond the words and symbolic actions. But in a sacrament, Jesus himself acts in and through the ritual, offering new life, forgiving sins, giving his own body and blood, healing, uniting, consecrating. Through the work of the Holy Spirit, the transforming grace of Christ's actions is poured into the hearts of those who are participating. So a sacrament does more than just symbolize a spiritual reality—it actually makes that spiritual reality present at the place and time the sacrament is celebrated. One term used to describe this reality is **efficacious**—the sacraments effect change in us and in the world because of God's power, not our own.

Just participating in a sacrament doesn't mean that you will be changed. You must be prepared for and actively participate in the sacraments if the grace given by God in them is to have an effect in your life. This inner attitude and readiness on our part is called our **disposition.**

With all this in mind, we can now understand the definition of *sacraments* provided by the *Catechism:*

> The **sacraments** are efficacious signs of grace, instituted by Christ and entrusted to the Church, by which divine life is dispensed to us. The visible rites by which the sacraments are celebrated signify and make present the graces proper to each sacrament. They bear fruit in those who receive them with the required dispositions (number 1131).

You've probably noticed that **grace** is a word that is frequently associated with the sacraments. Grace is the religious name we give to the free and undeserved gifts we receive from God. Through the centuries theologians have categorized and described different kinds of grace (see the article "Kinds of Grace," on page 146), but when it comes right down to it, grace is the experience we have of being loved as a child of God. The love we receive, in all its various forms, empowers us to live lives of love ourselves, in service to God and others.

In the biggest sense, Jesus Christ is the sacrament of salvation because God's gift of grace has its fullest expression in the saving actions of Jesus' life, death, and Resurrection. In the same way, the Catholic Church is also like a sacrament, because it is the symbol and living witness of all that God revealed through Christ. But then we have these seven official sacraments of the Church. Why are they so special?

The Seven Sacraments

The seven official sacraments of the Catholic Church are rooted in two things: (1) the life and ministry of Jesus Christ, and (2) the Tradition of the Catholic Church—the Church's wisdom, teaching, and practice handed down through the ages under the guidance of the Holy Spirit. As the Church grew in its understanding of what God revealed through Jesus' life and teachings, Christians came to recognize seven primary ways that God's grace is active in our lives:

- We are brought to new life.
- We are strengthened by the Holy Spirit.
- We share in Jesus' sacrifice, death, and Resurrection.
- Our sins are forgiven.

Looking Back

The Council of Trent

An ecumenical council is a gathering of the world's bishops, called by the Pope, to share the responsibility of teaching and guiding the Church. Pope Paul III convened such a council in 1545, to clarify Catholic beliefs and practices in response to the challenges of Martin Luther and other Protestant reformers. Many of these reformers did not believe there were seven authentic sacraments, but only three or two, or even one. In its decrees on the sacraments, the Council of Trent decisively defined their meaning and number, clarified Catholic belief and dogma, and established uniform liturgical rituals and practices for each of the sacraments. The council also established seminaries for the academic and spiritual formation of priests, so they could be properly trained as sacramental ministers.

The sacramental reforms of the Council of Trent became sacramental practice in the Catholic Church for nearly four hundred years. The Council mandated that the liturgies of the Church be in the same language (Latin) and use the same ritual actions and words all around the world. This uniformity became a source of pride and distinction for many Catholics. Significant changes in the way Catholics celebrated the sacraments didn't occur again until Pope John XXIII convened the Second Vatican Council in 1963.

- We are healed of illnesses.
- Some serve others through a special call to minister in the Church.
- Some are called to share love and the creation of new life in marriage.

Eventually all seven of these avenues of grace were ritualized into what we now identify as the official sacraments of the Catholic Church. Remembering the definition of *sacrament,* these seven official sacraments are "efficacious signs of grace." That is, when one of these sacraments is celebrated, the promised grace or gift will be made present.

The seven sacraments help us remember that Christ is the sacrament of salvation, which we experience through the life of the Church. Through the seven sacraments, we remember the life, ministry, and message of Jesus, and celebrate anew his risen presence among us. The seven sacraments are primarily community celebrations of our belonging to the Body of Christ. The sacraments do this in the following ways:

- *Together the three sacraments of initiation—Baptism, Confirmation, and the Eucharist—initiate new members and help the community of faith remember the earthly Jesus and celebrate his risen presence within the Church today.* The words and water of Baptism are signs of death and life: the baptized person symbolically dies to all that is sinful and then lives in Christ. In Confirmation the anointing with chrism and the words of Confirmation symbolize and impart to the baptized person, the fullness of the Holy Spirit. In the Eucharist the baptized and confirmed person shares in the body and blood of Christ, and is committed to live out the death and Resurrection of Christ in his or her daily life.
- *The sacraments of Penance and Reconciliation and Anointing of the Sick are sacraments of healing.* In these sacraments the

Church celebrates its mission of spiritual and physical healing. Reconciliation centers on spiritual healing; God's forgiveness of the sinner is celebrated in the words of the sacrament. In Anointing of the Sick, the Church anoints and prays for and with those whose sickness has made it difficult or impossible for them to be active in the community.

○ *In the sacraments at the service of Communion—Holy Orders and Matrimony—the Church celebrates its ministry to all people.* In the sacrament of Holy Orders—through prayer and the laying on of hands—men are ordained to serve the Church as bishops, priests, or deacons. Matrimony celebrates the love between a man and a woman, as well as their vow to serve each other and bring new life into the world.

Each of these seven sacraments will be covered in more depth in the chapters that follow. However, the following chart will give you a quick overview of each sacrament's essential sacramental symbol, who the minister is, and whether or not the sacrament can be repeated.

Sacrament	Essential Sacramental Symbol	Minister	Repeated?
Baptism	Water poured over or immersed in water while saying, "I baptize you in the name of the Father, and of the Son, and of the Holy Spirit."	Bishop, priest, deacon, or anyone in an emergency	No
Confirmation	Laying on of hands and anointing with chrism (sacred oil) while saying, "Be sealed with the gift of the Holy Spirit."	Bishop or a designated priest	No
Eucharist	Wheat bread and grape wine and the words of consecration	Priest	Yes
Penance and Reconciliation	Laying on of hands and the words of absolution (forgiveness)	Priest	Yes
Anointing of the Sick	Anointing with the oil of the sick accompanied by the liturgical prayer of the priest	Priest	Yes
Holy Orders	Laying on of hands and the prayer of consecration asking for the gifts specific to that order	Bishop	No
Matrimony	Exchange of marriage vows	The couple being married	No, unless a spouse dies

Sacramentals

Other symbols and rituals are used in the Church besides the seven sacraments. These symbols and rituals are related to the sacraments and many help prepare us for the sacraments, but they were established by the Church rather than by Christ. They are called **sacramentals,** and we are encouraged to make use of them as part of our spiritual practices.

A sacramental is usually an action or an object that is sometimes accompanied by a special prayer. A popular sacramental is putting your hand in the holy water font when you enter the Church and making the sign of the cross as you silently bless yourself "in the name of the Father, and of the Son, and of the Holy Spirit." Some examples of other sacramentals are being sprinkled with holy water, having your throat blessed with blessed candles, and venerating the Bible or the cross by kissing or touching it. Priests lead most, but not all, sacramentals.

This statue of Saint Patrick shows him dressed as a bishop and holding a golden shamrock. According to legend, Patrick used the shamrock to teach the people of Ireland about the mystery of the Trinity.

Look at this list of objects that are used in the Church's sacramentals, and see if you can remember where and how they are used:

- holy water
- Paschal (Easter) candle
- votive lights
- crosses
- medals and statues of saints
- stations of the cross
- blessed palm branches
- blessed ashes
- icons (special pictures of saints)
- incense

A special type of sacramental is a blessing, a prayer that calls on God's power to care for a person, place, thing, or undertaking. A prayer of blessing usually includes praise for God and his gifts, and a request that those gifts be used in the spirit of the Gospel. Blessings are often used to mark changes or special occasions in a person's life (see the article "Develop Your Own Blessing," on page 150). As a baptized person, you can and should ask for God's blessing; try making it a regular practice in your life.

For Further Reflection

○ In your various experiences of the Church's worship, what symbol or ritual means the most to you? Why?

○ What sacramentals do you have in your home? How have you used sacramental objects to mark special occasions? What sacramental blessing or object could you introduce into your family's prayer life?

Saintly Profiles

Saint Patrick

Saint Patrick is one of the world's most popular saints. Saint Patrick was born in Roman Britain around the year 389. At age sixteen he was captured by Irish pirates and kept as a slave for six years. While herding sheep he had plenty of time to think, pray, and learn to trust in God. Eventually he escaped, found his family again, and studied for the priesthood. He returned to Ireland as a missionary after having a recurring dream in which the children of Ireland cried out to him, "Come and walk among us once more."

Patrick saw Jesus present everywhere, and looked to nature to explain Christian beliefs about God. According to popular legend, Patrick used the shamrock to explain the Trinity, and it has been associated with him and the Irish since that time. "The Breastplate" is a prayer attributed to Patrick. In it he invites Christ to be part of every aspect of his life. A later writer developed the prayer below from Saint Patrick's original version. Saint Patrick's feast day is March 17.

Saint Patrick's Breastplate
Christ be with me, Christ within me,
Christ behind me, Christ before me,
Christ beside me, Christ to win me;
Christ to comfort me and restore me;
Christ beneath me, Christ above me,
Christ in quiet, Christ in danger,
Christ in hearts of all that love me, Christ in mouth of friend and stranger.

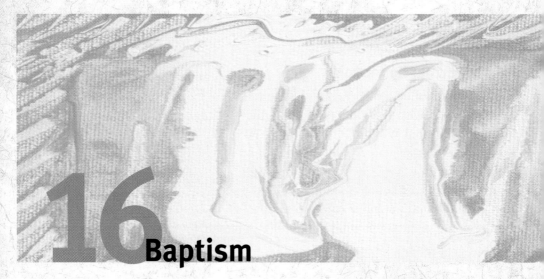

16 Baptism

Helen Keller was born in 1880. At the age of eighteen months, she became blind, deaf, and dumb. The loss of her senses shut Helen off from the world as a young child, and she lived scarcely more than an animal existence. Then at seven years old, she experienced a miracle:

> When I was about seven years old, my teacher and I walked down to the well-house. Someone was drawing water and my teacher placed my hand under the spout . . . [and] spelled out into the other the word *water*. . . . I stood still, my whole attention fixed upon the motion of her fingers. Suddenly . . . the mystery of language was revealed to me. I knew then that w-a-t-e-r meant the wonderful cool something that was flowing over my hand. That living word awakened my soul. . . . As we returned to the house every object which I touched seemed to quiver with life. That was because I saw

Words to Look For

- sacraments of initiation
- Baptism
- catechumenate
- catechumens
- sacramental character
- Baptism of blood

everything with the strange new sight that had come to me. (Helen Keller, *The Story of My Life*)

A new life, a new world opened up to Helen Keller because of her experience with water, a teacher who cared for her, and a supportive community. It is hard not to see the similarities to the sacrament of Baptism. Just as her experience at the well opened up the physical world to Helen, so our experience with Baptism opens up the spiritual world to us. Through water, those who are baptized are born again as God's children and as members of the Body of Christ, the Church.

The Sacraments of Initiation

The sacraments of Baptism, Confirmation, and Eucharist together are called the **sacraments of initiation.** These three sacraments are the foundation of the Christian life; every Catholic should receive all three. Children who are brought into the Roman Catholic Church through their families are usually baptized as infants, receive their First Communion as children, and are confirmed somewhere between sixth and tenth grade. But there are many variations on this timing. People who join the Church as adults receive all three sacraments during the Easter Vigil liturgy (see the article "RCIA," at right). And in the Eastern rite Catholic Churches (see the section "Liturgical Rites and Traditions," on page 105), infants are baptized, confirmed, and receive their First Communion in the same liturgy.

The sacraments of initiation are closely related. All three connect us more closely with the parish community, and in all three we receive the Holy Spirit and his gifts. But each sacrament has its special symbols and

RCIA

The Rite of Christian Initiation of Adults (RCIA) is the process by which adults become members of the Catholic Church. The process is a commitment, lasting up to a year or more. During the process those who hope to become Catholics spend time learning about the Catholic faith. They learn about our history, beliefs, rituals, spirituality, and much more. This is a time of learning and of forming close relationships with members of the parish.

The culmination of preparation of the catechumens happens during Holy Week each year. It is a time of intense preparation for the catechumens as they move toward becoming full members of the Church at the Easter Vigil.

During the Easter Vigil, the catechumens are baptized, confirmed, and participate in the Eucharist for the first time. Sometimes people who were baptized in other Christian Churches and are joining the Catholic Church are also confirmed as Catholics and receive Holy Communion at the Vigil. The ceremony is filled with the richness of our Catholic faith, and can be traced back to the way the first Christians were incorporated into the faith community. There is an atmosphere of celebration, and families, sponsors, and members of the parish community join together to welcome the newly baptized into the local parish and the universal Catholic Church.

effects. Baptism's primary effect is the beginning of new life in Christ. Confirmation's primary effect is to strengthen us to live more fully Christ's call to serve. And the primary effect of the Eucharist is to nourish us to live as Christ's disciples in our journey through this life. We will look at each of these sacraments in separate chapters, beginning with Baptism in this chapter.

A Short History of Baptism

The history of **Baptism** is a rich one. It begins with the many stories about water in the Old Testament. In creation God separates the waters from one another and the land (Genesis 1:9). Through God's intervention Noah saves his family from destruction by building an ark as shelter from the storm (Genesis, chapters 6–9). Moses parts the Red Sea with God's power, to save the Israelites from the Egyptians (Exodus 14:21–22). Later the Israelites enter the Promised Land by crossing the Jordan River (Joshua 3:14–17). All these events are early examples of God's saving power, which will be fully revealed in Baptism.

In this mural of Jesus' baptism, do you recognize the symbols of the Holy Trinity, Jesus' triumph over death, and his triumph over evil?

In the New Testament, Jesus himself submits to Baptism by John the Baptist, an event that is recorded in all four Gospels, thus demonstrating for us the importance of Baptism. He tells Nicodemus that no one can enter the Kingdom of God unless they are "born of water and Spirit" (John 3:5). And in Matthew his final words to his disciples are, "Go therefore and make disciples of all nations, baptizing them in the name of the Father and of the Son and of the Holy Spirit" (Matthew 28:19).

Thus the biblical evidence is quite clear that Christ established the sacrament of Baptism. It is no surprise that Baptism is the first sacrament the early Church practiced. The Acts of the Apostles describes group baptisms (2:41), individual baptisms (8:38), and baptisms of families or households (18:8). In these first years after Christ's Ascension, baptisms were focused on adult converts, and seemed to occur quickly without a lot of preparation.

But as the years progressed, we find that the Baptism ritual became more complex. We have evidence in the second and third centuries that it became common for people to go through extensive preparation, called the **catechumenate,** before being baptized and joining the Church. Those that were in the process of initiation were called **catechumens.** Their preparation would consist of study, prayer, fasting, and service to others over a period of two or three years. During this time each catechumen would be under the care of a sponsor, a mature Christian acting as model and guide.

All this preparation was building to the Easter Vigil, a special liturgy held the evening before Easter Sunday. During the weeks before the Easter Vigil, the catechumens entered a more intense time of prayer and fasting. At the beginning of the Easter Vigil, the catechumens would gather, men in one room, women in another. As the ritual began, they faced the west and denounced Satan and all his works. Then to symbolize their conversion, they would turn and face the east, the direction of the sunrise, and shout their commitment to Christ.

Then the catechumens went to rooms with pools, where they stripped off their old clothing. They were anointed with oil, and then stepped into the waist-deep waters. The bishop submerged each candidate three times—in the name of the Father, the Son, and the Holy Spirit. When they emerged they were no longer catechumens but newly baptized Christians. They were given new white robes, anointed again with oil, embraced in a sign of peace, and given a lighted candle. They were then led to a room in which the Eucharist was celebrated, and they received Communion for the first time.

Defend Your Faith

Q. Why do Catholics baptize babies? In the Bible only adults are baptized.

A. Catholics baptize babies because we believe they are being baptized into the faith life of the community and will be nurtured in faith by their parents and the community. During the ceremony the community is asked to help the parents and the godparents raise the child in the faith. The community agrees to support the family and to model the faith for the child. We know the practice of infant Baptism goes back to early in the Church's history; it may have begun in New Testament times.

Even infants suffer from the effects of original sin. With Baptism the baby enters into God's grace and is now free from original sin. We believe God's grace is freely given and is not earned, so even babies can receive it. This baptismal grace gives the baby the strength needed to grow up faithful and secure in God's love.

Q. Catholics don't have real Baptisms. To be truly baptized, you have to be totally dunked under the water, not just have a little dripped over your head.

A. Catholics do practice total immersion (being dunked under the water). The early Church used lakes and rivers for the ceremony. Over the years it became more practical to baptize infants through pouring water over their head. Vatican II encouraged the recovery of the ancient rituals of the early Church, and so immersion is once again being practiced. For the Church all these ways are valid.

Things changed around the fourth century, when Christianity became the official religion of the Roman Empire (see the article "The Conversion of Constantine," on page 162).

Whole families were converted and baptized, and soon almost all adults were Christian. In this way infant baptisms became the norm by the year 500 (although we have evidence of infant baptisms going back to the second century). As the doctrine of original sin was more widely taught, people wanted their children to be baptized as soon as possible because they thought (wrongly) that an unbaptized baby who died would not go to heaven. But now with so many Christians, bishops could no longer preside at every baptism. Priests began presiding over most baptisms, but they delayed the final parts of the ceremony (the final anointing with oil) until the bishop was available to "confirm" the initiation. That is how the sacrament of Confirmation became separated from Baptism.

When Catholic churches are built or remodeled, parishes are encouraged to include baptismal pools in them. In these pools, people who are being baptized are fully immersed in water, a powerful symbol of dying to sin and rising to new life in Christ.

Today we draw on all this tradition in our practice of the sacraments of initiation. In certain extreme situations, we baptize people quickly and immediately, for example, if they are near death. The early catechumenate process serves as the model for the Rite of Christian Initiation of Adults today. But the usual method is to baptize infants, who are then nurtured in their faith life by their family and the faith community.

When children are old enough, the Church assists the parents with the task of forming faith, by providing opportunities for religious education in preparation for receiving the Eucharist at the age of reason (defined as seven years old in Church law). Faith formation and religious education continue in preparation for receiving the sacrament of Confirmation with the bishop, sometime in junior high or high school.

The Effects of Baptism

Remember grace? Grace is another name for the gifts we receive from God (see the article "Kinds of Grace," on page 146). As *the* foundational sacrament for all Christian life, the grace we receive from the sacrament of Baptism has a number of important effects. Remember that these effects are not merely symbolic, they are guaranteed to occur.

Welcome into the Christian Community

Many groups have initiation ceremonies that new members go through to officially be part of the group. For the Church, Baptism is like that initiation ceremony. A baptized person is a member of the Body of Christ, the Church, with all the rights and responsibilities that it brings. But this is no mere human initiation ceremony. In Baptism it is Christ himself who is doing the initiating, who welcomes new members into his Body.

There is something special about being welcomed into a new community. If you have ever moved to a new town or attended a new school, you know how important it is to be welcomed into a new community. If you experience friendly people, you quickly begin to feel accepted and at home. But if you do not feel welcomed by anyone, you feel like you are on display, and life can be almost unbearable. We have a responsibility for making our churches friendly and welcoming places. This is not just a nice thing to do, it is an obligation of our own Baptism.

This brings us to another point. Through our Baptism we are called to share in the priesthood of Christ, which means that we are to participate in the sacramental life of the Church and to share in Christ's mission. Baptism is not our initiation into a social club. As baptized members of the Church, the Holy Spirit calls us to be people of prayer, to respect and obey our leaders, and to serve others—to share Christ's mission by being living signs of the Kingdom of God.

Pray It!

Blessing of Water

During the Easter Vigil, there is a particular ritual for blessing the water to be used for baptizing the RCIA catechumens. This prayer, from the *Rite of Christian Initiation of Adults,* reminds us of all the ways water has played a role in salvation history:

Father,
you give us grace through
    sacramental signs,
which tell us of the wonders of
    your unseen power.

In baptism we use your gift of
    water,
which you have made a rich
    symbol of the grace
you give us in this sacrament.

At the very dawn of creation
your Spirit breathed on the
    waters,
making them the wellspring of
    all holiness.

The waters of the great flood
you made a sign of the waters of
    baptism
that make an end of sin
and a new beginning of
    goodness.

Through the waters of the Red
    Sea
you led Israel out of slavery
to be an image of God's holy
    people
set free from sin by baptism.

Amen.

(Page 134)

Forgiveness of Sins

Through the grace of Baptism, all our sins are forgiven and we are given the grace to fight future temptation. This includes original sin as well as our personal sins. Original sin is the inherited disposition for choosing sin over God that all human beings have inherited from Adam and Eve (see the chapter Human Person). Through Baptism God wipes our slate clean, as if we had never done anything wrong before that moment. For people who are baptized as adults and who are aware of their sinful past, this grace can be overpowering.

Baptism does not magically remove all future temptation or ingrained sinful vices. Resisting temptation and ingrained patterns of sinful behavior is a lifelong call. But Baptism provides the grace for resisting temptation and breaking out of our sinful patterns.

Blessed Junipero Serra spent most of his priestly life as a missionary among the native people in California. Missionaries are people who are commissioned to share the Gospel message with those who have not yet embraced Christ.

Born into a New Life

Near the beginning of the Gospel of John, Jesus has an important encounter with a Pharisee named Nicodemus. In the conversation Jesus tells Nicodemus, "Very truly, I tell you, no one can enter the kingdom of God without being born of water and Spirit" (John 3:5). Jesus was speaking about Baptism, and he was telling Nicodemus that no one can enter the Kingdom of God without the rebirth that Baptism brings.

This rebirth isn't a physical birth, but a spiritual birth as a child of God. Through Baptism we leave a way of life that is headed for death and separation from God, and we enter a way of life that is destined for eternal life and union with God. In this new life, the separation from God caused through original sin vanishes, and we begin living the life that God intended for us from the beginning of creation.

There is one more aspect of this new life that has to do with spiritual reality. Every person's body has a sign of their physical birth, the belly button. In a similar way the Catholic Church teaches that every baptized person has a mark on his or her soul as a sign of spiritual rebirth. We call this mark a **sacramental character,** and it marks a person as belonging to Christ. Baptism's sacramental character is permanent, and therefore Baptism cannot be repeated. Once you have been marked for Christ, you belong to the family of God forever!

Receive the Holy Spirit

It is in Baptism that we first receive the Holy Spirit into our life. Christ gave us the Holy Spirit to be our comforter, our guide, and the source of our strength in living the Beatitude life to which we are called. Receiving the Holy Spirit is closely connected to the other effects of Baptism. The Holy Spirit moves through all the believers in the Christian community, tying us together as the Body of Christ. Through the Holy Spirit, our sins are forgiven. Jesus said it is through water and the Holy Spirit that we are born into new life. The Holy Spirit marks us with the permanent character of Baptism.

Some people mistakenly believe that we first receive the Holy Spirit at Confirmation. This is an understandable mistake, because an effect of Confirmation that is often emphasized is receiving the Holy Spirit in a deeper and more profound way. But everyone who has been baptized has already received the Holy Spirit into their life.

Necessary for Salvation

When you consider all the effects of the grace of Baptism, it becomes easier to see why this sacrament is necessary for our salvation. Salvation is the restoration of our relationship with God as God intended it to be. That relationship became fractured with the original sin of Adam and Eve. In a sense Baptism is the antidote for original sin. Where original sin separated us from God, Baptism unites us with

Saintly Profiles

Blessed Junipero Serra (1713–1784)

Blessed Junipero Serra was born in Majorca, Spain, in 1713, and was ordained a Franciscan priest in 1737. He spent most of his priestly life as a missionary in Mexico, Texas, and California. During his ministry Father Serra is believed to have baptized nearly six thousand people. He also established several missions up and down the coast of California, and was an important figure in the founding of our country. Father Serra was always known for his respect and kind treatment of the Native American people, even in a time when other missionaries may not have been so caring. He believed that all people were equal, and he helped fight for their rights as children of God.

Known as a gifted evangelizer, Father Serra was a key figure in helping to spread the faith in the New World. He worked tirelessly in sharing the love of God with all he met. California still honors him as an important historical figure. Pope John Paul II beatified Father Serra in 1988, calling him an "exemplary model of the selfless evangelizer."

The Serra Club, an organization that exists to promote vocations to the priesthood, is named for Father Serra. He is the patron of vocations, and we celebrate his feast day on July 1.

God. Where original sin separated human beings from one another, Baptism makes us one family again in the Church.

Does that mean that an unbaptized person cannot experience salvation? It has already been mentioned in other chapters that salvation is possible for those who through no fault of their own have not heard about Christ, but who follow the inner call God has placed in every person to live a good and holy life. And in those rare cases in which someone wishes to join the Church and is killed because of it (for example, in countries where Christianity is outlawed), that person is said to have undergone a **Baptism of blood,** and he or she will surely be saved. The Church also teaches that those who are catechumens preparing for Baptism will be saved even if they die before being baptized. And of course we believe in God's mercy for any child who has died before receiving Baptism. In our liturgy and our personal prayer, we pray for the salvation of all these people.

Constantine is depicted showing his companions the vision that caused him to convert to Christianity and to make Christianity the official religion of the Roman Empire. Can you recall a vision, a sign, or an event that turned your attention toward God?

The Baptism Rite

This brings us to the actual rite, or ritual, of Baptism. Every sacrament has symbolic words and actions that point to the spiritual reality of what is happening during the sacrament. Baptism's symbols and words are beautiful in their simplicity. The essential symbol is the blessed water that is poured over a person or the person is immersed in, while the minister pronounces, "I baptize you in the name of the Father, and of the Son, and of the Holy Spirit." These actions and words alone make for a valid Baptism. The complete ritual, however, is much richer.

Baptism for an infant or child usually begins with a formal welcome into the Church community, often during a Sunday Mass. Then the child being baptized, or their parents and godparents, is asked to reject Satan and all his works and proclaim their belief in the Holy Trinity and the Church. The water to be used for the Baptism is then blessed. This is followed by the pouring of water (or immersion in water) and the words of Baptism described above. After this the child is anointed with sacred chrism (scented oil blessed by the bishop), as a sign of the gift of the Holy Spirit. In the Roman Catholic Church, this is not Confirmation, but it does look forward to the child's future Confirmation.

Following the anointing the parents are given a white garment to put on the child. This garment symbolizes putting on Christ, and the white color symbolizes the purity of having our sins washed away. Finally, the child or the godparents are given a baptismal candle lit from the Easter candle. The Easter candle is a symbol of Christ, and the lit baptismal candle is a sign that the baptized person has received the light of Christ to share with the world.

The normal minister for a baptism is a priest, deacon, or bishop. But if it is necessary, any person can baptize by pouring water over the person's head while saying, "I baptize you in the name of the Father, and of the Son, and of the Holy Spirit." This would only happen if the person was near death and wished to be baptized and a priest or deacon was not available. The fact that any member of the church can perform a Baptism, though, is a sign that we all share in Christ's priesthood through our own Baptism.

For Further Reflection

○ Imagine that you have been asked to be a small child's godparent. Some people write letters to their godchildren that they are to read when they are older, say, before Confirmation. What would you write to your godchild in such a letter?

○ How is Baptism celebrated in your parish? What is your favorite part of the baptismal ritual? What do the symbols and words used mean to you?

Looking Back

The Conversion of Constantine

In the first century of Christianity, Christians were sometimes blamed for the problems of the Roman Empire. When the feelings got particularly intense, they were even persecuted and put to death, often killed in Roman games at the Coliseum. Today, in many areas of Rome, you can visit the catacombs used in secret by Christians. Catacombs are underground areas where the early Christians gathered to worship and where many are buried. Those who were killed—the martyrs—inspired the Christian community and sustained them through these terrible times.

The last great persecution of Christians happened under the Roman emperor Diocletian, in 303. Then something remarkable happened. The two emperors of the Roman Empire, Constantine in the west and Licinius in the east, issued the Edict of Milan, which made Christianity an approved religion of the Roman Empire. Legend has it that Constantine had a vision of Christ that led him to victory in battle. Whatever the real reason, he became an avid supporter of Christianity, and was baptized before his death in 337. Christianity grew rapidly, and quickly became the "official" religion of the empire by the end of the fourth century.

17
Confirmation

Think for a moment about the wind. Wind can be a gentle breeze, bringing comfort on a hot summer day. Or it can be a mighty gale, toppling trees and even buildings. Over time a steady wind reshapes shorelines and rock formations. Though it is unseen, the wind is constantly changing the world we live in.

It is not surprising that wind is also a symbol of the Holy Spirit. Although unseen, the Spirit moves in our lives and in the world. Like a gentle breeze, the Spirit comforts us in times of hardship and loss. Like a mighty wind, it empowers us to bravely confront evil. The Holy Spirit is the primary gift that we receive in Confirmation, so that we can grow even stronger in our calling to be Christ's disciples.

The Gift of the Holy Spirit

As with all the sacraments, all three persons of the Holy Trinity participate in Confirmation, but in this sacrament we call

Words to Look For

- Confirmation
- sacramental character
- confirmands
- chrism

particular attention to the Holy Spirit. Because of Confirmation we have a better understanding of the Holy Spirit and the gifts he brings into our life. This chapter, however, does not go into depth on the work of the Holy Spirit. For more information on the Holy Spirit, check out chapter 10, The Holy Spirit.

Confirmation is one of the sacraments of initiation that were introduced in the preceding chapter. Baptism, Confirmation, and the Eucharist together celebrate a person's new life in Christ and her or his membership in the Church, the Body of Christ. All three sacraments are sometimes celebrated as part of the same ritual, such as at the Easter Vigil, during which unbaptized adults become fully initiated into the Church. Each of these sacraments shares the same core meaning, yet each has its unique character and special grace to give to those who receive them.

This is why the Church strongly encourages all its members to receive the sacrament of Confirmation. You might be tempted to wonder why you should go through the hassle of preparing for Confirmation when you are already a member of the Church. The *Catechism* teaches, "The reception of the sacrament of Confirmation is necessary for the completion of baptismal grace"[1] (number 1285). Although this isn't a perfect analogy, it is sort of like not moving on from a junior varsity team to the varsity team when you are ready to do so. Confirmation builds on the gifts you have already received, and brings you more closely into God's ultimate team, the Church.

Pray It!

Prayer for the Holy Spirit

As part of the liturgy of Confirmation, the Bishop extends his hands over the candidates and prays for the outpouring of the Holy Spirit:

> Give them the spirit of wisdom
>   and understanding,
> the spirit of right judgment and
>   courage,
> the spirit of knowledge and
>   reverence.
> Fill them with the spirit of
>   wonder and awe in your
>   presence.
> We ask this through Christ our
>   Lord.
> Amen.
> (*The Rites of the Catholic Church*,
>   volume 1, page 490)

When you reflect on the gifts of the Spirit, you can use your own words or a prayer like this one:

> Dear God, you have poured out
>   your Spirit upon me.
> Help me to accept your gifts
>   wholeheartedly,
> develop them fully, and share
>   them by serving others.
> May your Spirit within me
> help me become the person you
>   are calling me to be.
> Make me more like Christ every
>   day,
> and help me to spread Christ's
>   presence wherever I go.
> Amen.

A Short History of Confirmation

In the Old Testament, even before the Holy Spirit was known to be part of the Trinity, it was understood that the spirit of

God came on certain individuals destined for a particular mission. For example, the prophet Isaiah announced:

> The spirit of the Lord GOD is upon me,
>   because the LORD has anointed me;
> he has sent me to bring good news to the
>   oppressed,
>   to bind up the brokenhearted,
> to proclaim liberty to the captives,
>   and release to the prisoners;
> to proclaim the year of the LORD's favor.
>
> (Isaiah 61:1–2)

Jesus began his own ministry by quoting these words of Isaiah, in the Gospel of Luke (4:14–21). The Gospels go on to indicate that the mission of Jesus and the mission of the Holy Spirit are closely entwined. For example, the Spirit descends on Jesus at his Baptism (Matthew 3:16). John the Baptist tells his followers that the one coming after him (Jesus) "will baptize you with the Holy Spirit and fire" (Luke 3:16). And Jesus promises to send his Spirit to his disciples, to comfort and guide them after his departure (John 14:16–17, 16:13–14).

Then in the experience of Pentecost (see chapter 10, The Holy Spirit), the Apostles receive the Holy Spirit in an awesome and profound way (Acts 2:1–13). The Holy Spirit empowers the Apostles with the courage to go out and preach about Jesus, although they know it will anger the authorities. With this experience it is not surprising that they understood that receiving the Holy Spirit was a necessary part of being a follower of Jesus Christ. The Apostles also knew that the gift of the Spirit was closely associated with the new birth of Baptism.

The previous chapter, on Baptism, has told how, in the first centuries of the Church, Baptism, Confirmation, and the Eucharist were given together in one sacramental ritual. The three sacraments became separated when it became impossible for the bishop to perform all the Baptisms. So priests became the ordinary ministers for Baptism. The Roman Catholic Church and the Eastern Catholic Churches (see the article

Saint Frances Xavier Cabrini is photographed in the traditional habit of her time. *Habit* is the term for the basic clothing worn by the members of a particular religious order. Black symbolized simplicity and giving up the colorful trappings of the world.

"Liturgical Rites and Traditions," on page 105 handled this in two different ways.

In the Roman Catholic Churches, the Baptism of an infant or child includes anointing with sacred chrism (oil). Later, when that child grows older, the bishop confers the sacrament of Confirmation. In the Eastern Churches, the sacraments have remained connected. The priest who performs the Baptism also confirms the infant or child and gives Holy Communion in the same ritual.

The two practices each emphasize a different but important meaning of the sacrament. The Roman Catholic practice more clearly expresses the communion of the fully initiated Christian with the bishop, and through the bishop, with the universal Church. The Eastern practice more clearly shows the traditional unity between Baptism, Confirmation, and the Eucharist, and emphasizes that the Holy Spirit is given in all three sacraments.

The Effects of Confirmation

The sacrament of **Confirmation** has two primary effects. The first is that the confirmed person's bond with the Church is strengthened. The second is that the person is enriched with an outpouring of the Holy Spirit. Both of these effects bring to perfection the grace that is first received in Baptism, and are the basis for the following specific ways that the sacrament impacts the life of a Christian.

United More Firmly with Christ

Confirmed people more closely identify with Jesus Christ. They reflect more deeply on how living by Jesus' values impacts their

Saintly Profiles

Saint Frances Xavier Cabrini (1850–1917)

Francesca Cabrini was born in northern Italy in 1850, the youngest of thirteen or more children. As a child she dreamed of being a missionary to faraway lands. When she was eighteen, she tried to join a religious community, but was turned away because of her poor health. She taught for a while, and then went to work at an orphanage. At age thirty she took the name of the great missionary Francis Xavier, and founded her own religious order. As the head of the Missionary Sisters of the Sacred Heart, she was called Mother Cabrini. She wanted to travel to China, but when she met with Pope Leo XIII to get his approval, he sent her to America to help provide pastoral care to the thousands of Italian immigrants settled there.

Mother Cabrini and six other sisters arrived in New York in 1889, and soon founded an orphanage for Italian American children. In spite of poor health, a fear of ocean travel, and many other obstacles, Mother Cabrini eventually opened sixty-seven schools, orphanages, and hospitals across the United States, as well as in Latin America, France, Spain, and England. Mother Cabrini made good use of the Holy Spirit's gifts of wisdom, understanding, right judgment, and courage to serve people who were in need. She became a citizen of the United States in 1909, and was canonized in 1946, the first American citizen to be proclaimed a saint. Her feast day is November 13.

relationships with friends, family, and strangers. They desire to be Christ's hands and feet, reaching out to serve others who are in need. They hope that when other people hear their words and see their actions, those people see a reflection of Christ acting in the world today. This is one of the reasons the programs preparing you for Confirmation usually have a strong focus on the life of Jesus.

Jesus anointed the Apostles, who in turn anointed more bishops, and so the chain has continued through the centuries. Therefore the bishop who anoints you at Confirmation is connecting you directly to Christ himself!

Deeper Participation in the Church

Confirmed people are drawn into deeper participation in the life of the Church. They have a desire to be active in their own parish's ministries. They serve as lectors, catechists, mentors, and volunteers of all kinds. They participate in youth ministry, service projects, and Bible studies. They are not afraid to be identified as a member of the Church when they participate in community activities. They look forward to Sunday Mass, to celebrate the Lord's Supper with their brothers and sisters in Christ.

Strengthened to Spread the Faith

Confirmed people are proud to be Catholic and want to share the joy and support they experience as a member of the Church with others. They enter into religious discussions with others, sharing what they have learned and believe. They invite their interested neighbors or friends to church activities or even to Sunday Mass. They are not afraid to let others know about their faith in Christ and the hope and joy they experience as a Christian.

Increased Gifts of the Holy Spirit

Confirmed people experience a growth in the spiritual gifts of the Holy Spirit: wisdom, understanding, right judgment, courage, knowledge, reverence, and wonder and awe. These gifts help us grow deeper spiritually, in order to deepen our faith and grow closer to God. They help us live holy, happy, and healthy lives by making good moral choices. And they prepare us for being of service to others.

Just as with Baptism, Confirmation imparts a permanent **sacramental character** on your soul. This spiritual mark signifies that you belong to Christ, fully initiated into the Body of Christ. Because this mark is permanent, Confirmation cannot be repeated. Once you are a fully initiated member of the Church, you cannot be more fully initiated.

The Confirmation Rite

Confirmation requires some things from the person who wishes to be confirmed. It requires that you be of the age of reason (defined as seven years old in Church law), so that you have an understanding of the meaning of the sacrament. You must be baptized and must freely profess the Catholic faith. You must be in a state of grace, which means that you are following the laws of Christ and the Church and are not guilty of any serious, unconfessed sins. Finally, you must wish to be confirmed and must be willing to be a witness for Christ.

If you meet these requirements and have gone through the preparation required by your parish and your diocese, you are ready to celebrate the rite of Confirmation. Most Confirmations take place as part of a Eucharistic liturgy or Mass. In the Roman Catholic Church, the bishop is the usual minister of Confirmation, although in special cases he can delegate that responsibility to priests.

The Confirmation Mass often begins with **confirmands** (Confirmation candidates) and their sponsors processing in before the bishop. The Mass then proceeds as usual until after the bishop's homily. This is when the actual rite of Confirmation begins. The bishop asks the candidates to renew their baptismal vows, rejecting Satan and evil and professing their belief in the Holy Trinity and the Church. Then the

LIVE it!

Choosing a Confirmation Sponsor

Choosing a Confirmation sponsor is important, and the Church spells out some basic requirements. A sponsor needs to be mature, a member of the Catholic Church, and already fully initiated through the sacraments of Baptism, Confirmation, and the Eucharist. When a baptismal godparent also serves as the Confirmation sponsor, it clearly shows the connection between Baptism and Confirmation, and strengthens an existing relationship.

But these are just minimal requirements. The word *sponsor* comes from the same root as "responsible," and a well-chosen sponsor can help you grow in your faith. Don't pick a sponsor because he's a lot of fun or she hasn't had a turn yet. Pick a sponsor who is actively practicing his or her faith, and who will assist you as you prepare for Confirmation, present you to the bishop for anointing, and support you in the years ahead as you discover how the gifts of the Holy Spirit are unfolding in your life. Your parish may encourage you to have both a sponsor and a mentor, the first to stand with you at the Confirmation ceremony, and the second to support you in your preparation.

bishop extends his hands over the confirmands and prays that they will receive the Holy Spirit. Following is a part of this prayer:

Sacred Chrism

Chrism is special oil used as a visible sign during the Confirmation ritual. Chrism is made of olive oil mixed with fragrant balsam. The oil is a symbol of strength, and the perfume is a symbol of the "fragrance of Christ," which Christians must spread. The name *Christ* means "the anointed of the Lord," and chrism marks our total belonging to Christ, our sharing in his mission, and our connection to the universal Church. Chrism is consecrated by the bishop and distributed to the churches for use in Baptism, Confirmation, and ordination.

At a special Chrism Mass, on Holy Thursday morning, or another day during Holy Week, the bishop consecrates the chrism and blesses the oil of catechumens and the oil for anointing the sick. The Chrism Mass expresses the fullness of the bishop's priesthood and shows the unity of priests in his diocese. The liturgy includes a renewal of commitment to priestly service. Oils blessed and consecrated at the Chrism Mass are brought back to the parishes, carried in procession at the Holy Thursday liturgy, and used for sacramental anointings throughout the year.

All-powerful God, Father of our Lord Jesus Christ,
by water and the Holy Spirit
you freed your sons and daughters from sin
and gave them new life.
Send your Holy Spirit upon them
to be their Helper and Guide.

(*The Rites of the Catholic Church,*
volume 1, page 490)

Following this prayer the confirmands come forward to stand or kneel before the bishop. The sponsor stands behind and places a hand on the candidate's shoulder. Then the bishop anoints each candidate's forehead with the sacred **chrism** (oil), placing his hands on her or him, and saying, "Be sealed with the Gift of the Holy Spirit." This is often followed by a handshake or embrace with the bishop, welcoming the newly confirmed person into full membership in the Church. The anointing, the laying on of the bishop's hands, and the words, "Be sealed with the gift of the Holy Spirit" are the essential symbols of the sacrament. After this the Mass continues as usual.

Three main differences are found in the celebration of Confirmation in the Eastern Catholic Churches. First, Confirmation is given to infants or children in the same ritual as Baptism. Second, the ordinary minister of Confirmation is the priest rather than the bishop. Third, rather than just anointing the forehead, the eyes, nose, ears, lips, chest, back, hands, and feet are anointed as well. This is to symbolize that the whole person belongs to Christ.

Notice that nowhere does this chapter mention that Confirmation is about becoming an adult Catholic. Sometimes people talk about the meaning of Confirmation in this way, but it is incorrect. Confirmation is about becoming a fully initiated Catholic. You may or may not be an adult when you are confirmed. But the gift of the Holy Spirit will help you live a fully Christian life appropriate for whatever age you happen to be. Confirmation is not a graduation. Rather it is the beginning of living the Christian life with all the passion and enthusiasm that God is calling for.

For Further Reflection

- What does it mean to you to belong totally to Christ?
- Read the characteristics of a confirmed person in the section "The Effects of Confirmation." Whether or not you're confirmed yet, reflect on how your own attitudes measure up to the descriptions.
- What are you doing to prepare for Confirmation? If you've already been confirmed, what difference has it made in your life?

Looking Back

Soldiers of Christ

As the water bath of Baptism and the anointing of Confirmation became separated, an understanding of Confirmation developed in the fifth century that focused on strengthening Christians for their battle with the devil. Over the years the bishop's caress on the cheek—a sign of peace—was given more and more quickly. By the Middle Ages, it looked like a slap and represented the suffering we must endure for Christ. Gradually the slap on the cheek came to be standard practice, and the idea that Confirmation would make someone a "soldier of Christ" caught on in the Church. For several centuries this "soldier of Christ" idea shaped people's understanding of Confirmation.

Older Catholics remember the "slap on the cheek" that used to be part of the Confirmation rite. In 1971, when the new rite of Confirmation was introduced, the slap was dropped and the sign of peace was restored. When your parents or grandparents were confirmed, they may have worried about how hard the bishop would hit them. You don't have to worry about that!

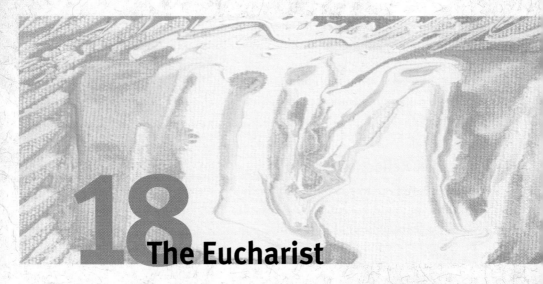

18 The Eucharist

If there is one thing that distinguishes Catholics from other
Christians, it is our devotion to the sacrament of the Eucharist.
Though all the sacraments are important, the Eucharist is the
spiritual center of Catholic life. Through the Eucharist we
remember what God has done for us through Jesus Christ,
when we gather every Sunday. We celebrate the Eucharist as
part of other sacramental celebrations, such as Confirmation
or marriage, making those sacraments fuller and more complete expressions of the mystery of our faith. We celebrate the
Eucharist at retreats, pilgrimages, and other spiritual events,
giving those activities Catholic identity. And we celebrate the
Eucharist when Catholics gather for important meetings, as a
sign of our unity. The traditional language we use to express
these varied celebrations of the same sacrament is that the
Eucharist is the "heart (or source) and the summit" (*CCC*,
number 1407) of the life of the Church.

Words to Look For

- *Paschal lamb*
- *Eucharist*
- *reparation*
- *assembly*
- *consecration*
- *transubstantiation*
- *liturgy of the word*
- *liturgy of the Eucharist*
- *Eucharistic prayer*
- *Holy Communion*

Why does the Eucharist hold such an esteemed place in Catholic life? It is because the Eucharist brings together in a single ritual all the important elements of the Catholic faith. In it we recall what God has revealed to us through history in the liturgy of the word. Through the power of the Holy Spirit, we remember and make present the life, death, and Resurrection of Jesus Christ. We actually receive Jesus Christ—physically and spiritually—when we receive the consecrated bread and wine, which becomes the body and blood of Jesus Christ. In our celebration of the Eucharistic liturgy, we are united across time and space with the communion of saints, who are praising God on earth and in heaven, all celebrating the same divine liturgy.

A common complaint of many teens— and a few adults—is that Mass is boring. There is no denying that many people experience this feeling as part of their spiritual journey. But if you understand what is happening during the Eucharist, you can never say that it is unimportant. Important things are not always exciting, especially if they become routine. But you may find that if you put your heart into it, the Mass will no longer seem as boring as you thought.

A Short History of the Eucharist

The roots of our celebration of the Eucharist are found in the Old Testament story of the Exodus. It is the story of how God freed the people of Israel from their captivity in Egypt. One particular event, the Passover, involved a sacrifice and a meal (Exodus, chapters 11 and 12). The Passover is connected to the tenth and final plague that God sent to convince Pharaoh to let the people go. In this plague God's messenger killed the firstborn of every Egyptian family and the firstborn

Pray It

Eucharist Meditations

One way to participate more fully in the Eucharist is to spend time reflecting on what the celebration means. Give some prayerful thought to the insights quoted below. Write one or more of them down, so you can carry it with you and read it before or after Mass next weekend.

Jesus said to them, "I am the bread of life. Whoever comes to me will never be hungry, and whoever believes in me will never be thirsty." (John 6:35)

God has no body now on earth but yours; no hands but yours; no feet but yours. Yours are the eyes through which the compassion of Christ must look out on the world. Yours are the feet with which He is to go about doing good. Yours are the hands with which He is to bless His people. (Saint Teresa of Ávila)

This holy Mass, this Eucharist is clearly an act of faith. . . . This body broken and this blood shed for human beings encourage us to give our body and blood up to suffering and pain, as Christ did—not for self, but to bring justice and peace to our people. (Oscar Romero)

Be what you see, and receive what you are. (Saint Augustine)

of all the livestock. To be spared, every Israelite family had to kill a young lamb (called the Passover or **Paschal lamb**) and spread its blood over their doorway. Then the angel of death would "pass over" their household, and their oldest son would live. They were to cook the lamb and serve it with unleavened bread, as their final meal in the land of Egypt. The Israelites were commanded by God to celebrate this Passover meal every year to remember their escape from slavery through God's divine power.

In this image of the Last Supper, servants, cooks, and even angels surround Jesus and the Apostles. Why is this meaningful?

Jump ahead now to Jesus' earthly mission. Jesus was always eating and drinking. In fact, he and the disciples were accused of being gluttons and drunkards (Luke 7:34). Jesus loved a good meal and conversation; mealtimes often became teaching moments (Luke 11:37–52, 14:1–24, 19:1–10). Jesus also could not stand to see people go hungry. One of his greatest miracles is the multiplication of the loaves and fishes, a story found in all four Gospels (Matthew 14:13–21, Mark 6:30–44, Luke 9:10–17, John 6:1–15).

The story of the loaves and fishes in chapter 6 of the Gospel of John is particularly important, because in it Jesus goes on to teach about the Eucharist. This chapter is a summary of what the early Christians came to understand about the Eucharist. Here are a few highlights of Jesus' words in chapter 6:

- "I am the bread of life. Whoever comes to me will never be hungry, and whoever believes in me will never be thirsty" (verse 35).
- "I am the living bread that came down from heaven. Whoever eats of this bread will live forever; and the bread that I will give for the life of the world is my flesh" (verse 51).
- "Those who eat my flesh and drink my blood have eternal life, and I will raise them up on the last day; for my flesh is true food and my blood is true drink. Those who eat my flesh and drink my blood abide in me, and I in them" (verses 54–56).

All this emphasis on eating and drinking, on hunger and thirst, on flesh and blood reached its culmination in Jesus' Last Supper with his Apostles. Again, this event is recorded in all four Gospels, although the Gospel of John has a different emphasis (Matthew 26:17–30, Mark 14:12–25, Luke 22:7–23, John 13:1—17:26). The meal Jesus shared on this occasion with his closest followers was the Jewish Passover meal. Jesus knew that his death was at hand, and he wanted to leave his disciples a special memorial as a sign of his continued presence with them. So Jesus blessed bread, broke it, and passed it to them, saying, "Take, eat; this is my body." Then he did the same with the cup of wine saying, "Drink from it, all of you; for this is my blood of the covenant, which is poured out for many for the forgiveness of sins" (Matthew 26:26–28).

After Jesus' death, Resurrection, and Ascension into heaven, the early Church put together the Old Testament understanding of the Paschal lamb and sacrifice with the words and actions of Jesus. They understood that although the sacrifice of the original Passover lamb saved the firstborn from physical death, Jesus' sacrifice saves us all from the eternal death that is separation from God. He is the new Paschal lamb (John 1:29, 1 Corinthians 5:7). The old sacrifices by the Israelite priests were not enough to overcome the damage caused by original sin, but Jesus' sacrifice completely restored our relationship with God once and for all (Hebrews 10:1–10). The Church understood that Jesus wants us to repeat the ritual of the Last Supper, and that when we do so, he will be physically and spiritually present (1 Corinthians 11:23–26). These are the core understandings of the Eucharist that we still celebrate today.

The Meaning of the Eucharist

Our look into the historical beginnings of the Eucharist has already begun to point out the meaning of this great sacrament. Like all

Looking Back

The Church Building

A church building isn't just a convenience. A church should convey a sense of God's presence and lead us to prayer. The U.S. Catholic bishops make this clear in their document *Built of Living Stones:*

> Just as the term *Church* refers to the *living temple,* God's People, the term *church* also has been used to describe "the building in which the Christian community gathers to hear the word of God, to pray together, to receive the sacraments, and celebrate the eucharist."[1] That building is both the house of God on earth *(domus Dei)* and a house fit for the prayers of the saints *(domus ecclesiae).* Such a house of prayer must be expressive of the presence of God and suited for the celebration of the sacrifice of Christ, as well as reflective of the community that celebrates there.
>
> The church is the proper place for the liturgical prayer of the parish community, especially the celebration of the Eucharist on Sunday. It is also the privileged place for adoration of the Blessed Sacrament and reservation of the Eucharist for Communion for the sick. Whenever communities have built houses for worship, the design of the building has been of critical importance.[2] . . . Every church building is a gathering place for the assembly, a resting place, a place of encounter with God, as well as a point of departure on the Church's unfinished journey toward the reign of God. (Numbers 16–17)

sacraments, the words and actions are a symbol of what is happening in the spiritual reality. The Church has developed some clear descriptions of the spiritual reality of the Eucharist that you should be aware of.

Saint Katharine Drexel, also known as Mother Drexel, started over one hundred missions and schools that served poor people in both rural areas and inner cities. Why do you think she is so happy?

Thanksgiving and Praise

The word *Eucharist* comes from a Greek word meaning "thanksgiving." In the sacrament we give God thanks and praise for all that God has given us: life, love, family, friends, creation, and most important, Jesus' sacrifice of love on the cross and the promise of the resurrection. Think for a moment about some of the prayers we say: "Glory to God in the highest," "Blessed are you, Lord, God of all creation," and "Holy, holy, holy Lord." They are all about praising and thanking God.

But in the spiritual realm, it isn't just we who are praising and thanking God, it is Christ himself, with us and through the Holy Spirit. Remember that one of the names for the Church gathered, is the Body of Christ. It is Christ himself, our high priest (Hebrews 8:3), who leads our praise and thanksgiving to the Father. Through the Holy Spirit, our earthly praise and thanksgiving is joined to the perfect worship of God by the saints and angels in heaven (Revelation 19:1–5).

Memorial of Christ's Passover Sacrifice

The Eucharist is also a memorial of the life, death, and Resurrection of Christ. This happens in a number of ways. In the Gospel reading and the homily, we hear and reflect on the meaning of a particular teaching or event from the life of Jesus. In the creed we profess our belief in the mysteries of our faith, including the saving events of Jesus' life. And in the Eucharistic prayer, we specifically recall the events surrounding his death and Resurrection.

But the spiritual reality is something much more than just remembering these events. In the Eucharist these saving actions are made present, and we are actually participating in these events! Through the words and actions of the priest, Jesus himself is blessing the bread and wine. Jesus is making his body and blood present in the form of bread and wine. The saving power of Jesus' Passover, that is, his sacrifice on the cross, strengthens us and renews us. It isn't that we are resacrificing Jesus, but making his original sacrifice real and present during the sacramental ritual.

As a sacrifice, the Eucharist is also **reparation** (making amends) for the sins of the living and the dead. Part of the prayer tradition of Catholics is consciously to remember someone during the Eucharist who has died, and to pray that his or her journey to heaven will be swift. You may have noticed that often a particular person is prayed for during the prayers at Mass. People arrange for this by contacting their parish office to ask that a Mass be designated as a memorial for someone they know who has died. And many people remember a special person or need in their personal prayers before or after Holy Communion. This is something you can do at any Mass.

Presence of Christ

In the Eucharist Jesus is present in the fullest possible way. He is present in the **assembly,** the people gathered as the Body of Christ. He is present in the word, the Scripture readings that are proclaimed at every Mass. Christ is also present in the priest or bishop who presides over the Eucharist. But he is particularly present in the bread and wine, which, after the **consecration** (the part of the Mass in which the priest prays over the bread and wine, repeating Jesus' prayers from the Last Supper), become the body and blood of Jesus, through the power of the Holy Spirit.

The technical word for the transformation of the bread and wine into Jesus' body and blood is **transubstantiation.**

Saintly Profiles

Katharine Drexel (1858–1955)

Katharine Drexel, also known as Mother Drexel, was the daughter of a wealthy Philadelphia banker. She devoted her life and her considerable inherited wealth to serving the poor. At the age of thirty, she joined the Sisters of Mercy and began to live a vow of poverty. She felt a special call to serve the African and Native American communities in the United States, and in 1891, she founded a new religious community of women, the Sisters of the Blessed Sacrament.

Katharine established over a hundred missions and schools on Indian reservations, in rural areas, and in inner cities. In 1915 she started a teachers' college that eventually became Xavier University of Louisiana, the first and only predominantly African American Catholic university. Throughout her life she fought for and funded civil rights' causes.

Today the Sisters of the Blessed Sacrament continue Katharine's Gospel-inspired mission of witnessing to the power of the Eucharist, by dedicating their whole life to practicing justice and fostering unity among all peoples. Katharine was the second American-born saint, and was canonized in October 2000. Her feast day is March 3.

This is perhaps one of the hardest things for us to understand. It is a belief that separates Catholics from many other Christians. But we have Jesus' own words to testify to this

reality (Matthew 26:26–29). To help you understand this mystery better (we will never completely understand it!), you may wish to review the section "Symbols and Rituals," on pages 146–148, in chapter 15, Introduction to the Sacraments. The bread and wine become a sacramental symbol that points to and makes real the spiritual reality: that we are receiving Jesus in a real and physical way. Although the bread and wine retain their physical forms, they have truly become Jesus' body and blood, nourishing us to live as his disciples.

Different colors of chasubles are worn by priests at different times during the liturgical year. Can you name the colors that are worn during each liturgical season?

The Eucharistic Rite

The Eucharistic rite, or ritual, is the most complex of the sacramental rites. The Lord's Supper, the Holy Sacrifice, the Holy and Divine Liturgy, Holy Communion, and the Mass (from the Latin word *missa,* meaning "sending forth") are all names for the Eucharistic liturgy. The entire rite consists of four parts: (1) the gathering rite, (2) the liturgy of the word, (3) the liturgy of the Eucharist, and (4) the dismissal rite. The **liturgy of the word** and the **liturgy of the Eucharist** are the two main parts; together they create one single act of worship. The chart on this page outlines the words and actions that typically occur in each part.

An Outline for the Eucharist

The movement of the Sunday Mass usually follows this outline:

1. Introductory Rites
   - Entrance (usually with gathering song)
   - Act of Penitence
   - Kyrie ("Lord, have mercy . . .")
   - Gloria ("Glory to God . . .")
   - Collect ("Let us pray . . .")

2. Liturgy of the Word
   - First Reading (usually from the Old Testament)
   - Responsorial Psalm (usually sung)
   - Second Reading (usually from the New Testament letters)
   - Gospel Acclamation
   - Gospel Reading
   - Homily
   - the Profession of Faith (the Nicene Creed)
   - Prayers of the Faithful (prayers for the needs of the Church and the world)
3. Liturgy of the Eucharist
   - Preparation of the Altar and the Gifts
   - Eucharistic Prayer (The central prayer in which the priest thanks God for all his gifts, calls down the Holy Spirit, and consecrates the bread and wine, making it the body and blood of Jesus. Includes the preface and the "Holy, Holy, Holy.")
   - Communion Rite (This includes the Lord's Prayer, the Rite of Peace, the Breaking of the Bread, the reception of Holy Communion, and a song of praise or silence.)
4. Concluding Rites
   - Greeting and Blessing
   - Dismissal (usually with a closing song)

The gathering rite prepares us for the celebration of the Eucharist. It comprises a song played when the priest or bishop processes in with the other liturgical ministers, a penitential rite for the forgiveness of minor sins, the Glory to God, and an opening prayer by the priest. We then move to the liturgy of the word, the time in which we receive Christ through the words of the Scriptures. On Sundays the liturgy of the word comprises a Scripture reading from the

Did You Know?

Liturgical Clothing and Colors

The celebrant's vestments (special religious clothing) reflect the ordinary clothing worn by men in the Roman Empire during the fourth century. Here is a brief description of some of the liturgical vestments worn today:

- **Alb.** This is the long, white robe that the celebrant wears over his regular clothes. The alb signifies Baptism, and may be worn by any baptized person.
- **Stole.** Priests and deacons wear this long scarflike vestment around their neck to signify their ordained ministry. In ancient times, people wore scarves to designate their official status.
- **Chasuble.** This is a colorful outer garment worn over the alb. The colors are carefully chosen in light of the liturgical season or feast.

The color of the vestments sets a tone and indicates the nature of the liturgical feast or season.

- **White** symbolizes purity and hope, and is worn during the seasons of Christmas and Easter and also at funeral masses.
- **Red** signifies the outpouring of blood, and is worn on Palm Sunday and Good Friday. It is also worn on the feast days of the Apostles and martyrs. Red also symbolizes the fire of the Holy Spirit, and so is worn on Pentecost and for the sacrament of Confirmation.
- **Green** symbolizes hope, and is worn during Ordinary Time.
- **Violet or blue** is worn during Advent to signify preparation and during Lent to signify penance.

Old Testament, a psalm that is sung or recited, a reading from the letters of the New Testament, and a reading from one of the Gospels. This is followed by a homily in which the readings are explained and applied to our life today. The liturgy of the word finishes with the recitation of the Nicene Creed and the gen-eral intercessions, in which we pray for the needs of the Church and the world.

Serving as a lector is one way of taking an active role during the liturgy. In what ways are teens involved in the Sunday Eucharist in your parish?

The liturgy of the Eucharist begins when the gifts of bread and wine are brought to the altar. Only simple, unleavened wheat bread and grape wine may be used. A prayer is said over these gifts ("Lord, accept these gifts of bread and wine"), and then the priest prays the preface to the **Eucharistic prayer,** to which the assembly responds with "Holy, Holy, Holy." The priest then prays the Eucharistic prayer on behalf of the gathered community. You will recognize this prayer because it begins with the priest saying, "Lift up your hearts," and we respond, "We lift them up to the Lord."

The Eucharistic prayer is the longest prayer of the Mass, and has a number of different parts. The priest can choose from several forms of the prayer. No matter which form is used, though, the core of the prayer is always the same. The priest extends his hands over the bread and wine, and says the words of consecration used by Jesus at the Last Supper: "This is my body, which is given for you. . . . This cup that is poured out for you is . . . my blood" (Luke 22:19–20). The bread and wine and these words are the essential signs of the sacrament.

After the Eucharistic prayer, the assembly recites the Lord's Prayer, exchanges a sign of peace, and processes up to receive the Eucharist. The dismissal rite includes a final blessing, the sending forth, and usually a closing song as the priest and servers recess out.

Only priests and bishops can preside at the Eucharist. It is Christ himself, the high priest of the New Covenant, who offers the Eucharistic sacrifice through the ministry of the ordained priest. Ordination gives them the special character needed to represent Christ, allowing them to consecrate the bread and wine so that they become the body and blood of the Lord.

Receiving the Eucharist

All Catholics have an obligation to "keep holy the Lord's Day" (the third commandment), that is, they must attend Sunday Mass. All Catholics are encouraged to receive the body and blood of the Lord whenever they attend Eucharist, and are obligated by the precepts of the Church to receive **Holy Communion** (another name for the consecrated bread and wine) at least once a year.

Although everyone is welcome to attend the Mass, under some circumstances people cannot receive Holy Communion in the Catholic Church. One situation is if a person is not Catholic. Because the Eucharist is a sign of our unity, it would be a false symbol for someone to receive it who is not in union with the beliefs and practices of the Catholic Church.

Another situation in which a person should not receive the Eucharist is if a person is guilty of a serious (mortal) sin and has not yet confessed it. Committing a mortal sin results in a serious break in our relationship with God, and only receiving absolution (forgiveness) in the sacrament of Penance and Reconciliation can restore the baptismal grace necessary to properly receive Christ. A person who seeks forgiveness for a mortal sin is encouraged to be part of the Eucharistic assembly, and to receive Penance and Reconciliation as soon as possible so she or he can again receive the body and blood of the Lord.

Receiving Christ in the Eucharist has a number of beneficial effects in our life. It builds up our relationship with Jesus, and it strengthens our relationship with his Body, the Church. It

Six Ways to Serve at the Liturgy

Your parish's liturgy depends on people using their gifts to fulfill special roles during the Sunday Eucharist. Read the descriptions of the following roles, and consider your own gifts and talents. Young people all over the country are serving in these ministries; might you be called to serve in one of them?

- **Greeters** (or ministers of hospitality) make sure that as people gather for Mass, they are met with a warm, genuine welcome.
- **Lectors** proclaim the first and second readings. They immerse themselves in the Scripture passages by reading them and praying with them before the liturgy.
- **Musicians** add joy, spirit, and reflection to the celebration, and foster a sense of unity among the people by leading the singing of hymns and prayers.
- **Gift bearers** bring forward the gifts of bread and wine—symbols of God's gift of creation and human work.
- **Extraordinary Ministers of Holy Communion** express their faith by assisting with the distribution of Communion.
- **Servers,** sometimes called **acolytes,** assist the priest by taking care of the books and objects used in the liturgy, so the celebrant can focus on the prayers and ritual actions.

unites all the members of the Church together, making the entire Church stronger and more vital. Participating in the Eucharist brings forgiveness for our venial sins and strengthens us to resist serious sin. The Holy Spirit sends us forth from the Eucharist, strengthened to be Christ's presence in the world. With all these benefits, why would anyone not wish to regularly attend Mass and receive the body and blood of Christ?

For Further Reflection

○ People often find that taking a few minutes to prepare for the Eucharist helps them receive more from the sacrament. Some ways of preparing include looking over the Scripture readings before Mass, remembering people you want to pray for during the liturgy, and getting to the church a few minutes early to silently pray and meditate before the liturgy begins. What could you do to better prepare yourself for the Eucharist?

○ The Sunday Eucharist is a time for the people of your parish to connect and grow together in Christ. Many new churches and remodeled churches include larger gathering areas so people can visit before and after Mass. How well does your parish encourage people to grow together as a community?

19

Sacraments of Healing

Which would you say is worse: physical illness, mental illness, or spiritual illness? You might be tempted to say physical illness, because it is easier to imagine the pain and the loss of function that comes with it. But mental illness can also be incapacitating and painful. Just ask someone who has a family member suffering from severe depression or schizophrenia. But Jesus and the Church consider spiritual illness—the sickness of the soul that is the result of sin—to be the worst type of illness we can have. Spiritual sickness can lead to spiritual death and the permanent separation from God's love that we call hell.

Jesus and the Church are concerned about healing all kinds of illness: spiritual, mental, and physical. This is why we have two sacraments called the **sacraments of healing:** Penance and Reconciliation, and the Anointing of the Sick. The sacrament of Penance and Reconciliation is primarily

Words to Look For

- sacraments of healing
- absolution
- act of contrition
- contrition
- repentance
- reparation
- penance
- oil of the sick
- vigil for the deceased

concerned with spiritual healing, while Anointing of the Sick is concerned with physical, mental, and spiritual healing.

This early Christian fresco shows the healing of the woman who had been bleeding for twelve years (Mark 5:25–34). Although she tried to remain unnoticed, the painting shows Jesus turning to her after he felt the healing power leave him.

A Short History of Penance and Reconciliation

Jesus was all about forgiveness. He was forgiving people all the time. He forgave the paralyzed man (Matthew 9:6); the woman caught in adultery (John 8:11), the woman who washed his feet with her tears (Luke 7:48), and even the soldiers who nailed him to the cross (Luke 23:34). He told great stories about forgiveness, like the one about the crazy-with-love father who forgave his prodigal son, even though the son wasted all his inheritance (Luke 15:11–32). And when Peter asked him if forgiving someone seven times was enough, Jesus replied, "Not seven times, but, I tell you, seventy-seven times" (Matthew 18:22).

Only God can forgive sins. Because Jesus was true God and true man, he could forgive people's sins during his earthly ministry. At the end of his earthly ministry, he shared that responsibility with the Apostles. After his Resurrection he tells the Apostles, "If you forgive the sins of any, they are forgiven them; if you retain the sins of any, they are retained" (John 20:23). Which means that if an Apostle forgives someone's sins in the Church, God also forgives the sins. As the successors to the Apostles, the bishops continue to have this power in the Church, and they share it with priests when they are ordained. This is why only a priest can forgive sins in the name of the Church.

In the early Church, the sacrament looked quite different from how we celebrate it today. Only the most serious sins (mortal sins) were confessed to the bishop. Often the repentant sinner then had to join a group called the "order of penitents," and spend extended time publicly in fasting and prayer, until the bishop decided she or he had truly reformed. To emphasize the importance of avoiding serious sin, in some regions people could join the order of penitents only once.

Monks from Ireland brought into the Church the idea of private confession. As part of a monk's formation, he was encouraged to confess his faults to a spiritual mentor. In the fifth century, the Pope encouraged the monks to be missionaries and convert the Germanic tribes to Christianity. The monks used their practice of individual confession with the new converts, and it became popular among the people. In fact, the people wanted to confess their sins to a priest repeatedly as an assurance that they were still loved and accepted by God. By the seventh century, the practice of private and frequent confession of one's sins was widespread.

Today the practice for the sacrament of Penance and Reconciliation continues to be private confession, in which an individual meets alone with a priest to confess his or her sins. The sacrament is practiced in three forms. In one form, the person seeking forgiveness meets only with the priest and there is no public liturgy. In the second form, communal (group) prayers and Scripture readings are followed by individual confessions and **absolution** (forgiveness by the priest). In rare situations in which there are more people seeking the sacrament than there are priests to hear individual confessions, the Church allows for a third form, in which there is a general confession and absolution without private confessions. However, that is only done with the understanding that people with serious (mortal) sins will go to private confession as soon as possible.

Pray It!

Act of Contrition

Expressing sorrow for our sins is an important part of the sacrament of Reconciliation. Telling God that you are sorry for your sins is also called making an **act of contrition.** You may have learned a short form of this prayer when you prepared for your first Reconciliation. Here is a popular version of this prayer:

My God,
I am sorry for my sins with all my heart.
In choosing to do wrong
and failing to do good,
I have sinned against you
whom I should love above all things.
I firmly intend, with your help,
to do penance,
to sin no more,
and to avoid whatever leads me to sin.
Our Savior Jesus Christ
suffered and died for us.
In his name, my God, have mercy.
(Catholic Household Blessings and Prayers, page 250)

The Effects of Penance and Reconciliation

The different effects of Penance and Reconciliation can be explained by the many different names used for this sacrament. Following are the different names for the sacrament and the effects they represent:

How to Make a Good Confession

The sacrament of Reconciliation is a good way to take a closer look at your life and make a fresh start, at least once a year. Many parishes offer communal Reconciliation services during Advent and Lent, and private Reconciliation is usually available at some time every week. Before you go, ask God for help in remembering your sins, specific actions, and general patterns of behavior.

Following is an outline of what you can expect. The priest will be glad to help you.

- **Go to the priest.** You can kneel behind a screen or sit and face him. He will welcome you, and you will both make the sign of the cross. The priest will pray for you and may read a Scripture passage.
- **Confess your sins.** The priest will discuss your sins with you and provide spiritual advice.
- **Receive a penance.** The priest will talk to you about doing something as a sign of your desire to change. It may be saying some prayers or doing a loving action.
- **Tell God that you are sorry.** You can use your own words or an act of contrition that you have memorized.
- **Receive absolution.** The priest proclaims the words of absolution and God forgives your sins.
- **Conclude.** The priest says, "Give thanks to the Lord, for he is good," and you respond, "His mercy endures forever." The priest will dismiss you, and you can respond, "Thank you" or "Amen."

○ **Sacrament of Conversion.** Conversion is the turning away from sin and the turning toward God that happens through the sacrament. Through conversion we recover the grace we lost through turning away from God's love.

○ **Sacrament of Confession.** In the sacrament we confess our sins. The very act of revealing our sins to another person brings peace and a clean conscience.

○ **Sacrament of Forgiveness.** In the sacrament God forgives our sins through the absolution of the priest. If we were in a state of serious (mortal) sin, we are freed from the consequence of eternal separation from God (hell).

○ **Sacrament of Penance.** Penance is the whole cycle of conversion, forgiveness, and making reparation (repaying any debt) for our sin. It is perhaps the best description of the sacrament. The sacrament strengthens us to enter the world and resist the future temptation of sin.

○ **Sacrament of Reconciliation.** Through the sacrament we are reconciled with God and with the Church, the Body of Christ. Our relationships with other Christians are restored, although we may still need to seek forgiveness from those who were directly affected by our sin, and if possible make amends for any damage or harm we have caused.

Receiving Penance and Reconciliation

A person first receives the sacrament of Penance and Reconciliation before receiving their first Eucharist (unless they are an adult catechumen, who is being baptized and confirmed, and receives first Eucharist at the Easter Vigil). The forgiveness of all sins committed since Baptism helps restore the original grace of Baptism before receiving the Eucharist. This is part of the sacramental reality—that we should be in a state of grace before receiving the body and blood of our Lord. For this reason the Church gives two other laws regarding Penance and Reconciliation.

The first is that we should confess serious sins at least once a year, sort of an annual "soul checkup." This law is one of the precepts of the Church (see pages 230–232). The second law is that if we are guilty of a mortal sin, we must not receive the Eucharist until we have confessed the sin. Why? Because a mortal sin means you have intentionally turned away from God, and receiving Jesus Christ in the Eucharist after that would be a lie. Once you realize you have committed a mortal sin and you are sorry, you should privately ask the forgiveness of God and then receive the sacrament of Penance and Reconciliation as soon as you can. When you are guilty of a mortal sin, receiving the sacrament is the only sure way of reconciliation with God and with the Church.

Penance and Reconciliation starts with our personal acceptance that we have sinned and done wrong in the sight of God. Our heart is moved to sorrow from the knowledge that we have failed to act in love and have distanced ourselves from our creator. We should also have a firm conviction to sin no more. This hatred for our sin and our commitment to not sin again is called **contrition,** and having a contrite heart is essential for receiving the sacrament. Receiving the sacrament is simple (see the article "How to Make a Good Confession," at left), and there is no reason to be afraid or hesitant to do so. Priests know they represent Christ, and they have nothing but compassion and understanding for those who come to receive forgiveness. Furthermore they are under a sacred seal never to reveal under any circumstances what has been confessed to them.

Perfect and Imperfect Contrition

In Baptism our sins are forgiven and we receive God's sanctifying grace. Even when we sin, this grace continues to work in us, to inspire us to turn away from sin and to seek God's forgiveness when we do sin. But what prompts us to seek God's forgiveness? The Church challenges us to examine our motives. Ideally our repentance should be inspired by the fact that our sin has injured our relationship with God and others. When repentance is motivated by our love of God, it is called "perfect" contrition, or contrition of charity. But when repentance is motivated by our fear of going to hell or losing heaven, it is called "imperfect" contrition, or contrition of fear. Even if your motive is imperfect, your sins will still be forgiven in Penance and Reconciliation. As your relationship with God grows, your motive for seeking God's forgiveness will also grow more perfect.

When you receive the sacrament, three main actions on your part are necessary. The first action is **repentance,** that is, expressing your sorrow to God. The second action is the confession of your sins. You need to confess all the serious sins that you remember making since your last confession. The Church also recommends that you confess your venial (less serious) sins too, although that isn't absolutely necessary. The third action, **reparation,** is your intention to do what you can to correct the damage your sins have caused. Usually the priest will suggest or talk with you about what actions you can take to repair the harm your sins have caused and to avoid these sins in the future. These actions are traditionally called your **penance.**

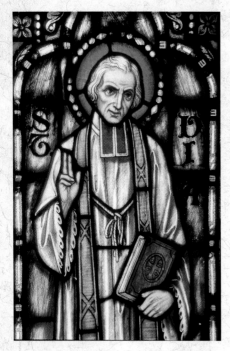

Saint John Vianney was famous for his kindness and wise advice, especially when hearing people's confessions. Yet his difficulties with school almost prevented him from becoming ordained.

The priest who hears your confession will try to make it as comfortable as possible. You always have the choice of remaining anonymous by staying behind a screen, or you can receive the sacrament face-to-face. After trying it many people prefer face-to-face confession because its personal nature makes the experience of forgiveness even stronger. As the representative of Christ, the priest's main action in the sacrament is to forgive your sins. After your confession he extends his hand over you or places his hand on you and says these traditional words of absolution (forgiveness):

God, the father of mercies,
through the death and the resurrection of his Son
has reconciled the world to himself
and sent the Holy Spirit among us
for the forgiveness of sins;
through the ministry of the Church
may God give you pardon and peace,
and I absolve you from your sins
in the name of the Father, and of the Son, and of the Holy Spirit.[1]

(*CCC,* number 1449)

A Short History of the Anointing of the Sick

The Bible contains even more stories about Jesus healing the sick than about his forgiveness of sins. We find more than twenty different accounts of the healing of individuals in the four Gospels (see the "Events, People, and Teachings" index of *The Catholic Youth Bible* for a list). Jesus healed lepers, people who were blind and deaf, people who were possessed by demons, and many others. His healings were motivated by compassion and love, and were a sign of the coming of the Kingdom of God—a time when sickness and death would no longer exist. But even Jesus was not able to heal everyone if people lacked faith in him (Matthew 13:58).

Jesus invited his disciples into his healing ministry. In the Gospel of Mark, Jesus sent out the Twelve on a mission, and it was reported that "they cast out many demons, and anointed with oil many who were sick and cured them" (6:13). And after his Resurrection, Jesus says that those who believe in him "will lay their hands on the sick, and they will recover" (Mark 16:18).

We also have a brief glimpse into how healing was a part of the earliest Church. The Letter of James has this interesting passage: "Are any among you sick? They should call for the elders of the church and have them pray over them, anointing them with oil in the name of the Lord. The prayer of faith will save the sick, and the Lord will raise them up" (5:14–15). It is from these passages that Tradition has recognized the sacrament of Anointing of the Sick.

It is unclear how consistently the sacrament was practiced in the first several hundred years of Church history. But around the ninth century or so, the sacrament took

Saintly Profiles

Saint John Vianney (1786–1859)

Saint John Vianney was born near Lyons, France, in 1786. He worked as a shepherd boy on his father's farm, and only attended the village school briefly when he was nine. When he entered the seminary to study for the priesthood, he really struggled with his studies, and it was questionable whether he would be ordained. He especially had trouble with Latin, the language used for all his classes. A parish priest tutored him privately and arranged for special exams. The seminary officials were impressed with his goodness, and the bishop ordained him in 1815.

In 1817 Saint John Vianney was assigned to Arsen-Dombes, a remote village of less than 250 people (which is why he is sometimes called the Curé d'Ars). He restored the church, visited every parishioner, and taught the Catechism. Although his sermons were often about hell and the Last Judgment, he was a compassionate priest, and was loved and respected as a confessor and spiritual counselor. He developed a reputation for working miracles, and attracted many visitors. For the last fifteen years of his life, he preached every day, and spent long hours hearing confessions and offering spiritual counsel to the thousands of visitors who came to see him. He was canonized in 1925 and named the patron saint of parish priests. His feast day is August 4.

on a significantly different meaning. Rather than being a sacrament of healing, it was used to prepare people for death. During that time it was called extreme unction, meaning "last anointing." It was usually combined with the sacraments of confession and Holy Eucharist, so that a person would be fully prepared to meet the Lord after death.

The liturgical reforms of the Second Vatican Council (1963–1965), however, restored the original intention of the sacrament. Renaming it Anointing of the Sick, the bishops of the Council said that the sacrament should be used to give God's special grace to those who were suffering from grave illness or old age. Although it is still used for those who are in danger of death, today it is used more often as a source of spiritual and physical healing for those who are suffering from serious illness or disease.

People receive the Anointing of the Sick for a variety of needs: when facing surgery, when battling illness or disease, and when nearing death. Do you know anyone who might benefit from receiving the sacrament?

The Effects of Anointing of the Sick

Like all the sacraments, the grace given in Anointing of the Sick has a number of effects. One effect is that it unites our suffering to the Passion, or suffering, of Christ. Jesus suffered for the sake of all humanity, and through the sacrament we can join our suffering with his. In some small way, our suffering becomes a participation in Jesus' redemptive (saving) suffering, for ourselves and for the whole Church. The sacrament also leads to the forgiveness of a person's sins if the person is unable to receive the sacrament of Penance and Reconciliation. Another effect is that the sacrament strengthens us and gives us peace to endure the inevitable suffering that comes with sickness and old age. We are far better witnesses to the power of God's grace when we accept illness and our own possible death with peace; the sacrament helps us to do that.

The sacrament of Anointing of the Sick also helps a person regain mental and physical health, if this is God's will for us, and will lead to the health of the soul. But the sacrament is no guarantee of a return to physical and mental health—it doesn't force God to perform a miraculous healing, as some people may think. Finally, the sacrament helps prepare a person for her or his death. It strengthens a person for the final good-byes: to let go of this life peacefully and to have faith in the promise of eternal life with God.

Receiving the Sacrament of Anointing of the Sick

There are two times when a priest should be contacted for the sacrament of Anointing of the Sick. The first is if someone is in danger of death. You do not need to wait until the person is on his or her actual deathbed; it is better to do it sooner, so the person can experience the grace that comes with receiving the sacrament. The other time is if someone is seriously ill or advanced in years. Many people receive the sacrament before surgery or before receiving chemical or radiation therapies. There is no limit to the number of times you can receive the sacrament, so if the illness gets worse, do not be afraid to ask to receive the sacrament again.

Only a priest or bishop can administer the sacrament of Anointing of the Sick. You may need to take the initiative to contact a priest by checking with the chaplain of the hospital or by calling your parish. In today's large parishes, priests may not always know who is ill or in the hospital. The actual rite of the sacrament is quite simple. The priest uses the **oil of the sick,** which has been blessed by the bishop (or if none is available, the priest can bless the oil himself), and anoints the sick person on the forehead and on the hands. He also says this prayer of healing:

> Through this holy anointing
> may the Lord in his love and mercy help you
> with the grace of the Holy Spirit.
> May the Lord who frees you from sin
> save you and raise you up.
>   (*The Rites of the Catholic Church,* volume 1, page 784)

Did You Know?

Wake Services

When someone dies, those who were close to her or him grieve the loss. Death leaves a hole in people's lives. The Church's ministry to those who grieve is one of gently accompanying them on their journey through sorrow to hope. One formal way this is done is through a wake service, or as it is officially known, a **vigil for the deceased.** In the days before the funeral, family and friends gather at the funeral home or the home of the deceased. The service consists of readings from the Scriptures, intercessory prayers, silent prayer, and a blessing. It may also include a homily, music, sharing of memories, and other elements, according to the wishes of the family.

The next time someone you know dies, attend the wake service. It is one way to celebrate the person's life, comfort the family, and witness to your belief in Christ's Resurrection.

Sometimes the sacrament of Anointing of the Sick is received during a healing Mass. When this is done, the anointing takes place after the liturgy of the word and before the liturgy of the Eucharist.

For Further Reflection

○ Think about the last time you received the sacrament of Penance and Reconciliation. What did it feel like to tell your sins to the priest and receive absolution?

○ How often do you go to confession? What stops you from going more often? What would be the benefits of doing so?

○ Think about people in your family who are seriously ill, facing surgery, or reaching old age. How could the sacrament of Anointing of the Sick help those people and your family?

20

Sacraments at the Service of Communion

When people ask, "What do you want to do when you graduate?" the usual answer is, "I want to be a teacher (or a doctor, or get into politics, and so on)." These answers have to do with your career, the kind of work you do. It is important to find a career that makes use of your gifts and interests. But in listening to God's call, you will find a deeper question about the vocation you are being called to. A **vocation** is the committed state of life that God calls us to. Are you called to be married? to be single? to become a priest or deacon? to be a member of a religious community?

All these vocation choices are ways in which we serve God and one another. Two of these vocations—married life and the priesthood, or diaconate—the Church recognizes as having been instituted by Christ, and thus as sacraments of the

Words to Look For

- vocation
- sacraments at the service of Communion
- Holy Orders
- ordained ministers or clergy
- priesthood of the faithful
- bishop
- priest (presbyter)
- permanent deacons
- marriage (Matrimony)
- annulment

193

Church. These sacraments are known as the **sacraments at the service of Communion.** In the Roman Catholic Church, you can be called to one or the other, but not both (unless you are a permanent deacon—more about that later). And some people are called to neither marriage nor the priesthood, or diaconate, but to a different vocational choice.

The Origins of the Priesthood

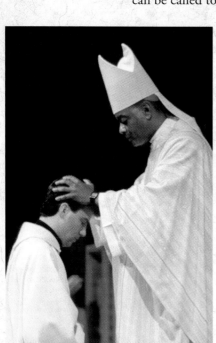

The origins of the priesthood go back to the Old Testament. One of the tribes of ancient Israel, the tribe of Levi, was set apart for priestly service (Numbers 3:5–10). Their role was to stay with the ark of the Covenant and to offer the required sacrifices for the people's sins. Later, after Solomon built the first Temple, their duties included leading the prayers and sacrifices offered at the Temple and interpreting the Law of the Old Covenant. They continued this role into the time of Christ.

A man receives the sacrament of Holy Orders in a ceremony called an ordination. An ordination is an occasion of great joy for the whole Church.

During his earthly ministry, Jesus was never identified as a priest. But after his Resurrection, the Apostles understood that everything the priesthood of the Old Testament pointed toward, found its fulfillment in Jesus Christ. He is the "one mediator between God and humankind" (1 Timothy 2:5). "Unlike the other high priests, he has no need to offer sacrifices day after day, first for his own sins, and then for those of the people; this he did once for all when he offered himself" (Hebrews 7:27). For these reasons the early Church recognized that "Christ came as a high priest of the good things that have come" (Hebrews 9:11).

In the Acts of the Apostles and the letters of the New Testament, the Apostles took leadership roles in the early Christian community. They started new communities of Christians in major cities, and were seen to represent Christ in the early communities. The successors to the Apostles became known as bishops, a word meaning "overseer." To help with needed works of service, the Apostles began to choose men of certain qualities to assist them (Acts 6:1–6). Eventually these assistants became known as deacons, taken from the Greek word meaning "service." The First Letter to Timothy, which was written thirty to sixty years after the Resurrection of Christ, gives the qualifications needed for bishops and deacons (3:1–13), indicating that these had become established ministries in the Church.

The development of the order of priests is a little less clear in the Scriptures. We do know that in the early years, the first Christians gathered in people's homes to share the Eucharist. An elder in the community often led these gatherings. These elders were also called presbyters (from the Greek word for "elder"). They assisted the bishops with their work, and gradually, over time, this role became an established ministry in the Church. The presbyters were also called priests, because as celebrants of the Eucharist, they represented Christ, the high priest.

Before we look further at the role of bishops, priests, and deacons in the Church today, we need to clarify some language. The sacrament is called **Holy Orders** because it is a way of consecrating (designating and making holy) people for the three orders (categories) of ministry in the Church: bishops, priests, and deacons. The rite of the sacrament of Holy Orders is also called ordination. Those who have received the sacrament are called **ordained ministers or clergy.** Sometimes the particular role (bishop, priest, or deacon) is called their office.

Ministries of Ordained Ministers

All baptized people share in the priesthood of Christ by virtue of their Baptism. As the First Letter of Peter says, "Let yourselves be built into a spiritual house, to be a holy priesthood" (2:5). The Church calls this the

Diocesan and Religious Priests

You may not have realized that two kinds of priests serve the Church. The vast majority are diocesan priests, who make promises of celibacy and of obedience to their bishop and who serve the Church within a particular diocese. They cannot leave that diocese to serve in another diocese without special permission. Most parish priests are diocesan priests.

Other priests are members of religious communities (like Benedictines, Franciscans, Jesuits, and Dominicans), and take vows of poverty, chastity, and obedience to their religious superior. All religious orders developed in response to what their founders perceived as the needs of the Church at a particular time in history. See articles about Saint Benedict (page 341), Saint Dominic (page 289), Saint Francis (page 73), and Saint Ignatius (page 131) for more information about the founders of some religious orders for men. Religious priests may be involved in ministries all over the world, and often live a simple lifestyle in community. Some of them also serve as parish pastors with the permission of the local bishop, but they serve in other dioceses and other ministries as determined by their religious community.

common **priesthood of the faithful.** Within this common priesthood, some people are called to unique participation in the mission of Christ through the sacrament of Holy Orders.

Discerning Your Vocation

Have you ever wondered if God is calling you? The answer is, "Yes!" Through Baptism God calls everyone—to ministry, to holiness, to Christian witness.

Here's a harder question: How can you figure out what vocation God is calling you to? Although a foolproof recipe for discerning your vocation hasn't been discovered yet, we do know many of the necessary ingredients:

- Trust that God wants you to discover your vocation. God has planted his call within your heart, and you simply need to be faithful in discovering it. Be honest about your deepest feelings, and do not be afraid of the vocation you are attracted to.
- Look for clues in things that you are attracted to. Do you enjoy being part of a community of people who are dedicated to God? You should take a good look at religious life. Do you love to be with children and cannot imagine not having children of your own? It is probable that marriage is your vocation.
- Serve God in any way you can. Try out different ministries in the Church: liturgical ministries, catechetical (teaching) ministries, ministries of charity and social action. These will help you discover your gifts and interests.
- Spend time with people you admire. Learn from them what a religious sister is about, what the ministry of a deacon entails, how a married couple live out their faith together.

Their role is to serve the Christian community in the name of Christ, and to represent Christ in the community. Because Christ is the head of the Church, this means that ordained ministers exercise a leadership role in the liturgy and in community life.

The role that bishops, priests, and deacons play in community life does not make them more important in the eyes of God than any other person. Nor does it mean that they are holier than laypeople—God calls us all to lives of perfect holiness according to our vocation. However, the priesthood of the men called to ordained ministry is different in its essence from the common priesthood of all the baptized. It isn't that they have *more* priesthood than the laity. They have a *different* priesthood, one that gives them unique responsibilities that no layperson can fulfill. These unique responsibilities fall into three areas: teaching, divine worship (the liturgy), and Church leadership or governance.

As our brief history has already pointed out, three degrees of Holy Orders have existed from the beginning of the Church: bishops, priests (presbyters), and deacons. All three ministries are necessary for the effective functioning of the Church; without any one of these ministries, the Church would be incomplete.

The **bishop** receives the fullness of the responsibilities of Holy Orders. Through the bishop's ordination rite, he becomes a successor to the original Apostles and takes on all the responsibilities that Christ entrusted to them. He becomes a member of the college of bishops, so that with his brother bishops, he must lead the entire Church in union with the Pope. But a bishop is uniquely responsible for the diocese that he has been designated to lead as chief shepherd. Only the bishop can ordain priests. The bishop is the ordinary minister for Confirmation. He blesses the sacred oils that are used in the sacraments by all the parishes in the diocese. The bishop is the chief catechist (teacher) of the diocese, and is responsible for ensuring that the Catholic faith is correctly taught. Through the diocesan offices, the bishop provides support and direction for parish and diocesan ministries.

When the bishop ordains a **priest,** he is extending a portion of his apostolic authority to the priest. This makes the priest a coworker with the bishop of the diocese. All the priests of a diocese, united with the bishop, are called the presbyterium of the diocese. The presbyterium is responsible for the spiritual life of the diocese. The bishop assigns each priest to a particular parish or diocesan ministry, and the priest is responsible for leading it in the name of the bishop. Priests can celebrate all the sacraments except Confirmation (unless given special permission) and Holy Orders.

The ministry of deacons is different from that of priests. A deacon is ordained for works of service and liturgical ministry, as directed by the bishop. They may or may not be assigned to a parish. A deacon assists the bishop and priests with the celebration of the Eucharist, including the proclamation of the Gospel, giving homilies, and distributing Holy Communion. Deacons can also baptize, bless marriages, and preside over funerals. But they also dedicate themselves to works of charity and compassion in the community. The Church has both transitional deacons

Looking Back

Transitional and Permanent Deacons

In the early Church, people with special roles of service were called deacons or deaconesses. Deacons assisted the bishops in works of charity and in the celebration of the Eucharist. When Baptism by immersion was common, deaconesses assisted female candidates for Baptism. By the sixth century, the role of deaconesses had died out and the order of deacons had also died out as a permanent life state. Rather than being an official order in and of itself, the diaconate was made part of the process of becoming a priest. Even today this is true. Transitional deacons are men who are ordained as deacons on their way to being ordained as priests. You may have had a transitional deacon serve in your parish as his last step before being ordained a priest.

In 1967 the Second Vatican Council restored the diaconate as a permanent order in the Church. Following years of preparation and study, men who are ordained deacons can baptize, preach, distribute Communion, witness marriages, preside at wakes and funerals, and engage in works of service to the Christian community. Permanent deacons must be at least thirty-five years old and may be married or celibate. Deacons presently serve in every state in the United States. They serve in nearly every diocese of the country as well. More than one in five ordained Catholic clergy in the United States are permanent deacons. You may have a permanent deacon at your parish.

and permanent deacons (see the article "Transitional and Permanent Deacons," on page 197). **Permanent deacons** may be single or married; however, if they are single when they are ordained, they promise to remain single, and if they are married when ordained, they promise not to remarry if their spouse should pass away.

The Rite of Ordination

There are three different ordination rites (rituals) corresponding to the three ordained ministries. The bishop is the ordinary minister for all three rites. The essential symbol for all three rites is the bishop laying his hands on the man to be ordained and praying that he receives the graces of the Holy Spirit necessary for his ministry.

In addition, when a bishop is ordained, he receives the book of the Gospels as a sign of his authority to teach the truth, a ring to signify marriage to the Church, a miter (the unique pointed hat) to represent authority, and a shepherd's staff to symbolize that he is to model his leadership after Jesus, the good shepherd. When a priest is ordained, he is clothed in the special vestments of his office (see the article "Liturgical Clothing and Colors," on page 179), his hands are anointed with oil, and he is presented with a paten (plate) and chalice (cup) as a sign of his role in the Eucharist. The ordination of a deacon also includes being clothed in special vestments, and he receives the book of the Gospels to symbolize his ministry of preaching.

Like Baptism and Confirmation, the sacrament of Holy Orders imprints a permanent character upon a person's soul. Thus an ordination can never be repeated. More important, though, an ordained person never loses the powers he receives. So, for example, a priest who has been released from his responsibilities and is free to marry can give the sacrament of Anointing of the Sick to a dying person in an emergency when no other priest is available.

Saint John Baptist de La Salle is the patron saint of Saint Mary's Press, the publisher of this book. His life inspires us in our commitment to educate the whole person, serve poor people, and help teens find God in everyday life.

The Catholic Church ordains only baptized men because Jesus chose men, not women, to be his Apostles, and the Apostles did the same when they chose the ones to share in their ministry. For this reason the Church is bound by Jesus' choice to ordain only men. The Magisterium of the Church has consistently upheld that this practice is part of the Tradition that has been revealed by God and cannot be changed by human beings.

The Roman Catholic Church also has a discipline of priestly celibacy. This means that the priests and bishops promise never to marry, so they can be free to focus their attention and energy on their ministry in the Church. It means a total commitment to God and the Body of Christ. Priestly celibacy is a human law and is not required by God. For example, many Eastern Catholic Churches permit their priests to marry (but not their bishops).

Marriage in the Bible

From the beginning the Bible teaches that **marriage (Matrimony)** is part of God's plan. We read in Genesis, "The LORD God said: 'It is not good that the man should be alone; I will make a helper as his partner'" (2:18). God created men and women so that the two sexes would be a complement to each other and form a natural union in which love might be shared. God wants this union to be fruitful and lead to new life, according to his command, "Be fruitful and multiply, and fill the earth and subdue it" (Genesis 1:28). The fact that some form of marriage exists in all cultures testifies that it is a desire God has placed within the human heart.

The importance and beauty of married love is found throughout the Old Testament. The Law of the Old Covenant carries severe

Saintly Profiles

Saint John Baptist de La Salle (1651–1719)

Saint John Baptist de La Salle was born to a wealthy family in northern France at a time when education was reserved for the rich. He was ordained a priest in 1678, and got involved in teaching almost by chance. He was uncomfortable around poor people, but he came to see that providing a quality education for poor children was his mission from God. At first he just recruited teachers for poor children and helped to train them. Later he formed a community of teachers, the Brothers of the Christian Schools (also known as Christian Brothers), and gave away his wealth to live with them.

Saint John Baptist de La Salle integrated prayer and the Gospels into all aspects of school life, and encouraged his students to live in God's presence. Every half hour a bell would ring and someone would announce, "Let us remember that we are in the holy presence of God." He taught his followers to look for God's purpose in their life and to see every event through the eyes of faith. He saw teaching and every act of service as a way to pray. As Saint John Baptist de La Salle experimented with effective techniques, he introduced methods like classroom teaching and individual reports about students' progress that are considered common practice today. He was canonized in 1900, and named the patron saint of schoolteachers in 1950. His feast day is April 7.

penalties for adultery and other sins against marriage. The faithful love in the Books of Ruth and Tobit are inspirational examples of the goodness of marriage. And the love poetry in the Song of Solomon has always been considered symbolic of the passionate love that God has for the chosen people and for the Church. In fact, some of the prophets speak of God's love for Israel being like a bridegroom's love for his bride (Isaiah 62:2–5).

The miracle at the wedding feast of Cana is one of the biblical stories that shows Christ blessing married life. How have you seen the holiness of marriage?

This positive attitude toward marriage is carried over into the New Testament. Jesus' first public miracle in the Gospel of John is at a wedding feast (2:1–12). The Church places great importance on this story as a confirmation by the Lord of the goodness of marriage and its place in God's plan. In Jesus' own teaching, he emphasized the permanence of marriage as something willed by God. Further, he said that the only reason divorce was allowed in the Law of Moses was because of their hardness of heart (Matthew 19:3–9). Through his support of and teaching about marriage, Christ made matrimony one of the seven sacraments.

But Christ does not place this demand on us—the demand to stay married without divorce—without also providing the grace needed to live it. Christ gives us the power through the Holy Spirit to live in a permanently committed love relationship. The same power that unites Christ and the Church also unites a wife and husband. This is what Saint Paul meant in the Letter to the Ephesians:

> Husbands, love your wives, just as Christ loved the church and gave himself up for her. . . . In the same way, husbands should love their wives as they do their own bodies. . . . For no one ever hates his own body, but he nourishes and tenderly cares for it, just as Christ does for the church, because we are members of his body. . . . This is a great mystery, and I am applying it to Christ and the church. (5:25–32)

Thus the Bible teaches us that the sacrament of Matrimony (another word for marriage) signifies the union of Christ and the Church. The permanent nature of the marriage union symbolizes God's unending love for all humanity. The sacrament gives a husband and wife the grace to love each other as Christ loves the Church. It strengthens their unity, makes them a sign of God's love in the world, and helps the couple perfect their holiness on their journey to eternal life.

The Meaning of Married Love

A sacramental marriage has several meanings. First, a marriage is intended to bring unity between the spouses. This doesn't mean that they agree on every single thing or that they have to like all the same things. This unity is the underlying understanding that no matter what happens in their lives, they will always love and cherish each other. They will have no other person come between them. A marriage is also meant to be indissoluble, that is, the spouses are committed to each other until "death do us part."

Finally, a marriage is intended to be open to new life. Children are part of God's plan, and married couples must be open to having children. True love is not closed in on itself, it is open to new life. A married couple that refuses to have children is rejecting God's supreme gift. Not every married couple can have children, and those marriages will be fruitful in other ways.

If you understand these meanings of the sacrament of Matrimony, it becomes clearer why certain acts are sins against marriage. Adultery and polygamy (more than one spouse) are both sins against the unity of marriage. Divorcing your lawful spouse and marrying another person is a sin against the indissolubility (permanence) of marriage. Artificial contraception is a sin against the openness to new life.

A person who divorces a living, lawful spouse and marries another person is living in direct contradiction to the law of

Pray It!

Anniversary Prayer

Just like weddings, anniversaries are times to pray and rejoice. Here is a prayer you can pray for your parents or other couples you know who are celebrating an anniversary:

Dear God,
Bless _____ and _____ on their anniversary.
In their love for each other, they reveal your love to the world.
Give them grace to live out their marriage covenant,
provide them with strength when times are hard,
and shower them with joy in the company of family and friends.
Open their eyes to the gifts you have given them
in order to serve you by serving others.
May they enjoy many more years together,
growing closer to each other and to you.
May they love and honor each other all the days of their lives. Amen.

God as taught by Christ. Although that person is not separated from the Church, he or she cannot in good conscience receive Holy Communion.

An **annulment** is not the same thing as a divorce. An annulment is a special decree granted by the Church, after closely examining the circumstances, declaring that a particular union was not a sacramental marriage. The judges granting the decree have determined that an impediment, or obstacle, was present at the time of the marriage, preventing the free and full consent by one or both spouses. A person who has received an annulment is free to receive Holy Communion and to marry again in the Church.

A sacramental marriage isn't about just the two people who are getting married. God intends for the love of a husband and wife to be life giving for their families and for the rest of their community.

The Rite of Matrimony

To be married a couple must both wish to be married and have no obstacles to prevent them from giving their free and full consent. Pregnancy, mental illness, a secret addiction could all be obstacles that prevent free and full consent. This is one reason why the Church requires a period of preparation that often includes some type of assessment to help determine a couple's readiness. Free consent is very important for a couple to have a faithful and fruitful marriage.

Although some people might prefer to get married privately, with just the spouses exchanging vows before a justice of the peace, that is not a sacramental marriage. The Church requires that weddings take place in the Church before witnesses that represent the Christian community. Having the wedding in the Church establishes its religious dimension. And having a public celebration emphasizes that a Christian marriage is a public state of life. The married couple represents God's love to the community as well as to each other. For this reason the sacrament of Matrimony is ideally celebrated as part of a Mass, although it isn't required.

In a Catholic wedding, the spouses are the ministers of the sacrament. The essential sacramental sign is the exchange of vows, thereby expressing the couple's consent before the whole Church. The priest or deacon witnesses the marriage as a representative of the Church, but he is not the minister of the sacrament. Other elements of the marriage rite include the liturgy of the word (even if the marriage is not held as part of the Eucharist), the exchange of rings, and the nuptial (marriage) blessing.

The sacrament of Matrimony is the foundation for the Christian family. The Christian family is the place where children first learn the love of God through the love of their parents. The family is the domestic Church, or the Church of the home. Families need to work together to be little communities of God's love and of prayer, to practice Christian virtues, and to serve those who are in need. In this way family life becomes the basis for the life of the Church, in keeping with God's plan!

For Further Reflection

- Think of all the different responsibilities that deacons, priests, and bishops have. Which ones do you think would be the most enjoyable? Which ones do you think would be the most difficult? Ask your pastor or another priest what he likes best about his vocation.
- Think about two people that you believe have a good marriage. What makes their marriage a good one?

Part C

Christian
Morality

I am the LORD your God: you shall not have strange Gods before me.
You shall not take the name of the LORD your God in vain.
Remember to keep holy the LORD's Day.
Honor your father and your mother.
You shall not kill.
You shall not commit adultery.
You shall not steal.
You shall not bear false witness against your neighbor.
You shall not covet your neighbor's wife.
You shall not covet your neighbor's goods.

(CCC, pages 496–497)

21

Introduction to Christian Morality

Have you ever thought about how many decisions you make in the course of a day? Getting out of bed, deciding what to wear, hanging out with your friends, doing your homework, and chatting with your family all involve decisions. Fortunately most of our decisions are habits that come easily and don't require much thought. If we had to scrutinize every decision we make in the course of a day, we wouldn't get much done! Every decision we make has a right or a wrong value, even if we rarely think of it that way.

Go back for a moment to your decision to get up this morning. Waking up may not have been your conscious choice, but the decision you made to stay awake and start your day has a right or a wrong implication. What if you refused to get up and get going? How would that have been a right or a wrong decision?

When we venture into the territory of deciding between right and wrong, we are talking about **morality,** "the goodness

Words to Look For

- morality
- Beatitudes
- free will
- conscience
- mortal sin
- venial sins
- vices
- virtues

or evil of human acts" (*CCC,* page 888). Morality can be a sensitive subject. Who decides what is moral: the Church? the government? the family? individuals? Some people would say that morality is just a matter of personal opinion.

Living in a society with freedom of speech and freedom of religion means that many voices are clamoring for our attention, suggesting different moral attitudes and actions. Undoubtedly people, culture, and the events in our life shape our morality. But God's gift of free will means that we have the ability to make conscious choices. So our question is, "How do we live the right way?" which for Catholics means, "How does God want me to live?"

Fortunately we have the Scriptures and Tradition to help answer that question. Although these sources of God's Revelation do not provide easy or precise answers to every situation, they include principles, guidelines, and rules that come from thousands of years of human experience. The Catholic Church has been a strong moral voice throughout history, and becoming familiar with what the Church teaches about morality can help us to "do the right thing." In this chapter we will look at some foundational principles for making good moral decisions.

Living as a Beatitude Person

The foundation of morality, of doing the right thing, is found in the first chapter of Genesis: We are made in the image of God, "God created humankind in his image, / in the image of God he created them; / male and female he created them" (1:27). From the moment you were conceived, you were made in God's image, meaning that you—and every other person on earth—are first and

Do the Right Thing

Q. One of my teammates told me that the brand of basketball shoes our team is required to wear is made at a factory run by people who underpay and mistreat the workers. I want to respond to this injustice. But I also want to play on the team, which means wearing the shoes. Am I morally wrong to do so?

A. Let's evaluate this situation by looking at the three sources of morality: (1) the action you want to do, (2) your intention, and (3) your circumstances. Let's look at the action—is it fundamentally right or wrong? It is hard to see how using something that was created in a system that mistreats people can be a good thing, so the action must be judged to be wrong. So, although you have a good intention—being on the team—the choice is still wrong. The final question revolves around your circumstances. Is any force taking away your freedom to make this decision? You are probably under some strong peer pressure, but it is hoped that you have the will to resist.

It would seem that your only moral choice is to refuse to wear the shoes. Explain your moral position to your coach, and maybe she will make an exception. Maybe the whole team will join your protest. This is the way the world becomes a better place, starting with one person refusing to cooperate with sin.

foremost essentially good. When we choose wisely, we are acting in accordance with our true nature. This is why doing the right thing ultimately makes us happy.

Happiness is not determined by what we normally see in magazines, on television, or in the movies. Our source of happiness is not material success, fame, or unending hours of leisure and pleasure. Rather, what God intends for us is complete joy and a sense of well-being. Our ultimate destiny is to be eternally happy with God in heaven.

Jesus gives us a glimpse of this destiny in the **Beatitudes** (Matthew 5:3–12 and Luke 6:20–26). *Beatitude* means "perfect happiness or blessedness." Jesus describes Beatitude people with statements like, "Blessed are the poor in spirit, for theirs is the kingdom of heaven." These statements are at the heart of Jesus' message (*CCC*, number 1716). They help us to understand what being a Christian is all about, so that one day we will share God's eternal life (*CCC*, number 1717).

Jesus taught about morality by using parables, such as the parable about the good Samaritan (Luke 10:25–37), illustrated here by Vincent Van Gogh. What is Jesus teaching us about who our neighbor is through the story of the good Samaritan?

Being made in God's image does not make us perfect; God gave us a soul, intellect, and **free will** to make our own choices. Although God wants each of us to be part of the Kingdom that Jesus spoke about, free will means that we have the freedom to accept or reject God's will. Adam and Eve exercised this freedom in the second Creation story, found in chapter 3 of Genesis. They chose to go against God's plan for them to live in harmony with all that God had created. They experienced the same choice that all humans have had to face: whether or not to do good and avoid evil.

Adam and Eve's decision to eat the forbidden fruit affected you, everyone who came before you, and those who will come after you. Their decision left us with a tendency to do the wrong thing, despite the promptings of our conscience. This inclination to choose evil and make moral mistakes is called original sin. (For a thorough explanation of original sin, see chapter 5, The Human Person.)

This is the dilemma each person faces. God created us in his image with a natural desire to follow the moral law, to do good and avoid evil. At the same time, because of original sin, we are inclined toward sin, or choosing to do the wrong thing. The ability to use reason to distinguish between right and wrong is the work of our conscience. Our **conscience** is the interior voice that helps us to know right from wrong and then to act on that knowledge. We will talk more about the role of conscience in chapter 23, Sources of Moral Truth.

Moral development never stops, no matter how old we get, until we reach our final glorious destiny with God in heaven. The Scriptures and Church Tradition are our roadmap on this lifelong journey. The Beatitudes give us Jesus' vision for how to build a moral life. Being poor in spirit, merciful, and pure of heart describe the kind of person that Jesus was, and the kind of person we are called to be.

The world tells us that it's not cool to be meek (gentle and humble) or to stand up for what we know to be just and true or to act as peacemakers. But no matter what the world says, Jesus emphasizes the importance of these attitudes. He calls them blessed because they help us find the true happiness that God created us to enjoy.

Looking Back

Words of Wisdom from John Paul II

To be truly free does not at all mean doing everything that pleases me, or doing what I want to do. . . . To be truly free means to use one's own freedom for what is a true good.
(Pope John Paul II, *Dilecti Amici*)

Human Freedom and Moral Choice

Did you ever stand in front of the refrigerator with the door wide open, staring at its contents? You know you want something, but you don't really know what. You try a slice of leftover pizza. That doesn't quite do it, so you go for a bowl of the triple-fudge-ripple ice cream with marshmallow fluff. After eating that you're full, but still not quite satisfied. You want— and need—something more.

The same is true of our need for God. It is easy when living in the wealthiest nation in the world to try to satisfy our yearning for God with worldly values, like having lots of things, keeping ourselves constantly busy, or finding a boyfriend or girlfriend. If Adam and Eve had a tough time resisting their forbidden fruit, imagine how much more

Pray It!

Examination of Conscience

Use the following questions to evaluate how you are doing with your moral decision making.

1. Is my heart set on God, so that I love him above all things? Or am I more concerned about the things of this world?
2. Do I have a genuine love for other people, whether or not I like them?
3. Have I contributed to the well-being of my family by patience and genuine love?
4. Do I share my possessions with those who are less fortunate?
5. Does my life reflect the mission I received in Baptism, that is, to be a disciple of Jesus?
6. Am I concerned for the good and prosperity of the human community, or do I care for only myself?
7. Have I been truthful and fair, or have I injured others by lying and cheating?
8. Have I done physical or emotional violence to others?
9. Have I kept myself chaste and pure, especially by avoiding pornography and all sexual activity before marriage?
10. If I have been injured, have I been ready to forgive, or do I harbor the desire for revenge?
11. In my life choices, am I led by the hope of eternal life?
12. Have I tried to grow spiritually by regular attendance at Mass, through prayer, meditating on the Scriptures, receiving the sacraments, and living simply?
13. How have I used my time, my health, and the gifts God has given me? Have I fallen into the trap of alcohol or other drug use?

(Adapted from The Rites of the Catholic Church, volume 1, pages 625–628)

challenged we are by thousands of messages that tell us true happiness can be found in the kind of car we drive, or the fashions or gadgets we "gotta have." The restless pursuit of popularity, pleasure, or prestige gets in the way of the authentic happiness that God promises.

But that's where our free will comes in. We can consciously choose the truly good life. Unlike animals whose instinct drives their actions, we can think about the moral aspects of our behavior both before and after we act. Of course, this gift of human freedom has a flip side. We are also responsible for the choices we make. Freedom and responsibility go hand in hand. Getting a driver's license gives you a greater degree of freedom to get places on your own, but it also means increased responsibility for your own safety as well as for the safety of others. Safe driving requires knowledge of traffic rules, but it also requires using your reasoning skills to recognize and avoid dangers that may not be covered in the drivers' handbook.

Moral freedom and responsibility are similar to the process of learning to drive. At first it is your parents and other adults who drive your moral decisions, teaching you right from wrong, getting you to the point where you can make those decisions on your own. As they let go and let you practice making your own choices, they expect that you will be able to respond to situations in the right way. As you become capable of assuming freedom and the accompanying responsibility, you accept the credit or the blame for the choices you make. If you choose a sinful course of action, you must also accept the blame. You must admit that you knowingly and deliberately did something wrong.

Although we are responsible for our actions, some factors may lessen the blame when we choose the wrong course of action. If you are obeying all the traffic laws and an accident happens due to the actions of another driver, you are not at fault. Fear can drive us to do bad things we would not otherwise think of doing. Likewise, psychological problems or the difficult circumstances of our life may also lessen the moral responsibility that we would normally have to accept for our actions. Even courts of law take into account mitigating circumstances and recognize the mental state of some people who commit terrible crimes.

Although circumstances may weaken our ability to choose good over evil, freedom—and the responsibility that comes with it—cannot be taken away. God has built it into us. Our freedom, however, does not give us the right to say or do anything we please. "If it feels good, do it" may make a clever slogan, but living that way is irresponsible, and can lead to sinful choices that will ultimately hurt others and ourselves.

What Makes Something Moral?

Three factors determine the morality of any human action: (1) whether the action itself is inherently good or evil, (2) the intention of the person doing the action, and (3) the circumstances of the action. All three of these elements help determine whether a particular act is good or bad. This all sounds rather complicated, but it really is a simple formula. A morally good act requires that the action be good (or morally neutral), that your intention be good, and that no circumstances exist that diminish your freedom to decide. Therefore we can't judge the morality of someone's action only by the act itself, or by considering only the intention or circumstances—we must take into account all three elements.

The Seven Deadly Sins

Church teaching identifies and cautions against seven particularly harmful sins. They are sometimes referred to as "capital" sins—meaning "most serious or influential"—because they lead to and reinforce all sorts of other sinful actions, thoughts, and omissions. The sins are deadly in that they increase our tendency to sin and cause us to turn away more and more from God. For example, the capital sin of envy can lead to spreading rumors about people who have more than you do or to lying or stealing to get the things you want. Here is a list of the seven deadly sins with present-day definitions:

- **Pride.** Believing you are better than others, often resulting in despising or disrespecting other people
- **Avarice (greed).** Greediness; hoarding money and things
- **Envy.** Resentment that we direct at others who have some success, thing, or privilege that we want for ourselves
- **Wrath.** Strong anger that makes us want to seek revenge and prevents reconciliation
- **Lust.** Undisciplined, unchecked desire for self-enjoyment, especially of a sexual nature
- **Gluttony.** Excessive eating or drinking
- **Sloth.** Habitual laziness; failing to put forth effort and take action

Do you struggle with any of these sins? Have you noticed in your own experience that these seven sins make it hard to resist other sins?

Let's use murder as an extreme example. We know that the act of killing another person is objectively wrong; it is an inherently bad act. However, your intention and the circumstances can create a situation in which this inherently bad act is morally justifiable. For example, if in self-defense you kill a person who is attacking you or another innocent person, your action is morally justified. Your direct intention was not to murder the other person but to keep the person from harming you or another innocent person. Because your intention was good, your action is morally justifiable.

What about doing the right thing for the wrong reasons? Signing up for your youth group's annual ski trip is a good thing to do—unless your intent is to make it a wild weekend of partying and breaking the rules. When your motivation is wrong, the good act is no longer a good decision.

In this icon of Saint Edith Stein, notice how the barbed wire turns into a rose stem and ends as a beautiful rose. How is this symbolic of how Edith Stein lived and how she died?

Of course, circumstances or good intentions can never justify some acts. A person cannot commit an evil act so that good can come from it. Rape would be one example of something that is always wrong. Being drunk, feeling pressured by circumstances, or just wanting it at the time will never make such an act morally right. Rape is an evil that violates your own humanity as well as the dignity of the other person. Another more typical example would be physical or verbal bullying. Although it may enhance your own social standing, it is not morally right. Ever.

Sin

Discussing morality in a theoretical way can help us make good decisions, but at the heart of this discussion are real relationships. When we choose to do wrong instead of doing good, we commit sin, and we hurt our relationship with our self, with others, and with God. Sin is any word that we speak, action that we perform, or desire that we have that is contrary to the law that God has inscribed in our heart at the very moment we are conceived. When we sin we reject God's will for us to be good; like Adam and Eve, we are guilty of disobedience. When we sin we are not following the example of Jesus, who was obedient to God in all things.

It may seem like most sin hurts only the sinner, but even the most private acts have a social dimension. Let's take pornography as an example. Who is that hurting, you ask? Well, if you are male, pornography will affect the way that you view women in your life. You will begin to judge them based on their physical attractiveness rather than on who they are as people. It will be easier to lust after women as objects for your pleasure rather than as people with whom to have a real relationship. Over time it will affect the women in your life, as you lose the ability to relate in healthy, positive ways. If you take the time to reflect on any sin, it becomes obvious how it negatively affects you, your relationships with others, and ultimately your relationship with God.

There are different kinds of sin. A **mortal sin** is a serious offense against God, one that destroys the virtue of charity within us, which helps us to love God and our neighbor. A mortal sin involves serious immoral acts, or what the Church calls "grave matter." The Ten Commandments specify the issues that constitute grave matter. Jesus referred to the Ten Commandments when he spoke to the rich young man who asked him how to inherit eternal life (Mark 10:19). Jesus implied to the young man that these sins, if unrepented, would keep us from eternal life. This is the reason they are called mortal sins; *mortal* means "death," and these sins have the power to cause eternal death, that is, eternal separation from God.

Mortal sin also requires full knowledge and complete consent on the part of the person committing the seriously wrong act. We must know how wrong an action is, and then

Saintly Profiles

Saint Edith Stein (1891–1942)

Edith Stein was born to a Jewish family in Breslau, Germany (now Wroclaw, Poland). As a teenager she turned away from Judaism and professed atheism. Years later, after becoming a noted philosopher, Stein was drawn to Catholic thought. Her reading of the autobiography of Teresa of Ávila influenced her greatly. After closing the book, she remarked to herself, "This is the truth." Stein was baptized in the Catholic Church in 1922. In 1933 she joined a religious community, the Carmelites at Cologne, and took the name Teresa Benedicta of the Cross.

In the late 1930s, because Hitler was in power and anti-Jewish sentiment was on the rise, Stein left Germany and sought refuge in the Netherlands, but her safety was short-lived. During World War II, the Nazi government ordered that all Christians of Jewish descent living in the Netherlands be rounded up for resettlement. Stein, along with her sister, who also converted from Judaism, was arrested and then gassed to death at Auschwitz. She was canonized in October 1998, and has been named a co–patron saint of Europe. Her feast day is August 9.

deliberately and freely choose to do it. You cannot unintentionally commit a mortal sin. Accidentally seeing a few answers on your classmate's test paper is not a mortal sin. Making specific plans to cheat on the next exam, knowing that it's wrong and then doing so anyway, is a mortal sin against the seventh commandment: You shall not steal.

Venial sins are less serious than mortal sins because they do not destroy our relationship with God. But they do damage it. Venial sins involve a lesser degree of evil, or they may be seriously wrong acts committed without full knowledge of just how wrong they are. A venial sin may involve a seriously wrong act, such as failing to attend Mass on Sunday (a sin against the third commandment), which is lessened by some unintended circumstance, like forgetting to set your alarm.

This illustration is from an instruction for monks living in the sixth century. The monks struggle to ascend to heaven, but sin pulls them off the path. What pulls you away from the path to God?

Venial sins are closely associated with **vices.** Vices are the opposite of **virtues,** which are habits of good actions. When we keep repeating venial sins, we are in danger of forming bad habits, called vices. The danger of developing a vice is that it makes it easier to commit sin without seriously thinking about it. Ultimately this makes it easier to commit mortal sin. Let's return to the example of cheating on a test. Let's say that one day you just didn't have time to study properly, and you "accidentally" see an answer on someone else's test for a question you aren't sure of, and you use it. It worked so well that you repeat this venial sin by copying an answer or two on most tests. You are developing a vice for cheating. Then one day someone offers you a complete test with all the answers, stolen from a teacher's file. This is clearly a serious sin, but the vice you have developed for cheating makes it much harder to turn it down.

Christian morality, then, is being the person God created you to be—a person who chooses to be good. You grow into a moral person by choosing good acts, carefully examining your motives to be sure your intentions are good, and avoiding circumstances that lessen your ability to choose freely. The benefits of choosing to act morally and avoiding sin are greater self-esteem, healthier relationships with others, and a deeper sense of the love of God coming through loud and clear in your life.

For Further Reflection

○ What are some of the most difficult moral issues that you face?

○ How does studying and talking about morality help you to be more aware of right and wrong? Why is it important to have these discussions with other faith-filled Catholics?

Pray It

Dear God

Give me the courage to do right in the face of wrong.
Instill in my heart
a set of values that prompts me to think of others
instead of just myself.
Give me the willingness to
stand up for what I believe in—
not following the crowd.
Give me the strength to
look evil in the eye
and withstand it.
Because I know
with you at my side
all things are possible.

(Theresa Vonderwell, in
More Dreams Alive, page 28)

22 Social Justice

War. Terrorism. Poverty. World hunger. Homelessness.
Pollution. Ecological threats to the planet. Does Christian
morality have anything to say about these issues? Of course it
does. By our very nature, we are social beings, linked to the rest
of humanity whether we like it or not. The choices we make
affect others, even if we are unaware of it. Even the most
private thought or act changes us, and therefore has the potential to affect others. How much more impact do our acts
have on others when thousands or millions of people are
making the same choices? One person driving a gas-guzzling,
polluting automobile will have a small impact, but a million
people doing the same thing will change the world.

In God's infinite wisdom, we came into this world
dependent on those around us, and we will exit this world
having left some great or small impression on the strands of
life. We will be held accountable, not only for the things we

Words to Look For

- ○ society
- ○ social justice
- ○ common good
- ○ social encyclical
- ○ human rights
- ○ human dignity
- ○ human solidarity

do but also for the things we do not do. When it comes to the social impact of our moral decisions, the things we do not do may be as important as the things we do. In this chapter we explore how morality is not just about us but about society as well.

Social Justice

When we say that we are made in the image and likeness of God, it means that we reflect what God is like. But what is God like? One way to answer this question is to examine our belief in the Holy Trinity, the three persons in one God. The Trinity tells us that God isn't just a lone individual; God is a community of persons, living in perfect love and charity. If we are to live out our divine destiny, we must treat one another in a way that resembles the unity of the three persons in one God.

In a famous scene found in all four Gospels, Jesus drives the moneychangers, merchants, and their animals out of the Temple. Through his words and actions, Jesus taught that God has little patience for people who practice hypocrisy and injustice.

Because every human being is made in the image and likeness of God, each person has infinite value. Our relationship with God calls us to be in right relationship with the beings he created in his image and likeness, that is, other people! It doesn't matter whether those people are our best friends or our worst enemies. Our love for God must translate into a love for all people and a commitment to treat them justly.

Recent scientific discoveries support this basic religious belief. Geneticists can now chart the DNA of each person's uniqueness, yet testify to the existence of the common strands of life that link us together. Anthropologists and sociologists know that humans have always been social beings who organize themselves into families, tribes, neighborhoods, and communities. These groups of people that are organically bound together and that go beyond the individuality of any one person are called **society.** The moral principles God calls society to follow and the moral judgments God calls society to make in order to ensure the rights of individuals and groups is called **social justice.**

Did You Know?

Catholic Service Organizations for Charity and Justice

The Catholic Church in the United States has long been a leader in both works of charity and action for justice. Look for information on these organizations in your parish or diocesan office, or on the Internet.

- **Catholic Relief Services** (CRS) assists poor people in other countries with disaster relief. It is one of the largest relief agencies in the world. CRS also sponsors development and self-help projects aimed at the causes of poverty. It educates U.S. Catholics about poverty, and provides tools for getting involved in both charity work and promoting justice. The Web site is *www.catholicrelief.org*.

- **Catholic Campaign for Human Development** addresses the root causes of poverty in the United States, through grants for community self-help projects. These projects have helped create jobs, provide affordable housing, and organize communities to address local injustices. People being helped are involved as decision makers. The Web site is *www.usccb.org/cchd/index.htm*.

- **Catholic Charities** is the largest private network of social services in the United States. A range of direct services is offered, such as counseling, adoption, drug abuse treatment, prison ministry, and refugee assistance. Services are often provided through agencies with names like Catholic Social Services. Justice is addressed through social-policy advocacy. The Web site is *www.catholiccharitiesusa.org*.

Social justice has deep roots in the Bible. The prophets of the Old Testament were outspoken advocates for justice in society. Isaiah prophesied in the Lord's name:

> Is not this the fast that I choose:
>   to loose the bonds of injustice,
>   to undo the thongs of the yoke,
>   to let the oppressed go free,
>   and to break every yoke?
> Is it not to share your bread with the
>   hungry,
>   and bring the homeless poor into your
>   house?
>
> (Isaiah 58:6–7)

And the prophet Amos condemned those who "trample on the poor and take from them levies of grain" and who "afflict the righteous, . . . take a bribe, and push aside the needy in the gate" (Amos 5:11–12).

Jesus, however, was the prophet who most exemplified the values of social justice. He told his disciples: "When you give a banquet, invite the poor, the crippled, the lame, and the blind. And you will be blessed, because they cannot repay you, for you will be repaid at the resurrection" (Luke 14:13–14). He also told the story of the rich man and Lazarus, the poor beggar who sat at the rich man's door. When the rich man died, he was sent to hell because he had ignored the needs of poor Lazarus (Luke 16:19–31).

Finally, when Jesus describes the final judgment in Matthew 25:31–46, he tells how he will separate those who were charitable and just from those who were not. Those who were charitable and just will go to heaven and those who were not are destined for hell. Those who are being sent to hell do not understand why:

"Lord, when was it that we saw you hungry or thirsty or
a stranger or naked or sick or in prison, and did not take
care of you?" Then he will answer them, "Truly I tell you,
just as you did not do it to one of the
least of these, you did not do it to me."
(Matthew 25:44–45)

Jesus is telling us that ignoring social needs is
just the same as causing them.

Social Justice Principles

Catholic social-justice teachings are based on
some key concepts. By applying these
concepts to different social issues, the Church
makes judgments about the correct direction
to follow. In this chapter we will look briefly
at the following four key concepts. In the
chapters that follow you will see how these
concepts affect social issues raised by the Ten
Commandments.

The Common Good

It seems that every day in the news, we
hear stories about murder, theft, child abuse,
and war. We need to remind ourselves that
human beings are essentially good. Consider
the outpouring of love and concern that en-
gulfed the world in the days after the terrorist
attacks on September 11, 2001. Strangers
donated their blood and their money, family
members took stock of their blessings, and
stories of heroism revealed the true nature of
individuals in a society united in a time of
crisis. When conditions exist in society that
allow all people, either as groups or individuals, to reach their human and spiritual fulfillment more fully and more easily, the
common good is achieved. The concept of
the common good is an important element of
all Catholic social teaching.

Pray It!

Praying with Dorothy Day

Dorothy Day was a tireless advocate for justice and for poor
people. She was the cofounder of
the *Catholic Worker*, a newspaper
that began publication in 1933,
and was the basis for a movement
that resulted in houses of hospitality all over the country that were
run by volunteers who were committed to charity and justice.
Today over 185 Catholic Worker
communities remain committed to
nonviolence, voluntary poverty,
prayer, hospitality for the homeless, and protesting injustice, war,
racism, and violence of all forms.
Pray these words of Dorothy Day's,
and reflect on what God asks of
you:

What we would like to do is
change the world—make it a
little simpler for people to feed,
clothe, and shelter themselves
as God intended them to do.
And . . . by fighting for better conditions, by crying out
unceasingly for the rights of the
workers, of the poor, . . . we
can to a certain extent change
the world. . . . We can throw
our pebble in the pond and be
confident that its ever-widening
circle will reach around the
world. . . . Dear God—please
enlarge our hearts to love each
other, to love our neighbor, to
love our enemy as well as our
friend.
(*Dorothy Day, Selected Writings*,
page 98)

It is important that we understand what the common good really means; it isn't just doing the greatest good for the greatest number of people. For example, although it is a good thing to provide electrical power, it would be wrong to do so if it meant exposing even a few people to unsafe radiation. The decision's impact on each and every person must be taken into account.

The sign this Peruvian protestor is carrying says, "One Heart for Social Justice." Why is it important for us to call on our governments and businesses to act justly?

Also the common good is not what is best only for the country we live in. Jesus Christ taught us that every person in the world is our spiritual brother or sister. Our membership in the family of God takes precedence over our allegiance to our country. This is a difficult challenge for those of us living in the United States, where 4 percent of the world's population uses 25 percent of the world's resources and creates 50 percent of the world's pollution. On a much grander scale of global society, we should recognize the importance of creating and supporting institutions that improve the conditions of human life for all.

When any government, whether it is the student government in your school or the representatives of a national government, exercises the authority given to them, they must keep in mind not only the common good of the group but also the way that it is achieved. If authorities make laws that are unjust (even if the outcome may seem good), the people are not morally bound to follow the law. A classic example of unjust laws is the legal system that prevented African Americans from obtaining their human rights. Although lawmakers in the United States at the time thought that such laws were necessary for public order, the means they used were morally wrong. It is clear now that both white and black people were adversely affected by this abuse of power.

Responsibility of Political Authority

Although some people may be cynical about politics and government, the Church teaches that political authority (also called the state) has an important role: to defend and promote the common good of civil society. Political authority is based on human nature, and therefore belongs to the same moral order established by God. In other words, our political leaders have a responsibility from God to make decisions for the common good. They do not have some special God-given right that lets them establish their moral order; they must follow the same moral law that God has implanted within every human being. They must create laws and structures that ensure people's freedom to live moral lives.

Policy makers at all levels of government should ensure that each person has access to the resources needed to lead a truly human life: "food, clothing, health, work, education and culture, suitable information, the right to establish a family, and so on"[1] (*CCC,* number 1908). These needs are often referred to as basic **human rights.**

The United Nations is an institution that recognized these basic human rights in 1948 with the Universal Declaration of Human Rights. Although the world has a long way to go in fulfilling these rights for all people, the Catholic Church strongly supports this document. These are God-given rights, the conditions or things that any person needs to be fully what God created them to be. To achieve these rights for every person in the world, it is critically important that society have organizations like the United Nations to provide for the common good of all.

Human Dignity

Another fundamental concept of social justice calls on us to reflect on the meaning of the Great Commandment: we are to love God and our neighbor as ourselves. As tough as it may be sometimes, we are called to

Looking Back

What Is a Social Encyclical?

An encyclical is an authoritative teaching letter issued by the Pope to the universal Church. It follows in the spirit of the biblical letters of the New Testament. A **social encyclical** addresses issues in society such as social justice, peace, human rights, solidarity, and the common good. Modern popes have issued social encyclicals to challenge us to work together to right the wrongs in the social structures of our world. Following are the names of a few of the social encyclicals and the issues they address. You can find them online at *www.papalencyclicals.net.*

- *On the Condition of Workers (Rerum Novarum),* by Pope Leo XIII in 1891, is the first modern social encyclical. It addresses unjust conditions created by the industrial revolution. It affirms the rights of workers to form unions and the need for just wages and safe working conditions.
- *Peace on Earth (Pacem in Terris),* by Pope John XXIII in 1963, gives a systematic presentation of human rights and corresponding duties. It addresses the problem of war and the conditions for peace. He calls for disarmament and the creation of a world authority to protect the common good.
- *On the Hundredth Anniversary of Rerum Novarum (Centesimus Annus),* by Pope John Paul II, affirms that the social teachings of the Church are an essential part of proclaiming the Gospel, and that the Church makes a preferential option for the poor. It states that the dignity of the human person is central. A strong critique of capitalism is given.

respect and love the other as "another self," whose rights flow from the same source as our own—**human dignity.** The homeless man on the street, the immigrant who crosses our borders illegally, even the prisoners in our jails all share the same human dignity that we have (remember Matthew 25:31–46). Because of this God calls us to consider each and every human being as "another self" (*CCC*, number 1944).

A belief in the equality of all human beings is acknowledged in our country's founding documents. We know in our heart that this belief is true because it flows from the moral law that God placed in every human being. The equality of all people flows from the human dignity we share.

Yet sinful inequalities keep large segments of the human population from obtaining the absolute necessities of life, while others enjoy rich abundance. God did not intend for the world to be this way. With the intellect and free will that we possess, we have the ability to solve local and global problems, as vast and complex as they may be. For the child who is starving, for the mother who cannot survive without medicine, and for the father who cannot find work within his own community, there is a great urgency to eliminate the huge gaps between the rich and the poor. As individuals examine their conscience for their own sinful actions and attitudes, so must society consider the lack of human rights as a grave matter that cannot be put off by telling ourselves that we can do nothing about it, or that it has always been this way.

ELIZABETH SETON.

Née le 28 Août 1774. Morte le à Janvier 1821.

Saint Elizabeth Ann Seton responded to Christ's call to use her wealth to serve poor people. How can you share what you have right now with those who have less?

Human Solidarity

A final key concept in Catholic social teaching is the principle of **human solidarity.** Solidarity means that we are to think in terms of friendship and charity toward our brothers and sisters in society. We are one. It's like being connected by invisible threads to every other person in the world. When one of us is suffering, that suffering is transferred down that invisible thread to all of us. As a starting point, solidarity means distributing the world's resources so that each of us gets our fair share and no one is suffering because of physical need. Maybe we cannot always share resources equally, but we can always share enough to meet everyone's basic human needs.

If we are to be in solidarity with one another, we need to strive to break down barriers between employees and employers, between rich people and poor people, and between nations and peoples. Within our own social circles, we must find ways to include rather than exclude. We all have a responsibility to work at creating a society whose very structure encourages people to live generously and justly. Instead of promoting the vices of greed and jealousy, society should promote virtues such as generosity, concern for the environment, and tolerance for different views and opinions.

The virtue of solidarity gives us motivation to act for justice. The belief that we are all God's children has motivated people for centuries to perform acts of charity and lead movements of justice that have changed lives and transformed society. We are capable of the same. When we serve those who are poor or on the margins of society, we live out the call to care for the least of God's children. And if we ask the questions, "Why are they poor?" and "Why do I have so much, and yet true joy eludes me?" we have taken the next step toward social justice. By asking the questions—and acting on the answers—we live more fully our destiny as the Body of Christ.

Saintly Profiles

Saint Elizabeth Ann Seton (1774–1821)

Elizabeth Ann Seton is a great American saint who was born wealthy but found her happiness in serving the poor. She was born in New York City into a wealthy Episcopalian family. She was home schooled by her father, and she read voraciously. At the age of nineteen, she married the wealthy merchant William Magee Seton, and they had five children. With her "soul-mate" and sister-in-law Rebecca Seton, she went about doing works of mercy. In 1797 she founded the Society for the Relief of Poor Widows with Children. Six years later her husband died. Attracted by the Catholic faith, she became a Catholic in 1805, facing rejection by her family.

Encouraged by others, Saint Elizabeth Ann Seton founded the Sisters of Charity of Saint Joseph, whose priority was to serve poor people in works of charity and through Catholic education. She is credited with founding the first Catholic school and the first orphanage in the United States. She was canonized in 1975, making her the first saint born in the United States. We can be inspired by her life to reach out to those in need and experience the joy of serving Christ in the process. Her feast day is January 4.

Service and Justice

Throughout this chapter we have talked about our response to social injustice as having two components. On the one hand

Two Feet of Service and Justice

Keep Going ↑

Works of Justice

(removing the causes of those problems)

You need both feet to walk and keep your balance.

Works of Service or Charity

(helping people survive their present crisis)

↖ **But you must move on to the next foot.**

↖ **If you are new, start here.**

we must try to alleviate immediate needs by giving food to the hungry, clothing to the naked, comfort to the sick and the imprisoned, and so on. This is sometimes called the work of service, or charity. On the other hand, we must also work to change the structures of society that keep people hungry or poor or cause them to commit crimes. This is called the work of justice. Charity and justice are like two feet that walk together in our faith.

Both service and justice are needed as part of our response to social injustice. Works of service are more immediate, and often the results are easier to see. Works of justice are more long term, more complex to deal with, and the results may never come. But Christ calls us to be faithful—though not necessarily successful—and he will strengthen and guide us in this work.

The morality chapters on the commandments that follow this chapter will highlight issues of both personal morality and social morality. Some of the social-justice issues are war, abortion, workers' rights, world hunger, and the environment. Think of how you can respond to each of these issues with works of service and works of justice. Your good works, combined with the good works of thousands and millions of others, will make a difference.

For Further Reflection

○ What problems do you see in your own community that trouble you, as a person who is concerned with social justice? What are the global problems that most concern you?

○ What ideas do you have for structuring society so that it would be easier for those who are poor to obtain what they need for a full life?

Working for Justice

Here are some ways you can get involved in working for social justice through prayer, study, and action:

- Pray each day for greater justice and equality for poor and oppressed people.
- Study by searching the Web for information, using key words from this chapter and sites such as *www.paxchristiusa.org,* which has an impressive list of links, and *www.usccb.org/sdwp*, the bishops' department of social development and world peace.
- Check with your parish and diocese for suggestions.
- Join with others and take a step into action! A journey of a thousand miles begins with the first step.

23 Sources of Moral Truth

Have you ever opened a gift only to find out that it needs to be put together? A detailed instruction book is included, so that you know exactly how to make it work the way the manufacturer intended. People face this situation in two different ways. One type of person reads the instruction manual from cover to cover before doing anything else. The other type launches into putting the device together, only referring to the instruction manual if she or he gets stuck or has some parts left over at the end! Which type of person do you tend to be?

In living the moral life, we face two similar choices. Each of us has a natural ability to tell right from wrong. Some people rely on this natural ability when making most of their moral choices. But because of outside influences, this natural ability can often be mistaken or in error, which is why God has also provided us with "instruction manuals," found in the Scriptures and Tradition. It is important for us to know these

Words to Look For

- natural law
- Old Law
- Decalogue
- New Law
- precepts of the Church
- Magisterium
- doctrines
- infallibility
- conscience

laws and teachings—particularly as they are taught by the Magisterium (the pope and bishops)—in order to live the moral life God intends for us to live. In this chapter we take a look at these different sources of moral truth.

Natural Moral Law

Law and order. Without laws we would live in a chaotic world. Laws help us to order our life according to God's plan for us. Just as physical laws govern the universe (for example, what goes up must come down), moral laws govern the relationships that human beings have with God and with one another (for example, treat others as you want to be treated). The moral law is God's instruction, God's way of teaching us the ways and the rules that will lead us to eternal happiness. As a parent guides a child away from the dangers of the world, so God's moral law prevents us from falling prey to the ways of evil.

The moral law that we are born with is called **natural law,** because it is part of our human nature. Saint Thomas Aquinas (see his Saintly Profile on page 27) describes natural law as "nothing other than the light of understanding placed in us by God; through it we know what we must do and what we must avoid"[1] (*CCC,* number 1955). Because we are made in God's image, the natural moral law enables us to participate in God's wisdom and goodness. It's like having a 24/7 hot line to the answers that will ultimately make us happy.

This ability to use our reason to do good and avoid evil is universal. Every human being comes equipped with this ability; it is not dependent on any religion. The founders of the United States proclaimed that we hold certain truths to be self-evident. We just know them. The Declaration of Independence affirms the natural moral law that all human

Pray It!

A Prayer for Moral Courage

Spirit of Truth,

Lead me to true freedom
   not just exterior freedom, where
      rights are guaranteed by law
   but interior freedom, given to
      the children of God
   who live according to the Spirit
   are guided by moral conscience
   and choose what is truly good.

Help me follow the commandments
   keep me from taking life away,
      mistreating the gift of
      sexuality
   keep me from stealing and lying
   keep me from dishonoring
      my parents, family, and
      neighbors
   keep me from lying to myself
      that small decisions do not
      matter.

Help me to become a person of
      conscience
   a person of principles
   a person who inspires trust
   a person who is credible.

Let me experience you looking
      upon me with great love
   and remember that you call me
   to a full, profound, authentic,
      and eternal life!

Amen.

beings have fundamental rights and duties, including the pursuit of true happiness.

The Golden Rule is a good example of a natural moral law. Call it common sense or basic moral sense, but natural law dictates that we should treat people the way we want to be treated. Jesus reminds us of the wisdom of the Golden Rule (Matthew 7:12), but Christians have no monopoly on it. Other great world religions, including Judaism, Islam, Buddhism, Hinduism, and Taoism, espouse it as well, although they may have a different way of saying it. Even people who profess no belief in God adhere to the Golden Rule.

Because natural moral law is an expression of God's moral law, it does not change with time. Regardless of the culture or religious belief, common principles bind us together and form the basis for all other moral rules and civil laws. Any community that wishes to embody justice and goodness will develop civil laws that reflect—and do not contradict—natural law.

Basically, then, natural law is part of our humanity—part of our nature. To be moral is to be fully human. The phrase *man's inhumanity to man* and the word *inhumane* express what happens when we do not live morally, that is, when we are no longer acting as human beings. However, it is obvious from much of the evil in the world that not everyone perceives clearly and immediately the positive dictates of natural law. So God provides other ways of revealing moral truth to us.

The Ten Commandments summarize the Old Law that God gave his Chosen People, the Jews. In bringing the New Law, Jesus gave the Ten Commandments even more force by challenging us to make our entire lives consistent with the values the commandments represent.

Old Law and New Law

The Law of Moses, also called the **Old Law,** was the first stage of God's Revelation to us about how we are to live as people made in God's image. This Old Law is summarized in the Ten Commandments that God revealed to Moses on Mount Sinai (Exodus 20:1–17). These ten laws are also referred to as the **Decalogue.** The Ten Commandments are a special expression of natural law, making perfectly clear through God's Revelation what he had already placed in the human heart.

As holy, spiritual, and good as the Old Law is, as Christians we believe that this Law is still imperfect. The Ten Commandments show what must be done, but they do not give us the strength, or the grace of the Spirit, to do it. The Old Law is the first stage on the way to the Kingdom of God, preparing us for conversion and faith in Jesus. In this way the Old Law is a preparation for the Gospel.

The **New Law,** or the Law of the Gospel, is the perfection of God's moral law, both natural and revealed. Jesus modeled the New Law, and taught the core of it in his Sermon on the Mount, when he gave us the Beatitudes to teach us what we must be like to inherit the Kingdom of God. Jesus' New Law does not abolish or devalue the Ten Commandments, but instead releases their full potential. Let's consider one example from the Sermon on the Mount:

> You have heard that it was said, "An eye for an eye and a tooth for a tooth." But I say to you, Do not resist an evildoer. But if anyone strikes you on the right cheek, turn the other also; and if anyone wants to sue you and take your coat, give your cloak as well; and if anyone forces you to go one mile, go also the second mile. (Matthew 5:38–41)

Does this strike you as a little crazy? What was Jesus saying here? Well, first he reminded his listeners that the Old Law limited the just revenge you could take on someone. If someone put out your eye, the most you could do to them was to put out their eye. But the New Law taught by Jesus is about love. Rather than exacting revenge (even if it was limited revenge), the morality of the New Law shows people the love of God through forgiveness, patience, and even outrageous

Looking Back

Veritatis Splendor

In 1993 Pope John Paul II wrote an encyclical letter titled *Veritatis Splendor* (Latin, meaning "The Splendor of the Truth") to the people of the world, addressing fundamental questions about the moral teaching of the Church. Prayerfully meditate on the following quotes from the encyclical:

The question: "Teacher, what good must I do to have eternal life?" arises in the heart of every individual, and it is Christ alone who is capable of giving the full and definitive answer. (Number 25)

When people ask the Church the questions raised by their consciences, when the faithful in the Church turn to their Bishops and Pastors, the Church's reply contains the voice of Jesus Christ, the voice of the truth about good and evil. In the words spoken by the Church there resounds, in people's inmost being, the voice of God who "alone is good," (cf. Matthew 19:17) who alone "is love" (1 John 4:8,16). (Number 117)

generosity. Who could live this way? Only the kind of people Jesus describes in the Beatitudes, people who are meek, who are pure in heart, who are merciful, who are willing to suffer for righteousness' sake (making things as God intended them to be).

The prophet Jeremiah describes in beautiful language the promise of this New Law: "I will make a new covenant with the house of Israel. . . . I will put my law within them, and I will write it on their hearts; and I will be their God and they shall be my people" (Jeremiah 31:31–33). It is truly amazing that God wrote the natural law into the hearts and minds of all people, made it even clearer in the Ten Commandments, and when we still didn't get it, God became one of us to reveal the perfection of the divine law. Even further, the gift of God's grace and the power of this New Law is communicated to us each time we receive the sacraments, nurturing us so we can communicate love to others.

Saint Thomas More chose to go to his death rather than violate his conscience. Why would a person make such a choice?

Church Law

As members of the Church, the Body of Christ, we are called to live a moral life. Christ has given the Church the responsibility of being a light to the world and a model of his New Law of love. The Church does this through its moral teaching. In addition, the Church has laws for its members that help guide us toward the moral life, the good actions and attitudes that are our ongoing spiritual worship.

The most basic laws are called the **precepts of the Church.** They are meant to be "the very necessary minimum" that will guarantee that we grow in love of God and neighbor (*CCC*, number 2041). The precepts of the Church direct us to participate in the sacramental life of the Church so that we might be nourished for living a moral life. Following are the precepts of the Church as designated by the Catholic bishops of the United States:

1. To keep holy the day of the Lord's Resurrection; to worship God by participating in Mass every Sunday and on the holy

days of obligation; to avoid those activities that would hinder renewal of the soul and body on the Sabbath (for example, needless work or unnecessary shopping).

2. To lead a sacramental life; to receive Holy Communion frequently and the sacrament of Reconciliation regularly—minimally, to receive the sacrament of Reconciliation at least once a year (annual confession is obligatory only if serious sin is involved); minimally also, to receive Holy Communion at least once a year between the first Sunday of Lent and Trinity Sunday.

3. To study Catholic teaching in preparation for the sacrament of Confirmation, to be confirmed, and then to continue to study and advance the cause of Christ.

4. To observe the marriage laws of the Church; to give religious training, by example and word, to one's children; to use parish schools and catechetical programs.

5. To strengthen and support the Church—one's own parish community and parish priests, the worldwide Church, and the pope.

6. To do penance, including abstaining from meat and fasting from food on the appointed days.

7. To join in the missionary spirit and apostolate (work) of the Church.

Catholics are obligated to follow these precepts. Rather than seeing them as a burden, we can approach them as a way of being. They are really minimum requirements for being Catholic, a part of the rich faith tradition of the Church, which provides the nourishment we need, through liturgy, to live morally and to fulfill what it means to be a Christian.

Saintly Profiles

Saint Thomas More (1478–1535)

Saint Thomas More is perhaps the most famous English saint because of the play and subsequent movie based on his life, *A Man for All Seasons*. Thomas More was an educated man who was also deeply religious. He considered becoming a priest before deciding on the married vocation and a career as a lawyer. He had a rich family life, raising three daughters and one son, and after his first wife died, he married again. Thomas spent every Friday in prayer, and his family read Scripture at mealtimes and shared evening prayer.

Unfortunately Thomas More, along with many others, was the victim of King Henry VIII's persecution of Catholics. The unusual thing was that Thomas More was a good friend of the king, who admired Thomas More's wit and loyalty. King Henry rapidly promoted Thomas through a series of public offices to chancellor, a position second only to the king's in power and authority. Then King Henry made a series of demands that in essence declared the king to be the supreme religious leader of the Church of England, instead of the Pope. Thomas More refused to give in to the king's demands. As a result Thomas was imprisoned for fifteen months, lost all his titles and lands, was convicted of treason in a bogus trial, and was beheaded. His last words were that he remained "the king's good servant, but God's first." His feast day is June 22.

The moral guidance of the Church goes beyond the few precepts listed above. Previous chapters have already presented how God has given the **Magisterium,** that is the bishops of the world united with the Pope, the responsibility for passing on and teaching the Tradition. Tradition includes the moral teaching of Christ's New Law, and so the Magisterium is always applying Christ's moral teaching to modern situations. In recent times they have given moral direction on such issues as genetic testing, the use of embryos in medical research, abortion, the death penalty, and welfare laws. The people who make civil law do not always accept the moral truth spoken by our Church leaders, but the Church's voice is an important part of the dialogue when people make important decisions about moral issues.

Catholics, on the other hand, have a special obligation to listen carefully to what the Pope and bishops say about moral matters. When they speak to us, they are the Magisterium, the "living, teaching office of the Church, whose task it is to give an authentic interpretation of the word of God, whether in its written form (Sacred Scripture), or in the form of Tradition" (*CCC,* p. 887). The Magisterium ensures that we stay faithful to the teaching of the Apostles in matters of faith and morals. When the Pope and the bishops agree on a matter of faith and morals, they speak with infallible authority. It means that the Holy Spirit guides them to teach the truths, or **doctrines,** of our faith without error.

Infallibility is a great gift God has given to the Church; it means that we can rely on the Church's teaching as being true. Thus we as Catholics are obliged to believe the doctrine of the church. The gift of infallibility applies to all doctrine, including moral doctrine, that is necessary for our salvation. The role of the Magisterium is to see that these truths of the faith are preserved, explained, and observed. To be clear, not every statement of every pope or every bishop is an infallible statement. If you apply a technical definition of infallibility, few of the Magisterium's many statements qualify as infallible in the strictest sense. However, because of the special charism (gift) they have received, we must take seriously all their teachings.

The Magisterium also does not claim to speak with absolute certainty in areas outside of religious doctrine. But religious doctrine sometimes overlaps other areas, such as scientific truth. You may have heard the famous story about the Church condemning Galileo's theory that the Earth revolved around the sun. The Magisterium at the time taught that because human beings are made in God's image and likeness, the Earth must be the center of the universe and the sun must revolve around the Earth. The Magisterium was correct in teaching the religious truth that human beings are made in God's image and likeness, but they were wrong about the scientific truth. Pope John Paul II publicly apologized for this mistake and the harm it caused Galileo.

Talking about doctrine, dogma, and infallibility can be somewhat confusing to people who may not understand all the ins and outs of the language of the Church. What is important to know is that the Church is the graced presence of God in the world. We, the people of God, are not alone on our journey of deciding what is moral and what is sinful. Jesus, the divine teacher, is still with us in his Church.

Conscience

Now that you know about natural law, the Law of Moses, the New Law of the Gospel, and the Magisterium of the Church, you are fully equipped to make moral decisions, right? Don't we wish it were that easy! Wouldn't it be great if we could go online, pop in a CD-ROM, or speed dial a hot line with all the answers to our moral questions? But we know that in the course of everyday life, we face situations in which we are not sure what to do.

On the Precepts of the Church

Q. What are the holy days of obligation in the United States?

A. The six holy days of obligation are Christmas (December 25), the Solemnity of the Blessed Virgin Mary, the Mother of God (January 1), the Ascension of the Lord (the Sunday that follows forty days after Easter), the Assumption of the Blessed Virgin Mary (August 15), All Saints (November 1), and the Immaculate Conception of the Blessed Virgin Mary (December 8).

Q. When do I have to fast, and when do I abstain?

A. Fasting is a companion to prayer. In Church law it means to eat one main meal and two smaller ones, and nothing in between. Catholics are obliged to fast on Ash Wednesday and Good Friday. Abstinence, refraining from eating meat, is a Catholic responsibility during Ash Wednesday, the Fridays of Lent, and Good Friday. It applies to people of good health who are age fourteen and older; fasting is required for those between eighteen and sixty (but you can certainly start younger if you wish!).

Q. If I haven't committed any mortal sins (see page 213), do I still have to go to confession every year?

A. The obligation to confess once a year is absolutely necessary only if you have committed a serious sin. But the habit of examining our conscience and going to confession leads us to holiness even when our sins are not mortal, but venial.

Top Ten Ways for Forming Your Conscience

1. **Receive the Eucharist.** At Mass, our way of thinking is attuned to the life-giving sacrifice of Jesus for the world. The love of God in turn strengthens our desire to seek truth and act morally.
2. **Examine your conscience.** Written examinations of conscience can be found in prayer books and missalettes, on Catholic Web sites, or at public penance services during Lent and Advent.
3. **Go to confession.** Receive the sacrament of Reconciliation often.
4. **Study, pray, and practice the Scriptures.** The word of God is the principal shaper of conscience.
5. **Pray.** Pray always, seeking the gifts of the Spirit.
6. **Discover what the Church teaches.** Study the teachings of the Church. Having this book is a great start! Listen to your priest, your religion teachers, and your parents. They are charged with helping you form your conscience.
7. **Every choice counts.** Examine the moral choices you make each day. They lead to habits, and habits lead to virtues (or vices). For example, holding back from premarital sex helps you to stay faithful in marriage.
8. **Garbage in—garbage out.** Read and watch stories that inspire virtue.
9. **You are my hero.** Look for friends, mentors, and heroes that lead virtuous lives.
10. **Seek truth.** Don't settle for gossip or popular opinion. Seek information from people who have studied the issues.

This is why God gifted us with a **conscience,** the ability to make a judgment based on practical reason, to recognize what is moral and what is not according to God's law. Our conscience is not like the cricket in the Pinocchio story or the angel sitting on a cartoon character's shoulder, warning us to do the right thing and to avoid those things that get us into moral trouble. Yet we do have an interior voice, one that is bonded with the natural law written on our hearts and in our minds. Our conscience helps us recognize the moral quality of a particular act.

A correctly formed conscience will lead you to make a right moral judgment, in keeping with God's desires. But your conscience isn't always right. If your conscience hasn't been properly formed, it can lead you to make an erroneous moral judgment, one that will lead you into sin and away from God. Even though you might have thought you were doing right, you might still be at fault if the reason your conscience led you into error was because you didn't take reasonable steps to inform it.

That is why it is so important that your conscience be fed and exercised. Shaquille O'Neal has natural ability on the basketball court, yet he and all other athletes must practice if they are going to reach their full potential. Exercising your conscience is just as necessary if you want to reach your potential to live a truly moral life, an authentically happy life. You need to find the time and take the effort, availing yourself of all means of forming your conscience and acting on that formation.

Here's another reason to work at informing your conscience: At times you will be faced with moral choices, on a moment's notice. You may not have time to consult anyone else. In those times you have to depend on your conscience to guide you in making a right judgment, one in keeping with reason and Revelation.

Many voices in the world today try to tell you what is right and what is wrong. Many of them are giving you advice that is contrary to the Law of Christ. That is why in forming your conscience it is essential that you stay connected to your Church and the opportunities it provides for dialogue, reading, and reflection. The Scriptures and Tradition can light the path in our conscience formation, but only if we absorb it in faith and prayer, and put it into practice. Acting on things that you know are good is the kind of practice that will keep your conscience in shape. The article "Top Ten Ways for Forming Your Conscience," at left, gives you some practical ideas for how to do this. The remaining chapters in this morality section are devoted to giving you the Church's teaching on particular topics, to help form your conscience.

One final thing: When it comes right down to it, you must always obey the certain judgment of your conscience. But that word *certain* is a big qualifier. For Catholics, the green light to follow our conscience means that we know and try to follow the teachings of the Church, while considering our intentions and the circumstances of our decisions. When you pay the premium of good conscience formation in accordance with God's laws, you are guaranteed peace of mind. That is an insurance policy that money can't buy!

For Further Reflection

○ When do laws and rules help you to know the right way to act or be in a certain situation? Which laws do you find the most difficult to follow?

○ Look over the "Top Ten Ways for Forming Your Conscience," at left. Pick three things from that list that you will do in the next month, and make a commitment to follow through.

24

Honoring God

Have you ever heard the expression "written in stone"? This cliché is used to describe something that is not negotiable and can't be changed. The phrase comes from Moses and the stone tablets on which God wrote the Ten Commandments. Picture books and Hollywood have created for us a mental picture of Moses coming down from Mount Sinai with the Decalogue (meaning the "ten words"), held high for the people to see.

The Ten Commandments were given to God's Chosen People, the Israelites, as a sign of their special relationship with God. They symbolized the law, which if lived faithfully would lead them to holiness. But the law was meant for everyone. We are able to understand the truth God revealed in those commandments because they are based on the natural law God has implanted in every person's heart. But sometimes we ignore that natural law. So God revealed the Ten Commandments to Moses to make his truth clearer.

Words to Look For

- idolatry
- superstition
- sacrilege
- simony
- atheism
- venerate
- blasphemy
- perjury
- Sabbath
- Lord's Day

God did not give us ten suggestions; the commandments contain serious obligations. Obedience to these serious obligations implies that we must also follow lesser, but related, obligations. For example, "You shall not kill" also covers other kinds of violence, including physical and verbal abuse. The Ten Commandments cover a lot of territory in teaching us how to be in right relationship with God, our neighbors, and all creation. We are able to live out these laws by the grace of God, who is always with us, loving us and nurturing us so that we can live as the people we were created to be—human beings made in God's image.

The first three commandments concern the love of God. The next seven commandments concern love of neighbor. These commands are inseparable. We can't love God unless we love our neighbor, and the opposite is also true. In this chapter we will explore the first three commandments—the ones that show us how to be in right relationship with our Creator.

The First Commandment

Imagine for a moment that your family was among those who escaped from the Egyptians, across the Red Sea and into the desert. Moses had promised your parents a new land, a place where you could be free, and where milk and honey (gourmet food in those days) would be plentiful. The old ones—Moses and his generation—are sticking by their story that the Promised Land is right around the corner, but you and a lot of the others are getting restless. In fact, there are some in the camp who are saying that the God of Moses isn't worth following anymore, and that there is this golden calf that represents a much more powerful god (Exodus, chapter 32). You are torn between the competing voices. Who are you going to follow? Who will be your God?

How hard it is for us to be faithful to God! Although the Chosen People had been led out of slavery, provided with miraculous food and drink, and had seen God's glory on Mount Sinai, they still doubted, and looked for answers in

Worshiping a golden calf may seem silly to us today, but it made sense at a time when people put their faith in statues and figurines. What "golden calves" are we tempted to put our faith in when times get tough? Will these seem silly a thousand years from now?

idols. This is why the first command from God that Moses delivered was, "I am the LORD, your God: you shall not have strange gods before me." The first commandment is a summons—a call for us to believe, to hope, and to love God above all else. It comes first because it is the basis for our life and happiness.

This commandment also tells us that we must adore God, pray to God, and offer worship that belongs to God alone. Adoration, prayer and worship, and fulfilling our promises to God acknowledge the great and infinite wisdom of the One who made us.

Worshiping, adoring, and praying to God may sound pretty basic, but as a young person in the world today, you face competing voices about who and what to worship. Most of us cannot imagine worshiping a golden calf, yet we may idolize the false gods of power, pleasure, popularity, or money. To idolize these things or anything else is **idolatry**, a sin against the first commandment. It is making them more important in our life than God.

We can sin against God's first commandment in other ways. In all ages, we find people who have turned worship of the true God into **superstition.** This is the practice of assigning magical power to certain practices or objects, like charms or omens. When items like crystals or good-luck charms become more than just decorations, there is the danger of superstition. Some people even use religious symbols or rituals in superstitious ways, actually believing that they can influence God. Although expressing your desires to God through prayer is good, believing that God will fix the outcome of a game because you made the sign of the cross is wrong.

Hobbies and games that lead individuals to believe in magic or the occult can be sinful. They, too, are not compatible with true Christian belief and worship of God. Believing in creatures, devices, or objects as if they had divine power is a

Pray It!

Avoiding False Gods

Good and gracious God,
   you have called my name,
   you have loved me,
   you have never left me alone.

I am sorry for the times I forget you,
   when I spend my time and talent
      in pursuit of possessions,
   when I judge others by the
      clothes they wear or the car
      they drive,
   when I crave pleasure and
      popularity for myself,
   when my self-esteem is tied to
      the quality of my possessions.

God, give me, I pray,
   the eyes to see the false gods
      that I put before you,
   the strength to avoid the things
      that turn my attention away
      from you,
   and the courage to pursue the
      true greatness that comes
      from putting
   other's needs before my own.

In Jesus' name I pray. Amen.

serious sin. Satanism, astrology, palm reading, and attempts to call up the dead or see the future are wrong because "they contradict the honor, respect, and loving fear that we owe to God alone" (*CCC,* number 2116).

Sacrilege is another sin against the first commandment. It is the abuse of the sacraments, persons, things, or places that are consecrated to God. Some movies, television shows, and celebrities poke fun at objects or actions that are specifically Catholic. There is nothing funny and everything wrong about belittling the symbols and rituals of our faith.

Simony is a term that is probably unfamiliar to you. It describes an old practice of buying and selling spiritual things and favors, and is also a sin against the first commandment. A modern-day example would be a television preacher promising people miraculous cures if they only send in so much money. Although it is permissible to expect a contribution for goods and services so that the ministers of God can earn a living, someone who tries to buy or sell spiritual power, or con unsuspecting people with promises of God's favor, is guilty of sin.

Finally, there is **atheism**—a serious and common problem of our time. Atheism is the denial of God's existence, and is the ultimate violation of the first commandment that assures us of God's loving and ongoing presence in our life. It can have many faces, including the belief that humans aren't dependent on God. Atheistic political systems, like communism, deny the existence of God and blame religion for the economic and social oppression of people.

Although the first commandment forbids us to worship images, like the golden calf, it is permissible, and indeed good, to use images like crucifixes, statues, pictures, or icons to symbolically represent the sacred and holy. If you have been in other Christian churches, you may have noticed how different they are from Catholic churches. They have no statues, no vigil lights, no stations of the cross. Catholics have sometimes been

Looking Back

Love God with Your Whole Self

This, after all, is the rule of love that God has set for us: *You shall love,* he says, *your neighbor as yourself; God,* however, *with your whole heart and your whole soul and your whole mind* (Mark 12:30–31, Leviticus 19:18, Deuteronomy 6:5). Thus all your thoughts and your whole life and all your intelligence should be focused on him from whom you have received the very things you devote to him. Now when he said *with your whole heart, your whole soul, your whole mind,* he did not leave out any part of our life, which could be left vacant, so to speak, and leave room for wanting to enjoy something else. (Saint Augustine, in *The Works of Saint Augustine,* page 115) criticized because of the mistaken perception that we worship these things. But the veneration of saints, sacred objects, and images is different from worship and adoration, which is for God alone. To **venerate** means to give honor and respect; it does not violate the first commandment.

The Second Commandment

God calls each one of us by name. Everyone's name is sacred. It demands respect as a sign of the dignity of the one who bears it. God's name is no different, and indeed, should be treated with even more respect. Some Catholics even bow their heads slightly when they say or hear the name of Jesus. Sadly, in our culture, many people have lost that sense of the sacredness of God's name, forgetting the second commandment, "You shall not take the name of the LORD your God in vain."

If you were to listen carefully to your own speech, the conversations of others, and the spoken media for an entire day, how many times do you think you would hear God's or Jesus' name? How many of those times do you think it would be used respectfully? All too often we hear people use the expressions, "Oh, God!" "Jesus Christ!" or even "Holy mother of God!" as a way to express humor, surprise, or anger. Rarely is it a situation in which people really intend to call on our God and Savior! To speak in vain means that what we say has no positive result or real value. Using the name of God improperly is a subtle sign that we are losing the awe and respect due to him.

Far worse, though, than a casual curse is using the name of God, of Jesus Christ, of the Virgin Mary, or of the saints in an intentionally offensive way. This is called **blasphemy.** In Jesus' time blasphemy was considered so serious that a person could be put to death as punishment. Jesus' claim to be the Messiah and the Son of God was considered blasphemous by those who wanted to kill him. Although today we would not put someone to death for blasphemy in this country, perhaps we have become too used to the offensive use of God's name.

A time when we publicly use God's name in a reverential manner is when someone takes an oath promising to uphold the law or to tell the truth in court and ends by saying, "so help me, God." This oath is a sacred promise because it is asking God to be a witness to the truthfulness of a person's commitment or testimony. A false oath calls on God to be witness to a lie. That is why the crime of **perjury,** lying under oath, is a serious sin. If we can't trust individuals who swear to tell the truth, then the law and order of our community is threatened.

So many people have a deep desire for a sense of the sacred, a connection to the holiness that is God. Yet so much of popular culture seems to poke fun at anything that is sacred or to belittle people who treasure God and holy things. The second commandment is all about keeping holy things holy. Keeping the second commandment requires a conscious effort not to give in to the many subtle ways God's name and holy symbols are belittled. God wants us to use his name only for good purposes: to bless, praise, and glorify it.

The Third Commandment: Origins of the Lord's Day

Have you ever considered that the word *recreation* literally means "to create again"? It is so important that we take time for recreation that God gave us a special day just for this purpose. "Remember the Sabbath day, and keep it holy. Six days you shall labor and do all your work; but the seventh day is a Sabbath to the LORD your God; you shall not do any work" (Exodus 20:8–10). With its origins in the Jewish observance of the **Sabbath,** Sunday has become the day of rest for Christians (see the article "Sabbath and Sunday," on page 242). Sunday is also when Christians celebrate the day

Saintly Profiles

Joan of Arc (1412–1431)

Joan of Arc, while still in her teens, was burned at the stake because of her faith in God. She had been born into a peasant family in France, and was a child at the time of the Hundred Years' War between France and England and the civil war that pitted the French houses Orléans and Burgundy against each other. She convinced the French king that she had heard messages from saints telling her to save France. She was given troops to try to defend Orléans, and had the honor of leading them into battle.

After victory at Orléans and other military successes, Joan was accorded the privilege of standing next to the new king at his coronation. The next year, however, she was captured by the duke of Burgundy and imprisoned. The French king did nothing to save her. She was tried for and convicted of heresy. After refusing to deny that the voices she heard were from God, she was condemned to death. Joan was only a teenager when she was burned at the stake, gazing at the cross and calling the name of Jesus. A quarter of a century later, a commission appointed by Pope Callistus III reversed the verdict and declared Joan innocent. She was canonized in 1920, and is one of the patron saints of France. Her feast day is May 30.

of Christ's Resurrection, and so Sunday is the known as the **Lord's Day.**

In the Bible God set a good example for us, resting on the seventh day of Creation (Genesis 2:2–3). If God rested and was refreshed, we too ought to rest and encourage others to take a day of rest. There is no denying that finding time to honor the Lord's Day can be a challenge. Day planners, handheld computers, cell phones, and beepers remind us of our hour-to-hour, minute-to-minute commitments. All that activity—studying, working, extracurricular activities—can make a person tired and weary. Things to do, places to go, people to see keep us on a daily treadmill of high intensity. This is not what God intended. We need to set aside time to pray and play. Time to worship our God and leisure time are fundamental human rights.

Businesses that are closed on Sundays give witness to the importance of obeying the third commandment. What changes could you make in your life to better "keep holy the Lord's Day"?

Observing the Lord's Day

As the Sabbath evolved into the Lord's Day, Christians preserved God's original command to us: "Remember to keep holy the LORD's Day." We are to use this day to praise God in community with one another. Going to Mass on Sunday is an essential part of being Catholic. The Church requires us to celebrate the Lord's Day and other holy days of obligation by participating in the Mass. The Sunday celebration of the Lord's Day and his Eucharist is at the heart of the Church's life.

You might ask, "Why is it so important to go to Mass on Sundays?" One reason is that the practice dates back to the days of the Apostles. The Letter to the Hebrews reminds the faithful to "not [neglect] to meet together" (10:25). A few centuries later Saint John Chrysostom was asked why not just pray in the privacy of our home or in some other place that is sacred to us? He replied:

You cannot pray at home as at church, where there is a great multitude, where exclamations are cried out to God as from one great heart, and where there is something more: the union of minds, the accord of souls, the bond of charity, the prayers of the priests.[1] (*CCC,* number 2179)

Saint John's language probably seems old and dated, and yet the reasons he gives make sense today. You can and should still pray in the privacy of your home, outside in nature, or in some special place that helps you communicate with God. But the Sunday Eucharist (also celebrated on Saturday evening) is the opportunity to praise God through song, prayer, and the Scriptures, and to receive the body and blood of Christ with the whole community on the day of rest that God set aside for us.

Another reason to participate in the Mass on Sunday is that the family of God is like any other group of people who are bonded by family or friendship. It is important that the members of the Christian community come together on a regular basis. God insists that his people set aside Sunday so that nothing else gets in the way of that date with one another and with our God. We should arrange the rest of our life—our work, study, and business—so that we can be available for Mass and for time to properly relax our mind and body. For example, when you apply for a job, do you make it clear that you cannot work on Sundays, or at the very least, Sunday mornings?

As Christians we should pause and think of ways that we can challenge the way we do business. We should never make demands on others that would keep them from observing the Lord's Day. When stores and restaurants are open around the clock, including Sundays, it is easy to lose respect for the third commandment. Truett Cathy, the owner of a successful chain of fast-food restaurants, lives out his Christian

Did You Know?

Sabbath and Sunday

Christians follow the command to "keep holy the Sabbath" on Sunday, but the Sabbath and Sunday are not the same day for everyone. The Jewish observance of the Sabbath on Saturday is derived from the story of God creating the universe in six days and resting on the seventh (Sunday is considered the first day of the week). Christians gather to celebrate the Eucharist on Sunday because that is the day Jesus rose from the dead. Early Christians probably observed the Sabbath on Saturday and gathered for the Eucharist on Sunday, but by the second century the Sunday gathering had replaced the Saturday Sabbath observance.

Earlier in the history of the United States, it was common for governments to enforce laws forbidding certain kinds of work, recreation, and commerce on Sunday. It was a way of encouraging people to devote the day to the worship of God. Very few of these laws, called blue laws, remain in force today. They fell out of use in the latter half of the twentieth century, as it was recognized that these laws favored the practice of the Christian religion. But still, no law says that Christians have to work on Sunday!

faith by intentionally closing all his stores on Sunday. He truly honors the Lord's Day by giving his workers the day off to worship and be with their families. That day is our opportunity to cultivate our family, community, social, and religious life, so that we can slow down and appreciate the many blessings that are the fruits of our labor.

Reclaiming Sunday as the Lord's Day by participating in the celebration of the Eucharist and taking the time for rest and recreation helps us remember God's original blessing in creation. We need to "re-create," so that we can be the kind of people God calls us to be. We know that this is a blessing—something that is good for us. It is one of those laws written on our hearts and minds, as well as in stone.

For Further Reflection

- In what ways does advertising tempt people to worship today's false gods?
- How does using God's name in situations other than true prayer or adoration harm the relationship we should have with God?
- Is it difficult for you to set aside Sunday as a day of worship, rest, and relaxation? What would have to change to make Sundays more holy for you, your family, and your friends?

LiVE it

Five Reasons for Controlling Your Tongue

"Sticks and stones may break my bones, but names will never hurt me." If you have ever uttered this saying to try to end someone's verbal attack, it was probably because the words hurt—not because they didn't matter.

Check out what James has to say on this issue (James 3:1–12), and think about the following reasons for being careful about what you say to others:

1. A word spoken with the intent to injure is like a small fire that can set a huge forest ablaze, causing far more damage than we ever intended.
2. Hurtful words can leave long-lasting scars and broken relationships.
3. The tongue is like a small rudder on a large ship. A verbal insult is like a small adjustment to the rudder's position, which can set the huge ship (our life) on the wrong course and result in disastrous consequences.
4. The mouth is like a source of water from which springs either clean or contaminated water, not both.
5. Loving our neighbor and loving God demands that we control our tongue so that we can speak healing words—words of affirmation, concern, reconciliation, and love.

25 Honoring Family

Have you noticed how many shows on television are about families? You can probably think of dozens of TV families, from the ideal *Brady Bunch* to the less-than-ideal *Simpsons*. We have even seen reality shows that film the daily lives of actual families. These media families portray funny, touching, and sometimes troubling scenes that may or may not be similar to our own experiences of family. If you had to pick a show that described your family, what would it be?

We don't get to choose our family ties, but the bonds that we share with the members of our family last a lifetime, for better or for worse. In the best of times, parents, children, and siblings enjoy and support one another. At other times, you may wish you could exchange a family member or two for the ones in a television show.

This brings us to the fourth commandment, "Honor your father and your mother." This is the first of the commandments that tells us how we are to love our neighbor, starting with those who are closest to us. As is true with all the

Words to Look For

- *civil authorities*
- *civil disobedience*
- *natural law*
- *society*
- *civil laws*

Why Isn't My Family Perfect?

Some families really struggle. Every family has its ups and downs, but some families struggle with serious issues like divorce, alcoholism, mental illness, and physical and sexual abuse. If you are living in a family that is struggling with problems like these, you probably want to cry out to God, "Why us?" And you should, because it isn't fair and it isn't the way God intends for us to live. If you are in a family situation like this, what can you do?

- **Find support.** See a counselor, join a support group, get active in your Church's youth group. Find a place where you can belong in healthy ways.
- **Talk to whoever in your family will listen.** If it is affecting you, it is also affecting other members of your family. You can work together to find little things to make your family better.
- **Take action.** If someone is being seriously hurt or neglected, don't accept it. Call the police or a social worker. Or tell a teacher, a parish priest, a school counselor, or a youth leader, and they will direct you to someone who can help. Sometimes it takes an intervention from the outside for a family to get healthy again.
- **Pray.** Share your heart with God. Jesus is with you, and wants to help share your burden. Pray for your family, that it can grow healthier. Pray for yourself, that you can find the strength you need.

commandments, it is about more than just your relationship with your parents. This commandment forms a bridge between the first three commandments, which deal with our relationship with God, and the last six commandments, which tell us how *not* to treat one another. Focusing on the responsibilities and duties that family members have toward one another is the first step in knowing how we are to act toward all people.

Honoring Parents

What do you remember about the first time you met your mother and father? Unless you were adopted when you more than three years old, most likely your memory doesn't go back that far. However, if you have ever watched a couple with their newborn baby, you might have an idea of how crazy your folks were (and still are) about you. And you have probably seen how children instinctively go to their parents for love and attention. The fourth commandment is based on this natural love between parent and child that God has placed in the human heart. Even though the fourth commandment is addressed toward children instead of parents, the Church teaches that it implies moral responsibilities that go both ways.

What does it mean to honor parents? [We recognize the reality that many teens live in single-parent households. To avoid the awkwardness of always saying "parents or parent," we will intersperse both in this section.] Instead of a typical list of chores, the Church defines the duties of this commandment as attitudes that lead to specific actions. The Church teaches that the attitudes children owe parents are respect, gratitude, obedience, and assistance.

Respect is the foundation of any healthy relationship. Respect, required by God's commandment, comes naturally when children experience the love and respect a parent has for them. When we are little, this usually happens pretty easily, because we look up to our parent with a belief that he or she can do no wrong. However, as we get a little older and develop our own desires and beliefs, parents and children may find that they have conflicting interests, and mutual respect becomes more challenging. Even so, respect requires that you listen to your parent with an open and patient attitude, doing your best to try to understand his or her point of view.

Another requirement of children is to show gratitude toward parents. Many parents sacrifice a great deal for their children. It is said that it typically costs over $100,000 to raise a child from infancy through college. And that doesn't count the hours taking children to and from school and extracurricular activities. Of course these are parents' responsibilities, but they occasionally need to know that you appreciate it! So don't wait until Mother's Day or Father's Day to tell your parents, "Thanks." Thank them for the gift of life—for saying yes to your coming. And express your appreciation for them providing you with what you need to grow physically, mentally, and spiritually.

Then there is the duty of obedience. That is a word few of us really like to hear. Most teens generally have no problem doing what their parent asks. Yet for some teens it is a constant challenge to listen to and do what a parent requests. You may protest, bargain, and delay just to make sure your parents really meant what they said. The commandment to honor your mother and father should help provide the motivation you need to trust your parent's judgment, even when you don't see her or his wisdom. The only exception to the obedience

Looking Back

John Paul II on Family

Pope John Paul II has a special place in his heart for the family. He commonly refers to the family as the "domestic church," meaning that the family is the first place where children learn about God's love. He also holds up the Holy Family—Jesus, Mary, and Joseph—as a model for all families. Here is an excerpt from one of Pope John Paul II's letters on the family:

For every believer, and especially for Christian families, the humble dwelling place in Nazareth is *an authentic school of the Gospel.* Here we admire, put into practice, the divine plan to make the family an *intimate community of life and love;* here we learn that every Christian family is called to be a small *"domestic church"* that must shine with the Gospel virtues. Recollection and prayer, mutual understanding and respect, personal discipline and community asceticism (simple living) and a spirit of sacrifice, work and solidarity are typical features that make the family of Nazareth a model for every home. (From the *Angelus,* Feast of the Holy Family, December 30, 2001, number 2) requirement is if your parents, your teacher, or someone else in authority is asking you to do something that you know is wrong. For example, an overzealous parent or coach suggests that you cheat to gain an advantage. That is a request you are not expected to follow.

Finally, in the list of duties for children is the responsibility that we have to assist our parents. Assistance may come in the form of regular chores, or just helping out when needed to baby-sit, carry in groceries, do yard work, or help your technically challenged parents with the computer. As you grow older, you will discover that the commandment goes deeper than that. It also means that grown children must care for their parents in their old age, giving them the moral and material support they need, especially when they are ill, lonely, or in crisis.

Mary and Joseph risked their honor and even their lives to bring Jesus into the world. Jesus also demonstrated his love for and obedience to his mother and foster father. How are their actions reflected in the relationships between parents and children today?

Parents' Responsibility for Children

We don't always like to hear the words, "This is for your own good," but parents are the ones who are supposed to know better than we do what is truly good for us. As an infant you received injections that your parents knew were painful, but the discomfort was necessary to prevent dangerous childhood diseases. Your parents winced as you protested those needles, but they knew what was good for you. In a similar way, God gives parents the responsibility to teach their children about God and the moral life and to make rules for your safety— even if it means telling you things you would rather not hear. Believe it or not, parents do not enjoy telling their children no. In fact, it would be much easier just to let children do whatever they want—but then what kind of a parent would such a person be?

Not only must parents provide for the physical, emotional, and spiritual needs of their children (those things you should be grateful for), but they must also be your first educators, especially when it comes to your faith life. Teaching you your prayers when you were little or seeing that you participate in Confirmation preparation are part of the responsibilities they accepted at your Baptism.

As you grow older, the natural progression that God created requires that parents give you more freedom as you make your own choices. This can be very hard for some parents to do. You are probably familiar with stories of parents who pushed their son or daughter to be a doctor, even though the child's talents and interests were more artistic or mechanical. Even Mary and Joseph had difficulty letting go when Jesus started to become more independent. When they found him in the Temple, after being lost for three days, they didn't understand his explanation of being about his Father's business. The Gospel tells us that Mary had to ponder his words in her heart, seriously considering what he was saying about his life's work (Luke 2:41–51).

Figuring out your life's vocation is something you have to do for yourself; a parent's responsibility is to encourage and support you in whatever vocation you choose. Of course the most important thing they can do is to teach you from an early age that your first calling is to follow Jesus. And being a follower of Jesus may take you on paths that were not in your parents' plans.

Responsibilities of Civil Authorities

Remember that the fourth commandment applies to more than the relationships in the family. Going one step further, the Church teaches that we should honor and respect other legitimate authority figures, which are established for the public good. For young people this includes most adults who are concerned with their well-being. Teachers, counselors, coaches, and youth leaders have the authority to help guide you. So do priests, principals, police, government

Did You Know?

Civil Disobedience

In 1990 Fr. Roy Bourgeois, along with a handful of people, began a protest at the School of the Americas in Fort Benning, Georgia. This military installation trained soldiers from Latin American countries. The training included learning how to torture people and put down popular uprisings. Many of the soldiers trained there returned to their countries and used their training to put down popular movements for democracy and justice. It is extremely likely that the men who assassinated Archbishop Oscar Romero were trained at this "school." Father Bourgeois wanted the U.S. government to close it down. He chose civil disobedience as his means of protest.

It is against the law to trespass on an Army base. The protesters created a solemn procession, honoring those killed by graduates of the School of the Americas, and crossed the boundary onto the military base. Many were arrested and jailed. The school still operates, but each November Father Bourgeois has led many people, including nuns, laypeople, and college students, across the line to face arrest and imprisonment. The small group that began protesting in 1990 has now grown to an annual gathering of over ten thousand people, with close to eight thousand people participating in civil disobedience (the school has been renamed the Western Hemisphere Institute for Security Cooperation). The protesters continue to draw attention to what they hope to accomplish: the closing of the school. Learn more at *www.soaw.org*.

workers, and at times your own peers, when they act in official leadership positions. That may seem like a whole lot of people telling you what to do. But you also may have experienced being an authority to others in your role as an older sibling, a baby-sitter, a scout leader, a class officer, or the assigned leader of a school, parish, or community group.

There is never a time in our life when we do not have to listen to the wisdom, experience, and instructions of authority figures. But being in charge carries responsibilities as well. No matter how important a person is, he or she must never violate another person's dignity. No one has the right to go against God's law, to ask you or force you to do something that is morally wrong. **Civil authorities,** those who make and enforce laws, must always respect people's dignity and rights, especially those of families and people who are disadvantaged.

The Church recognizes the holiness of married couples such as Blessed Luigi and Maria Beltrame Quattrocchi. In this photo, can you see the love they had for each other?

Church and State

The duties of authorities in a community, state, or nation are like the responsibilities that parents have for the welfare of their family. As members of the larger human family, called **society,** we must work together with our leaders to build up the moral environment of the world we live in, making it easier to be good. Our actions and attitudes must contribute to the good of society in a spirit of truth, justice, solidarity, and freedom.

Just as you must obey your parents unless you believe their expectations are morally wrong, so you must also obey the laws of your community. Like children who find it difficult to obey their parents, some people think traffic laws, tax laws, or trade laws don't apply to them. But unless a law is truly unjust, we are required to follow it.

Not every law is morally right. If we have good reasons to believe a law is morally wrong, then the opposite is true. We are obliged *not* to follow it. Refusing to follow immoral laws is called **civil disobedience.** Examples of citizens who practiced civil disobedience against unjust laws are many. Courageous people in Europe hid Jews from the Nazis when the law said they were to be turned in. Martin Luther King Jr. and other civil rights' activists landed in jail in Birmingham, Alabama, for refusing to honor laws that were racially prejudiced. People refuse to join the military or fight in wars on moral grounds. Medical personnel refuse to be part of teams that perform abortions. Today the citizens of a certain town in Georgia require every household to have a gun. If you were to live in that town, and owning a gun violates your conscience, you would be obliged to break that law. Thankfully, in a democratic country with checks and balances in the system, not too many laws require people to violate their conscience, but it is important to recognize injustice, refuse to participate in it, and work to change unjust laws.

The **civil laws** that leaders make for a society reflect a particular worldview, that is, an overall vision of what humanity is like and why we are here in this world. In a democratic society, we believe in the equality of all and the right of freedom of expression. Other societies may see the world and the purpose of each human being differently. Some countries' laws do not give women equal rights. Other countries make laws that oppress groups of people according to their ethnic background or their wealth.

God's law, **natural law,** should be clear to all people in all societies, but humanity is still learning. No community or nation has a monopoly on the truth of how we are to live. This is where the Gospel comes in. Jesus preached the Good News of the Kingdom of God. As human societies realize the full meaning of that Kingdom, we all come closer to living as God intends for us to live.

The Gospel can enlighten us about how we are to live together, but the Church encourages the separation of religious and political authority, or as some say, of

Saintly Profiles

Blessed Luigi and Maria Beltrame Quattrocchi

Two of the first people Pope John Paul II beatified in the new millennium were Luigi and Maria (Corsini) Beltrame Quattrocchi. Luigi and Maria were an Italian married couple who were married for forty-six years. They had four children, three of whom entered religious life. The Quattrocchi family was busy and active in the world around them. Maria wrote books on the mother's role in the education of her children. She accompanied sick people on pilgrimages to Lourdes, in France. Luigi was a lawyer, and worked for the Italian government. He was an active participant in several Catholic organizations. Every day this family prayed the rosary together, and they shared a daily devotion to the Eucharist.

The Quattrocchis knew what it meant to live in modern times, with the threats of war, disease, terrorism, and poverty. The family was involved in helping Jewish people escape Nazi persecution in Italy. Their strength was in their faith. Pope John Paul II beatified Luigi and Maria in October 2001. Beatification is the final step before being named a saint of the Church. This Italian family of our time reminds us of Jesus' family of ancient times, and both families are models for us today. Their feast day is November 28.

church and state. The Church is not, and does not want to be, the same as the political community; she wants to be a free voice that speaks for the dignity of the human person. And the Church encourages us to stand up for that dignity by being involved in our own political communities. History shows us that when people in a society forget God and moral principles, immoral forms of government can easily take over. Governments become totalitarian, seeking total control over people's lives, making material wealth and political power a higher priority than the dignity of the human person.

Imagine for a moment that society is made up of living cells. The family is the smallest cell. When we obey the fourth commandment, to honor our parents, we honor God, our Divine Parent, and we keep the family cells healthy. The healthier the family is, the better off society is. The fourth commandment speaks to children, adults, and the ever-widening circles of the human family. It is a positive statement about respect. The last six commandments show us how to live that respect.

For Further Reflection

○ Are you someone who finds it easy to obey your parents, or is that a challenge in your life? What kind of expectations do your parents have of you?

○ Think of one political issue that you care about: the environment, poverty, gun control, abortion, domestic violence, the death penalty. How does your faith help to inform your conscience about that issue? How could you become politically involved to make a difference about the issue?

Pray It!

Prayer for Your Family

God,

I pray for Mom and Dad, God, that you will help them to be good parents, strong in ways you want them to be, so I can look up to them with admiration and feel confident that their instruction is right.

Help me, dear God, to understand my parents. Remind me that when I don't get my way it is because they love me, and not because they want to be mean or deprive me of a good time.

Help me, God when I become stubborn and refuse to listen. Help me accept the fact that they have wisdom and experience because they were once teenagers, but I have never been a parent.

Put in my heart the respect and consideration they deserve for their years of hard work and sacrifice. They are raising me the best they can. Let me not repay them with grief or shame. Rather, help me to give them obedience, respect, forgiveness, and love. Amen.

(By Lindsey Krebs, a teenager, in *More Dreams Alive*, pages 44–45)

26 Respecting Life

In a recent interview, a wealthy man who had been a nonbeliever most of his adult life commented that watching the birth of a calf had brought him back to God. As he watched the baby animal emerge, he was overwhelmed by the miracle of life that he was witnessing. The only explanation for the miracle was, of course, God.

If the birth of an animal can move a person to believe in God, imagine how much more overwhelming a baby's birth is. People who have witnessed a child's birth often speak about it in religious terms. The natural law God has put in our heart tells us that every human life has eternal value. From the unborn child to the person who has lived more than one hundred years, every life is sacred. Despite the most advanced scientific discoveries and technologies, the mystery of life and death ultimately leads us to God.

Words to Look For

- legitimate defense
- capital punishment
- just war
- conscientious objection
- arms race
- abortion
- genetic engineering
- euthanasia
- suicide
- scandal

In this chapter we explore that mystery in light of the fifth commandment, "You shall not kill." God expects us to stand in awe of human life, to have profound respect for the

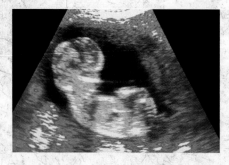

dignity of the human person. The word *respect* means "to look again." Generations of men and women have had to stop and look again at life issues that are related to the fifth commandment. But no generation before has had to consider so many complex and controversial issues that threaten the dignity of life.

Ultrasound images give expectant parents amazing views of their babies when they are just a few months old. Is it any wonder that we hold all human life sacred, from conception to natural death?

Human Life Is Sacred

We are made in the image of God—each and every one of us. No exceptions. From the first chapter of Genesis to the most recent edition of the *Catechism,* this statement about who we are and what kind of person God wants us to be is at the heart of morality. It is the foundation for loving other people, our God, and ourselves.

The Scriptures tell us that from the moment of conception, God knew us and loved us: "Before I formed you in the womb I knew you, / and before you were born I consecrated you" (Jeremiah 1:5). Sacred Tradition also speaks of the dignity of all life, confirming that every human life is sacred until natural death, from womb to tomb.

Sometimes the lives of others or even our own life may not be perfect, and life can make demands on us that are not what we want. Children and adults who are disabled or ill can require a great deal of demanding care. Sometimes other people can be annoying, inconvenient, or even our enemy. But each life is as precious to God as we are. We can never throw a life away. The beginning and end of every life is up to God, and only God.

When you hear the words, "You shall not kill," what probably comes to mind is the act of murder. Hopefully you will never be involved in a true homicide—a direct and intentional act of killing. Even without a commandment, you know how evil murder is. It wipes out the life of a human being, a horrible offense against the Creator of all life. However, studies show that by the age of eighteen, the average child will see sixteen thousand murders on television! Sadly, so much exposure to killing, from cartoons to news programs, has the effect of making us less sensitive to the horror of taking another human life.

Legitimate Defense

Although murder is clearly wrong, what about killing in self-defense? The Church teaches that we have the right to stop someone from inflicting harm on us or others. But if possible we must avoid taking the life of the one who threatens us. If a burglar wants to steal from you, it is far better to allow the theft than to try to kill the thief. The life of a person—even a thief—is always more valuable than an object. However, if a threat to your own life exists and you have no alternative except to kill or be killed, it would be permissible to kill in self-defense. This principle of **legitimate defense** of life is the only justification for killing; it is the principle that forms the basis for civil law.

Life Issues and the Fifth Commandment

Although individuals do not often face such do-or-die situations, those who are responsible for the lives of others in society must make difficult moral decisions about killing. Government and military leaders as well as law enforcement officers carry a heavy responsibility to determine what is legitimate self-defense as they try to protect their community and country. Let's look at the moral implications of several situations that are governed by the fifth commandment.

Capital Punishment

The issue of the death penalty presents a major challenge to society. The majority of the people in the United States

Did You Know?

Movements for Life

You can turn to many pro-life organizations for information on current issues. Here are some of the many you can find on the Web:

- **Amnesty International** *(www.amnesty.org)* works to protect human rights worldwide. Follow their links for information on the death penalty and other issues.
- **Birthright** *(www.birthright.org)* was founded by a Catholic woman, Louise Summerhill, in the 1960s. They provide nonjudgmental, material, emotional, and spiritual support for pregnant girls and women.
- **Pax Christi** *(www.paxchristiusa.org)* is a national Catholic movement for peace. They provide excellent literature to use in school projects.
- **The United States Conference of Catholic Bishops** *(www.usccb.org)* has many timely and well-researched statements on contemporary life issues.

support the use of the death penalty, also called **capital punishment.** However, the teaching of the Pope and the bishops is not guided by public opinion. They question the morality of capital punishment as it is used today.

Throughout most of history, the Church has accepted the use of capital punishment as a way to stop people who are considered a threat to society. Today the Church teaches that capital punishment is moral only when it is impossible to effectively defend human life in any other way. Because we have prison systems that can adequately protect society, Pope John Paul II has said that moral reasons for using the death penalty "are very rare, if not practically non-existent"[1] (*CCC,* number 2267). The Church recognizes that even the worst immoral act does not take away a person's God-given dignity. Imprisoning the offender to protect society is a better witness to the value of life than having the state kill that person to show that killing others is wrong.

The electric chair is still used as an instrument of capital punishment in some states. Why is the Church speaking out more strongly against capital punishment in our time?

War

War, as an act of self-defense, is another challenging issue when we talk about respect for human life. Although armed conflict can be a valid way of protecting against unjust aggressors, we know that war brings evils and injustices to all of society. News programs, magazines, books, movies, and television have made the horrors of war real to people who are not on the front lines. We see vivid pictures of the victims of war, from the young men and women who fight, to the refugees whose lives, homes, and livelihoods are threatened. Unfortunately sometimes the media glorify war in the name of entertainment. Movies, video games, and music that promote killing can lead us to believe that the violence of war is an acceptable way to solve problems.

In the Bible we see a growing awareness that love is incompatible with violence. The early history of the Old Testament is full of stories of war. Yet even in the Old Testament are glimpses of insight showing that God is not a God of violence but of nonviolent love. See Isaiah's prophecies of the Messiah (2:4) and of the suffering servant (52:13—53:12). When Jesus, the Prince of Peace, breaks into history, he tells us, "Blessed are the peacemakers" (Matthew 5:9), and "Love your enemies and pray for those who persecute you" (Matthew 5:44). By his own example of accepting humiliation and suffering rather than resorting to violence to protect himself and destroy his enemies, Jesus set a new standard.

So the Church teaches that all citizens and all governments must do everything they can to avoid war. Pope Paul VI, frustrated by modern warfare, affirmed this teaching when he said, "War no more; no more war!" Our reason and our faith tell us that it makes more sense to resolve conflicts without using violence in our homes, in our communities, and among nations.

The reality is that war still happens, and countries must defend themselves. The principles of legitimate self-defense are just as applicable for nations as they are for individuals. However, war must be a last resort, and over the centuries the Church developed criteria that must be met if a war is morally permissible. The criteria for a **just war** are:

- **Just cause.** You must have a just cause, that is, you are using war to correct a grave, public evil.
- **Comparative justice.** The good you achieve through war must far outweigh the resulting loss of life and disruption to society that will occur.
- **Legitimate authority.** Only duly constituted public authority may use deadly force or wage war.
- **Right intention.** You may use war only for a truly just cause and solely for that purpose.

Looking Back

Conscientious Objection

The Church supports both those who serve in the armed forces (as long as a country is abiding by the criteria of just war and legitimate self-defense) and those whose conscience will not allow them to participate in military service (**conscientious objection**) or in a particular war or branch of the military (selective conscientious objection). Here is a statement from the U.S. Catholic bishops.

We repeat our support both for legal protection for those who conscientiously refuse to participate in any war (conscientious objectors) and for those who cannot, in good conscience, serve in specific conflicts they consider unjust or in branches of the service (e.g., the strategic nuclear forces) which would require them to perform actions contrary to deeply held moral convictions about indiscriminate killing (selective conscientious objection).[1] . . . There is a need to improve the legal and practical protection which this country rightly affords conscientious objectors and, in accord with the just-war tradition, to provide similar legal protection for selective conscientious objectors.[2] (From the pastoral letter *The Harvest of Justice Is Sown in Peace*)

- **Probability of success.** War may not be used in a futile cause or in a case where disproportionate measures—for example, nuclear or biological weapons that would result in massive loss of life—are required to achieve success.
- **Proportionality.** The overall destruction expected from the use of force must be outweighed by the good to be achieved. In particular the loss of civilian life must be avoided at all costs.
- **Last resort.** Force may be used only after all peaceful alternatives have been seriously tried and exhausted.

If any of these conditions are not met, the war cannot be considered just, and believers should not participate. Christians have differing perspectives on this. For some, fighting in a just war fulfills a moral duty in a courageous manner. Others take Christ's command to love our enemies so seriously that they consider all war wrong. The Church teaches that nations must not force these conscientious objectors to serve as soldiers and should provide alternative ways for them to serve the needs of their country.

Because one of the criteria for a just war is to avoid harm to noncombatants, many people question whether a just war is even possible in modern times. Nuclear, biological, and chemical weapons kill soldiers and nonsoldiers alike. Mines and biological contaminants are left behind, to infect, injure, and kill the innocent, most often children. Even without a war, the **arms race** causes more harm than good. Even if we never use the weapons, the enormous sums of money spent creating weapons of mass destruction keep us from using those resources to provide basic human rights to the neediest people. Christians should do everything they can to end the arms race.

Abortion

One of the most controversial life issues in society today is abortion. **Abortion** intentionally stops the development of an unborn child. The ability to abort children has existed for a long time, but until recently both society and Churches considered this act a moral evil. In the 1970s, the United States made abortion legal, and many other countries have done the same. But remember: acts that are legal are not always moral. What is legal often becomes acceptable, and today abortion has become commonplace, though controversial. It is controversial because not everyone agrees with the Church that from conception, a child has the right to life.

The Church, however, has never wavered in her complete support of unborn children from the moment of their conception (when the egg and sperm unite). Abortion is a serious sin and strongly forbidden by the law of God. The only time an abortion would be justified is when it happens as the result of a procedure to save the mother's life.

People without well-formed consciences may not know how seriously wrong abortion is. But even those who know abortion is wrong might consider it anyway when they face the situation personally. Girls and women who find themselves unexpectedly pregnant often panic and are afraid of what their parents or society might think of them or do to them. Some feel pressured by friends or family to abort their baby. Another reason some women resort to abortion is that they do not think they will be able to provide for their child once it is born. Still others seek abortions because the child will be an inconvenience or get in the way of their life plans.

Boys and men who are responsible for an unexpected pregnancy are also tempted with the "we can fix it" attitude of abortion. Bringing a life into the world may disrupt their life, too, and years of child support can make abortion seem like a good financial alternative. But the issue of abortion touches the soul of men and women. The unborn child carries the genetic life of both parents; although it isn't the man's body that is directly affected, killing the unborn child creates a psychological wound for men as well as women.

Because abortion affects the whole community, preventing this tragedy is the responsibility of all who respect human

Five Ways to Promote Life

- Volunteer at a pregnancy support center and join in the March for Life in Washington on January 22 each year, to protest the Roe *v.* Wade Supreme Court decision legalizing abortions.
- Begin a local youth chapter of the National Coalition to Abolish the Death Penalty *(www.ncadp.org)*.
- Plant a Peace Pole at your parish or school. A Peace Pole is a handcrafted monument that displays the message and prayer, "May Peace Prevail on Earth," on each of its four or six sides, usually in different languages. There are more than 200,000 Peace Poles in 180 countries all over the world, dedicated as monuments to peace. Gather regularly at the pole to pray for peace.
- Volunteer in a local nursing home, listening with compassion to the life stories of the people you meet.
- Follow stories in the news where the value of life is denied or demeaned. Write a letter to the editor and to government leaders supporting life-affirming and nonviolent solutions.

life. Providing material, emotional, and spiritual help for women who face a crisis pregnancy is one way to help stop the number of babies who are aborted. Enabling women to see adoption as a loving alternative to abortion can help save lives, too. And, of course, greater respect for our sexuality will prevent the situation in the first place. We will get to that topic in the next chapter.

The Catholic Church stands as a strong voice for those who cannot speak for themselves. Faith communities can foster respect for life by communicating the evil of abortion, while finding ways to help women avoid this tragedy. The Church also takes the lead in offering forgiveness and reconciliation to women who have had abortions. If you or someone you know has had an abortion, only to realize later what a great wrong it was, programs like Project Rachel can help you find peace and reconciliation with God and the Church.

This featherless chicken is a product of genetic engineering. Though it may be efficient for the food industry, do we have the right to interfere with God's creation to this extent?

Abortion is not the only issue that involves the earliest forms of human life. Recent scientific and technological breakthroughs show that signs of life are present long before a mother and father are aware that they have conceived a child. Science can use this information to promote respect for life, or in ways that are not so respectful. There are serious moral questions about **genetic engineering,** cloning, and other ways of conceiving life in ways that God did not intend. Because we have the technology and knowledge to do something doesn't mean that it is morally right. The Church defends the rights of human beings from conception through all the stages of life. For that reason we must defend, care for, and heal embryos as we would any other human being.

Euthanasia

Moral issues exist on the other end of human life. One of those issues is **euthanasia,** also called mercy killing. Proponents of euthanasia make it an issue of human freedom, saying that people—or their family if the person is incapable of making their own decisions—have a right to choose to end their life. This is usually in the context of someone who is terminally ill and in severe pain. But the Church teaches that euthanasia is a serious moral wrong. The Church considers the act of intentionally causing the death of a human being to be murder, regardless of the motive or the circumstances.

Remember the three ways to judge the morality of an act: the act itself, the intention, and the circumstances must be good. In the case of euthanasia, the act itself is a violation of God's law. It violates human dignity and the respect that we owe to our Creator, the author of human life. Some people facing a long and difficult death want someone to put them out of their misery; family members often experience great anxiety as they watch their loved ones suffer. Dying with dignity is possible without resorting to euthanasia. Hospice programs, medical advances in relieving pain, and spiritual support can help us make that transition from death into new life with our God.

Suicide

Suicide is also a grave offense against the fifth commandment. As sacred as life is, it can certainly seem overwhelming at times. But **suicide,** the taking of your own life, goes against human nature. As human beings, created by God, we are meant to preserve our own life as well as the lives of others. Suicide is the ultimate rejection of love of self, love of God, and love of neighbor. It causes devastation to the surviving family and friends— those closest to us. But it also wounds the greater human family, which is prematurely deprived of the gift of the life of the person who commits suicide.

Pray It!

Seamless Garment of Life

Joseph Cardinal Bernardin was the beloved cardinal of the archdiocese of Chicago for fourteen years, until his death in 1996. Cardinal Bernardin was an outspoken advocate for the protection of all life, from natural conception to natural death. He coined the phrase "seamless garment of life" as a way of pulling together everyone working for pro-life, no matter what their favorite issue was. Cardinal Bernardin died of cancer. Prayerfully reflect on these words of his written before his death:

As my life now slowly ebbs away, . . . I am not anxious, but rather reconfirmed in my conviction about the wonder of human life, a gift that flows from the very being of God and is entrusted to each of us. It is easy in the rush of daily life or in its tedium to lose the sense of wonder that is appropriate to this gift. . . . The truth is, of course, that each life is of infinite value. . . . My final hope is that my efforts have been faithful to the truth of the gospel of life and that you and others like you will find in this gospel the vision and strength needed to promote and nurture the great gift of life God has shared with us. (Joseph Cardinal Bernardin, *A Moral Vision for America,* page 157)

Although suicide is always wrong, the Church recognizes that serious mental illness or suffering can contribute to why someone would take his or her own life. If you know someone who is thinking about suicide, it is essential that you do what you can to get the person the medical or psychological help they need, even if it breaks a promise of confidentiality. If you know someone who has committed suicide, you should not consider him or her forever lost to the love of God or condemned to hell. As the Church, we pray for those who have committed suicide, placing them in God's love and mercy.

Scandal

Respect for life also includes caring for the spiritual life of other people. **Scandal** is an attitude or behavior that deliberately leads another person to sin, causing harm to their spiritual life. Things we do, say, or wear can be scandalous. For example, offering alcohol to someone who is underage is scandalous behavior. Scandal can also be a sin of omission—something we failed to do. Skipping Mass on Sunday sets a bad example for others about their spiritual well-being. Scandal is particularly wrong when committed by those who are supposed to teach and educate. Remember Jesus' words, "If any of you put a stumbling block before one of these little ones who believe in me, it would be better for you if a great millstone were fastened around your neck and you were drowned in the depth of the sea" (Matthew 18:6).

This drawing shows Saint Maximilian Kolbe in his prison uniform. Sometimes standing for Gospel justice and truth means risking our freedom and even our lives.

Respect for Health

The fifth commandment, "You shall not kill," also covers respect for health as part of respect for life. We are wonderfully made—body, mind, and soul. When any aspect of our being is hurting, we cannot be whole, the way God made us. As individuals we must have respect for our own health, avoiding all kinds of excess: the abuse of food, alcohol, tobacco, or drugs.

Still other issues fall under the fifth commandment that you may not have thought of. For example, what happens when you get behind the wheel? Besides being against the law, disobeying speed and traffic laws on roads, on the water, or in the air is wrong because it endangers your safety and the safety of others.

How about getting proper exercise, getting enough sleep, and eating a healthy diet? These are also fifth commandment issues, and they are things that we face every day. Some people's primary motive for living a healthy lifestyle is to look sexually attractive. But the primary reason God wants us to live a healthy lifestyle is to take good care of the body and mind he has given us. When our focus for eating a healthy diet is on how we look, for example, it can easily lead to a skewed perspective, and even result in eating disorders like bulimia and anorexia. Remember, our intention for acting morally is as important as the act itself.

It may seem like the list of sins against the fifth commandment could go on and on. It is true that respect for life means more than avoiding murder; it cautions us to avoid all forms of physical and psychological violence against others or ourselves. All of the "shall not" commandments make short statements that cover a multitude of sins, but at the heart of each of them is the Great Commandment: to love our God and our neighbor as we love ourselves.

For Further Reflection

○ We live in a throwaway and convenience society. We easily dispose of and replace things that are no longer useful, worn out, or no longer convenient. Do you think

Saintly Profiles

Maximilian Kolbe (1894–1941)

Maximilian Kolbe was born in Poland in 1894 with the name Raimund Kolbe. He attended a Franciscan seminary as a teen, where he took the name Maximilian. Despite having tuberculosis, he was ordained a Franciscan priest and earned two doctorate degrees. He began publishing a spiritual newsletter that served more than 200,000 people of Poland, preparing a nation to persevere during the coming trials of Nazi terror and communist occupation.

After six years of missionary work in Japan, Father Kolbe returned to Poland in 1936, and continued his work as a theologian and newspaper editor, and he entered radio ministry. Then in 1939 the Nazis invaded Poland. After a brief arrest, Father Kolbe turned his monastery into a refuge camp for Polish refugees and 1,500 Jews. His papers took a Polish patriotic, anti-Nazi line. Within two years Father Kolbe was arrested for taking a stand against Nazi oppression.

Father Kolbe was sent to the prison camp at Auschwitz. Within the camp he continued his priestly ministry by hearing confessions and saying Mass with smuggled bread and wine. After some prisoners tried to escape, the warden chose ten men at random to die by starvation. Father Kolbe offered his life for the life of another man who had a wife and children. His last days were spent in a starvation chamber before he was finally killed with a lethal injection. Father Kolbe is a modern-day example of resisting evil with nonviolent love. His feast day is August 14.

this throwaway mentality leads to a lack of respect for human life? Why or why not?

- This country has been involved in war in your lifetime. According to the criteria for a just war, do you think these wars are morally right?

- What gifts do children bring to your life? What gifts do older people bring to your life? Can you imagine what your life would be like if the parents of a child you are close to aborted her or him? Can you imagine what life would be like if the last time an older person who is close to you was seriously ill, someone had chosen to end her or his life?

27

Respecting Sexuality

Do you remember when you first learned about sex? Were you a bit surprised about the way babies are made? When you were a child, it was probably hard to imagine that anybody would want a baby badly enough to do something that *gross*. Now that you are a bit older and wiser, it may be difficult to imagine that you ever felt that way about sex. You are a sexual being from the moment of conception until your last breath, but adolescence is a time when your changing body makes it difficult to ignore that you are either male or female. As young people enter puberty, sexual feelings become one of the most powerful and wonderful aspects of being human.

Most of the time, when we refer to the word *sex*, we think of our body, even though sexual acts also involve our mind, our emotions, and even our spirituality. The trouble is, many people try to take sex out of the larger picture, making

Words to Look For

- contraception
- in vitro fertilization
- artificial insemination
- adultery
- annulment
- chastity
- lust
- fornication
- masturbation
- pornography
- homosexuality

the gift much less than it was intended to be. It would be like taking a fine piece of art and using it for scrap paper. It will work, but you destroy the beauty and the real purpose of the masterpiece.

Adding to the problem is that the gift of sex has become a marketing tool to sell products—jeans, perfume, soft drinks, shoes, and cars—even appliances. The message of the media today is that sex is "no big deal." But both advertisers and the Church know that sex is a very big deal. The difference is that marketing experts have their own best interest in mind. The Church wants what is best for you.

The Church's teaching on sex and sexuality is like all her moral teachings. It is based on human reason, on the Scriptures, and on Tradition. Although some people think that the Church has nothing positive to say about the topic, the opposite is true. Both the Scriptures and Tradition begin with the basic teaching that sexuality is one of God's greatest and most beautiful gifts to us. The Bible even includes an entire book of somewhat erotic love poetry, the Song of Solomon. The sixth (You shall not commit adultery.) and ninth (You shall not covet your neighbor's wife.) commandments simply remind us that the misuse of such a great gift can cause great harm. They cover a lot of ground, but it is sacred ground that helps us to fully appreciate our sexuality as a beautiful gift from God.

God created the union of man and woman in marriage to be a holy, life-giving, and lifelong commitment. What do you think it takes for a marriage to last a lifetime?

Made in the Image of God

It doesn't take long for little children to discover that there are physical differences between boys and girls. The Scriptures tell us that not only are we made in God's image, God intentionally created us male and female (Genesis 1:27). As children grow, their curiosity about each other leads to an awakening about their own sexual identity and how they are supposed to relate to the opposite sex.

Understanding our intimate relationships with others begins with understanding our own sexuality. God did not intend for our sexuality to be separate from our heart, our mind, and our spirit. We can't remove our sexuality from who we are, any more than we can separate our brain from our body or our spirit from our mind.

But our sexuality is not just about us. Sexual activity, the physical expression of our sexuality, enables us to relate to another human being in a way that says, "This relationship is special." Sexual expression should be a sign of our commitment to the other person. Simple kissing, or even holding hands, says that we are more than just friends. Sexual expression that involves genital activity is reserved for real, permanent love relationships. Real sex belongs within a real love relationship that will stand the test of time. It belongs in sacramental marriage.

Why does the Church make such a big deal out of sex belonging only in marriage? To answer that question, we need to look at how God made the act of sexual intercourse different for humans than for any other species. Simply stated, God made sex for three purposes:

○ Sex creates new life.
○ Sex expresses loving union.
○ Sex brings us joy and pleasure.

It is important to keep all three purposes in mind, because they cannot be separated from one another; they are integrated—parts of the whole picture. If only one or two of these is present, God's plan is derailed.

If sex was *only* about experiencing pleasure would be more like animals than humans. People who have sex just because it feels good are missing the point. They are acting on instinct—body only, no heart or head involved. Likewise, if we use sex

Looking Back

The Theology of Sexuality

The communion of love between God and people, a fundamental part of the Revelation and faith experience of Israel, finds a meaningful expression in the marriage covenant which is established between a man and a woman.

For this reason the central word of Revelation, "God loves His people," is likewise proclaimed through the living and concrete word whereby a man and a woman express their conjugal [married] love. Their bond of love becomes the image and the symbol of the covenant which unites God and His people.[1] (Pope John Paul II, *Role of the Christian Family,* 1981, number 12)

The man and woman, who "are no longer two but one" (Matthew 19:6), help and serve each other by their marriage partnership; they become conscious of their unity and experience it more deeply from day to day. The intimate union of marriage, as a mutual giving of two persons, and the good of the children demand total fidelity from the spouses and require an unbreakable unity between them.[1] (Vatican Council II, *Pastoral Constitution on the Church in the Modern World [Gaudium et Spes],* 1965, number 48) only to procreate, to make babies, it takes away from the pleasure and the expression of loving union.

Some people think that love and pleasure are enough, that if you really love someone, then experiencing the pleasure of sex is okay. But that line of thought leaves out the life aspect. Anytime you have sexual intercourse, you have the possibility of new life. And once new life is on the way, and the couple is not married, there are no easy solutions.

The story of the woman who was caught in adultery teaches us about Jesus' compassion for sinners (John 8:1–11). Why do you think it is so difficult for people to forgive some kinds of sin?

The combination of love and pleasure without the permanent commitment of marriage is not good for the health and life of the couple, either. Emotional wounds, transmission of disease, and postponement of commitment are all proven negative consequences that hurt the individual as well as society. Just like any other action, there is a social dimension to sexual activity.

Dating is a temporary arrangement—a testing ground for relationships. Even being engaged is not quite permanent. Thus neither a dating relationship nor being engaged provides the commitment necessary for sexual intercourse. But Christian marriage does. It is the only relationship that ensures that all three aspects of sex are integrated, woven into the minds, bodies, and spiritualities of the couple.

Marriage

Marriage is a covenant, a sacred promise that people freely make and intend to keep faithfully. Sex is the sign of that covenant, that communion. Within that context "sexuality is a source of joy and pleasure" (*CCC*, number 2362) for a couple as they achieve the two purposes of marriage: "the good of the spouses themselves and the transmission of life" (*CCC*, number 2363). You can see how pleasure, life, and love are connected to the heart of marriage.

A sacramental marriage, one that is a sign of God's love, must especially honor the purposes of love and life. The expression of sexual love must be open to the gift of life. This is the basis for the Church's teaching on artificial birth control, or **contraception.** Although the Church recognizes that couples should act responsibly, the spacing of the births of children should be accomplished through natural methods that emphasize the union of the couple and their openness to life. Surgical sterilization, chemical contraception, and barrier methods such as condoms or diaphragms are not considered natural means, and are therefore morally wrong.

Eliminating the life aspect in the sexual relationship is not what God intended, but God did not intend for us to take the love or pleasure aspects out of creating new life, either. Although the desire to have a baby is good, couples cannot use artificial means to achieve that good. For conception to be morally right, the sperm and the egg must come together as the result of human sexual intercourse, a physical expression of love. This is the basis for the Church's laws against creating babies in test tubes and implanting them in the mother's womb (**in vitro fertilization**) or fertility techniques that implant sperm in a mother's womb (**artificial insemination**).

Obviously marriage is a major life commitment. So how do you know if you are going to love someone for the rest of your life? That is what the promise is all about. When two people publicly say that they will love and honor each other until death, they are saying that no one else and nothing else will get in the way of their marriage. That is why the Church takes such a strong stance against divorce. Divorce breaks the contract, the covenant. It harms the couple themselves, any children they may have, and the rest of the community.

The sixth commandment, "You shall not commit adultery," forbids any violation of the dignity of marriage. **Adultery,** having sexual relations with someone other than your spouse, is obviously wrong. It involves

Did You Know?

Divorce and Annulment

The Church teaches that marriage is meant to last forever, but what happens when it doesn't? When a couple divorces, the marriage is dissolved in the eyes of the state but not the Church. Divorced people remain full members of the Church, but are not permitted to remarry as long as their original spouse is alive. There is an exception to this, however. In some cases the married couple never truly achieves a sacramental or covenantal bond. Church officials can declare such marriages null (meaning that a sacramental marriage never existed), and the two former spouses are free to marry again. This declaration, called an **annulment,** is not a statement about the validity of the civil bond that existed or the legitimacy of the children born to the couple during their marriage.

Those who remarry without annulling an earlier marriage are excluded from receiving Holy Communion but are not separated from the Church. "They should be encouraged to listen to the Word of God, to attend the Sacrifice of the Mass, to persevere in prayer, to contribute to works of charity and to community efforts for justice, to bring up their children in the Christian faith, to cultivate the spirit and practice of penance and thus implore, day by day, God's grace"[1] (*CCC*, number 1651).

breaking the sacred promise to be faithful. It is harmful to all the parties concerned, whether or not they are all aware of it. Cheating on a spouse jeopardizes the marriage, the family, and the rest of society. Cohabitation, or living together before marriage, is also wrong because the couple live together as if they were married, without the complete commitment of a sacramental marriage. This commandment also forbids the practice of polygamy—having more than one wife or husband.

Finally, the command to avoid adultery and respect sexuality for the purposes of love, life, and pleasure is also the basis for the Church's strong stand against living together before marriage. Although common in our culture today, the idea of a trial marriage is not the same as a permanent commitment. When couples decide to experience the pleasure of sex without the vow, it is too easy to give up on each other, to walk away, to decide that the sign of committed love that sex was supposed to be wasn't that powerful a sign after all.

Chastity

We have talked quite a bit about the integration of sexuality with our body, mind, and spirit. The words *integration* and *integrity* come from the same root word, *integer,* meaning "whole." In fact, an integer in mathematics is a whole number. One of the greatest compliments you could receive is to be called a person of integrity.

Think about what that means. Integrity requires honesty and authenticity in what you say and what you do. Sexual integrity is about being honest with yourself and others about how committed you are to a relationship. Rationalizing or leading people on for the purpose of sexual pleasure is deceptive. The Church's term for

Ten Ways to Practice Chastity

1. Pray. Thank God for the gift of sexuality, and ask for the strength to live a life of chastity.
2. Seek out a parent or another adult that you can talk to when you have questions about sexuality.
3. Focus on making friends—not romance—with people of the opposite sex.
4. Learn to turn a critical eye toward media messages that use sex to sell products.
5. Remind yourself that your value is not dependent on whether and how much you date.
6. Stay away from drugs and alcohol. Impaired judgment on a date can lead to trouble.
7. If you are on a date and things get out of hand, call a friend or a parent for a ride home.
8. If you have a boyfriend or a girlfriend, communicate openly and set boundaries about touching.
9. Remember that more teenagers are not having sex than are having sex.
10. Make a pledge to avoid intimate sexual activity until you get married (visit the Web site *www.truelovewaits.com*).

sexual integrity is **chastity.** Christ is the model for chastity, a virtue that requires integration of our sexuality with the whole person—body, mind, and spirit. Every person, single or married, is called to be chaste, to be healthy and honest, and to respect the sexuality of self and others.

Chastity does take practice. Your body is telling you that sex feels good, and hundreds of cultural messages a day tell you it is okay to act on your sexual instincts. Some adults will bluntly state that teenagers are going to do it anyway. What those voices are suggesting is that young people don't have the discipline to practice sexual integrity, to be chaste.

The Church has more hope and higher expectations for you. The sexual passions young people feel today are no different from the days of Romeo and Juliet. Biology did not change. But attitudes did. Teens certainly experience more pressure to jump into the deep waters of sexual activity before marriage. But as the number of sexually active teens has gone up over the last forty years, the consequences have become more dangerous. So to avoid sexual sin, the Church teaches us to practice chastity, the art of mastering our sexual integrity. Being aware of the power of the life force within you can help you to use it in the way God intended. But it does require focus and discipline.

Sexual respect and integrity are so important that another commandment is devoted to these issues. The ninth commandment, "You shall not covet your neighbor's wife," is closely related to the sixth commandment against adultery. It speaks of **lust** and carnal concupiscence. These intimidating words simply mean that the life forces within us have a dark side. Men often experience this dark side as an overwhelming desire for sexual pleasure. Women often experience it as a need to have sex in order to hold on to a relationship. The gift the Holy Spirit gives us to keep our desires in check is the virtue

Pray It

True Love Waits

Dear Jesus, help me to live a life pleasing to you. Help me to do what is right and to be strong enough to say no to those things that are against your will. Let me be an example of your love and kindness to my family, friends, and all I meet. Help me to respect myself by avoiding places and people that would do injury to me. Especially, give me the courage and strength to live chastely, honoring the gift of my sexuality and avoiding sexual intercourse and other intimate sexual activity outside of marriage.

Jesus, you were always a friend to those in pain or trouble. If I should make a mistake and fail in these efforts, please forgive and heal me. I know that your love for me is sure, that you will always be with me to lift me up and show me the right way to go. Amen. (National Federation for Catholic Youth Ministry, True Love Waits program) called temperance. Temperance is about using our will to overcome our instincts.

The demons of the dark side will always be present, threatening our good intentions. **Fornication** is a biblical term that refers to sex outside of marriage. Television shows may influence you to think that casual sex is a sign of the times, and that everybody is doing it, but the reality is that more and more teenagers are questioning the wisdom of sex without permanent commitment. Recent studies show that the majority of adolescents who have had sex, said they wish they had waited. That message may be gaining in popularity. Between 1999 and 2001, the percentage of high school students who have had sex dropped below 50 percent.

Because Saint Maria Goretti was killed while resisting a rapist, she is often pictured with a white lily, a symbol of purity.

Masturbation, genital activity alone or with another person that does not result in sexual intercourse, is also a sin against chastity. It is all about pleasure without regard for life or real love. Sins against chastity include other forms of genital sexual activity that stop short of sexual intercourse, such as petting or oral sex. They are forms of exploitation, and are not appropriate sexual expressions for semicommitted love. These activities can also result in disease and emotional wounds that can prevent true intimacy in future relationships.

One of the most common offenses against the sixth and ninth commandments is **pornography.** The Internet has made this evil more accessible to young people. Pornography is dangerous because it violates human dignity. It takes the gift of sexuality and makes it an object to be exploited and abused. Even though models may agree to pose for these pictures, there is nothing right and everything wrong with viewing pornographic images. Pornography can become addictive, leading to serious disrespect and even violence, especially toward women.

Homosexuality

The issue of **homosexuality** is an especially difficult one in our discussion of sexuality. For reasons that are still unclear, some people experience a strong sexual attraction toward persons of the same sex. Although homosexuality has always existed, recently we have seen more social acceptance of people who have a homosexual orientation. The Catholic Church affirms that people with a homosexual orientation are children of God, and must be treated with respect, compassion, and sensitivity. It is never moral to discriminate, act violently toward, make jokes about, or look down on them.

Although the Church is clear about accepting our homosexual brothers and sisters—that is, gay men and lesbian women—as part of the Body of Christ, she also teaches that homosexual acts are against natural law because they do not allow for the possibility of life. All of us are called to practice chastity according to our station in life. For those who realize that they are sexually attracted to people of the same sex, avoiding genital sexual expression can be a cross to bear, requiring great effort at mastering will over instinct. An active prayer life and support from others within the faith community can help men and women with homosexual orientations to accept the gift of their sexuality through deepening friendships that are a sign of Christian love.

Purity of Heart

The list of sexual sins may seem long, and at times impossible to avoid. But practicing sexual integrity and chastity is easier if we develop attitudes that not only form our conscience the right way but also help us to live according to what we know is right. The sixth beatitude, "Blessed are the pure of heart, for they shall see God," is Jesus' message that fulfills the sixth and ninth commandments. What does it mean to be pure of heart?

Saintly Profiles

Maria Goretti (1890–1902)

Maria Goretti was mortally wounded while fending off a rapist at the age of twelve. She had been born in Italy to a peasant family that was too poor to send the children to school. Maria never had the chance to learn to read or write. After her father's death, she assumed responsibility for keeping house, while her mother and siblings worked in the fields. One day an eighteen-year-old neighbor, Alessandro, made sexual advances. When Maria resisted the attempted rape, the young man stabbed her numerous times. She died at the hospital the next day. As she lay dying in her bed, she forgave Alessandro "for the love of Jesus."

Her murderer was sentenced to thirty years for his crime. He remained unrepentant until one life-changing night, when he had a dream that Maria gathered up flowers and gave them to him. Upon his release from prison Alessandro went and begged forgiveness from Maria's mother. When Maria was canonized in 1950, Alessandro was among the crowd of 250,000 gathered to celebrate in Saint Peter's Square.

We celebrate Maria for her heroic commitment to the value of chastity and for her forgiveness of Alessandro. This is not meant to imply that women who are violently attacked should resist their attackers until the point of death. But Maria's commitment to defending Christian values serves as an inspiration for courageously following Christ in our lives. Her feast day as a martyr and virgin is July 6.

The *Catechism* refers to the heart as the seat of moral personality. Forming our conscience is the work of the head, but our heart "enables us to see *according* to God; . . . [Purity of heart] lets us perceive the human body—ours and our neighbor's—as a temple of the Holy Spirit, a manifestation of divine beauty" (*CCC*, number 2519).

The Temple in Jerusalem, described in the Old Testament, was a magnificent structure, but its most sacred territory was deep within. Only one person, the high priest, could enter the holy of holies—the innermost sacred rooms. Our bodies are magnificent too, but places deep within us are so sacred that they are to be protected in a special way. The virtue of modesty protects our intimate center. We don't tell just anybody our most private secrets; we should not let just anybody see or touch our sacred places. Although modesty does not require dressing in Victorian-era fashions, sexual respect means you should look again at how you dress and how you act sexually. The clothes you wear can send unintended messages, and outfits that leave little to the imagination may reveal more than you want. It is wrong to intentionally try to cause sexual excitement in another person. But respect goes both ways. It is never right to take advantage of someone sexually, regardless of his or her dress or behavior.

The road to sexual respect may seem difficult at times, but it is well worth the effort. Can you imagine a bride or groom wishing that they had sexual partners other than their beloved? The kind of discipline required for sexual abstinence before marriage is good practice for the lifelong commitment that you will make as part of your vocation. Rather than seeing chastity as a burden, consider the freedom that it gives: freedom from worry about pregnancy, disease, and emotional wounds that lead to the scar tissue of vulnerability. Sexual integrity is the freedom to be healthy and whole—according to God's design.

For Further Reflection

○ How does pornography—whether it is considered soft porn, like in movies, or hard-core porn, as in some magazines or on the Internet—exploit and cheapen the gift of sexuality?

○ Other than what you've read in this book, what other reasons can you think of for abstaining from sex until you are called to join a spouse in Catholic sacramental marriage?

○ Given all that you have read in this chapter about the beauty, integrity, and purpose of sexuality, why would someone choose to be sexually active before they're ready for marriage? What could you say to convince him or her to wait?

28 Respecting Material Goods

There is a little book about life called *All I Really Need to Know I Learned in Kindergarten.* The author, Robert Fulghum, says that most of what he really needed to know about how to live, what to do, and how to be, was learned when he was a young child. As he was playing in the sand pile, some of the most basic moral laws became clear to him: share everything, play fair, put things back where you found them, clean up your own mess, and don't take things that aren't yours. These simple insights are what the seventh commandment, "You shall not steal," and the tenth commandment, "You shall not covet your neighbor's goods," are all about.

But are these just personal rules for individuals to follow? Like all the commandments, the Church teaches that they have more far-reaching consequences than that. They apply to corporations, institutions, and governments as well. What if

Words to Look For

- plagiarism
- embezzlement
- reparation
- restitution
- almsgiving
- common good
- social doctrine
- stewardship
- vocation
- envy
- preferential option

those who run these groups really practiced in corporate life what they preach in private life? What if they truly shared their wealth, did not steal, and cleaned up all their messes? We would have far fewer corporate-accounting scandals, far less pollution, and far less danger to the earth and her resources. This is part of what we must work for as Christ's disciples in our world today!

Respect for the Goods of Others

Although it may be a stretch, imagine for a moment that God created the world like a giant kindergarten room, with enough toys, books, and snacks for everybody. The Garden of Eden was like that—a world of harmony with enough resources for everyone's material needs. That world is still possible if we follow the rules that our reason, the Scriptures, and Tradition teach us about respecting the goods of others in the giant kindergarten classroom called earth.

Many people who shoplift could easily pay for or do without the items they steal. What drives people to want to possess more things?

Let's start with the basics: "You shall not steal." Anytime we take something that doesn't belong to us without the permission of the rightful owner, it is stealing, and it is a sin— even if the owner never finds out or misses the item. If you shoplift and get away with it, you are still guilty of theft. You can tell yourself that the store will never miss it, or that the company makes enough money anyway, but your act is still wrong. Backing into someone's car, causing damage, and driving away without leaving a note is not only ruining someone else's property, it is taking money out of the owner's pocket (instead of yours) to get it fixed. Stealing ideas or information from others may be more abstract, but it is still wrong. This is a primary reason why cheating—whether on school tests or as a business practice—is sinful. **Plagiarism,** that is, copying someone else's words or ideas without permission or giving proper credit is a form of stealing; so is pirating music, videos, and software.

On a bigger scale, taking funds that are not yours from an organization, a community, or the government is a form of stealing called **embezzlement.** Also, business practices that are deceptive, costing employees or stockholders their rightful wages, dividends, or retirement savings, may not look like a burglary, but the deception is just as wrong.

Regardless of the kind of theft, those who take from others damage the harmony of society. What if you are guilty of having stolen something? Stealing requires confession, and **reparation** (making amends) or **restitution** (returning what you have stolen). You need to give it back or make it right, and ask for forgiveness. As with any serious sin, going to confession is important. And the priest can help you determine how best to give back what you have stolen or make up for it.

The story of the rich man and Lazarus the beggar (Luke 16:19–31) is about noticing people who are in need and sharing the goods we have with them. Who are the people in our time whose needs go unnoticed?

The Earth's Goods Are for All

A classroom—or a global community—can be affected in less obvious ways that violate the seventh commandment. If one child or one group of people hoards most of the toys and food, others will have a hard time getting their needs met. We know that God created the world with enough resources to go around. God also intended that the world's resources benefit all creation. Although it is okay to own private property, we have to be respectful so that we don't claim so much that others have little or no access to the goods necessary to survive. Our reason tells us that sharing is a matter of fairness, or justice. And our faith goes a step further. Charity, or love of neighbor, requires that the goods of the earth be available for everyone to use in a reasonable way.

If you have ever seen pictures or stories of starving people, you know that we fall short of justice and charity. Today, more than 800 million people are malnourished. Each day in the developing world, 30,100 children die from diseases associated with hunger. Although those statistics may seem beyond our comprehension or control, the people in the richest countries of the world have the means to share the wealth more effectively. The United Nations Development Program estimates that the basic health and nutrition needs of the world's poorest people could be met for an additional thirteen billion dollars a year. That may sound like a lot, but animal lovers in the United States and Europe spend more on pet food each year.

Our response when people are hungry and desperately poor is two-fold. Our first response, if we have the means, is to help ease the hunger or poverty by donating money or food. This is a work of charity (**almsgiving,** in traditional language) and is rooted in Jesus' teaching, "Whoever has two coats must share with him who has none; and whoever has food must do likewise" (Luke 3:11). Charity is pleasing to God, and is the easiest step for us to take. The second response is to work for social action to correct the situations that cause hunger and poverty. Social action means working for changes in laws or public policies, and is a long-term effort that doesn't bring immediate results. But it is also a work that is required by the Gospel and is pleasing to God.

All creation can thrive if we get our priorities in order. God entrusted human beings to manage the resources of the universe. Our moral duty to care for creation extends beyond today and tomorrow. We must have the foresight to see how our actions and lifestyle today will affect generations to come. Every day new information on the environment reminds us that we cannot continue to greedily use up the goods that God has entrusted to us. The seventh commandment says that we cannot steal the natural inheritance of future generations by consuming so much for ourselves that we use up or destroy what they will need. We must have respect for the integrity of creation, because it is not just our generation that is dependent on the planet's health, but all future generations.

Simple Living

Why would a person voluntarily give up things in life? Vast numbers of people in the world do not have a choice about living simply. They do not have the resources to meet even their most basic needs for food, shelter, clothing, health care, and education. This is poverty in its strictest sense. Then there are people who live by the motto, "Live simply so others may simply live." This is called voluntary simplicity, so that more resources can be available for those who do not have enough. Following the example of Jesus, we can all take steps to live a simpler lifestyle.

For example, if you have a closet full of clothes, you can choose to not buy more until you have a real need for more. You can even give excess clothing to those who need it. Before you purchase your next CD or junk-food item, stop and ask, "Do I really need this?" If not, don't buy it! You can make other choices, like watching a beautiful sunset or taking a walk through a park with a friend, instead of spending money on high-cost entertainment. Some people choose to eat less meat and more vegetarian because grains, fruits, and vegetables take fewer of the earth's resources to produce than does meat. You make a difference in the world—for better or for worse—with each decision you make!

Social Doctrine of Church

The Catholic Church has often spoken with the voice of moral authority about issues of economic and social justice, including hunger and pollution. Anytime social issues affect the **common good** (what is good not just for the majority or the richest but for all humankind), the Church has a responsibility to make moral judgments about those issues. The Scriptures and Tradition teach that concern for material needs is as essential as care for the soul. Thus the leaders of the Church cannot be limited to speaking only about spiritual issues. The teaching of the Church on social issues is called the **social doctrine** of the Church.

One of the foundations of the Church's social doctrine is that God gave human beings **stewardship** of the earth. That means that we have the will and intelligence to be in charge—not to dominate or overpower, but to create a just and reasonable society, using the earth's resources. It is up to us to see that the goods of the earth are distributed, in just and charitable ways, to every person in the world.

Some people blame those who are economically poor for their own situation. All children who enter school have the same teacher, books, and resources, right? If they would just listen and study hard, they could do well, graduate, and even go to college. But in reality it doesn't work that way.

We all have different abilities and different situations. Some children enter kindergarten knowing how to read. Others have learning disabilities, and reading comes much harder. Some children come from homes with one parent working for minimum wage. Those families may not have enough food—it's hard to learn when your stomach is growling. Not everyone enters life with equal circumstances. Good teachers recognize that some children need more help than others, and that just about every child will need special attention at times.

The Church's concern for people who are poor or disadvantaged is similar. The Scriptures tell us, "From everyone to whom much has been given, much will be required; and from the one to whom much has been entrusted, even more will be demanded" (Luke 12:48). The social doctrine of the Church realizes that those who have been given much should have special concern for those who are oppressed by poverty. Sometimes even equal treatment is not fair treatment. Our reason and our faith inform us that people who are poor or disadvantaged should get preferential treatment because their needs are greater or because their condition is a result of unjust circumstances (see the article "Preferential Option for the Poor," on page 284).

Vocation and Work

You can see that the seventh commandment has a lot to do with work and jobs. Working and paychecks are one way we participate in the distribution of the world's resources. Our work should be a reflection of who we are as whole persons. Work is part of our **vocation,** that is, God's call for our purpose in life. Our work should reflect our values, including our religious values.

As a young person, your call right now is primarily to study and learn, though you may also have other jobs in your family or the community. But as you grow older and find your vocation, the work you do has a higher purpose. By contributing your talents to society, you participate in the work of creation. And when you connect that work with Jesus, you discover that work does not have to be a burden, but part of the process of redemption, our ultimate purpose in life. Despite the glamour of television characters that don't seem to have real jobs, someone who leads

---

Pray It!

Prayer to Know Jesus in Those in Need

Jesus tells us in Matthew 25:31–46 that if we want a close relationship with him, we need to encounter him in the faces of the hungry, the thirsty, the poor, and the imprisoned. Read this Gospel passage. Then pray:

Jesus, open my eyes to see you in the face of those who are poor and suffer from injustice in our world. Open my hands in service to those who are hungry and thirsty. Warm my heart to welcome you in the immigrant, the refugee, and those who feel all alone. Grant me a spirit of simplicity in my life so more will be available to clothe the naked. Soften my heart with compassion for those who are ill and don't have basic medical services. Move my feet on the path of action for the "least" of your people. Give me the joy and deep peace of your presence as I serve you in my brothers and sisters in need. Amen.

a life of leisure all the time is certainly not living up to the potential of a person made in the image of God.

What does all this have to do with the seventh commandment, "You shall not steal"? Employers expect that workers will work to the best of their ability for the wages they are paid. Coming in late, slacking off at work, or leaving early is stealing from the boss and the company. It means others may have to do more than their fair share—plus your employer is not getting her money's worth.

However, employers have responsibilities too—to pay just wages, provide safe working conditions, and consider the economic and ecological effects on the rest of society. Dumping waste, causing air pollution, and depleting natural resources are all forms of stealing that affect the common good. Good business means that you clean up your mess and put things back where they belong.

When it comes to work and workers, we should be aware of one more social justice issue—slavery. Slavery still exists, and it exists because it provides some people with an economic advantage. There are an estimated twenty-seven million women, children, and men forced into economic slavery around the world. This slavery ranges from people forced into prostitution to people lured into another country and then forced to work in prison-like conditions. On the basis of moral law, the Church condemns any act that leads to the enslavement of human beings—persons bought, sold, or exchanged like merchandise.

Saint Vincent de Paul is honored for his commitment to care for poor and sick people. Do you know how many chapters (groups) of the Saint Vincent de Paul Society are in the United States alone?

Proper Use of Wealth

The complex problems of economic injustice clearly hurt poor people, but they also wound the hearts of rich people. When one child in the sandbox has too many toys, he is not necessarily better off. Having too much can be as bad for us as having too little. A different kind of poverty affects those of us with great material wealth. Poverty of spirit, like material poverty, leads to unhappiness.

Speaking of overload, can you estimate the number of advertisements that bombard you daily—one hundred? five hundred? one thousand? According to media experts, the number of advertising messages that the average American hears or sees each day is almost three thousand! Radio, television, the Internet, billboards, clothing with designer monograms or labels, store displays, even rolling advertisements on cars, trucks, busses, and taxis bombard us daily. Obviously we are not fully conscious of most of these ads. They are just part of our life. But ignorance may not be bliss. The power of advertising can be addictive, urging us to want to buy more, more, more.

Unfortunately, the "more, more, more" of excess consumerism doesn't make us happy. No matter how many music CDs, computerized gadgets, jeans, or pairs of shoes we have, somebody else is bound to have more than we do. That's where the tenth commandment and **envy** come in. It is just too easy for us humans to be jealous of our neighbor's things or our neighbor's talents. Instead of being happy with what we do have, we become sad when we see that someone else has more. We get caught up in wanting what they have.

When we let envy, which is a capital sin (see the article "The Seven Deadly Sins," on page 211), get under our skin, we run into all kinds of problems, such as broken relationships, bad-mouthing others, cheating, and stealing. The passion for riches, fame, or success can also make us seek power over others for all the wrong reasons (to have more things) in all the wrong ways (through manipulation, lying, and cheating).

That's why we have a commandment that challenges us to be careful about those feelings. The tenth and final commandment,

Saintly Profiles

Saint Vincent de Paul (1581–1660)

Vincent de Paul made a decision to serve the poor that changed his life and changed the world. He was born in France in 1581 into a peasant family. He progressed rapidly in school, and was ordained a priest at the age of nineteen. By 1613 he became an influential tutor for the rich and powerful Gondi family. During this time he also served as a village pastor. In ministering to the people of his parish, he became increasingly aware of the needs of the many poor and sick. He made a commitment to respond.

Throughout many villages Saint Vincent de Paul formed organized groups dedicated to helping those in need. His work also included ministering to prisoners and changing miserable prison conditions. He founded the religious community known as the Vincentians to serve the poor, and along with Saint Louise de Marillac, he founded the Daughters of Charity for the same purpose. He established orphanages and opportunities for education and employment. He organized drives to fund his efforts, inspiring some to sell their jewels.

Inspired by Saint Vincent de Paul's work, Frédéric Ozanam founded the Saint Vincent de Paul Society in 1833 as an association of laypeople dedicated to serving the poor in their communities. Today there are over one thousand chapters of the Saint Vincent de Paul Society throughout the United States, and almost a million members worldwide. Saint Vincent de Paul shows us the impact of one person's decision to make a preferential option for the poor. His feast day is September 27.

"You shall not covet your neighbor's goods," warns us about the human tendency to want what others have. We overcome that tendency by always acting morally toward others and by learning to be humble. Growing closer to God through the Scriptures and prayer makes us aware of how little we need material things to be happy. As Madaleva Wolf put it, "I like to go to Marshall Field's in Chicago just to see how many things there are in the world that I do not want." Jesus came to bring us life abundant, not in the material sense but in the deep authentic joy of knowing that riches will not make us ultimately happy. We must learn to be detached from material wealth, that is, to not make it the center of our life. He who dies with the most toys doesn't win. Just the opposite—it is love of God and neighbor, not things, that is essential for entering the Kingdom of God.

Looking Back

Preferential Option for the Poor

A **preferential option** for the poor is a choice to help poor people more than those who already have enough. The U.S. bishops, in their 1986 pastoral letter *Economic Justice for All*, talk about the roots of this concept in the Bible when they say:

> Jesus, especially in Luke, lives as a poor man, [and] like the prophets takes the side of the poor. . . . When [Jesus] states that the reign of God is theirs [Matthew 5:3], he voices God's special concern for them. . . . As individuals and as a nation, therefore, we are called to make a fundamental "option for the poor."[1] (Numbers 49, 50, and 87)

The bishops explain that making a preferential option for the poor is not to put down people with more wealth but because *"the fulfillment of the basic needs of the poor is of the highest priority"* (number 90).

For Further Reflection

- How can you be more aware of the power of advertising in your life? Make a list of all the commercials and ads you've seen in just the last week.
- Think about the things you have bought recently. How many of them did you really need for basic survival? How can you make good buying decisions in the future?
- Pope Paul VI said, "If you want peace, work for justice." How does injustice lead to conflict? Can you think of examples within your own family, your community, and the world where conflict resulted from an injustice?

Respecting Truth

Once upon a time in the not-so-fairy-tale world of teenagers, there was a guy named Judd. He was about fourteen years old, not quite legal to have his driver's license, but old enough to want a bit more independence than his parents were ready to give. One night, as Judd's curfew was getting close, he and his buddies decided on an after-hours party. To make that happen, however, everyone would have to go home first, check-in, and then sneak out after their parents were sound asleep. Meeting time in the park was 1:00 a.m.

The plan worked flawlessly. In fact, while they waited in their respective homes for their parents to drift off, they were able to go online, send a few instant messages, and invite a group of girls to join them in the park. So there they were—eight young people gathered in the middle of the night to have the time of their lives. Of course, not much is going on for teenagers at that hour, so they created their own fun. A few of the girls came prepared with rolls of toilet paper, and the adventure got more interesting.

Words to Look For

- detraction
- calumny
- slander
- reparation
- heresy
- confidentiality

What they had not counted on was the dog at the first victim's house. Suddenly awakened by a band of nocturnal visitors, Fluffy became a low-tech but incredibly efficient security system, alerting the owners of the house, the neighbors, and eventually the police. Caught red-handed, the toilet-paper-toting teenagers were taken to the police station to call their parents. When his parents demanded an explanation, Judd's defense was that he didn't exactly disobey or even lie to his parents. After all, he never asked, so they never told him specifically that he couldn't go out after midnight—as if that made it right!

In the world of morality, sometimes what is *not* said is as important as what is. The eighth commandment, "You shall not bear false witness against your neighbor," includes the sins of lying, deception, hypocrisy, and slander. But the heart of the commandment isn't about forbidding certain acts; it is about being a person of integrity who respects and lives the truth.

Lies are often seductive because they promise us something that isn't real. Does Eve look like she's enjoying the serpent's promises?

Living the Truth

Tell the truth—probably one of the first moral teachings that you heard as a child. Truthfulness is a virtue, a good habit that makes you a person of integrity, the kind of person who can be trusted. And trust is a big thing in the world of relationships. The eighth commandment commands us not to bear false witness against our neighbor. When we intentionally deceive, speak falsehoods, or keep relevant information a secret, we hurt our relationships with the people around us.

When teenagers list the important characteristics of a good relationship, romantic or otherwise, the word that surfaces most often is "trust." When Judd broke the rules set by his parents, he was deceiving them as well as disobeying them. It may be a long time before he can mend the broken trust with his parents.

Fortunately, by nature we are inclined toward the truth. Morally we are obliged to seek the truth, especially religious truth. And once we know what is true, we must live by it. Jesus tells us that he is the way, the truth, and the life (John 14:6). As followers of Jesus, we are bound by the truth of the Gospel.

The Impact of Lying

Because we as humans have a natural tendency to tell the truth, we have to be motivated to tell a lie. Some people lie to cover up something they did wrong; some lie to avoid punishment; others lie to make themselves appear more important. Well-meaning people sometimes lie to avoid confronting someone with an unpleasant truth. But any of these reasons for saying something false in order to deceive someone does not make it okay. The lie is still a sin.

Lying and deception can have unintended or unexpect-ed consequences. Getting away with a lie can still hurt and wound others, even if they never find out that you lied to them. Consider the following scenario: Jim and Joan are "going out" on a regular basis. They have a mutual understanding that their relationship is exclusive—that is, they don't date anyone else. But when Jim goes out of town one weekend, Joan goes out with his best friend, John. They figure that what Jim doesn't know won't hurt him. Are they correct in that assumption? Has the relationship between Joan and Jim changed in some way, even if Jim never finds out that his girlfriend broke the trust?

Or consider another form of deception—cheating on homework, quizzes, tests, or projects. How does cheating harm others if you get away with it? Is the teacher hurt if she never finds out? What about your classmates? How could they be negatively affected by your dishonesty?

The Church and the Media

The Church has a long history of providing moral guidelines for the media. Church leaders have addressed artists in the Middle Ages, printers in the sixteenth century, and now speak to the leaders of film, television, music, advertising, and cyberspace.

One of the most recent documents is entitled *Renewing the Mind of the Media: Statement on Overcoming the Exploitation of Sex and Violence in Communications.* In this document the U.S. Catholic bishops call on Catholics to encourage the media to portray what is truthful and good. They speak to the youth of the United States, encouraging them "to speak out against the abusive manipulation they are subjected to by media." Specific suggestions include these:

- Complain to corporations and businesses that profit from distributing objectionable programming.
- Contact at least one advertiser who sponsors commendable programming and one who sponsors objectionable programming, and ask them to continue or to withdraw their support, respectively.
- Challenge video stores and hotels/motels that distribute X-rated material.
- Use reliable sources (such as the U.S. Catholic bishops' movie review line, 800-311-4CCC, or the bishops' Web site, *www.usccb. org*) when deciding what to watch.

When we fail to be honest, at the very minimum, we negatively affect our own morality. And because every sin has social implications, the web of deceit often gets larger without us even realizing it. Sir Walter Scott's statement, "Oh, what a tangled web we weave when first we practice to deceive," is as true today as it was when God asked Cain where his brother was. Cain had murdered Abel, but tried to deceive God by answering, "I do not know; am I my brother's keeper?" (Genesis 4:9).

On the other hand, it is also wrong to use the truth as a weapon. Telling someone the truth with the intention of hurting the other person (such as making fun of a person who is overweight or doesn't dress fashionably) does not make it right. Remember the three sources of morality: the act, the intention, and the circumstances. All three must be correct for an act to be good.

Boasting, or bragging, is an offense against the truth also. Though it may feel good to inflate our own ego, lies of exaggeration usually catch up with us, damaging our own reputation. But damaging the reputation of others is even more serious.

Saint Dominic felt called to spread the truth about Jesus Christ by founding a society of preachers. You can recognize his followers by the initials OP (Order of Preachers) after their name.

Respecting Reputations

The children's old saying, "Sticks and stones may break my bones, but words can never hurt me," might be a good comeback on the playground, but it isn't true. Words can do violence to another person. Spreading a negative rumor about someone never serves any good purpose. Though a piece of gossip may be true, when we pass on that information unnecessarily, we injure someone's reputation. That kind of lying is called **detraction,** because it detracts from another person's good name. And if you pass on or create a rumor or story that is not true, you are "bearing false witness against your neighbor," an even more serious sin called **calumny,** or **slander.**

Putting ourselves in the place of the other person is a good way to avoid the moral pitfalls of gossip and slandering.

First of all, remember how it felt when someone gossiped about you. Then you can empathize with how that person might feel about your gossip. Only true empathy with other people can break the vicious cycle of rumors.

Reparations and Amends

As with the sin of stealing, we are morally obligated to make **reparation,** or amends, for sins against the truth. Owning up to our lies may be more difficult than telling the truth in the first place. But we must try to undo the harm we have caused. Sadly, sometimes the harm may be irreparable; we simply cannot repair all the damage.

Take as an example this true story. A high school cheating scandal began with two students finding and taking copies of a final exam in a required science course. As they made multiple photocopies for their friends, who in turn made copies for their buddies, the dishonesty spread like wildfire. By the time some students, who felt strongly about integrity, came forward to tell authorities, the damage had been done. Over a hundred students had seen at least part of the exam. A few students turned themselves in; others turned their friends in. Investigations led to expulsions from school, from sports teams, and from honor societies. Those who admitted guilt received zeroes on the exam, bringing their grade point average down. They were justifiably angry with classmates who apparently got away with the cheating, so friendships suffered. The scandal made the local paper, embarrassing the school, its administration, and its alumni.

Despite the damage, the students who came forward, confessed, and paid the

Saintly Profiles

Saint Dominic (1170–1221)

Saint Dominic de Guzman was a Spanish theologian and the founder of the Order of Friars Preachers. At age fourteen he went to the university to study theology and philosophy, and was ordained a priest as a young man. When a famine hit where he was studying, he sold his possessions and books to feed the poor.

When traveling through Europe, Dominic was overwhelmed by the number of people who were listening to Albigensian **heresy** (the denial of a revealed truth). The Albigensians taught that matter was evil and only God was good. Their teaching and lifestyle were popular with the common people, who were scandalized by the extravagant lifestyle of many priests and bishops of the time. Dominic knew Albigensian teaching was wrong because God revealed in the Scriptures that creation is good, and he wanted to win back people to the truth that God had revealed.

Dominic formed an order of preachers, also knows as Dominicans (they carry the initials OP after their name), who were devoted to penance, study, and preaching in order to win back those who were caught up in the Albigensian heresy. He knew that the clerical privileges often scandalized ordinary people, so he instructed those joining the order to live simple lives. He once told a bishop, "Heretics are more easily won over by examples of humility and virtue than by external display or a hail of words." Today thousands of men and women are in Dominican religious communities. Saint Dominic's feast day is August 8.

consequences were better off in the long run than those who continued to lie to the school and themselves. Confronting our own dishonesty can get us back on the track to integrity.

Failure to admit our wrongs is more likely to lead to future dishonesty. The school also confronted a problem that had been brewing for a long time; the crisis eventually brought about healing, and awareness of the importance of trust and honor in a community.

Confidentiality

Is it ever morally permissible to lie or to deceive others? A few circumstances might affect the morality of a dishonest act. Sometimes it is inappropriate to reveal the truth to someone who asks for it. The welfare and safety of others, respect for privacy, and the common good are sufficient reasons for being silent or discreet about the truth. You are not morally bound to tell the truth to someone who will use it to harm another person. For example, if you have a friend who is staying at your house because she is being harassed or abused by an ex-boyfriend, you have a duty to protect her. If the guy calls and wants to know if she is with you, it is morally permissible to deny that she is there.

However, exceptional circumstances are pretty rare. If the school calls your parents to verify your absence, it is not permissible to lie about their whereabouts, even if you think they would punish you for skipping school. In this case the deception does not serve a greater good; it covers up another wrong.

Sometimes **confidentiality** requires secrecy. Youth leaders, counselors, therapists, and doctors must not reveal what you tell them in confidence, except in unusual cases when keeping the secret might cause serious harm to you or someone else. Private information that could lead to prejudice against a person is confidential, unless

Pray It!

Squashing Rumors and Stopping Gossip

The wisdom writer Sirach tells us, "Whoever betrays secrets destroys confidence, / and will never find a congenial friend" (27:16). Gossip and rumors tear apart communities and destroy relationships. We've all witnessed the following:

- someone venting about their pet peeves of an irritating classmate, only to realize the person was overhearing the conversation
- something said in an angry moment about a friend being repeated to your friend in order to hurt your relationship
- someone repeating a rumor only to find out later that it was untrue and it caused great pain to the people involved

Gossip is appealing because it appears to make us popular or give us power. But it too often causes pain, guilt, and embarrassment. How do we rid ourselves "of all malice, and all guile, insincerity, envy, and all slander" (1 Peter 2:1)? As with any sin, we must experience a conversion. Take a moment to prayerfully examine your conscience. Have you been guilty of spreading rumors or gossiping about others? If so, ask for God's forgiveness, and pray for the insight to recognize when you are tempted to do it again.

a serious reason exists to tell it. The same kind of trust exists between friends. If a person tells you something in private, it is morally wrong to tell someone else without her or his permission—especially if the information could damage that person's reputation.

However, it is morally permissible—even morally necessary—to reveal a secret when a friend is in danger of harming herself or himself. For example, if your friend tells you that he is thinking about suicide, it is okay for you to go to an adult that you trust—a teacher, parent, counselor, coach, youth minister—and tell that person about your friend's plan, even if you promised your friend you wouldn't tell a soul! Your friend needs more help and support than you alone can give him at this time, and the best way for you to be a friend is to tell his secret. He may be angry with you for a while, but it's better to lose the friendship for a while than to lose the friend forever!

The one place where everyone's secrets are completely safe is in the sacrament of Penance and Reconciliation. The seal of confession is so sacred that a priest can never tell anyone what he has heard in someone's confession, even in the most serious circumstances.

Truth in Society

Telling the truth is as important in society as it is among individuals. We need to be able to trust other people in our community and beyond. When someone gives you information, you trust that they are telling the truth: "What time does the plane land?" "How much money do I have in my account?" "What grade did I get on my test?" Like trust among family and friends, truth is the glue that makes a society work harmoniously.

Copy and Paste: An Instant-Messenger Conversation

Below is an instant-messenger conversation between MadlyInLove (MIL) and LetsBeFriends (LBF). The words in parentheses are the truth that their lies misrepresent.

MIL: im going to the movies tonight, wanna come (I'll only go if I find a friend.)
LBF: the band's coming to practice (I'll be home alone, just don't want to go.)
LBF: susie wanted to go to the movies
LBF: shes online
MIL: i thought you didn't talk to susie (You said she lied to you and you'd never speak to her again.)
LBF: we talk sometimes (Actually all the time, but I know that will make you upset.)
MIL: i heard she broke up with her boyfriend after he had bought her this really expensive bracelet
LBF: he is a total jerk (I don't know him, only heard he was a jerk.)
MIL: my parental unit just came in the room
MIL: have to look like im doing homework (I'm yelling to them that I am doing homework.)
MIL: bye
LBF: bye

- Why do MadlyInLove and LetsBeFriends tell each other half-truths and gossip?
- How does this hurt relationships?
- How could you rewrite the above conversation to be truthful *and* make the friendship stronger *and* enable both MIL and LBF to become better people?

In modern society the media are our source of information about our community, our nation, and the world. We are blessed to have the freedom of the press enjoyed in the United States and Canada and many other nations. The public has the right to information based on truth, freedom, and justice. News reporters, talk show hosts, political analysts, and journalists should practice integrity in what they report and how they report it.

Freedom of the press comes with responsibilities. The media have a social responsibility, because they are such a powerful influence in the formation of public opinion. Ratings and the profits they bring in do not justify sensationalizing or misrepresenting the truth. Certain information is too confidential or in too poor taste to put on the air. Those in the media are called to make good moral choices about all issues. We can influence the mind of the media by carefully choosing what we watch. Our decisions as consumers can affect advertisers, who have an enormous impact on media decisions.

We all have to make daily choices about truthfulness. When you are a person of integrity, telling the truth is your default—a good habit that will serve you well. Jesus said to those who believed in him, "If you continue in my word, you are truly my disciples; and you will know the truth, and the truth will make you free" (John 8:31–32). Being truthful does lead to freedom: freedom from guilt and freedom from worrying about being caught in a lie. And that's the Gospel truth.

Looking Back

The Seal of Confession

A priest can *never,* under penalty of excommunication, reveal what he hears in confession. The Code of Canon Law says: "The sacramental seal is inviolable. Accordingly, it is absolutely wrong for a confessor in any way to betray the penitent, for any reason whatsoever, whether by word or in any other fashion" (number 983, paragraph 1). The seal of confession is so sacred that it binds a layperson who acts as an interpreter during confession. Even the Pope cannot permit a priest to divulge a sin. A priest cannot speak to you after confession about what you have confessed or reveal your sins after you have died.

A priest is expected to go to jail, and some even choose death, rather than reveal what was said in confession. Saint John Nepomucene, the archbishop of Prague, was drowned in 1393 by the king, when he refused to tell what the queen had said in confession.

For Further Reflection

- James A. Garfield, the twentieth president of the United States, said, "The truth will set you free, but first it will make you miserable." Can you think of examples from your own life that might illustrate this statement?
- Have you ever had to make a decision about revealing someone's secret—for their own good? What were the circumstances? How did you handle it? Do you wish you had done anything differently?
- Think of a time when telling the truth was difficult, but worth it. What happened? What was the result?

30

The Moral Life

There once was a young person who deeply envied the people she saw who moved with such grace and beauty on the school dance team. One day she decided to do something about it. She went to the greatest dance teacher in the city and said, "Teach me how to dance." The teacher said, "First you must learn the steps." For weeks she drilled the basic steps over and over. Then the teacher said, "Now you must learn to put the steps together into a dance." For months the girl practiced putting the moves together into complicated dance patterns.

Finally the girl approached her teacher and said, "I've been practicing for months and months. I know the steps, I know the patterns, but I still feel clumsy and awkward." And the teacher said, "There is one more thing you must do that I cannot teach you. You must forget trying to look good for others, and dance only for yourself and the One who created

Words to Look For

- cardinal virtues
- prudence
- justice
- temperance
- fortitude
- theological virtues
- justification
- grace
- sanctifying grace
- conversion

294

you. Tap into the rhythm that is already inside you, and let it move you so that your dancing is a free and joyful expression of your inner grace." And the girl did, and her dancing was an inspiration for all who saw her.

In the moral life, our heart tells us we want to learn to dance the right way, God's way. We have to use our head to learn the meaning of the commandments, which are the basic steps. We listen to the Beatitudes, which are the music that makes the steps come alive. But to best practice the moral life, we have to tap into the gifts God has placed within each one of us: the virtues, forgiveness, and grace. This final chapter on morality isn't about specific rights and wrongs; it's about making your life a beautiful testimony to God's love and presence in your life!

Cardinal Virtues

Virtues harness the good energy within us. They are habits that we develop over time to help us make good decisions. Like mastering skills in any sport, virtues capitalize on the abilities God has already placed within us. When you first learned to shoot a basket, to dribble a soccer ball, or to master a swimming stroke, someone had to show you the technique. As you practiced the basics, it became more natural, and you were able to advance to more complicated skills. When virtues become natural to us, we don't always have to think about the mechanics of moral decision-making.

There are two kinds of virtues—cardinal virtues and theological virtues. The **cardinal virtues** come with being human, regardless of religious belief. Jesus was a model for living the four virtues of prudence, justice, temperance, and fortitude. As you develop these four virtues in your life, you become a person of moral character. To have character means that you do the right thing, even under difficult circumstances.

Did You Know?

Other Virtues

The word *cardinal* is derived from the Latin *cardo,* meaning "hinge," something on which many other things depend. Thus the cardinal virtues of justice, prudence, temperance, and fortitude are the primary virtues that many other virtues depend on. If we develop these four good habits in our life, many other virtuous habits are possible. For example, if you develop the virtue of temperance, it is easier to also develop the virtues of patience and living a healthy lifestyle.

The Church doesn't have a comprehensive list of the virtues Christians strive to develop, but here are some examples: compassion, honesty, chastity, charity, caring for the earth, caring for our bodies, expressing gratitude, and respecting life. The life of Christian virtue is an ongoing journey. Do you notice that when you practice a good habit, it makes it easier to do other good things and to avoid bad habits?

Prudence is the opposite of being impulsive. Acting impulsively is okay when you are two years old. It may even be appropriate in certain settings that call for creativity or spontaneity. But making moral decisions impulsively can get you into trouble. Prudence requires that you approach moral problems with a degree of caution. Also called wise judgment, prudence relies heavily on our reason. In fact, Saint Thomas Aquinas called it "right reason in action"[1] (*CCC*, number 1806). Prudence helps you to stop and think before you act.

Justice is the virtue concerned with giving both God and neighbor what is their due. It is the habit of thinking about the needs of others as much as your own needs, and acting on what you know to be fair. It takes determination and dedication to be a just person. The Scriptures take justice a step further than fairness: justice is all about loving your neighbor. Justice is washing your own laundry; love is washing someone else's.

Temperance is about balance in your life. You know that stress, greed, or sickness comes from too much of a good thing. The pleasures in life must be balanced with moderation. Too much play isn't good; neither is all work and no play. Exercise is good for our body; too much can lead to an obsession. Food is another pleasure we must learn to balance. Good food nourishes our body and gives us pleasure; too much leads to obesity, too little and we develop an eating disorder. People must learn to drink in moderation or they will experience the tragedy of alcoholism. The virtue of temperance is about self-control in all areas of our life.

Fortitude is the moral virtue that strengthens us to overcome obstacles to living morally. It is easy to be good when we have no direct temptation in our life. When you

Looking Back

John Paul II on Life in Christ

Our daily experience tells us that life is marked by *sin* and threatened by *death,* despite the desire for good which beats in our hearts and the desire for life which courses through our veins. However little heed we pay to ourselves and to the frustrations which life brings us, we discover that *everything within us impels us to transcend ourselves,* urges us to overcome the temptation of superficiality or despair.

. . . There are the teachers of the "fleeting moment," who invite people to give free rein to every instinctive urge or longing, with the result that individuals fall prey to a sense of anguish and anxiety leading them to seek refuge in false, artificial paradises. . . .

There are also those who teach that the meaning of life lies solely in the quest for success, the accumulation of wealth, the development of personal abilities, without regard for the needs of others or respect for values, at times not even for the fundamental value of life itself. . . .

You can find the answer by yourselves, if you really try to live faithfully in the love of Christ (cf. John 15:9). Then you will personally experience the truth of those words of his: "I am . . . the life" (John 14:6) and you will be able to bring this joyful message of hope to everyone. (Pope John Paul II, message for World Youth Day VIII, 1993) are not feeling the ecstasy of being in love, the Church's teaching on premarital sex makes perfect sense. If you are not angry, nonviolence is a worthy ideal. But when you are in the heat of any moment, whether it is sexual passion or anger or some other strong feeling, fortitude gives you strength to overcome the temptation.

You must practice these virtues even when they don't come naturally. If you persevere, eventually they will become a more natural way of life for you. The good news is that God is with us in the struggle to live a virtuous life. With God guiding our efforts through divine grace, the cardinal virtues will bring our moral life to a higher level of integrity.

Theological Virtues

Human virtues are a source of energy for choosing good moral actions. But faith, hope, and love—the **theological virtues**—are the source of energy for perfecting our relationships with God and neighbor. *Theological* means "the study of God." These virtues are theological because in accepting them and using them, we are drawn into deeper knowledge of and relationship with the Holy Trinity. Faith, hope, and love flow from God and back to God, providing an eternal power source of divine energy.

Faith is belief in God. It is both a gift and a response. Faith is the gift of God inviting us to believe in him, never forcing the issue. Faith is also our response—we accept or reject the offer. Our belief in God then affects every dimension of our life; we can't just say we believe in God and leave it at that. As disciples of Christ, we must live our faith, confidently professing it and spreading it to others.

Hope in God is closely connected to our faith. Hope enables us to keep our eye on the prize of heaven and eternal life.

Pray It!

Prayer for a Virtuous Life

Good and gracious God,

When I feel the lure of excess and crave too much of a good thing, help me to develop temperance, the self-control that gives my life balance and wholeness.

When I feel driven to act on impulse, give me prudence, the wisdom to stop and think before I act.

When I find that I am preoccupied with myself, my own wants and worries, help me to see others with eyes of compassion and reach out to them with loving justice.

When I face obstacles to living morally that tempt me to move away from you, give me fortitude, the courage to overcome the temptation.

Amen.

It inspires us in this life, helping us to overcome discouragement. Even when our situation seems hopeless, maintaining our hope in God helps us remember our ultimate destiny and gets us through difficulties. Hope working together with faith and love gives us confidence to live the higher purpose of our life.

And then there is love, also called charity. This is the greatest of all the theological virtues. Saint Paul said, "And now faith, hope, and love abide, these three; and the greatest of these is love" (1 Corinthians 13:13). Love is the virtue that gives life to the commandment to love God above all things, and our neighbor as ourself. God is love, and love is God. More than a feeling—even though feelings of love are wonderful—love is an attitude. At times we must go beyond feelings, and will ourselves to love others. Love like this, like God, makes all things possible.

Saint Thérèse of Lisieux was more concerned with showing great love in the relationships of everyday life than in performing great spiritual deeds. How can we show extraordinary love in our daily relationships?

Forgiveness

A popular bumper sticker says, "Christians are not perfect, just forgiven." The question of forgiveness is important, because despite the fact that we are made in God's image and likeness, despite all the gifts that God has given us to follow his Law, we still sin. Sometimes we act impulsively, and we hurt others in our attempts to be funny or to be accepted, because we are scared, or because we just don't think. Other times we deliberately think about the wrong we are about to do, and then go ahead and do it anyway. Or we get into such bad habits, or vices, that virtue doesn't have a chance. Despite that, we are on the journey toward the perfection of mind, heart, and soul that is our inheritance as children of God, but we still have a ways to go.

But the Gospel message, the good news (*Gospel* means "good news"), is that God is always ready to forgive us! All we need to do is turn to him in true sorrow and repentance and our sins are wiped away, we are free to begin again. The psalmist knew this when he wrote, "As far as the east is from the west, / so far he removes our transgressions from us" (Psalm 103:12).

Jesus practiced this kind of forgiveness. Read the story of the woman caught in adultery (John 8:2–11). How do you think she felt when she heard Jesus' words: "Neither do I condemn you. Go your way, and from now on do not sin again"? There is no sin that can separate us from God's love and forgiveness.

The Church teaches that through our Baptism, we receive the grace of the Holy Spirit, who has the power to cleanse us from our sins and to communicate God's grace to us. Because Jesus died and rose from the dead for us, we are able to turn back toward God and away from sin. Each time we accept God's forgiveness, we are sanctified (made holy again) and renewed.

Forgiveness and **justification** are closely related topics. Justification means that are our sins have been forgiven and that we have been made right with God. Has anyone ever asked you if you have been justified? The question has its roots in the writings of Saint Paul, who speaks about being justified in Christ (Romans 3:21–26). The answer is: "Yes, I have been justified, because I have been baptized in Christ. I am assured of God's infinite and unconditional love because of Jesus' death on the cross." Justification is a term that most Catholics are not familiar with, but Christians in other denominations speak about it frequently. Justification is the most excellent work of God's mercy.

The sacrament of Penance and Reconciliation is also connected to justification and forgiveness. As human beings with reason and emotions, we need to experience God's forgiveness by being sorry for our sins and sincerely resolving to avoid those acts or attitudes in the future. Only God can forgive sins. The sacrament is the outward sign of God's forgiveness and grace, and through the absolution of the priest, who represents the

Saintly Profiles

Saint Thérèse of Lisieux (1873–1897)

Saint Thérèse of Lisieux, also known as the "Little Flower," was born in Alençon, France in 1873. While still a young girl, Thérèse longed to enter the Carmelite convent at Lisieux. When she was fifteen, the bishop gave permission, and she joined two of her older sisters there. Her life of prayer and work in the convent was hidden to others, but she became known to the world through her autobiography, *The Story of a Soul*, published in 1899. The book was translated into many languages and became widely popular. It was not her idea to write it. Her superiors saw a unique holiness in Thérèse, and directed her to write it.

In the book she describes her life as the "little way"—a simple life of spiritual childhood, characterized by acknowledging one's spiritual poverty, living with complete confidence in God's love, and dedicating one's days to the practice of love. Thérèse's little way to holiness emphasizes great love rather than great deeds, and has appealed to countless people seeking to be holy in the midst of ordinary life.

A short time before her death, Thérèse remarked that she would spend her time in heaven trying to do good on earth. She said she would send a "shower of roses" from heaven. She died at the age of twenty-four from tuberculosis, after much suffering. She was canonized in 1925, and declared a doctor of the Church in 1997. Her feast day is October 1.

faith community, we can be assured of God's forgiveness and our reconciliation with the Church. Receiving the sacrament of Penance and Reconciliation regularly provides a good checkpoint as we strive to live a moral life. Be sure to participate regularly in the sacrament; you might be surprised at how wonderful it will make you feel!

Grace

Grace happens. And it is amazing. We don't do anything to get grace. The most general definition of **grace** is that God is communicating to us at every moment of our existence (also see "Kinds of Grace," on page 146). It's like radio waves. As you read this, millions of sound waves are being broadcast, available for you to hear. But you need a radio to tune them in if you want to actually experience the music, news, or conversations that are happening out there in radioland. God is broadcasting too, but you need to tune in for grace to make a difference in your life.

We can locate God's station in multiple ways: stopping to give praise for all creation; being more aware of God's presence as we go about the routine of our daily life; prayer, worship, and the sacraments, of course, are guaranteed ways to experience God's grace. But we also experience grace through forgiveness. Through our Baptism and through the sacrament of Penance and Reconciliation, the Holy Spirit gives us **sanctifying grace** to heal our wounded soul and make us whole—and make us holy—again.

In the world of morality, tuning in to grace is especially crucial. Grace is the help that God gives us to respond to our vocation to be his adopted daughters and sons. Without any effort on our part, we become part of the divine energy of the Trinity. God's infinite love is there before we realize it, preparing us and inviting us to respond to the invitation to love God back. Our deepest desires connect back to God, who gives us the free will to choose to listen and then act on what we hear.

When we cooperate with God's gift of self-love to us, we benefit even more from the gift. Although we don't earn grace by being good, grace helps us to be good. When we are grace-filled, we are at our best, fulfilling our potential. To go back to the opening story in this chapter, we are most "grace-full" when we dance in harmony with God.

Conversion, our lifelong journey with and to God, is ignited and fueled by the energy of grace. The initial grace that leads to our conversion and Baptism is entirely God's work. Then when we act morally, we dance in the direction of God, and we actually increase the grace available to ourselves and to others. When we sin, we take a step backward, and God's grace is less available. But God's mercy is ever present, inviting us to a change of heart, a change in the direction we are headed, so that we can get back on track. When we respond to God's ever-present invitation, we discover how good it feels to be good. Being moral in this life is worth it, now *and* forever.

Being Catholic is like being online to God's Web site for moral living. We find moral principals, virtues, commandments, Beatitudes, Jesus' life and his teachings, the sacraments, and two thousand years of wisdom for us. There is moral support from parents, priests, youth leaders, teachers, counselors, and peers who share our values. The virtues, forgiveness, and grace are the gifts that help us put all this wisdom into action. You have everything you need to live a holy, happy, and healthy life. Now, just do it!

Further Reflection

○ Pick one of the cardinal virtues that you would like to work on. Make a plan for practicing this virtue intentionally for one week. Check yourself at the end of the week to see how your plan made a difference.

○ Reflect on a time when you needed forgiveness from someone. How hard was it to ask for forgiveness? How did you feel about being forgiven—or not forgiven? How hard is it for you to extend forgiveness to others?

Grace and Works

Q. A friend asked me why Catholics put so much emphasis on doing good things. Does this contradict our understanding of grace? Are we always assured of God's grace no matter what we do?

A. Grace is God's love given to us, all of us. It is free and undeserved—*never* earned. This gift is ours for the taking. We are free to reject God's gift, however. God gives us the power to love, but does not program us to love! What we do is important because our response to God matters. The good work that we do, however, is attributed first to God's grace and only secondarily to us. Think about this insight from Saint Augustine:

> Indeed we also work, but we are only collaborating with God who works, for his mercy has gone before us. It has gone before us so that we may be healed, and follows us so that once healed, we may be given life; it goes before us so that we may be called, and follows us so that we may be glorified; it goes before us so that we may live devoutly, and follows us so that we may always live with God: for without him we can do nothing.[2] (*CCC*, number 2001)

An often-quoted saying offers this insightful and practical advice: "Work as if everything depends on you. Pray as if everything depends on God."

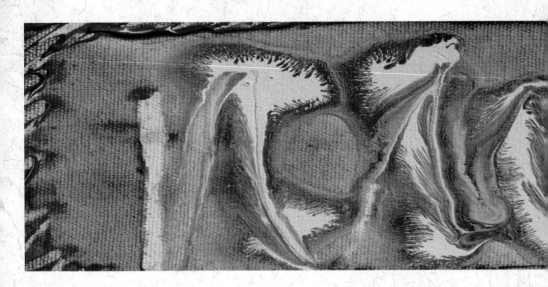

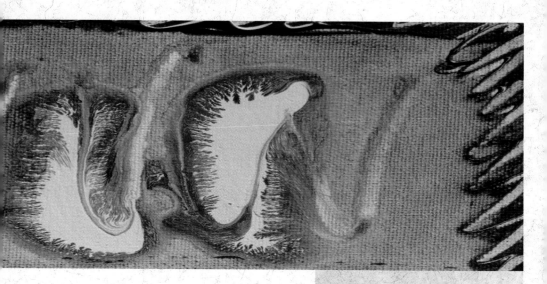

Father who art in heaven,
lowed be thy name.
kingdom come.
will be done on earth, as it is in heaven.
e us this day our daily bread,
forgive us our trespasses,
as we forgive those who trespass against us,
lead us not into temptation,
deliver us from evil.
en.

Part D

Christian
Prayer

31 Introduction to Prayer

Maybe you are outgoing: you make new acquaintances easily, you are often the first to speak, and new situations energize you. Or perhaps you are more introverted: you have fewer but deeper friendships, listening rather than talking is your strength, and you find predictability reassuring. Regardless of your nature, you know that making and keeping friends takes effort.

If you made a list of ways to develop good friendships, what would it include? Here are some things that many people would include on such a list:

- Make time for each other.
- Talk about things that are important, such as hopes and dreams.
- Do things together, just hang out.
- Listen to each other.
- Forgive each other.
- Give each other space when needed, but still stay in touch.

Words to Look For

- prayer
- humility
- laity
- domestic church

It might surprise you to realize that these and other facets of making and keeping strong friendships also apply to another important relationship—prayer. Prayer can become alive and vital when you experience it as a deep, personal relationship with God.

Prayer Defined

When you were young, you learned to talk by imitating someone else. Sounds and words gradually became yours, and you gained skill at stringing them into phrases and then sentences to express thoughts. This process carries over into prayer. You probably first learned to talk to God using someone else's words. These memorized prayers helped you express a child's faith. But as you have matured, you have likely used your own words in prayer to express who you are, what you think, how you feel, and what you need.

Sharing prayer with other people is one of the foundations of Christian life. How and where do you pray with others?

Approaching **prayer** as "talking to God" is a good starting point, but too much talk has its drawbacks. Sometimes we start out talking to God, only to end up conversing with ourselves. So, a question: In addition to talking to God, do you spend time listening to God too? Few of us can tolerate friends who do nothing but talk at us. Words are an important part of prayer, but just as relationships are more than words, so is prayer.

A classic definition of prayer says, "Prayer is the raising of one's mind and heart to God or the requesting of good things from God" (*CCC*, number 2590). In other words, in addition to words, prayer involves your mind and heart. It includes insight and affection, just like a good friendship.

Sometimes when you pray, you might experience insight, like a bright lightbulb going off in your head. More often when you raise your mind to God in prayer, your intellect is shaped so gradually and gently that you only notice the change over time, much like you come to appreciate the way a good friend or teacher has influenced your thinking, only years later.

Just as friendship is more about affection than insight, prayer is also more a matter of the heart. When you allow yourself to open your heart in friendship to God, you can hear

God's voice within saying, "I love you!" When this happens you experience the power of prayer to heal you and to help you become more loving in all your relationships.

The rosary is a meditative prayer that you can pray by yourself or with others. It is rooted in Catholics' deep love for and trust in Mary. If you have never prayed the rosary, ask someone to teach it to you.

Prayer as Covenant, Communion, and Gift

According to the Scriptures, it is the heart that prays. This doesn't refer to the hollow muscular organ that pumps blood through your body. Nor does it imply that prayer is a romantic endeavor. Biblically speaking, the heart is your hidden center, the place of decision and truth where as a person made in God's image, you speak to God, live in God's presence, and hear God speak to you. The heart is where your relationship with God unfolds.

Perhaps a couple of analogies can help you understand. If you were a computer, your relationship to God would be a part of your hardware that no software virus could corrupt. Or think of it as having something that resembles a satellite dish as part of your very essence. You were made to receive a special kind of signal, a communication with God in Christ that springs from the Holy Spirit. Prayer is this living relationship, this communion.

Although you might be hardwired for a relationship with God, that alone doesn't make you a person of prayer. You have probably noticed that some people are hard to get to know. In some cases this is because they are overly proud or constantly exerting their opinion and their will. Such people do not receive others as uniquely gifted, nor are they able to give of themselves to others. For friendship to grow, people have to approach one another with the opposite stance, with a humble openness to the gift and mystery of one another.

Similarly, the Catholic Church teaches that only when we approach God in prayer with humility are we able to receive the gift of this vital and personal relationship. **Humility** means that we are honest about who we are, that we acknowledge our weaknesses and sins as well as our gifts. Jesus illustrates this point in the parable of the Pharisee and the tax collector. The

Pharisee's prayer is a boast of his own goodness. He is too full of himself to receive anything. The tax collector humbly admits his sinfulness and is exalted with the gift of God's mercy (Luke 18:9–14). Later in this section, we will look at some of Jesus' other teachings on prayer.

Everyone Is Called to Prayer

When you really want to get to know someone, it is easy to get caught up in worrying about saying the right words and doing the right things. You can probably think of a time when you tried to impress someone else, but you ended up neither getting to know the person nor feeling like yourself. Hopefully you have learned that the best person to be when you are making friends is yourself.

The same is true in prayer. Because prayer arises from our being made in God's image, it is far less about the right words and techniques and far more about being who God made us to be: people who desire to be in relationship with the one who called us into existence. Everyone is called to prayer. This is because the desire for God is built into us; it is a response to God who first and tirelessly calls us to encounter him through prayer. It's like picking up the phone to call a friend and finding her or him already on the line, having called you first.

When you are your true self in a relationship, you learn about the other person and experience the joy of self-discovery at the same time. Similarly, in prayer God reveals himself to you, and you learn about yourself. This reciprocal call between God and humankind has been going on throughout the whole of salvation history. Prayer is a central way that God has revealed himself to humankind and shown us who we are.

Did You Know?

The Rosary

The rosary is one of the oldest forms of prayer in our Catholic Tradition. It is also one of the most popular. It is a meditative prayer, entered into by the repetition of an Our Father, or the Lord's Prayer, followed by ten Hail Marys. It can be prayed alone or with others.

The rosary is intended to move us to meditate on the mysteries of Jesus' life. The mysteries used are the five Mysteries of Light, the five Joyful Mysteries, the five Sorrowful Mysteries, and the five Glorious Mysteries. Praying the Hail Mary repeatedly helps you quietly reflect on these mysteries in order to enter into the life of Jesus. Saint Dominic (1170–1221) is believed to have received a vision from Mary, asking him to encourage people to pray the rosary. However, monasteries were using the rosary long before Saint Dominic.

Rosaries come in a wide variety of colors and styles. There are finger rosaries and very large rosaries. They are made of precious metals and gems as well as simple cord and wood. People often give rosaries as gifts on religious occasions. Because of this many people's rosaries have special memories attached to them. You can find directions for saying this prayer on pages 385–386 in the Catholic Prayers and Devotions appendix.

Prayer in the Old Testament

Prayer reveals the relationship between humankind and God that grows through historical events. The drama of prayer in the Old Testament reveals God's initiative, continually calling humankind deeper into relationship. Looking at some of the central characters in the Bible reveals the human heart at prayer.

Abraham's response to God's call to be in a covenant relationship shows the attentiveness of the heart at prayer, making decisions according to God's will. Abraham and Sarah welcomed the mysterious presence of God (see the story of Abraham and the strangers, in Genesis 18:1–15), and their hearts, like God's, have compassion for all humankind. Abraham's faith does not weaken when he is asked to sacrifice the son that God gave him. Praying with Abraham's faithfulness can enlarge your heart to trust more fully in God.

From the midst of the burning bush, God calls Moses to be his messenger. The heart of Moses balks because he feels unworthy and inadequate to the task (Exodus 3:1–4:17). In his prayer conversation with God, Moses gradually agrees to a role that calls to mind Jesus Christ's role as mediator between God and humankind. As mediator Moses doesn't pray for himself, but intercedes for God's people, often conversing at length and face-to-face with God. Moses can be an example for you of what the humble heart does in prayer (Numbers 12:3,7–8).

The heart of King David at prayer expresses loving and joyful trust in God, submission to God's will, praise, and repentance. So great was his joy that he danced before the Lord's presence in the ark (2 Samuel 6:14). David, inspired by the Holy Spirit, is credited with writing many of the Psalms, the masterpiece of prayer in the Old Testament. Read the story of David, and you will find that his enemies persecuted him,

Saint Francis de Sales wrote *Introduction to the Devout Life* to support the spiritual life of ordinary people. Here he is pictured doing his own spiritual reading. What reading can you do to grow in your faith?

he delighted in God, he was deeply repentant over his sin, and he experienced great grief over the death of those close to him—all of which is reflected in the Psalms. Written and collected over time, they reflect a deepening in prayer of the People of God.

The Psalms have a unique timelessness about them that makes them the prayer of the human heart for all ages. They are about God's work and they are about humankind's response. As a Jewish man, Jesus prayed the Psalms many times, because they are an important part of Jewish prayer. When you pray the Psalms, you are praying the same prayers that Jesus himself prayed! In ways that are both deeply personal and communal, the Psalms express every emotion of the human heart: anger, certitude, temptation, submission to God's will, praise, abandonment, desire, trust, confidence, and more. There is a psalm that can give expression to whatever you might be feeling.

Finally, in the prayer of the prophets, we see the human heart complain and argue but never flee from a world in need of change. Instead the prophetic heart remains attentive to God's word, intercedes for an unfaithful world, and awaits God's answer. When you feel like the world around you is going to the dogs, let the prayer of the prophets teach you to pray for the conversion of the world, while you remain steadfast.

The Prayer of Jesus as Model

As children of God, we are all made to be in a close relationship with God. Through prayer you enter that relationship with God through Christ by the power of the Holy Spirit. So what better teacher of prayer could there be than someone who is part of this communion? Jesus is that teacher. Let's take a closer

Saintly Profiles

Saint Francis de Sales (1567–1622)

Saint Francis de Sales was a bishop of Geneva, Switzerland, and is known as a doctor of the Church. Saint Francis lived a simple life and had a deep love for the poor and the sick. He was well known for his preaching, his writing, and his ministry. His book *Introduction to the Devout Life* is a spiritual classic. This book was unusual for the time because in it Saint Francis stressed that everyone is called to live a holy life, not just priests and members of religious communities. He was one of the first leaders of the Church to emphasize prayer and the spiritual life to the laity.

Saint Francis de Sales's simple approach to prayer and the spiritual life attracted many followers. He also founded several religious congregations, including the Missionaries of Saint Francis de Sales, the Oblates of Saint Francis de Sales, the Salesians of Don Bosco, and the Sisters of Saint Joseph. He became spiritual director for a young widow, Jane Frances de Chantal, and helped her found the Institute of the Visitation of the Blessed Virgin, for women who felt called to religious life but who did not have the means to join an order. The Church later declared her a saint too. Saint Francis de Sales is known as the patron saint of writers, of the Catholic press, and of the hearing impaired. His feast day is January 24.

look at how he prayed, what he taught about prayer, and how he hears our prayer.

As the Son of God who became human, Jesus prayed just as we do. As a child he learned the prayer words and rhythms of his people from his mother. In this way he was like many of us. The Gospels tell us that he prayed at decisive moments in his ministry, before his Father's witness to him in his Baptism and Transfiguration, and before the fulfillment of his Father's plan by his Passion (Luke 3:21, 9:28, 22:41–44). He also prayed at key moments involving his Apostles. When you pray at decisive moments in your life and in the lives of your friends, like Jesus you humbly commit your will to the will of God.

Jesus emphasized that we should bring the correct attitude to our prayer. Beginning with the Sermon on the Mount, he taught that for our hearts to pray in faith, we must undergo conversion, which is turning away from sin and toward God. We must reconcile with others, love our enemies, pray for our persecutors, pray sincerely and not to look important, pray for forgiveness from the depths of a pure heart, and make seeking the Kingdom of God our top priority (Matthew 5:23—6:33).

Because Jesus is the Son of God, his prayer is to his heavenly Father. When Jesus' disciples make the request, "Lord, teach us to pray" (Luke 11:1), he tells them that they, too, must pray to the Father. Through our Baptism we, too, have become daughters and sons of God, and so our prayer is also primarily addressed to the Father. In the chapters on the Lord's Prayer, we will look more closely at the way Jesus taught us to pray to the Father.

Jesus tells his disciples that when they pray in faith and "ask in my name" (John 14:13), whatever they need will be provided. Above all, Jesus will ask his Father to send the Holy Spirit, who contains all gifts. As Catholics we understand this

Looking Back

Spiritual Direction

Spiritual direction is about an ongoing relationship between two people or a group of people who want to be serious about their spiritual life and who meet on a regular basis. It is an old and traditional practice in the Church. It is common among priests, seminarians, and religious men and women, but it is also gaining popularity among the **laity** (non-clergy). The directee is the person who seeks the relationship in order to uncover the mystery of his or her own journey with God and to God. He or she meets with a spiritual director, someone who has been trained to help others grow in their prayer life and their relationship with God. Building a strong relationship of trust between the directee and the director is important, so that sharing and the desire to grow in God's love can be honest and sincere. If you are interested in spiritual direction, ask your youth minister or priest to recommend someone you could visit.

to mean that even though we pray to the Father, we pray "in the name of Jesus," because it is through his sacred humanity that the Holy Spirit teaches us to pray to the Father. If you remember the analogy of having a satellite dish as part of your very essence, you can think of the Holy Spirit as the signal that God is constantly sending. It is the Holy Spirit who draws us on the way of prayer.

You might be saying, "I pray, but does anyone hear my prayers?" We can look to Jesus for the answer. He heard the prayers that were expressed to him in words by the leper, by Jairus, by the Gentile woman, and by the good thief (Mark 1:40–41; 5:21–24, 35–43; 7:29; Luke 23:39–43). He also heard the silent prayers—those needs indicated by actions, not by words—of the bearers of the paralytic, of the woman with a hemorrhage, and of the sinful woman who anointed him (Mark 2:5, 5:28; Luke 7:37–38). The traditional prayer known as the Jesus prayer (see the article "The Jesus Prayer," on page 62) has its roots in the urgent request of the blind man (Matthew 20:29–34, Mark 10:46–52, Luke 18:35–43), whom Jesus heard and responded to, and the humble tax collector, whom Jesus holds up as a model for prayer (Luke 18:9–14). Have faith that just as Jesus heard the prayers of all these people, God will also hear your prayer. You may not get everything you ask for, but you will receive everything you need. Part of prayer is placing our complete trust in God, for God knows better than we do what we truly need.

The Prayer of Mary

Mary also stands as a model of prayer for us. Before the Incarnation and the outpouring of the Holy Spirit, her human heart was completely attuned to the will of the Father. Her response to God's messenger, "Here

How God Answers Prayers

Responding to the question, "What kind of answer do you expect from God when you pray?" Jackie Mahoney, a 2001 graduate of O'Gorman High School, in Sioux Falls, South Dakota, wrote:

I have always lived by the old saying, "The Lord works in mysterious ways." The older I get, the more I realize how much this is true. When we are younger we expect immediate results, and if we don't get them, then we are not fully satisfied. I remember thinking to myself, "Surely if God is all-powerful and so wonderful, he could grant me one simple request, such as having a snow day off school or getting my secret crush to notice me."

Now I believe God answers prayer the way he thinks will be most beneficial to me. The Lord always has our best intentions in mind, and sometimes what we want is not really necessary. While we may think it is cruel punishment to not get what we ask for, sometimes this is for the better if it is God's will. When I pray, I expect God to listen to me and to simply give me a push in the right direction. I don't look for some sort of sign from heaven. Instead I listen to my heart, where I believe God puts the answers.

I am, the servant of the Lord; let it be with me according to your word" (Luke 1:38) shows us how to be wholly God's and that he is worthy of our complete trust. From her we learn that we, too, are capable of such faith.

Mary is not only the mother of God, she is the mother of the Church, of all Christians (see pages 121–122). Because of this the Church has developed a tradition of praying to Mary for special needs. We do not adore Mary, or imagine that she bestows special favors—although like any good mother, we expect her to sympathize with our needs and concerns and to bring those needs before God. The Catholic Church teaches that when we pray to Mary, we are acknowledging her special role in God's plan. Along with Mary, we praise God for the great things he does for us and for all humankind (see Mary's special prayer, the Magnificat, in Luke 1:46–55).

After being blessed by her relative Elizabeth, the pregnant Mary spontaneously praises God in a beautiful prayer called the Magnificat (Luke 1:46–55). Have you ever been moved to spontaneous prayer in a moment of great joy?

Guides for Prayer

Have you ever asked advice of someone concerning a relationship with a friend, because of a disagreement, a lack of communication, or feeling like things were just plain "stuck"? You probably thought about it beforehand and chose someone with experience in the same kind of issue. When it comes to this relationship called prayer, there are many you can turn to for advice. One source we can turn to is the saints. Through their writings, their lives, and their continued prayer, the saints will inspire your prayer life.

Another source to look to is the rich spiritual traditions started by some of the saints in the Church. For example, many prayer traditions are associated with Saint Francis, Saint Benedict, Saint Ignatius, Saint Teresa, and Saint Francis de Sales. The Church uses the beautiful image of light refracting through a prism to get across the idea that these many ways of praying all come from the one pure light of the Holy Spirit. The different schools of Christian spirituality share in the living tradition of prayer and are precious guides for the spiritual life. You have met many of the holy men and women who began these spiritual traditions already, and you will meet many more in this section.

Another guide for prayer is our family. We noted that for most of us, home is where we first learn to pray. For this reason the Catholic Church has long called the family the **domestic church,** and teaches that the Christian family is the first place for education in prayer. Perhaps you can think of some ways to build up the prayer life in your home.

Finally, priests, deacons, religious, catechists, prayer groups, and spiritual directors can each be seen as avenues of support in your prayer life. If you need help with prayer, ask one of these people for some assistance.

For Further Reflection

- Where and from whom did you first learn to pray? What did you learn? How do you pray now? When you think about prayer as a relationship, which areas of that relationship need attention?
- When you look at the attitudes and dispositions of the human heart that Jesus says are necessary in order to pray in faith, what simple things could you do each day to make these more a part of your life?

Pray It!

A Simple Way to Pray

Is prayer a regular part of your life? There is a simple way to begin to pray regularly that will help you use the Scriptures and quiet time. Find a passage in the Scriptures. It doesn't have to be long. A good guideline is to use one of the Mass readings of the day. You can also use one of your favorite Bible stories. Calm yourself, and ask God to help you. Read the passage and then sit quietly. Try not to think about anything. Just let the passage settle in you. Now go back a second time and read the passage again. Take note this time of a word or phrase that might jump out at you, something you are drawn to. Take some quiet time to just think about your word or phrase. Don't try to analyze it. Just let the words rest in your mind and in your heart.

Read your passage a third time, and this time ask God what it is he wants you to understand about your word or phrase. Then write down your word or phrase and carry it with you for a day or a week, to remind you of what you have experienced. When you are ready, you can move on to another Scripture passage. This prayer experience can also be done with your friends. It will help you to see how God is working differently in your lives. It will also help you to support one another.

32 The Forms of Prayer

Friendships are based on many things, and you would probably agree that friends bring out different aspects of your personality. One friend brings out the clown in you. With another you share more serious thoughts. Friends on a team or in an activity help you achieve your best and challenge you to work well with others. With some friends you just take it easy and soak in whatever life offers.

Although each friendship brings out a part of you, you probably aren't comfortable sharing everything about yourself with everyone. It is true that most of us have a few faults and insecurities that we feel others might find hard to accept. It is hoped that you have one of those rare and special friends with whom you can be completely open and honest.

The really wonderful thing about prayer is that it is *the* relationship where you can share all of your self and know that you are loved. In the last chapter, we used the analogy of a satellite dish and signal to say that it is the Holy Spirit who

Words to Look For

- *blessing*
- *adoration*
- *petition*
- *Kyrie Eleison*
- *novenas*
- *intercession*
- *thanksgiving*
- *praise*
- *doxology*

teaches you to pray. No part of you is out of range of the Holy Spirit. God wants to be in relationship with you in every aspect of your life—in all your concerns, gifts, faults, and feelings. This gives rise to different forms of prayer—blessing (and adoration), petition, intercession, thanksgiving, and praise—that connect to different times and situations in your life. In the next few pages, we learn more about each of these prayer forms.

Blessing and Adoration

"Gesundheit!" "Bless us, O Lord, and these thy gifts . . ." "Bless me, Father, for I have sinned . . ." What do we mean by these and other blessings?

The prayer form blessing is a two-step movement. First God gives us a gift, and then we respond with joy and gratitude. If you have ever watched the loving exchange between a parent and an infant, you have glimpsed the basic rhythm of **blessing.** The parent, who provides for the baby's every need, pours care and devotion over the child. The infant, rejoicing in a love that it can barely fathom, coos and squeals with delight. Like a baby's delight, our prayers of blessing in response to God's many gifts ascend in the Holy Spirit through Christ to the Father.

"Blessed is he who comes in the name of the Lord. Hosanna in the highest" is an example of a blessing we pray at Mass. "I will bless the LORD at all times; / his praise shall continually be in my mouth" (Psalm 34:1) is a blessing from the Psalms. Just remember that it is because God first blesses us that the human heart can in return bless the One who is the source of every blessing.

Adoration is closely related to blessing. When you adore God, you acknowledge that you are a creature before the One who created you. Adoration, which is reserved for God alone

Looking Back

An Aspiration of the Heart

There are so many of them [beautiful prayers in books] it really gives me a headache! and each prayer is more beautiful than the others. I cannot recite them all and not knowing which to choose, I do like children who do not know how to read, I say very simply to God what I wish to say, without composing beautiful sentences, and He always understands me. For me, prayer is an aspiration of the heart, it is a simple glance directed to heaven, it is a cry of gratitude and love in the midst of trial as well as joy; finally, it is something great, supernatural, which expands my soul and unites me to Jesus. (Page 165)

Saint Thérèse of Lisieux wrote these words in her autobiography *Story of a Soul.* The book describes her prayer experiences as a teenager and a young adult. Her words echo the underlying truth to prayer, that no matter what the form may be, we express the simple yet profound sentiment, "I love you, Lord."

(Exodus 20:2–7), can take the form of "joyful noise" (Psalm 95:1) or respectful, humbled silence.

In some blessings, you or someone else actually invokes God's power and care on another person, place, thing, or undertaking. The gestures or touch that often accompany these blessings symbolize the bestowal of God's grace on the receiver. In Numbers 6:22–27 God instructs Aaron to bless the Israelites. The blessing at the end of Mass, the familiar Irish blessing, and the blessing of animals on the feast of Saint Francis are other examples of this kind of blessing.

In the most famous conversion story in the Bible, Saint Paul has an encounter with the risen Christ that turns his life around 180 degrees. Read the description of it in Acts of the Apostles 26:4–23. How does Paul's story speak to you?

Petition

"Why didn't you just *ask?*" When friends say this, they express willingness to be there for each other and to help with any need. If you would do anything for a friend, how much greater is God's willingness to provide all that you need? Jesus once told his disciples: "Is there anyone among you who, if your child asks for bread, will give a stone? . . . If you then . . . know how to give good gifts to your children, how much more will your Father in heaven give good things to those who ask him!" (Matthew 7:9–11).

The prayer form **petition** is asking God for something you need. At some level most of us know this, and probably make petitions, the most common form of prayer, dozens of times a day without even realizing it. "Help me pass this test!" "Give me a break, Lord!" "God forgive me!" "Lord, tell me what to say!" And when learning to drive, "Yikes, Lord, keep me safe!"

Petition is prayer's most usual form because it is the most spontaneous. It arises naturally from the depths of our heart, where we are aware of our relationship with God, where we know that we are dependent on our Creator. In this prayer form, which is also called supplication, we ask, beseech, plead, invoke, entreat, cry out, even struggle in prayer.

You know how hard it is to have an honest conversation with a friend when you've had a falling out? It is even more difficult to ask for a favor. This uneasiness often spills over into other relationships making them uncomfortable as well. Jesus knew this, and in the Sermon on the Mount, he said to be reconciled with others before prayer (Matthew 5:22–24). Therefore, the Catholic Church teaches that the first movement of petition is always asking forgiveness: acknowledging our shortcomings and turning back to God. The **Kyrie Eleison,** (Lord have mercy, Christ have mercy, Lord have mercy) said at Mass, is an example of this call to forgiveness as a prerequisite to prayer.

Even when things are going great with our friends, it can be awkward to ask for things. Jesus had something to say about that. Right after he taught his disciples the Lord's Prayer, he told two parables about prayer that he summarized by saying, "Ask, and it will be given you; search, and you will find; knock, and the door will be opened for you" (Luke 11:9). Pray with confidence and perseverance, he said, and the Father will give you all you need, above all the Holy Spirit. **Novenas,** prayers for a particular intention, are an example of perseverance. These devotions span nine consecutive days or nine weeks, and are based on the number of days Mary and the Apostles waited for the coming of the Holy Spirit, from the Ascension to Pentecost.

You might be thinking: "What about those times when I don't know *what* to ask for?" "What about the times when I feel so confused that I don't even pray?" In response to these questions, Saint Paul had an encouraging insight. He reminded believers, "The Spirit helps us in our weakness; for we do not know how to pray as we ought, but that very Spirit intercedes with sighs too deep for words" (Romans 8:26). How reassuring to know that the Holy Spirit backs us up in prayer!

Saintly Profiles

Saint Paul, Apostle to the Gentiles

Saint Paul's story unfolds in the Acts of the Apostles and in the letters of the New Testament. His original name was Saul, and he was a devoted Jew who initially persecuted Christians he thought were corrupting the Jewish faith. While traveling to Damascus, he had a dramatic experience of the resurrected Christ (Acts 9:1–19). He was baptized, and changed his name to Paul to reflect the new person he had become. When the Jewish Christians doubted his conversion, God sent Paul to preach the Gospel to the Gentiles (non-Jews). He had several missionary journeys in which he traveled for years throughout the Mediterranean, establishing churches in major cities. While he was on the road or in prison, Paul wrote letters to those first Christian communities, reminding them of what he had taught, correcting them, and encouraging them to live lives of holiness.

These letters from Saint Paul instruct and model all five forms of prayer. To the Ephesians he writes, "Blessed be . . . God . . . who has blessed us in Christ" (1:3). Paul asks the Romans to intercede for him, "I appeal to you . . . to join me in earnest prayer to God on my behalf" (15:30). He tells the Philippians, "In everything by prayer and supplication [petition], . . . let your requests be made known to God" (4:6). In his Second Letter to the Corinthians he announces, "Thanks be to God for his indescribable gift!" (9:15). To the Hebrews he says, "Through [Jesus], then, let us continually offer a sacrifice of praise to God" (13:15). Saint Paul shares a feast day with Saint Peter, June 29.

Intercession

"Put in a good word for me!" In the ordinary circumstances of life, you might speak a supportive word on behalf of a friend to a possible employer, a secret crush, a teacher, or a coach. It's quite natural for friends to hold each other up in this way. **Intercession** is a prayer of petition in which you do something very similar. You ask God's help for another person.

In the last chapter, you read that Moses interceded for his people because his heart was attuned to God's will for them. Catholics pray for others, following the example of Jesus, who intercedes for all (Romans 8:34). We believe that intercessory prayer has great power. When you offer a prayer of intercession, you join your love for another person with God's love for the person you are praying for. If you have ever played with a magnifying glass on a sunny day, you know that you can take a ray of sunlight and intensify it by passing it through the glass. Intercessory prayer works in a similar way. When you pray for another person, you establish or strengthen your bond of love for her or him. God's love, like the ray of sunlight, is already there. You allow your heart to become like a magnifying glass, channeling God's love in a way that will forever change you and the person you are praying for.

Just as putting in a good word for a friend comes quite naturally, it is easy to pray for those who are closest to you—your family and friends. Intercession invites you to broaden your circle of concern, to see your self as part of something much greater. Jesus taught us to pray for the coming of God's Kingdom. In prayers that reach out to Church and world leaders, and to the lonely, sick, and forgotten people throughout the world, every baptized person can work for the coming of the Kingdom. These more expansive prayers are also the basis for the prayers of interces-

Lord, Hear Our Prayer

The intercessions in the Mass are a type of the petition prayer form. Called the prayer of the faithful, they connect the liturgy with real life, making us consciously aware of the people and needs we name in the intercessions. In the prayer of the faithful, we pray for the Church, for public authorities, for the salvation of the whole world, for those oppressed by any need, and for the local community.

These prayers are sometimes called general intercessions because they are meant for general, not private needs (although we do pray for members of the community who are ill or who have died). So if you are asked to write general intercessions for the prayer of the faithful, do not pray, "For my friend who is going through a hard time." It would be okay to pray, "That all people experiencing rejection and loneliness would experience God's loving presence." Get the difference?

sion during Mass (see the article "Lord, Hear Our Prayer," at left.

You might ask, "But what about Jesus' command to pray for our enemies and those who persecute us?" (Matthew 5:43–44). These can be the hardest prayers to offer with a sincere heart. When you stretch yourself to pray for someone you are in conflict with or someone who has hurt you, you are affirming your belief that no person or concern is outside the love and care of God. It can be difficult to know how to pray for our enemies. Try asking God to help you understand the person with God's own heart. Pray that God's light and peace surround that person and sink in, and pray for healing in your relationship.

Thanksgiving

Have you ever sat down to write a list of one hundred things you are grateful for? It can be slow going at first, but something wonderful happens when you rise to this challenge. In the process you become aware of the many gifts God has given you, and you move into an attitude of gratitude.

In **thanksgiving** we remember that we are creatures and God is our Creator. The more we pray thanksgiving, the more we grow in awareness that all we have comes to us as a gift from God's abundant love. The Greek word *eucharist* means "thanksgiving." Early Christians prayed with a grateful spirit in the "breaking of bread" (Acts 2:42–47). At Mass, Catholics join in this prayer of thanksgiving with Christ, and offer back to the Father all that he has accomplished in Christ. Many people offer their personal prayers with the prayer of the Church by spending the quiet moments after the Communion rite in thanksgiving.

Saint Paul tells us the real test of a grateful heart is to "give thanks in all circumstances" (1 Thessalonians 5:18). This

Pray It

The Divine Praises

The divine praises are a form of adoration. These praises name some of the wonderful blessings of our faith. Pray them from time to time as part of your adoration of God.

Blessed be God.
Blessed be his holy name.
Blessed be Jesus Christ, true God and true man.
Blessed be the name of Jesus.
Blessed be his most sacred heart.
Blessed be Jesus in the most holy sacrament of the altar.
Blessed be the great mother of God, Mary most holy.
Blessed be her holy and immaculate conception.
Blessed be her glorious assumption.
Blessed be the name of Mary, virgin and mother.
Blessed be Saint Joseph, her most chaste spouse.
Blessed be God in his angels and in his saints.

(*Catholic Household Blessings and Prayers*, pages 334–335)

may sound a little phony to you, but Paul isn't telling you to put on a false front. What he means is that you can have confidence that God is loving you, even in the middle of difficulties, even when you can't see the purpose for your suffering, even when there is no end in sight. Such gratitude involves deep faith in the Paschal mystery—the mystery that life and growth come through death and suffering. Through the lens of the Paschal mystery, broken friendships, addictions, illness, and death become windows into the vastness of God's abiding love, and the Christian heart wells up in gratitude.

Perhaps you know this because you have become stronger or more loving through an experience of loss. Many people find that as they grow older, the prayer of thanksgiving comes more naturally, because they can look back over their life and see how God was acting even in the difficult times.

This is an early Christian painting that was found in a catacomb. Notice the raised arms of the woman in prayer, a posture people often use when praising God. What postures do you use in your prayer?

Praise

Which would you rather have, friends who love you for what you can do, or friends who love you for who you are? Most of us would choose the latter as the freest, purest, most authentic kind of love. It is love for its own sake, not because we have earned it or because the other person owes it to us, but simply because we exist.

The Church teaches that **praise** embraces all other forms of prayer and carries them to God, who is our source and goal. Praise is the form of prayer that expresses our love for God simply because God IS. You know if you have felt this natural, self-forgetful kind of love for God welling up in you for no particular reason. When this happens, the Holy Spirit is working in you to inspire you to glorify God. Saint Paul told the Ephesians to be filled with the Spirit "as you sing psalms and hymns and spiritual songs among yourselves, singing and making melody to the Lord in your hearts" (Ephesians 5:19).

Praise often finds its expression in music. The Gloria we sing at Mass echoes the angels' song of praise that beckoned the shepherds to worship the newborn Jesus. In this hymn we sing, "We worship you, we give you thanks, we praise you for your glory." The thanks we offer in the Gloria is not for what God has done, but simply because he exists and is so glorious. Many other traditional prayers express praise. *Alleluia* literally means "Praise the Lord." It comes to us from our Jewish roots, and has been the Easter cry of the Church from the time the first Christians celebrated Christ's victory over death. Many of the psalms are prayers of praise. **Doxology** is a word for the Christian prayers of praise that are usually directed to the Trinity.

Now that we have considered these five forms of prayer, here are a few final thoughts for your consideration:

- The Holy Eucharist embodies all five forms of prayer perfectly. The next time you are at Mass, look for examples of all five prayer forms.
- You might be wondering: Who decided that these are the only forms of prayer? Can there be new ones? As in the other aspects of the Catholic faith, the Scriptures and Tradition are our guides in prayer. Through the guidance of the Holy Spirit, these five forms of prayer are part of the living transmission of faith that comes down to you like a treasured family heirloom.
- Working in you and the entire Church, recalling all that Jesus said, and instructing the human heart in the life of prayer, the Holy Spirit inspires new expressions of prayer using the same basic forms of blessing, petition, intercession, thanksgiving, and praise.

Attitude of Gratitude

The words *thank you* express a recognition that what is held, what is seen, what is experienced is a gift. Little children teach this sense of wonder and thankfulness; just watch them take joy at even the smallest and simplest things. Admittedly life presents us with all kinds of experiences: joy and happiness, pain and sadness. When we are presented with painful or disappointing experiences, we do have a choice about how to respond. We can choose to respond with resentment and self-pity, or we can respond with gratitude. Learn to respond with gratitude! Learn from this reflection written by Carrie Mach, a teenager who was dying of cancer (also see the article "Holiness in Daily Life," on page 67):

I encourage each of you to look at your own lives . . . and stop to think about what you are thankful for. Don't go for the easy ones either. Of course you're thankful for your house and food. Stop and really appreciate your parents. . . . Look at the little things, too. When you don't get the A you wanted on a test, be glad you're even getting an education. . . . When you're on your feet all day, be glad you can walk. Even when you just have a bad hair day, thank God for hair. Remember that the little things you take for granted, aren't taken for granted by everyone. Take a new perspective this week. Look at your life from the point of view of someone else. You will be amazed at how many good things you can find. (Quoted in Laurie Delgatto with Marilyn Kielbasa, *Church Women*, page 124)

For Further Reflection

- What is your favorite form of prayer? Why do you like this form of prayer the most? What do you express when you pray this way?
- Try your hand at writing your own prayers. Write a prayer for each of the five prayer forms: blessing, petition, intercession, thanksgiving, and praise. Tape them in different places (for example, by a mirror, on your nightstand, on your desk), where you will see them and be reminded to pray.

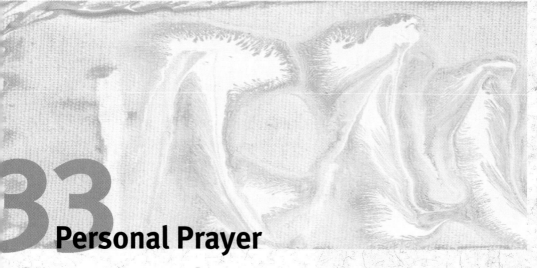

33 Personal Prayer

Whether or not you have done much dating, the topics of
courtship and marriage are common in our culture. Because
these topics have to do with the growth of personal relationships, they can help you understand the various expressions
the life of personal prayer takes. This isn't as farfetched as it
may seem. Jesus referred to himself as a bridegroom (Matthew
25:1–13) and to the kingdom of heaven as a wedding feast
(Matthew 22:1–14).

In courtship two people build a healthy love relationship
by following a gradual pattern of coming to know each other.
When they first start dating, conversation is important. They
share significant ideas and values as well as their day-to-day
thoughts. The foundation of the relationship is built on
speaking with a sincere heart.

As things progress, engagement celebrates the deepening
relationship. Though conversation remains important, during

Words to Look For

- vocal prayer
- forty hours'
  devotion
- first Friday
- novena
- meditation
- contemplation
- mysticism

this next stage, partners ponder various aspects of their life together and grow in knowledge of their love for each other. The heart is in a process of active discernment.

Couples who marry and continue to grow in love still converse and still continue to reflect on various aspects of their relationship. But they also enjoy rich wordless moments in each other's presence, abiding in each other's heart.

To some degree these stages of courtship and married love resemble the major expressions in the personal prayer life of Christians: vocal prayer, meditation, and contemplative prayer. In each expression the heart must be present and open to the beloved, who is God, and earlier expressions remain important as the relationship deepens.

Vocal Prayer

When you want to get to know someone, you might strike up a conversation. At first, you usually focus on simple things: school, music, sports. As you get to know each other better, you begin to share about topics of greater importance: your beliefs, your worries, your dreams for the future. **Vocal prayer,** which uses words either spoken aloud or recited silently, is similar to this kind of sharing because it focuses on your conversation with God that grows over time. Memorized prayers are the first way most people learn to pray vocally. You learn these prayers in your family and in religious education classes. You will find most of the common memorized vocal prayers of the Catholic Church beginning on page 380, in the Catholic Prayers and Devotions appendix.

As you grow in your relationship with God, you will probably find that you express yourself more in your own words. God wants us to share our joys and trials, hopes and frustrations. We can be angry with God, confused, or just plain goofy. God is big enough to accept whatever is in our heart and on our mind. The Gospels show that Jesus shouted at God both in joy to the Father (Matthew 11:25–26) and in agony on the cross (Mark 14:36).

This is a picture of a Hispanic family's beautiful home altar. Where and how can you create a space in your home for prayer? It doesn't have to be as elaborate as this!

324

You have probably heard the expressions "lip service" and "talk is cheap," to indicate that people don't always mean what they say. Sometimes the deception is intentional. Perhaps, as can be the case in memorized vocal prayer, they have said the same words over and over to the point where the words have lost their meaning. Fifth-century bishop Saint John Chrysostom (whose name means "golden-mouthed") was a preacher who knew the importance of making words count. He advised, "Whether or not our prayer is heard depends not on the number of words, but on the fervor [passion] of our souls"[1] (*CCC,* number 2700). For vocal prayer to be effective, you have to mean what you say.

If you are like most people, from time to time you've caught yourself reciting memorized vocal prayers without feeling. There are a few things you can do to put the passion back into this expression of prayer. Begin by truly focusing on the words themselves. This presence of your heart to vocal prayer can refill the words with power and meaning. The Catholic Church teaches that we also bring a bodily presence to prayer. As people who are both body and spirit, it is part of our human nature to involve our senses in prayer. Bring passion to your vocal prayer through trying different postures (standing, kneeling, sitting yoga style) at prayer.

LIVE it

Prayer Spaces and Times

No matter the type or types of prayer you practice, it is important to deliberately schedule a time and place to pray each day. Consider morning prayers (a Christian song, with petitions for friends and people you have promised to pray for), a walk at lunch each day to quietly meditate on a scriptural quote, or time before bed to read quietly or pray some favorite prayers. A prayer space may be a corner of the breakfast table with a prayer book; rosary beads kept in a car ashtray; a candle, icon, or cross on a dresser near your bed; or a favorite chapel you can walk to or drive past each day. Remember, prayer is a discipline. It takes time to make it part of your daily routine. But the rewards are eternal.

Meditation

To continue the courtship analogy, as a love relationship deepens, partners find themselves spending a fair amount of time thinking about each other. They become the object of each other's thoughts, imagination, and emotions. In a relationship characterized by real love, not infatuation, this isn't preoccupation or daydreaming. Rather it is a process of discernment that desires the best for the other. The prayer expression that resembles this kind of active reflection is meditation.

Some Catholic Devotions

The Word of God became a particular man in a particular place (Palestine) at a particular time (two thousand years ago) in a specific culture (Judaism). The Church continues to bring the Word of God into particular places, times, and cultures. When the people of a particular culture seek to express their faith, devotions are created from the rhythms of people's lives. Farmers moving pebbles from one pocket to another as they said one hundred and fifty Our Fathers gave rise to rosary beads. When people wanted to express their love for Jesus in the Eucharist in a special way, the **forty hours' devotion** was created. In this devotion people arrange their schedules so that someone is at prayer before the Blessed Sacrament (the consecrated bread) for forty continuous hours.

First Friday devotions began when Jesus revealed to Saint Margaret Mary Alacoque, in 1675, that receiving Communion on the first Friday of every month would demonstrate devotion to the Sacred Heart of Jesus. Many parishes today celebrate first Fridays by making Communion visits to sick people. The nine-day mourning rituals of the Greek and Roman cultures led to the **novena,** the practice of praying for a particular person or intention for nine days in a row. Some people combine the first Friday devotion with the novena, praying for a special intention by attending Mass on Friday for nine weeks in a row.

Meditation is a term used broadly and somewhat loosely. The word goes back to a Greek root meaning, "care, study, and exercise." You can tell by these meanings that in its truest sense, meditation involves real activity. The *Catechism* uses the active word *mobilize* to describe the use of thoughts, imagination, emotions, and desires in meditation. When you meditate you use these faculties to ponder God's presence and activity in your life and in the world, to discover the movements that stir your heart, and to say, "Lord, I want you to be the focus of my life."

There are as many and varied methods of meditation as there are spiritual guides, even in the Christian Tradition. Catholics often use the Scriptures as a springboard to meditation, as in *lectio divina,* which you will learn about in the next chapter. Liturgical texts of the day or season, holy writings, the rosary, icons, and all creation are other doors through which you can enter into meditation. Regardless of how you enter, Christian meditation is not Zen or Eastern meditation or relaxation or mere psychological activity, but a path to the knowledge of the love of Christ and union with him.

Contemplative Prayer

We noted earlier that lovers enjoy rich wordless moments in each other's presence. **Contemplation,** called "silent love" by Saint John of the Cross, is the expression of prayer that resembles this experience.

Like meditation, *contemplation* is a word that has held different meanings throughout the history of spirituality. This kind of union, or awareness of oneness, is the central element of **mysticism,** another term used to describe experiences of profound union with

God. What is consistent in descriptions of contemplation is that it always has to do with deep awareness of the presence of God arrived at not by rational thought but by love. It is the experience of oneness with God that Jesus speaks about in the Gospel of John, with words like "Abide in me" (15:4) and "I in them" (17:26). Contemplation is union with the indwelling Christ that takes place in the heart at prayer.

You might be thinking, "Okay, really holy people can do this, not me!" Remember, we are all called to holiness in the ordinary events of our everyday life. It doesn't take holiness to pray, but prayer will make you holier. Also, try not to think of contemplation as something to "do." It is God who loves you and draws near to you. Contemplation is God's gift to you, and you can only accept it in humility. The Psalms offer an image that conveys the truly simple nature of contemplative prayer. Think of it as climbing into God's lap, like a child rests in his mother's arms (Psalm 131). It is simply dwelling in God's love.

If after reading all this, you don't feel drawn to contemplation, that's okay. Not all these expressions of personal prayer are required for following Jesus. And contemplation tends to be a prayer form that people are drawn to as they get older. It tends to develop over time and with experience. But if you wish to try this expression of prayer in your life, see the article "Centering Prayer," at right, for a description of one way to begin.

Challenges of Prayer

Like all relationships, the relationship of prayer has its challenges. The great teachers of prayer all comment that prayer is a battle, a fact you might find very discouraging. Often

Pray It!

Centering Prayer

Centering prayer is a method to develop skills for contemplative prayer, to quiet yourself and rest in God. To try centering prayer, choose a time when you have some energy and a place you can sit comfortably and undisturbed. Choose a sacred word that expresses your intention to surrender to God, a word from the Scriptures or a word that describes God for you. Begin by praying, "Dear Father, Son, and Spirit, I place myself in your loving presence," or something like it to place yourself in God's presence. Then close your eyes and gently repeat in your mind the sacred word you have chosen, returning to it every time other thoughts invade. Your goal is to let go of all distractions and thoughts, and simply rest in silence in God's presence. Continue to sit comfortably, breathe deeply, and seek interior peace and silence for as long as twenty to thirty minutes.

When all distractions are gone, you can even let go of repeating your sacred word, seeking interior silence. In this silence the language of God is the experience of the ultimate mystery; the communion among the Father, Son, and Spirit; between you and God; and of all creation. At the end of your prayer time, say a vocal prayer, or simply start talking to God, for several minutes before opening your eyes again.

a close look at a difficult relationship helps us understand how to overcome its problems. Let's take a closer look at the difficulties that accompany prayer.

In her prayer Saint Teresa of Ávila sometimes experienced union with God so joyful and complete that those unions were called raptures. Many people cannot imagine having that kind of experience during prayer. Do your ideas of prayer limit your encounters with God?

Misperceptions of Prayer

First of all, a lot of misperceptions exist about prayer. Just as having the wrong idea about a person hinders getting to know him or her, having the wrong idea about prayer will work against you. Begin by dismissing thoughts about prayer as mere psychological activity or the rattling of memorized words. These are not part of healthy human relationships, and are also not true prayer. Nor is prayer something that requires expertise. In prayer there are no black belts, no summa cum laudes, no five-stars. Anyone can pray, and you probably already do!

For example, do you ever sit in your room listening to music, caught up in the rhythm and how the verses express your own thoughts and feelings? Do you ever look at a tiny infant or a beautiful sunset and think, "Way to go, God!" When you are caught in a difficult situation, do you turn to God and ask for help? If you do any of these things, you are already praying. Most people pray at some level, even if it is only occasional and unplanned. What God wants you to do is to be more disciplined and consistent in your prayer—to make him a regular part of your life.

Difficulties in Prayer

Those who do attempt prayer will sooner or later face other difficulties, particularly distractions and periods of dryness. When this happens, take heart. Those great saints who said that prayer is a battle, learned to fight the battle well and left advice for how to handle these difficulties. We will talk about some of that advice here and in the next chapters of this section. Always remember, you are not alone. The Holy Spirit prays with you and will see you through.

Distractions in prayer are similar to what happens when you try to carry on a conversation and keep getting interrupted. Some days it seems the moment you bow in prayer, a dozen alarms go off in your head at once, all calling you away from the relationship of prayer: "Oh, no! I forgot to call Sue!" "I wonder what I should wear to the dance." "I've got to get that job application in by tomorrow." The moment you quiet one distraction, another pops up, like a game of mental jack-in-the-box.

Spiritual guides tell us that these distractions reveal our preferences and attachments, and therefore which master we serve (Matthew 6:21,24). They advise against hunting down distractions because that is precisely the trap—to get you chasing around instead of praying. Respond just as you would to interruptions in conversation. Turn your focus back to the Lord, with whom you want to be. In doing so you demonstrate which master you choose to serve. This is vigilance: constantly seeking God instead of allowing other things to draw you away.

The next difficulty, dryness, is akin to those times in even the best friendship when the spark seems to have faded. You seem to be growing apart; you no longer have as much fun when you are together. Remaining faithful to your friend and exploring new activities together are important if you do not want the friendship to die. In prayer, dryness is experienced as feeling separated from God. When this happens, the strength, joy, and peace of prayer runs dry, and nothing you do seems to change the situation. Sometimes these periods of dryness, or darkness, are the gift and work of God, liberating you from imperfections and attachments. If this is the case, keeping faith will see you through.

Saintly Profiles

Teresa of Ávila (1512–1582)

Saint Teresa of Ávila was a mystic, a teacher of the art of prayer, a spirit-filled leader of a religious order, a woman of great courage, and an individual who lived life to the full. Born in Spain, she was one of ten children to her father's second wife. A beautiful, extroverted teenager, she lost interest in faith, instead falling in love with boys and books of chivalry when she was twelve. When she was fifteen, her mother died. Teresa was placed in the care of Augustinian nuns, where her love of God was rekindled. At twenty she entered the Carmelite monastery. There she suffered repeated and serious illnesses, and struggled with prayer and a desire to be appreciated by others. In her forties she experienced transforming mystical visions of Christ and began her work as a reformer, establishing a new convent against much opposition. She is recognized as a doctor of the Church (someone whose writings have had a major impact on the Church) for the spiritual path she outlined in her writings, a path many have followed to holiness.

Teresa spoke of prayer as an intimate sharing between friends, taking time frequently to be alone with God. In her book *The Interior Castle,* she describes the union of our soul with God: "It is as if a tiny streamlet enters the sea, from which it will find no way of separating itself, or as if in a room there were two large windows through which the light streamed in: it enters in different places but it all becomes one." Her feast day is October 15.

At other times dryness is the result of a lack of devotion to the relationship. In marriage, couples can focus too much on other things—raising children, making money, other friends—and grow lax in devotion to each other. The couple has to radically reorient their priorities to mend their marriage. If your prayer is dry because of lax practice or carelessness of heart, the remedy is conversion. Conversion involves a radical change of heart, turning away from the things that draw you away from God, and returning to God.

All this talk of difficulties may have you feeling discouraged. Listen to this modern-day parable: The devil takes a man on a tour of hell and proudly shows off all his storehouses brimming with the seeds of sin. There is lust and jealousy, anger and envy, and so on—a large storehouse for each big sin. But the man points out another storehouse larger by far than all the rest. "What do you keep in there?" he asks. "Oh, that," responds the devil, "that holds the smallest but most effective seed of all. That is overflowing with seeds of discouragement." Prayer can be such a wonderful and life-giving relationship that you want to take great care not to allow the seeds of discouragement to grow there. Remember, even an infinitesimal seed of faith grows to the size of a mustard tree, whose roots and shade hold back despair, hopelessness, and fear (Luke 17:5–6).

For Further Reflection

○ What is your favorite vocal prayer? What do the words mean to you?

○ Which expressions of prayer—vocal, meditation, and contemplation—have you experienced? How can you go about making each expression a part of your prayer life?

○ Many wonderful resources are available to help you in your personal prayer life. If you have access to a computer, do an Internet search for "Catholic prayer." You will be amazed at how many sites you will find. You can also visit a Catholic bookstore or ask your parish leaders for suggestions.

Looking Back

The Body at Prayer

We are a sacramental people, believing that the divine mystery can be experienced in visible ways, can be embodied (in a body). Certain postures and gestures express our attitudes at prayer. *Standing* straight, tall, and free asserts our dignity as children of God. *Facing east,* the direction from which the sun—the symbol of Christ—rises, dates to cultures that held the sun as an important symbol of the divine. *Kneeling* appears in the Scriptures (in Acts 20:36, Paul kneels in prayer), and is a sign of adoration, penance, and supplication. *Prostration* (lying on the floor, arms outstretched) also appears in the Scriptures, when Jesus falls prostrate in the Garden of Gethsemane (Matthew 26:39). Priests will use this posture at their ordination and at the beginning of Good Friday liturgies.

Genuflection (bending the knee) is a sign of adoration and greeting directed to the divine presence in the Blessed Sacrament in the tabernacle. *Bowing,* before the altar and before the word of God, is a sign of humility that dates to the practice in the oriental court. *Sitting* has no religious significance, except as a posture for listening. It became popular when seats were introduced into churches in the sixteenth century. Try a new posture or gesture with a prayer you say often.

34 Praying with the Scriptures

Which of these best describes the way most of your relationships get started: Do you usually initiate conversation with someone new, or do you wait for someone to talk to you? Are you the first to send an e-mail, or do you wait until someone e-mails you and then respond? If you are outgoing, you probably answered that you are the one to start a conversation or the first to send an e-mail. But if you are quieter, waiting for someone to talk first or send an e-mail first probably seemed more like you.

Whether or not you feel like you initiate most of your friendships, it might surprise you to learn that when it comes to prayer, you don't make the first move. It may seem that way, because you start the conversation with God in your prayer. But what most of us fail to realize is that God has already made the first move in ways we do not recognize. The late Swiss Catholic Cardinal Hans Urs von Balthasar put it this way, "Prayer . . . is communication, in which God's word has the initiative, and we, at first, are simply listeners."

Words to Look For

- *theological virtues*
- lectio divina
- *Ignatian Gospel contemplation*

God speaks to us through the people and events of our life every day. He especially speaks through the Scriptures, the liturgy of the Church, and the virtues of faith, hope, and love to get the relationship of prayer started and keep it going. All these things are sources of prayer. The next chapter will look at the liturgy of the Church as a central source of prayer in Catholic life. In this chapter we look at the theological virtues and the Bible as sources of prayer.

Faith, Hope, and Love

If you have been reading this handbook from the beginning, you have already encountered the **theological virtues** of faith, hope, and love as the foundation for Christian morality. When you pray, the Holy Spirit works through the theological virtues to draw you into relationship with God.

Think of things you do to get a relationship started. You might call someone on the phone, sit with her or him at lunch, or look for that person at a game or dance. But before the talking or the eating or the looking, you seek and desire this friendship. In prayer you can use all kinds of words and techniques, but prior to all these, faith brings you to seek and desire God in prayer. The Holy Spirit works with the faith God has planted in your heart to stir up the desire for prayer in you.

You know that prayer isn't just about asking for things and hoping God will grant them to you. But where does hope fit into the relationship of prayer? Again, thinking about relationships helps you understand how hope works in prayer. Ideally you can name at least one person whom you know will listen to you and be there for you when you need him or her. Just knowing this can be all you need to get through a rough spot. Such a friend gives you hope. Through

Where to Turn in the Bible for Prayer

Where do you turn when you wish to pray with the Scriptures? Following are some suggestions to get you started:

- When you are feeling unloved: Isaiah 6:1–8, 43:1–4; Jeremiah 1:4–10; John, chapter 15
- When you need encouragement: Psalms 23, 42, 43
- When you are not sure what to do: Matthew 22:34–40, 25:31–46; Ephesians 4:25–32
- When you are anxious for someone you love: Luke 12:22–34, John, chapter 17
- When you want to thank God: Psalm 107, Ecclesiastes 3:1–15, 1 Thessalonians 5:18
- When everything is going from bad to worse: 2 Timothy, chapter 3; Hebrews, chapter 13
- When you are jealous: Psalm 49; 1 Corinthians, chapter 13; James 3:13–18
- When you are bored: 2 Kings, chapter 5; Job, chapter 28; Revelation (with footnotes)
- When you need to forgive: Matthew 5:43–48, 6:12; Luke 23:34
- When you need to be forgiven: Psalm 51; Isaiah, chapter 53; Matthew 16:18–19

our relationship to God in prayer, the Holy Spirit teaches your heart to have hope, to know that God listens to you and is there for you. Saint Paul tells us to "abound in hope" (Romans 15:13), and the Psalms are full of language telling us to fix our hope in God. Like faith, hope is God-given. Perhaps you can think of a time when prayer made you more hopeful.

Just as the glance of a good friend from across the room touches the heart, even a brief moment in prayer can reassure you of God's love. It is true that sometimes the friends we count on disappoint us. Perhaps our expectations are too high, we think they are someone they are not, or they fail us simply because they are human. Saint Paul tells us that because of God's perfect love, our hope in God will not disappoint us (Romans 5:5). God's love is the source and summit of prayer. Drawn to prayer by faith, and nourished in hope, we experience the love of God poured into our heart in prayer. Spiritual writers describe profound experiences of God's love in prayer, but you don't have to be on the Olympic Prayer Team to have felt this for yourself. Prayer is above all else a relationship of love.

Have you ever been part of a Bible-based sharing group? A Bible-based sharing group is a great way to pray with other people and to grow spiritually.

The Living Word

One of the primary ways two people express love for each other is through words, sometimes spoken, sometimes written. The Scriptures are like God's love letter to us. Whether it's the commandments, the words of the prophets, or the words of Christ, all of God's word is an expression of his love for us.

For this reason the Scriptures have an important place in prayer. Often when we pray, we fill the silence. Just as none of us are inclined to appreciate a one-sided conversation, we want to take care that we don't let our prayer become one-sided. Saint Ambrose reminds us, "We speak to him when we pray; we listen to him when we read the divine oracles [the Scriptures]"[1] (*CCC*, number 2653). When we accompany prayer with reading the Bible, we move from a lopsided conversation into dialogue with God.

The Scriptures do more than move you into dialogue with God; they change you. You know that words can be very powerful. Words can cement relationships, launch dreams, or start wars. Even words that may not seem profound to the person who speaks them can touch a heart in need and transform it. God's word is even more powerful. The author of the first chapter of Genesis expresses this truth when God speaks and all things come into being.

You might be thinking, "The Bible was written so long ago, how can it mean anything today?" But the Bible is no ordinary book; it was not written just for the people of one time and then quickly outdated. It is God's word, and it continues to have creative power in the lives of those who read it today. The Letter to the Hebrews calls the Scriptures "living and active" (4:12), to express the truth that, though written long ago, comes to us with newness and relevance for our life. Those who pray with the Scriptures regularly find this to be so. They will tell you that they can return to the same passage over and over, like drawing water from a well, and find something they have never experienced before, something that speaks to their life in the present moment.

God's word is powerful because it changes us. Your geometry book might temporarily change your life, because it means homework, and it also has the long-term effect of providing a needed job skill. The Scriptures are similar in that they prepare you for the Christian life. We read in Second Timothy that they are "useful for teaching, for reproof, for correction, and for training in righteousness" (3:16). But the Bible is far more life changing than your geometry book. The Scriptures have the power to transform you into the person God intends you to be.

Looking Back

Dei Verbum

Throughout Church history, the Scriptures have led and formed the People of God. In the 1400s the Gutenberg Press made it possible to put the Bible into the hands of ordinary people. One of the struggles of the Reformation, in the 1500s, was over interpretations of the meaning of the Holy Scriptures. The Catholic Church was concerned about untrained people misinterpreting the Bible, and so Scripture reading by laypeople was not encouraged.

In 1965 the air was cleared when the Second Vatican Council released the encyclical *Dogmatic Constitution on Divine Revelation* (*Dei Verbum* in Latin). The 3,500 bishops gathered at Vatican Council II urged all the Christian faithful "to learn by frequent reading of the divine Scriptures," because "ignorance of the Scriptures is ignorance of Christ"[1] (number 25).

The document also defined the methods we should use to correctly interpret the Scriptures: *(a)* recognize that truth is expressed differently in historical, prophetic, poetic, and other forms of literature, *(b)* understand how time and culture influence the author's intention, *(c)* utilize modern scholarship and archaeology to understand past cultures when the Scriptures were written, and *(d)* allow the whole of the Scriptures to inform the interpretation of just one part.

Getting Started

When you pick up the Bible as a source of prayer, where should you start? Some people have the curious habit of reading the last chapter of a book first, but most of us start at the beginning, possible glossing over the introduction. In the case of the Bible, neither of these strategies serves too well. Beginning with the end means starting with one of the most difficult books to understand. The mere size of the Bible makes a front-to-back read a staggering experience, especially for the first-time Bible reader.

These Franciscan monks are praying the Liturgy of the Hours, the official prayer of the Catholic Church. Many monasteries have times when the public can join in their prayer. Is there a monastery in your area?

Keep in mind that the Bible is less like a novel and more like a library. In it you find many books by different authors, writing over a course of hundreds of years. Each uses a different style and writes for a different community of people, addressing the community's particular needs and cultural and historical circumstances. A Bible like *The Catholic Youth Bible* has some excellent reading plans, to give you a start in picking passages to pray with.

How should you approach the Bible as a source of prayer? Start with an up-to-date Catholic Bible that accurately translates the Bible texts, which were written in Hebrew and Greek, into modern English. Popular modern translations are the New American Bible and the New Revised Standard Version: Catholic Edition. In addition to providing you with more accurate and clear texts, these translations give you the benefit of introductions and footnotes to aid your understanding. Next, as with any relationship, allow yourself some time to get acquainted. Page through your Bible. Find your favorite stories and the passages that you think might have something to say to you. If you don't know where to start, consult a teacher, a friend, or a priest. Ask them to point you to a few passages they have found fruitful for prayer.

Prepare yourself for your time with God as you would prepare for time with a special friend. Mark the passage that you intend to read, just as you would make plans with a friend. Find a place where you can be with God uninterrupted and uninhibited. Then relax and become peaceful. You can tell when your friends are distracted and not fully attentive to you. In the same way, you want to come to prayer without other distractions. Become aware that you are in God's presence, and when you are ready, begin reading the passage you have marked.

Most of all, consider that prayer is not the same as Scripture study. Studying the Bible is good, but the primary focus of study is the intellect, where you analyze and evaluate things. Recall that it is the heart that prays. The heart focuses thoughts, feelings, concerns, and questions. Approach the passage as you would a love letter that contains a personal message for you. Think of it as drawing near to God, who has an incredibly deep love for you and accepts you for who you are. You need not read extensive passages or spend long periods of time dwelling on the text. Like quickly touching base with a good friend, your encounter with the Lord in the Scriptures may take only ten to twenty minutes. The point is to listen attentively, savor each word that you hear, and respond with your heart. The following are two time-proven ways people use to pray with the Scriptures: *lectio divina* and Ignatian Gospel contemplation.

Lectio Divina

Lectio divina is a method of prayer from the monastic tradition of Christianity. The Rule of Saint Benedict makes reference to it, as do most traditions of Christian spirituality. It is translated as "holy reading," "meditative reading," or "spiritual reading." The method is divided into five steps with Latin names: *lectio, meditatio, oratio, contemplatio,* and *actio.*

Pray It!

Praying the Psalms

Open the Bible in the middle, and you will fall into the wisdom books. Go a few pages backward or forward, and you will stumble on one of the most beautiful treasures ever set to paper, the Psalms. The Psalms are three-thousand-year-old songs that Israel used in its Temple worship. These beautiful poems, whether read silently, proclaimed aloud, or set to music, help us express every possible human emotion and share that experience with God. By praying the Psalms, we come to the awesome realization that God has always shared in all our joys and sorrows.

The Psalms are part of each Sunday liturgy: a sung response with a cantor singing or speaking the verses. The Psalms are part of morning and evening prayers of the Divine Office. Some famous lines from the Psalms follow. Look them up and pray the entire psalm.

- Psalm 16: "You show me the path of life."
- Psalm 22: "My God, My God, why have you forsaken me?"
- Psalm 23: "The LORD is my shepherd, I shall not want."
- Psalm 27: "The LORD is my light and my salvation; / whom shall I fear?"
- Psalm 51: "Have mercy on me, O God, . . . / blot out my transgressions."
- Psalm 63: "My soul thirsts for you."
- Psalm 91: "Under his wings you will find refuge."
- Psalm 104: "Send forth your spirit, . . . Renew the face of the ground."
- Psalm 145: "His compassion is over all that he has made."

To prepare yourself to use *lectio divina,* select a passage of the Scriptures that you wish to pray, assume a comfortable position, and allow yourself to become silent. Then follow these steps:

HAVE LIFE MORE ABUNDANTLY

This is a bishop's crest, and this bishop has taken as his motto part of a verse from John 10:10. What Bible verse would you take as a personal motto?

○ *Lectio* (lex-ee-oh). This word means "reading." This step evolved from the practice of having a lector read and reread a passage to an assembly that listened. When you practice *lectio divina* by yourself, read slowly and allow God's word to wash over you and sink in. Pause for a minute or so after each reading. You will probably want to read the passage at least three times, each time listening carefully for a word or phrase that seems to stand out to you. You may even want to read the passage aloud. Some advise that you listen for a word or phrase that speaks to you today.

○ *Meditatio* (med-it-tots-ee-oh). The word translates to mean "meditation," and describes the movement into thought that occurs in this step. In this step you engage your intellect, seeking to understand what God might be saying to you in the passage. You may wish to read a short commentary on the passage, if you have a Bible commentary. Or if you have found a word or phrase that speaks to your heart, allow it to interact with your thoughts, hopes, memories, and desires. Try to understand: "What is God saying to me in this passage?" "Why does this particular word or phrase stand out?" "How does this passage relate to my current situation?" Probe these questions for a while.

○ *Oratio* (or-ot-see-oh). This is the Latin name for "prayer." In this step you respond to what you have received. After reflecting in *meditatio,* you are drawn into conversation with God, following any of the prayer forms: blessing, petition, intercession, thanksgiving, or praise. Here you also make an offering to God of the parts of you that were touched by his word in the previous step. In this way you acknowledge that you allow these parts of yourself to be changed by God's word.

○ *Contemplatio* (con-tem-plot-see-oh). *Lectio divina* closes in contemplation. In this step you simply rest quietly in the presence of the One who loves you. This is like the moment in a love relationship when no words are necessary.

○ *Actio* (ax-ee-oh). This word means "action." This is not an actual step in the prayer, but it is a reminder that our time with God's word will have an effect on the way we live our life. As you finish your prayer, you might want to consider if what you've heard is calling you to some action.

Sometimes in *lectio divina,* you will return to reading several times, to savor the line or phrase that you have been given that day. Other times you may seek a new word or phrase. The purpose of *lectio divina* is to be in God's presence praying with the Scriptures. Don't worry about doing it well or experiencing deep insights and emotions. Think of it as a special moment with a best friend.

Ignatian Gospel Contemplation

Imagination is a wonderful thing. Through it you can discover possibilities, break down barriers, and solve problems. It is such a powerful tool that songs and poems have been written to praise the amazing things that people have accomplished because they dared to imagine the world in new and different ways.

The power and beauty of the human imagination were not lost on Saint Ignatius of Loyola. He developed a method of prayer that uses the imagination to immerse the person who is at prayer, into a story from the Bible. With this method you visualize in your mind the details of the Gospel story. As it comes to life in your imagination, you are drawn to a personal and real encounter with Jesus in the present moment. Here is a suggested format to follow for **Ignatian Gospel contemplation:**

Scriptural Mottos

The call arrives to tell you that you have been invited to serve as a bishop. Just days after your acceptance, you make an appointment to have your head measured for your zucchettos and miters (the beanies and tall hats that bishops wear). You sit down with a friend who is an artist to design your coat of arms, and you decide on your own personal motto.

A motto is a phrase that guides and inspires your actions. Many bishops choose a phrase from the Scriptures; others take their motto from holy writings. Following are some bishops' mottos and the Scripture passages on which they are based:

- God will provide. (Genesis 22:8)
- What shall I return to the LORD? (Psalm 116:12)
- Thy Kingdom come. (Matthew 6:10)
- Nothing is impossible with God. (Luke 1:37)
- It is the Lord! (John 21:7)
- I belong to Christ. (1 Corinthians 1:12)
- God's grace suffices. (2 Corinthians 12:9)

Discover the motto of the bishop of your diocese. Look for a motto from the Scriptures to guide and inspire you.

○ Prepare yourself for prayer by assuming a comfortable position and allowing yourself to become silent. Select a passage from the Scriptures with which to pray. It is usually best to begin with the Gospels, because the details and story line are especially suited to this method. With some experience you will be able to spot other passages in the Scriptures that also work well.

○ Read the passage through once, paying special attention to the characters and the concrete details: What does this place look, feel, smell, and sound like? Who is there? What action unfolds? What words are spoken? You may wish to reread the text several times to absorb all the details.

○ Next, enter into the story in your imagination, just as if you were there. Employ your senses to allow the details of the story to come alive. Listen, taste, feel, smell, and see all that you can. Either be yourself or imagine yourself as one of the people in the story. Converse and interact with the people in the story. Allow the story to unfold in your imagination without changing any of the essential details from the Bible passage.

○ As you experience the story, pay careful attention to all your reactions, all that you are feeling and thinking.

○ Respond to this experience in prayerful conversation with Jesus.

The Rule that Saint Benedict (pictured on the left) created for his monks covered many things, including eating. Imagine that you had to create rules to live by for a group of Christians. What would your rule include?

As an example, let's take a look at the passage in Matthew 8:23–27, where Jesus calms the storm at sea. With this story you imagine the gentle rocking of the boat as you first set out, the smell of the salt air, gulls calling, the warmth of the sun, each of the people in the boat with you, and the easy conversation and laughter. You sit casually in the boat. As events unfold in your mind, you feel the wind come up, the seas roughen, and the tension mount. What kind of dialogue transpires now? How do you sit in the boat now? As the storm becomes more intense, you experience your anxiety and that of the others, and then your amazement that Jesus is sleeping. Who wakes him? How do you feel when he asks, "Why are you afraid, you of little faith?" (8:26). What feelings do these words bring to the surface from deep in your heart? As Jesus calms the storm, what do you feel? Then speak with Jesus about this experience.

You might be thinking: "This is all just imagination. It isn't real!" Recall that the Scriptures are the "living Word." Those who pray with this method have very real encounters with Jesus, and find that in the experience, God touches them. They are comforted, healed, and challenged by the living Christ when they meet him through the doorway of the imagination. They find things in the story that they might have overlooked before.

As the "living Word" of God, the Scriptures have a unique contribution to make in the dialogue of prayer. The two methods presented in this chapter are simple ways to start a conversation with God's Word and keep it going. If you aren't in dialogue with God's Word, take the opportunity when you pray today.

For Further Reflection

○ How might it affect your prayer to know that God initiates this relationship? When have you felt faith, hope, and love at work in you?

○ Which of the two methods for praying with the Scriptures in this chapter do you feel most drawn to? What passage of the Scriptures would you select for prayer? Why?

Saintly Profiles

Saint Benedict of Nursia (480–547)

Much of what we know about Saint Benedict comes from legends, and is debated by scholars. Legend holds that he was born in the mountains northeast of Rome, and that he fled the eternal city as a young man to become a hermit. He went on to found monasteries south of Rome, writing a Rule for the monks to live by.

The Rule of Benedict was followed by the formation of thousands of monasteries in Europe. Those following Benedict's order own nothing personally, although they have enough food, drink, and clothing. They work with their hands for about six hours a day. Their leisure is spent reading Scripture and holy writings and praying with the community. A large focus of the Benedictine rule is to show great compassion and hospitality to strangers, the young, the old, and the sick.

Saint Benedict's love and knowledge of the Scriptures shaped his Rule. In it he often quotes the Gospels, for example, "Let all guests who arrive be received like Christ, for He is going to say, 'I came as a guest, and you received Me' (Matthew 25:35)" (Rule of Benedict, chapter 53).

The Rule of Benedict was also written for ordinary Christians who want to develop a pattern of living like Christ. The spiritual wisdom of Saint Benedict continues to lead over twenty thousand monastic men and women and uncounted oblates (lay associates). His feast day is July 11.

35 Praying Together

You would be hard pressed to name something that you do constantly. Of course you continually breathe; your heart continually beats; and your cells go about the continual process of division, growth, and renewal. But these are not conscious activities. Imagine if you constantly had to tell yourself: "Lungs, breathe in! Heart, beat! Lungs, breathe out! Cells, divide!" In God's great wisdom and deep love for you, he has freed your higher consciousness for more important things, primarily the activity of responding to his love.

For this reason Saint Paul advises, "Pray without ceasing, give thanks in all circumstances; for this is the will of God in Christ Jesus for you" (1 Thessalonians 5:17–18). Prayer without ceasing is your response to God's invitation to be in loving relationship with you. You might be thinking, "Always?" This would be an impossible task if it meant that you should engage in verbal prayer, meditation, or contemplation every waking

Words to Look For

- Eucharistic prayer
- Eucharistic adoration
- Blessed Sacrament
- exposition
- benediction
- Liturgy of the Hours
- tabernacle
- monstrance
- breviary

moment. But perhaps there is another way to think about prayer becoming an integrated part of your life.

Praying Always

The Church teaches that it is always possible to pray. Saint John Chrysostom notes, "It is possible to offer fervent prayer even while walking in public or strolling alone, or seated in your shop, . . . while buying or selling, . . . or even while cooking"[1] (*CCC,* number 2743). Psalm 131 tells us that even our resting can be prayer.

"But how is this prayer?" you might respond. To become a believer in constant prayer, you need only be a person of regular prayer. Those who pray regularly feel its constant effect in their life. They report clarity in decision making, calm in the face of adversity, strength in the face of temptation, and growth in loving other people. They also note that in the absence of prayer, it is much easier to fall back into sin. Through their experience of its constant impact on their life, many people have come to believe what the Church teaches: that regular prayer is a vital necessity.

So to "pray without ceasing" doesn't mean you should be dropping to your knees in the intersection when you are supposed to be driving to school. Nor will gazing heavenward with your arms lifted in prayer, when you should be listening to the biology lecture, help you graduate. What the Church is really saying is that all your life *can* be prayer, that prayer and Christian life are inseparable. Bless God each morning for the new day. Ask God regularly for all you need and for the needs of others, each moment you think of them. Thank God for all creation. Praise God in every moment. Make every moment of your life an offering to God. When you unite your life to prayer and prayer to your life, it is possible to "pray without ceasing."

Why Sunday Mass Is Important to Me

Like many college students, I have a busy life: school, homework, meetings, keeping up with friends, and I still have to try and find some time for myself. When I fall into bed at night, I am usually asleep before my prayers are finished. I want to spend more time with God, but it's hard.

That's why I look forward to Sundays. When I go to Mass, I get a whole hour where I don't have to think about anything but my faith. I get a chance to thank God for all the good things I have received over the past week. I get a chance to praise him through song and prayer, and I get a chance to ask him to guide my way through my next week.

Receiving the Eucharist allows me to get even closer to God and Jesus. For the most part, faith is something we cannot physically touch. But I am very much a physical person, so sometimes I just need something right there in front of me that is a part of what I believe in. When I receive the Eucharist—Jesus' body and blood— well, he can't get much closer than that.

(Kari, age 20)

However, the Church invites us to be in constant prayer in one other important way: by praying together as a community. None of us can pray all the time. But as a worldwide community, we can be assured that Catholics in the world are at prayer seven days a week, twenty-four hours a day, every minute of every hour. Although we have talked about some of the ways of praying in other chapters, let's take a closer look at why and how praying with a community is an essential aspect of Catholic life.

The highlight of World Youth Day, an international gathering of youth and young adults, is the closing Mass. What reasons would you give to explain why sharing prayer, particularly the Eucharist, is so essential to the Christian faith?

The Importance of Communal Prayer

Chapter 32, The Forms of Prayer, describes praise, the prayer that expresses love for God simply because God is. This prayer form begins as a natural, self-forgetful kind of love for God that wells up in you for no particular reason. Because we do feel called to prayer in this natural and personal way, we could mistakenly conclude that prayer is an individual relationship.

But by the very nature of what it means to be a Christian, prayer is more than your own personal response to God's initiative. When you were baptized, you were clothed with a white garment, and told, "You have clothed yourself in Christ." Think carefully for a moment about this image. When you put on a shirt, you become enveloped by it—you are *in* your shirt. In Baptism you put on Christ—you are *in* Christ. Only Christ is not a lifeless shirt, but the living Son of God. This means that when you pray in Christ, Christ prays with you to the Father through the power of the Holy Spirit. Your voice is not yours alone, but Christ's voice in communion with the Holy Trinity.

This by itself is amazing, but it doesn't stop there. The Body of Christ that you became part of in Baptism is made up of many members (Romans 12:1–8). Christ promised, "Where two or three are gathered in my name, I am there among them" (Matthew 18:20). When you pray, your voice is joined both to Christ's and to the voice of Christ in every member of his Body. For this reason Christians believe that the liturgy of the Church is the most authentic expression of what it means to be a member of Christ's Body.

Keep in mind that one of the central truths the mystery of the Holy Trinity teaches is that God is a community of three persons in one. Because God made us in his image and likeness, we are also in our very essence created for community. In communal prayer, when you join your voice to the voices of other believers, you affirm the truth that faith is not a private matter. To maintain that you only need to pray by yourself, that you never need to participate in prayer with a community, is to deny an essential part of yourself that was created by God.

The Centrality of the Eucharist

The communal prayer of the Church finds many expressions, but the fullest of these is the Eucharist, where we gather as the People of God, are nourished by his real presence, and are sent to be the Body of Christ in the world. The first Christians knew Jesus personally. They walked with him, talked with him, felt his healing presence in their life, and witnessed it in the lives of others. They experienced his death, and his glorified and resurrected body. When he was no longer physically present, they recalled the words he had spoken at the Last Supper (Luke 22:14–20), gathered in his name and broke bread together (Acts 2:46), and felt him once again present in their midst. The Christ they experienced as they gathered and broke bread was not a vague, fuzzy recollection, but the real, living, healing, transforming presence of the One who had walked with them and changed their lives.

The Catholic Church teaches that Christ continues to be present in the Eucharist: body, blood, soul, and divinity. It is because of this real presence that the encounter with Christ in the Eucharist is as real and transforming today as it was in first-century Palestine. You know that what you eat

PrayIt

"From Age to Age We Gather"

In the Mass we celebrate the **Eucharistic prayer** as the center of Mass and the center of our life as people of God. The Eucharistic prayer is the long prayer the priest says while the bread and wine are consecrated (turned into the body and blood of Christ). It helps us to enter fully into the saving work of Jesus. This is our prayer, the communal prayer of the Church:

Father, you are holy indeed, and all creation rightly gives you praise. All life, all holiness comes from you through your Son, Jesus Christ our Lord, by the working of the Holy Spirit. From age to age you gather a people to yourself, so that from east to west a perfect offering may be made to the glory of your name. And so, Father, we bring you these gifts. We ask you to make them holy by the power of your Spirit, that they may become the body and blood of your Son, our Lord Jesus Christ, at whose command we celebrate this Eucharist. (Eucharistic prayer 3, in *The Sacramentary*, page 552) for breakfast, lunch, or dinner becomes a part of you. It is assimilated in your body, and becomes tissue, muscle, and probably fat too. But the Eucharist is different. When you consume the Body of Christ, you become part of the Body of Christ.

For this reason the Eucharistic liturgy is the central prayer of the Church. The liturgy is the summit and source of spiritual life in the Church. Think about these images. We are always moving toward the next celebration of the Eucharist, gathering the moments of our life on the way to the summit moment, when we are united with Jesus and the entire Body of Christ. Nourished and transformed by Christ, who is the source of all our hope and strength, we are then sent to nourish a spiritually thirsty world, to be the fountain from which Christ's love flows into the world.

Notice the reverence of the priest as he holds the monstrance containing the body of Christ. How do people in your community show reverence and adoration for the presence of Christ in the Eucharist?

Eucharistic Devotions

During every age some people have found the Church's teaching on the Eucharist difficult to believe. Jesus knew that many would find it hard to believe (John 6:60–71). During the thirteenth century, some people challenged the belief that Christ is truly present in the Eucharist. In response, faithful Catholics developed private and public expressions of prayer before Christ's real presence in the Blessed Sacrament. At first the laity made private visits, to pray in adoration before the consecrated bread that had been placed in a vessel that allowed it to be seen. People would take turns at this prayer, making sure that someone was always present, creating another form of prayer without ceasing.

From these beginnings **Eucharistic adoration** has taken on the prayer form of meditation or contemplation. The contemplation of the **Blessed Sacrament** (the body and blood of Christ in the form of bread and wine) can be thought of as a gaze of faith fixed on Jesus. Later in the thirteenth century, in response to the popularity of Eucharistic adoration, public processions with the Blessed Sacrament became common throughout Europe on Corpus Christi, the feast that celebrates the sacrament. **Exposition,** the custom of taking the Eucharist from the tabernacle and placing it in a special vessel called a monstrance, designed to hold a host and make it visible, would normally last as long as the faithful are there to pray. **Benediction** is a special prayer ritual and blessing with the Blessed Sacrament, given by a priest. These devotions developed as extensions of Eucharistic adoration.

The Second Vatican Council, back in the 1960s, clarified some of the practices around Eucharistic devotions. The bishops wanted to be sure that personal devotion to the Eucharist maintained its relationship to the Mass as the source and summit of Christian life. Done correctly, Eucharistic devotions help us to better appreciate and participate in the Eucharistic liturgy.

Liturgy of the Hours

If you have a priest or a religious brother or sister in your family, or if you have ever spent time with one on a trip or a retreat, you may have noticed that once or twice a day they pray out of a thick red or black book. This person was probably praying morning or evening prayer from the **Liturgy of the Hours.** Bishops, priest, deacons, men and women religious, and many laypeople make a commitment to pray the Liturgy of the Hours every day. It is the official nonsacramental, communal prayer of the Catholic Church, although it can also be prayed privately. It is one way that the Church prays always.

Christians are not the first people to desire to make all of life a prayer. The Jews had a practice of making holy the days and the hours by reciting the Psalms. The psalmist says, "Seven times a day I praise

Did You Know?

The Tabernacle

The ark of the Covenant is first revealed in the Old Testament stories in the Book of Exodus. Here we are told that a box was made of gold to honor and protect the tablets of the Ten Commandments (Exodus 25:10–22). The ark was the location of the special presence of God. As the Israelites wandered in the desert, the ark traveled with them, symbolizing God's commitment and presence. The ark of the Covenant foreshadowed the **tabernacle** in a Catholic church. The tabernacle is the place where the consecrated hosts are kept, as a reminder that Jesus continues to dwell among us. You will notice that the priest or an Extraordinary Minister of Holy Communion returns the unused consecrated hosts to the tabernacle right after Communion. A candle is always lit near the tabernacle when it contains consecrated hosts, as a sign that Christ is present.

A common practice of many years ago was to make a visit to Church to spend some time in prayer, in the presence of Jesus dwelling in the tabernacle. Tabernacles are often gold like the ark of the Covenant, although they come in various shapes, sizes, and materials. A **monstrance** is also gold, and is the ornate crosslike container used during benediction and anytime the Blessed Sacrament is publicly exposed for prayer. The ark of the Covenant, the tabernacle, and the monstrance are ways the people of God have come to revere God's presence among us, to remind us of God's covenant with us and to invite us to honor God in prayer.

you" (119:164), and we read that the prophet Daniel prayed throughout the day (Daniel 6:10). Early Christians, who were originally Jews, continued the practice of going to the Temple to pray at regularly fixed hours (Acts 3:1).

This thirteenth-century painting of Saint Clare of Assisi includes images that tell eight stories from her life. If someone were to paint a similar picture of your life, what stories would it include?

Under Roman rule the empire bell rang at certain hours of the day to regulate the opening and closing of shops, breaks, and meals. At some point Jewish prayer hours became attached to the regular sounding of the empire bell. Though Christianity eventually moved outside of its Jewish origins, Christians continued to gather for hours of prayer in their homes. Because several families would gather together at these house churches, prayer with the hours evolved as a communal prayer of the Church. Thus the Liturgy of the Hours as a Christian practice was born.

Although the principal hours of morning and evening prayer would continue to be popular with laypeople for centuries, in the third and fourth centuries, the desert fathers (leaders of desert monastic communities) took Paul's mandate "pray without ceasing" even more seriously. Rather than praying at scheduled hours of the day, they rotated choirs that read the psalms for three hours and then passed it on to the next choir, which in turn did the same.

The practice of celebrating the Liturgy of the Hours, which was always prayed in Latin, endured long after the laity understood Latin. Therefore it gradually became the prayer of the clergy and the vowed religious, who used a shortened version called the **breviary.** When the Second Vatican Council restored the liturgy to the language spoken by the people, it envisioned the renewal of the Liturgy of the Hours as the prayer of the whole Church, so the entire course of the day and the night might be made holy.

When you think about it, it is a wonderful concept, really. You know that because of time zones, every hour of the day exists somewhere in the world. As Christians everywhere pray the Liturgy of the Hours, they are always passing the prayer on to the next choir somewhere else around the world, in the manner of the desert fathers. This practice adds another dimension to understanding communal prayer. At any one time, even if prayed alone, this prayer unites us with the Body of Christ throughout the world.

Today the Liturgy of the Hours consists of a structured pattern of prayers that includes hymns, psalms, antiphons, Scripture meditation, the Lord's Prayer, and other readings and responses. The Liturgy of the Hours follows a four-week cycle, with adjustments for the feasts and seasons of the liturgical year. It can be prayed seven times a day, though the primary hours are morning and evening prayer. If you are unfamiliar with the Liturgy of the Hours, ask a priest, religious, or layperson who prays it to show you how.

Other Ways of Praying with Groups

Eating, shopping, studying, dancing, car trips, and many forms of exercise are among things you can do alone, but probably find more enjoyable when you do them with others. Don't neglect to think of praying with others as something that can be rich and exciting too. There are many forms of prayer with groups, including some that are less formal and structured than those we have already discussed.

Family life is full of events that can be lifted in prayers. Many families pray grace at meals, and a rosary or other prayers before bed. Births, adoptions, injuries, deaths, anniversaries, birthdays, promotions, graduations, good grades, failures, meals together, and every ordinary moment are deepened when we pause to connect our life with God, who gives us life. If someone in your family is

Saintly Profiles

Saint Clare of Assisi (1193–1253)

Saint Clare of Assisi was of noble birth, but when she was eighteen, she was so moved by the Lenten sermons of Saint Francis of Assisi that she renounced all her possessions to become a nun. Her family and friends tried hard to change her mind and bring her home, but she would not be moved. She was deeply in love with God and wanted to live a holy life. Saint Francis recognized something special in Clare, and urged her to return to Assisi, and she and Saint Francis became close friends and spiritual associates. Clare became the founder of the Poor Clares, and lived twenty-seven years beyond the death of Saint Francis. Deep humility, a deep commitment to poverty, and a deep longing for God marked her life.

On Christmas Day, shortly before her death, Clare was sick and could not join her community and the friars in praying. She acknowledged her loneliness to God, and suddenly she began to hear the singing and praying of her sisters and the friars. She also had a vision of Jesus in the manger. Clare was able to see the rest of the service as she lay ill on her bed. Later she told her sisters: "Blessed be my Lord Jesus Christ who did not abandon me even when you were all gone. By His grace I was allowed to participate in the entire service" (Gerard Thomas Straub, *The Sun and Moon Over Assisi*, page 396). Because of this miracle, Clare has been named the patron saint of television! She is also the patron saint of women in childbirth and people suffering from eye diseases. Her feast day is celebrated on August 11.

good at leading prayer, see if you can establish a few more moments of praise, thanksgiving, adoration, or reconciliation at your home. Many beautiful prayer books are available for Catholic families, to help you in this effort.

Books can also be helpful if you want to organize a prayer group with other students, coworkers, or friends. Some prayer books include the readings for the liturgy of the day and a written reflection. Many people discover an appreciation for the Scriptures through this kind of prayer. Other books focus on specific topics. Many good prayer books are written for teenagers, but you need not rely on books. Many prayer groups simply gather to offer petitions and thanksgiving, and close with the Lord's Prayer.

Music is a wonderful avenue for prayer. If you sing or play an instrument, think about forming a group. Rather than having performance be the goal, allow the time you spend together to be a prayerful lifting of one another's joys and needs in song.

Some friends connect as prayer partners. This one-on-one prayer can happen in different ways. You can take a walk, share hopes and concerns, and conclude with words holding each other up to God. Many prayer partners end the day with a prayer phone call.

The ways you can connect with others in prayer are limitless. Any group can pray together, and anyone can create a prayer. There are no special formulas or requirements. Don't worry whether you are getting it right, just do it. Some Web sites offer prayer suggestions and bulletin boards, where you can post prayers. Think of at least one way you might make your prayer life richer by praying with others.

For Further Reflection

○ What are two things you can do to make your life a constant prayer? What do you feel might be holding you back from "praying without ceasing"?

○ What do you think is the most important aspect of communal prayer? Which of the regular prayers of the Church do you find most significant for your life now? What communal forms of prayer talked about in this chapter would you like to try?

Looking Back

Monastic Prayer

Nestled in the hills of Kentucky is one of the most famous monasteries in the country, Gethsemani. It is one of the earliest religious communities established in the area, and is visited by many people each year. The climate of silence and the sense of holiness are important to the visitors, and to the monks who call Gethsemani home. These Trappist monks rarely leave the community. They participate in gardening, building, farming, baking, and more, in order to provide the basics for themselves. It is prayer, however, that unites them and forms the core of their ministry. The monks withdraw from the world and modern society to pray for the world and to live a life centered on God.

Their entire day is centered in the act of praying the Liturgy of the Hours. The cycle begins when the monks pray Vigils and Matins in the middle of the night, a time of silence and waiting for the dawn. Next they gather for Lauds, the prayer at daybreak, expressing joy and thanksgiving for the new day. Terce is the midmorning prayer to the Holy Spirit, asking for strength for the day. Sext is prayed at noon, asking for perseverance. Nones is prayed midafternoon, reminding us of Jesus' death. At the end of the day, the monks pray Vespers in thanksgiving and Compline before retiring for the night. These are the official prayers of the Church being prayed around the world, so the Church is in constant prayer (based on Bob O'Gorman and Mary Faulkner, *The Complete Idiot's Guide to Understanding Catholicism*, pages 193–194).

36 The Lord's Prayer
God's Glory

If you were to write an essay on the topic "All I Really Need," what would you write about? You might be surprised to learn that Jesus gave us a basic outline for such an essay in the form of a prayer. At the Sermon on the Mount (Matthew 6:9–15), he taught his disciples seven petitions (requests) commonly known as the **Lord's Prayer.** We call it the Lord's Prayer because the Lord Jesus Christ gave it to us (it is also called the Our Father, after the opening words). Because this prayer is a summary of all that we need to live the Christian life, the Church teaches that the Lord's Prayer is a summary of the entire Gospel.

The Lord's Prayer has a key place in the prayer life of Christians for two reasons: first, it comes to us directly from Jesus, and second, this prayer lays the foundation for all our desires in the Christian life. In fact, it is referred to as the "quintessential (perfect example of) prayer of the Church" (*CCC*, number 2776), which is why the Our Father is said almost anytime Catholics gather. The first Christians prayed it

Words to Look For

- ○ *Lord's Prayer*
- ○ *petition*
- ○ *heaven*
- ○ *Kingdom of God*
- ○ *Parousia*
- ○ *doxology*

three times a day. Today we pray it at every Eucharistic liturgy so that the entire Church prays together for the things that Jesus taught us to ask for.

Chances are you have prayed this prayer hundreds, even thousands of times. In the second chapter of this section, we note how easy it is to fall into a mechanical recitation of vocal prayers. The Lord's Prayer in particular is a prayer you do not want to repeat mechanically, because it asks God for all you really need. This chapter and the next one look at the wording of this prayer, in order to help you make your approach to it fresh and personal. Remember that Jesus, who gave you this prayer, also gives you the Spirit to help you pray with a sincere heart. Take care when you pray the Lord's Prayer, that your voice might unite with the Son and the Spirit to place the desires of your heart before God.

The Structure of the Lord's Prayer

The Lord's Prayer begins with an address: "Our Father who art in heaven." Then seven petitions follow. A **petition** is a request for God to do something for us. But because Jesus gave these petitions to us, they are more than just simple requests. They teach us what we really need to live holy, happy, moral lives.

The opening address helps us to place ourselves in the presence of God and in the proper frame of mind. The first three petitions are theological, that is, they are oriented toward God, to help draw us closer to God and his glory. The last four petitions are oriented to human need. They teach us to ask for what we truly need, not just for ourselves but for the whole human family. By studying each of these elements of the Lord's Prayer, we can learn a lot about ourselves and about God.

Top Ten Ways for Seeking God's Will

Are you faced with a difficult decision at home, at school, or with a friend? Have you asked for God's help? Christians use the word *discernment* to refer to the process of choosing the best loving action, under the guidance of the Holy Spirit. No one has time to discern everything, but faithful Christians consciously invite God into their major decisions. Here are some ways to approach a decision with discernment:

1. **Pray about it.** Ask God for the grace to make a good decision.
2. **Put it in writing.** Clearly state the decision you want to make.
3. **Do your research.** Collect solid information and consult people you trust.
4. **Consider your options.** List the pros and cons and the relative weight of each.
5. **Use your imagination.** Imagine what benefits and problems might result.
6. **Tune in to your feelings.** Reflect on how God might be speaking through your attractions and desires.
7. **Make your decision and offer it to God.** Ask God to help you live it out.
8. **Look for fruits of the Spirit.** Watch for qualities like charity, peace, patience, faithfulness, and self-control.
9. **Stay open.** Be willing to make adjustments as you live out your decision.
10. **Persevere.** Make discernment a part of your life.

Because the Lord's Prayer is so central to Christian life, two chapters are devoted to it. In this chapter, you read about the opening address and the first three petitions, which address the glory of the Father, the sanctification of his name, the coming of the Kingdom, and the fulfillment of his will.

Our Father in Heaven

Words are kind of like suitcases. The letters are like the exterior shell, which is capable of holding the contents. All kinds of meaning can be packed inside a word. First of all, words carry their basic dictionary meaning. But, just as a suitcase on a long trip gets filled with mementos, words acquire additional meanings for us based on our personal and cultural experiences. As a result words can have different meanings or even cause different feelings for different people. If we want to understand and be understood, it becomes important to "unpack" the meaning of the words we use. In this chapter and the next, we will look at the words in the Lord's Prayer, with all their layers of meaning.

One of the most famous Catholics of the last century is Mother Teresa. Why was her simple life and total commitment to caring for poor people so inspiring for so many people?

Our

This book has emphasized the Catholic teaching that we are called to follow Jesus not as solitary individuals but always as part of a community. We see this truth again in the fact that Jesus begins the prayer with "Our Father" rather than "My Father." The use of "our" in the Lord's Prayer has several meanings:

- It is a sign of the new covenant accomplished in Christ. It means we are God's people and he is our Father.
- It expresses the certitude of our hope in God's promise that we will one day be with him in the new Jerusalem. We are God's children forever.
- It is a profession of the Trinity, because when we pray to the Father, we adore and glorify him together with the Son and the Holy Spirit.

- It acknowledges that we pray with the whole Church, all the baptized.
- It leaves our individualism behind because the love we receive from God frees us from divisions and oppositions and establishes our relationship with all God's people.
- It is an expression of God's care for all people, even those who do not yet know Christ.

Father

When we hear "Father," we understand the word in light of our experience of earthly fathers and mothers. It is hoped that you have been raised in a home with loving parents, and your image of a father is a positive one. However, even the best parents are still human, and are bound to hurt and disappoint us on occasion. Not so with God. The Church tells us to remember that God as Father is more than any earthly image we might have. We have to get beyond our personal experiences of father and mother to meet the Father that Jesus reveals to us.

For Christians, Jesus is the starting point for understanding God. We can invoke God as Father because Jesus Christ revealed him to us. Most children bear a resemblance to their parents. Ask any parent of a newborn how much of the conversation centers on whom the child looks like: "She has your eyes." "He has his father's nose." These natural human connections are a glimpse of how we come to know God as Father through Jesus. Jesus reveals who God is, not in terms of physical appearance, but through his actions and his words. Furthermore, because Jesus is God, the resemblance is identical.

We can all-too-easily take for granted the power and beauty of this Revelation. God

Looking Back

Mother Teresa's Simple Path to God

Mother Teresa (1910–1997) grew up as Agnes Bojaxhiu in Skoplje, Albania. She joined the Sisters of Our Lady of Loreto in 1928, and taught for many years in a Catholic school for girls in Calcutta, India. But then she heard God calling her to serve the poorest of the poor. Mother Teresa touched the lives of thousands of people because of her willingness to do the will of God. The following quotes illustrate her simple path to God:

Holiness does not consist in doing extraordinary things. It consists in accepting, with a smile, what Jesus sends us. It consists in accepting and following the will of God. (José Luis González-Balado, *Mother Teresa*, page xiii)

If you are searching for God and do not know where to begin, learn to pray and take the trouble to pray every day. You can pray anytime, anywhere. You do not have to be in a chapel or a church. You can pray at work—work doesn't have to stop prayer and prayer doesn't have to stop work. You can also consult a priest or minister for guidance, or try speaking directly to God. Just speak. Tell Him everything, talk to Him. He is our father. He is father to us all whatever religion we are. We are all created by God, we are his children. We have to put our trust in Him and love Him, believe in Him, work for Him. And if we pray, we will get all the answers we need. (Mother Teresa, *A Simple Path*, page 8) the Father was never fully revealed until Jesus Christ walked among us. "No one knows the Son except the Father, and no one knows the Father except the Son and anyone to whom the Son chooses to reveal him" (Matthew 11:27). Through Jesus we are invited into a new relationship with God. When Jesus accomplished our salvation through his death and Resurrection, he brought us into God's presence, called us his brothers and sisters, and made us the adopted children of God (Hebrews 1:3, 2:12–13). Praying the Our Father brings us into communion with God our Father and his Son, Jesus Christ, our brother.

This painting is of Saint Joseph playing with Jesus and a puppy while Mary looks on. What qualities of Saint Joseph's emerge from this simple image?

Who Art in Heaven

The last words of the first phrase of the Lord's Prayer are "who art in heaven." When you were small, like most children you probably imagined heaven as a distant place up in the sky somewhere. As you have grown, you have come to realize that "up" is a relative concept. On a round planet, up for you, is down for someone halfway around the world.

No one on earth knows exactly what heaven is like. In fact, Saint Paul reminds us in First Corinthians, "No eye has seen, nor ear heard, / nor the human heart conceived, / what God has prepared for those who love him" (2:9). What we do know, as Saint Paul indicates, is that **heaven** has to do with being in God's love. For this reason we say that heaven is more a way of being than a place, a state of deep happiness and loving communion with God. Our earthly experiences of the happiness and joy that are a part of Christian life help us to glimpse the loving communion with the Trinity that we will experience if we die in union with God.

So when you pray "who art in heaven," your words are not an expression of place or distance. They are an expression of your desire to be in union with God, who is holy, majestic, and transcendent. They express our desire that God dwell in our heart and help us to love as he loves. When we love this way, we experience something of the loving communion we long for at the end of our life.

"Who art in heaven" also refers to our eternal destiny. This world is only our temporary home. We are made for something greater than this life. We are God's people, who long for our true home in heaven with him. (See chapter 13, The Last Things, for more on heaven and the afterlife.)

This first phrase of the Lord's Prayer addresses God and draws us into his presence. The first three petitions that follow draw us even deeper into God's glory.

Hallowed Be Thy Name

Knowing someone's name gives you a certain amount of power. You can build the person up by saying good things, and you can tear the person down just as easily. You can report the person to the authorities for doing something illegal. When you remember the name of someone you met recently, it can be very affirming. The first petition of the Lord's Prayer reminds us of the power of God's name and of our responsibility to treat it with great care.

The petition asks God to "hallow" his name. *Hallow* means "to make holy," and we know that only God makes things holy. Why, then, does Jesus tell us that our first request from God should be to make holy his name? Because Jesus was instructing us to recognize God's name as holy and to treat God in a holy way.

For the people of the Old Testament, revealing your name was pretty much the same as revealing who you were as a person. Thus God doesn't reveal his name at first to Abraham, because the people are not ready for it. He reveals an aspect of himself to Moses and the Israelites when he gives his name as "I AM WHO I AM" (Exodus 3:14). God commands the people, "You shall be holy, for I the LORD your God am holy" (Leviticus 19:2).

Saintly Profiles

Saint Joseph

Saint Joseph was the husband of the Blessed Virgin Mary, the mother of Jesus. Joseph was a just and compassionate man, and protected Mary from shame when he discovered that she was pregnant, even though he did not understand that her unborn child was the Son of God. We see evidence of Joseph's deep faith when he changed his plans in response to messages from God.

Although God is Jesus' true father, Joseph fulfilled that role in daily life. He loved Jesus and treated him as his own son (Luke 4:22). He provided for the safety of his family (Matthew 2:13–14), and taught Jesus his trade (Mark 6:3). There are no more references to Joseph in the New Testament after the family's pilgrimage to Jerusalem (Luke 2:41–52), so he may have died before Jesus began his public ministry. Joseph is known as the patron saint of fathers and workers. We celebrate two feast days for him, March 19 for Joseph the husband of Mary, and May 1 for Joseph the worker.

God's name is only fully revealed in Jesus. Not only does Jesus tell us to call God "Father," but he also establishes the New Covenant whereby we are made holy because Jesus is holy. In his priestly prayer, Jesus prays, "Holy Father, . . . for their sakes I sanctify myself, that they also may be sanctified in truth" (John 17:11,19). When Jesus passes from death to new life, the Father gives him the name that is above all names: "Jesus Christ is Lord, / to the glory of God the Father" (Philippians 2:11).

In Baptism we are made holy in the name of Jesus and the Holy Spirit (1 Corinthians 6:11) and called to holiness in the whole of our life. We cannot make God unholy. However, because our Baptism draws us into God's plan, his name is blessed when we live well and cursed when we do not. You can draw a comparison with earthly parents. Their goodness isn't changed by their children's behavior, but how well their children act is often reflected back on them.

When you pray "hallowed be thy name," reflect on how your life is holy. Do the people who know you and watch you see how you honor God in everything you do? Do you make choices that are not honoring God? The first petition is a summary of all the petitions that follow, because it calls us to hallow God's name in everything we do.

Thy Kingdom Come

If you have been reading this handbook from the beginning, you learned about the **Kingdom of God** in chapter 7, Jesus' Message and Mission. Recall that this Kingdom lies ahead of us, is brought near in Jesus, is proclaimed throughout the Gospel, and, since Pentecost, has been coming through the work of the Spirit.

Pray It!

In Your Own Words

Through the ages people have wrestled with the true meaning of the Lord's Prayer by putting it into their own words. Saint Francis of Assisi wrote a lengthy paraphrase of the Lord's Prayer that starts out like this:

Our Father most holy,
our Creator and Redeemer,
our Saviour and our Comforter.

This modern paraphrase changes the wording just enough to make its meaning a little easier to understand:

Abba in heaven, your name is holy!
Your justice come, your will be done, on earth as in the heavens.
Fill us this day with all that we need.
Teach us to heal as you have healed us.
Bring us not to the test, but deliver us always from the power of evil.
You alone are God, and all belongs to you!
(Edward F. Gabriele, *Gathered at Table in Prayer and Song,* page 25)

How would you put the Lord's Prayer into your own words?

You have probably heard talk of the Second Coming of Jesus. It is often veiled in frightening terms, with plagues, destruction, and death. Early Christians did not fear the Second Coming, but anxiously anticipated it. The **Parousia,** the glorious return and appearance of Jesus at the end of time, as judge of the living and the dead, was hoped for with great joy. In the Second Coming of Christ, all of history and all of creation would achieve their fulfillment. This is a great thing, and this is the coming Kingdom for which you pray in this petition.

The petition "thy kingdom come" primarily refers to this final coming of the Reign of God through Christ's return. But the Church is also a sign and presence of the Kingdom of God in the world right now. So when you pray this petition of the Lord's Prayer, you are also saying that you commit yourself to Jesus' mission here on earth. How are you helping to bring love, peace, and justice into the world? Is God calling you to be part of some work of service or justice?

Thy Will Be Done on Earth as It Is in Heaven

As with God's name, some people use "God's will" in vain. People justify prejudice and war as God's will. Pain and sorrow are explained away as God's will. If you find this confusing, you are on the right track. For Christians it should be difficult to reconcile such things with the God of love and mercy revealed to us in Jesus. So just what is God's will?

The commandment Jesus gave his disciples at the Last Supper, "Just as I have loved you, you also should love one another" (John 13:34), summarizes God's entire will. This means that love is mandatory for Christians. Many of the stories in the New Testament illustrate love of others, although perhaps none

The Doxology

Have you ever prayed the Lord's Prayer with friends and noticed that their prayer went on longer than yours did? Have you wondered why Catholics usually don't end the Lord's Prayer with the words, "For yours is the kingdom, the power, and the glory," except at Mass?

In Judaism it was normal to conclude prayers with a formal **doxology** (short expression of praise), and the early Christian communities often followed this Jewish practice. They ended the Lord's Prayer with the doxology, "For yours are the power and the glory for ever." We know this because it is quoted in an early Christian paper called the *Didache,* written before A.D. 100.

Some of the earliest copies of the Gospels added the doxology to the Lord's Prayer in Matthew, chapter 6, and other copies did not. The manuscript that Saint Jerome used in the fourth century to translate the New Testament from Greek into Latin did not include the added doxology. Thus it was not included in Catholic Bibles. The manuscript that was used in the early 1600s to translate the King James Bible included the doxology, which is why it is in many Protestant Bibles.

more clearly than the parable of the good Samaritan (Luke 10:30–37). God's will is that we love everyone, even our enemies, with a love that includes serving, forgiving, and sometimes suffering, without receiving love in return. Praying to our heavenly Father develops in us the will to become like him, and fosters in us a humble and trusting heart.

When you pray "thy will be done," think about how wonderful it would be if everyone followed God's plan for us, starting with yourself. Are you following the commandments, which contain the moral will of God? Do you honor your parents, teachers, and civil authorities who reflect God's will in their concern for your safety and personal growth? Do you follow the teachings of the Church, which reflect God's will for your spiritual growth?

For Further Reflection

- Pick one of the words or phrases from the first half of the Lord's Prayer. What new insights do you have now about the meaning of this word or phrase?
- When you hear the word *obedience,* does it raise positive or negative feelings in you? Why? Could you describe to someone why obedience to God's will is a positive thing?

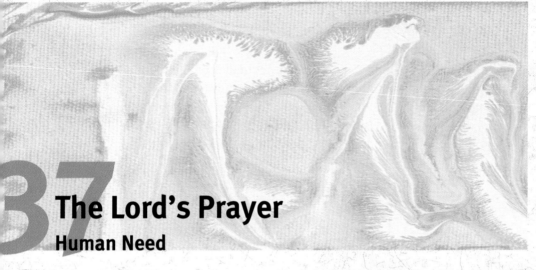

37

The Lord's Prayer
Human Need

The wishes of the human heart are a universal theme. Nearly every culture has a tale with a genie or some other figure with the power to grant three wishes. The story gets played out in different ways, depending on the goodness of the grantor and the wisdom of the requester. What would you ask for if you had three wishes?

The final four petitions of the Lord's Prayer can be thought of as Jesus' answer to the desires of the Christian heart. He teaches us to boldly ask that our lives be nourished, healed of sin, and made victorious in the struggle of good over evil. As in the previous chapter, we "unpack" the meaning of some of the words in these petitions, in order to come to a fuller appreciation of the Lord's Prayer.

Give Us This Day Our Daily Bread

On whom do you ultimately depend? Believe it or not, how you answer this question might depend somewhat on your

Words to Look For

- temptations
- discernment
- Christ's Parousia
- Satan
- exorcism

gender. Men would tend to answer, "Ultimately I depend only on myself," because in U.S. culture men are taught in many subtle ways that true strength is in being independent. Women would tend to answer, "Ultimately I depend on my family and friends," because our culture teaches women to cooperate and build relationships. Both of these answers contain truth. Yet in the Lord's Prayer, Jesus teaches that they are only part of the bigger answer, which is that ultimately and in every moment, we depend not on our own abilities or the abilities of others, but on God.

Looking Back

"Give Us This Day Our Daily Bread"

In a homily to the Italian bishops in November 2001, Pope John Paul II expressed the sense of gratitude and shared responsibility that underlies our prayer for daily bread, in the Lord's Prayer:

> When teaching this prayer to the disciples, Christ asked them to trust in the goodness of God the Father, who rejoices to give all creatures, especially human beings, what is necessary for life. At the same time, having us say *"today"* and *"daily"* reminds us that this gift must not be taken for granted, but must always be asked for and received in a spirit of thanksgiving.
>
> Moreover, it is important that Christ taught us to ask for "our" bread, and not that each one ask for "his" own. This means that children of the same Father are co-responsible for the "bread" of all, so that everyone may live in dignity and together with the others thank the Lord. (*Angelus*, number 1, Sunday, November 11, 2001)

Give Us This Day

The words *give us* sound like a child's selfish plea, don't they? The very phrasing recalls our relationship as children before God our Father. We ask him in trust for our needs, and in doing so acknowledge the goodness of the One who gives to all the living "their food in due season" (Psalm 104:27). Jesus tells us to say "give us" with the confidence of children who rely on their parents for basic care. He teaches us, "Ask, and it will be given you; search, and you will find; knock, and the door will be opened for you" (Matthew 7:7). Jesus illustrated this teaching by comparing the good gifts earthly parents give their children to the even greater gifts of the heavenly Father (Matthew 7:9–11).

In asking only for our daily bread, the petition emphasizes our radical dependence on God. It doesn't ask God for our monthly bread or our yearly bread. The prayer asks only for bread for a day; tomorrow we will have to ask again. Every day we must acknowledge our need for God's bounty. The accumulation of material things can get in the way of recognizing our daily dependence on God. Remember Jesus' story of the rich man who decided to store many years' worth of grain and goods so he could relax, eat, drink, and be merry?

Then God said: "You fool, this very night your life is being demanded of you. And the things you have prepared, whose will they be?" (Luke 12:20).

Our Daily Bread

As the basic staple of life in many cultures, bread stands for all the nourishment that life requires. So the petition is not asking just for bread, but for all the essential things we need to sustain our lives. This, of course, means food and water. In Catholic social-justice teaching, it also means things like housing, employment, education, and medical care. All these things are part of our daily bread.

You might be thinking, "If we are truly trusting God to provide all these things, does this mean we can quit our jobs, pray, and get all we need?" In response, Saint Ignatius cautions, "Pray as if everything depended on God and work as if everything depended on you"[1] (*CCC*, number 2834). God does not want idleness on our part. He does want us to be confident that our needs will be taken care of (Matthew 6:25–34). At the same time, one of the ways that God provides is by giving each person unique gifts to share with the world.

For example, the presence of hunger in the world is not a sign of God's neglect. Rather it is the point where God's goodness and our gifts meet. There is plenty of food in the world, but some people have much more than they need and others have none. When Jesus taught us to pray this petition, in addition to teaching us to trust in God's care, he was reminding us to reflect God's care for all people by distributing the world's abundance responsibly. Like the yeast that makes dough rise, we are called to be people who work for change, who work for the

Teens Can Fight Hunger!

Get the facts:

- One half of all children's deaths around the world are hunger related.
- Most people are hungry because they lack land of their own to grow food or work that pays a living wage.
- There *is* enough food to feed the world. Hunger is more often caused by politics than by the lack of food.

Take action:

- Collect food for a local food pantry.
- Prepare and serve food for a soup kitchen in your area.
- Plan a food fast with your friends or youth group, to learn more about hunger.
- Hold a Work of Human Hands sale at your church or school, and support artisans from all over the world.
- Participate in Operation Rice Bowl during Lent, and collect money to improve the lives of people close to home and far away.

Catholic Relief Services (CRS) has the information and connections to help you make a difference. CRS works in more than eighty countries in Africa, Asia, Latin America, the Caribbean, Europe, and the Middle East. Find out more at *www.catholicrelief.org*.

establishment of social justice. We are to put our unique gifts and talents to work in doing our part to make sure others have their "daily bread."

The needs of the world addressed by this petition are not limited to material needs. Jesus reminds us in the Gospel of Matthew, "One does not live by bread alone, / but by every word that comes from the mouth of God" (4:4). The petition calls us to ask for and share spiritual nourishment as well. It especially reminds us that Jesus is the bread of life: both the Word of God and the Body of Christ that we receive in the Eucharist.

In this famous event, Pope John Paul II extends his forgiveness and reconciliation to the man who shot him. Following his example, do you have people in your life to whom you need to extend the hand of forgiveness?

Forgive Us as We Forgive Others

When you stop and think about it, this next petition is astonishing. We know that through Christ's sacrifice our sins have been forgiven. But the phrase, "Forgive us our trespasses, as we forgive those who trespass against us," places a strict requirement on us. The two parts of the petition are joined by the word *as,* which means that our request to be forgiven will not be heard unless we first forgive others.

And Forgive Us Our Trespasses

We begin this fifth petition of the Lord's Prayer with a confession of our sinfulness and our need for God's mercy. We can pray for God's forgiveness with confidence because Jesus has revealed to us a Father who is rich in compassion and full of mercy. The parables of the lost sheep (Luke 15:1–7), the lost coin (Luke 15:8–10), and the prodigal son (Luke 15:11–32) portray a God who not only forgives but waits, seeks, and longs to do so. In Christ we know that "we have redemption, the forgiveness of sins" (Colossians 1:14).

As We Forgive Those Who Trespass Against Us

The second half of the petition tells the rest of the story. Another parable, the parable of the unforgiving servant, spells out the meaning of this petition (Matthew 18:23–35). You might recall the servant who is forgiven a large debt, something like fifteen years' wages. In turn he throws into prison a fellow servant who owes him a small amount, roughly a day's wages. On learning of his servant's wickedness, the master hands him over to be tortured. The parable ends with these daunting words: "So my heavenly Father will also do to every one of you, if you do not forgive your brother or sister from your heart."

A lack of forgiveness hardens our heart. Think of a friend who holds a grudge against someone. Even if the person your friend is angry with does something kind, your friend may be unwilling to soften her or his view of that person—this is what it means to have a "hardened heart." The outpouring of God's forgiveness cannot penetrate a hardened heart. Nor can a hardened heart receive love. "Those who do not love a brother or sister whom they have seen, cannot love God whom they have not seen" (1 John 4:20). Only when we forgive others and confess our own sins are our hearts softened and opened to God's grace.

Here's the hardest part: Forgiving *as* God forgives includes forgiving our enemies. Jesus tells us that only when we are capable of this are we truly children of our Father in heaven, "for he makes the sun rise on the evil and on the good, and sends rain on the righteous and on the unrighteous" (Matthew 5:43–45). We can't pretend that this is easy. Sometimes people do terrible, violent things to others. If we have been victimized by such terrible acts, how is it possible to forgive those who are responsible, so that our inner healing can be complete? It is only by the power of the Spirit that we can accomplish this. (However, forgiving someone does not mean that you blame yourself for the other person's evil actions or that the person does not accept the consequences for the action.)

When you pray this petition, recall any sins that you still need to ask forgiveness for. Then consider if you have friends

Pray It!

Ignatian Examen

Saint Ignatius of Loyola, the founder of the Jesuits, was noted for his practical approach to spiritual matters. He encouraged his followers to use an orderly process each evening to reflect on their day and how they had experienced God in it. He called this an examen, or examination of conscience, but he didn't want his followers to focus only on their sins. You can use this process to reflect or journal about your day too.

1. Pray for light. Ask God to help you see what God wants you to see in your experiences and encounters.
2. Review your day. Take a careful look back. Stop to say thanks for the gifts you received. Pause to notice the feelings that surface.
3. Choose a feeling. Focus on a feeling that caught your attention, and pray about it. Use your own words of praise or petition, whatever fits for you.
4. Imagine what tomorrow will bring. Invite God to be with you in the day ahead.

or family who have sinned against you that you still need to forgive. Finally, think about the people you consider your enemies and how you have responded to them. Allow the Spirit of God to soften any hardness you have left, so that God's mercy and love can live in you.

In this painting, Saint Ignatius of Loyola has a vision of the name of Jesus Christ, represented by the initials IHS. His devotion to the name of Christ led him to name the religious community he founded the Society of Jesus, or the Jesuits.

Lead Us Not into Temptation

Would God *lead* us to be tempted? In the original Greek, *lead us not* means both "do not allow us to enter" and "do not let us yield." So to rephrase the petition, we are asking God "not to allow us to enter situations of temptation" or "not to let us yield to temptation." Of course, God would never lead us into evil. God wills that all of us have eternal life with him.

"Do not enter" and "yield" are like the road signs. In this petition we ask God not to allow us to take the road that leads to sin. The Holy Spirit acts like a "do not enter" sign in the hearts of those who pray, by helping us to identify and respond to temptations. **Temptations** are invitations or enticements to commit an unwise or immoral act that often include a promise or a reward to make them more appealing.

The greatest difficulty lies in being able to identify temptations for what they are. Like the fruit of the tree in the Garden of Eden, temptations masquerade as good, desirable, and a "delight to the eyes" (Genesis 3:6). You can probably think of a time when you chose to do something because it seemed like it would be fun, but in the end it led to hurt and sorrow. Through **discernment** the Spirit can help us determine that which is truly good from that which is evil in a tempting disguise.

Most of us aren't faced every day with temptations that lead to mortal sin. We usually face smaller temptations, like passing on a little gossip, or cheating on one question on a test. The danger with these small temptations is that giving in to them puts us on the wrong road. Once we give in to temptation, we are weakened. It is easier to give in again and again.

That little white lie can lead to a bigger lie, and then an even bigger lie, all to cover up the first little lie. The Letter of James describes this situation: "But one is tempted by one's own desire, being lured and enticed by it; then, when that desire has conceived, it gives birth to sin, and that sin, when it is fully grown, gives birth to death" (James 1:14–15).

Probably the most famous story of temptation in the Bible is the story of David and Bathsheba (2 Samuel, chapter 11). You might want to read it; it illustrates the way that giving in to one temptation leads you further and further into sin. What begins as coveting another man's wife, gives way to adultery. Adultery gives way to lying. Lying gives way to murder.

Fortunately, with God's great mercy, taking the wrong road doesn't have to lead to the point of no return. David's expression of repentance in Psalm 51 is a model prayer for requesting forgiveness when we have failed. When we do fall to temptation, we can learn from our mistakes. Being tempted does not mean that we have done anything wrong. We know that Jesus was tempted in the desert (Matthew 4:1–11, Mark 1:12–13, Luke 4:1–13). In the world we live in, it is almost impossible to go a day without facing some kind of temptation. In Second Corinthians (12:7–10) Saint Paul talks about how a testing of our inner strength can lead to growth. Origen, a great theologian of the early Church, also counseled that there was a certain usefulness to temptation, "In this way we discover our evil inclinations and are obliged to give thanks for the goods that temptation has revealed to us"[2] (*CCC*, number 2847).

Through regular prayer the Holy Spirit makes us vigilant to the possibility of temptation. When you pray, "lead us not into temptation," you are inviting the Holy Spirit into your

Saintly Profiles

Saint Ignatius of Loyola (1491–1556)

Ignatius of Loyola was the youngest of eleven children in a noble family in Spain. As a young adult, his goal in life was to achieve fame and fortune. At the age of thirty, he was seriously injured in a battle. During the long months of his recovery, he had the opportunity to examine his life and read about the saints. Ignatius never did anything halfway. Once he realized that God was calling him, he devoted all his energy to discerning God's will and then doing it. In search of what he ought to do, Ignatius encountered setbacks, closed doors, and even imprisonment. He was convinced that God could be found in all things, and was guided by an inner peace that comes from knowing one is doing the will of God.

Ignatius developed the Spiritual Exercises, a practical guide for those who want to live a truly Christian life, and shared them with his companions. Ignatius called his community the "Company of Jesus." Today they are known as the Society of Jesus, or the Jesuits, one of the largest religious communities in the world. Besides the three vows of poverty, chastity, and obedience, members take a fourth vow of obedience to the Pope. Saint Ignatius's feast day is July 31.

heart to awaken you and keep watch with you. When you pray this petition, think about the situations and people that tempt you to do things you know are wrong. How can you avoid these situations? What kind of relationship do you need with the people who tempt you, to minimize their temptation?

This ivory relief shows Jesus driving the evil spirit from a possessed man. What forms of evil are dangers to us today?

But Deliver Us from Evil

The last petition of the Lord's Prayer continues the theme of the sixth petition, the struggle of good over evil. It moves away from our personal struggle with evil to pray with the whole Church about the distress of the world. We ask to be delivered from evil, and strengthened to persevere against the evil in the world until **Christ's Parousia** (Christ's Second Coming). It echoes the prayer of Jesus to the Father at the Last Supper, "I am not asking you to take them out of the world, but I ask you to protect them from the evil one" (John 17:15).

Evil in this petition is not an abstract concept, but refers to **Satan,** the evil one, the fallen angel who opposes God and all God's works. This petition anticipates the great battle against evil symbolized in the vision in chapter 12 of the Book of Revelation. In the opening scene, the pregnant woman represents Israel, from which the Messiah will come. The dragon waiting to devour her is the symbol for Satan. The child, who will rule all the nations, is the Messiah, Jesus Christ.

The conflict moves from heaven to earth when Satan fails to devour the child and is thrown down from his place in heaven. Through Satan, "the father of lies" (John 8:44), sin enters the world. He works tirelessly against God's plan. As the "prince of the world," he continues to pursue the woman on earth, who now represents the Christian churches. The dragon angrily persecutes her because he was not successful in devouring her child.

John wrote this symbolic passage to the Christians of his time because they were facing real evil in the form of persecution. The symbolic language he used encouraged them to have hope, because in the end Christ, already victorious over sin and death, will completely destroy Satan. We too face real evil today. In the last section, we noted how evil often subtly masquerades as goodness and delight, luring us into temptation. At other times the veil is completely lifted, and we are able to see evil in all its horror. September 11, 2001, is for many a stark reminder that the world is in the power of the evil one (1 John 5:19). Like John's community we need to be reminded that our hope is in the salvation already accomplished in Christ.

Evil does touch each of us personally, but the focus of this petition is the deliverance of the whole human family from all evils. It is a fitting finish to this prayer, which deals throughout with issues that, though personal, also have a universal dimension. Jesus taught us to pray for *us.* Even when we pray the Lord's Prayer in private, we pray in communion with the whole Church for the needs of the entire human family.

For Further Reflection

○ Pick one of the petitions from the Lord's Prayer covered in this chapter. What new insights do you have about the meaning of the words in this petition? Which insight from this chapter is especially helpful for you?

○ What temptations do you face on a regular basis? What have you learned about yourself from temptation? Why are temptations so dangerous?

Exorcism

What is the worst evil that you can imagine needing to be delivered from? For followers of Jesus, it was being possessed by a demon. In his earthly ministry, Jesus delivered people from demonic possession. This power has now been given to his Church, and is called **exorcism.** The *Catechism* defines *exorcism* as "the public and authoritative act of the Church to protect or liberate a person or object from the power of the devil (e.g., demonic possession) in the name of Christ" (page 878). Only a priest with the permission of the bishop can perform a major exorcism. However, a simple form of exorcism is part of the Baptism rite. Here is a prayer of exorcism from the *Rite of Baptism for Children:*

> Almighty God,
> you sent your only Son
> to rescue us from the slavery of
> sin,
> and to give us the freedom
> only your sons and daughters
> enjoy.
>
> We now pray for these children
> who will have to face the world
> with its temptations,
> and fight the devil in all his
> cunning.
>
> Your son died and rose again to
> save us.
> By his victory over sin and death,
> bring these children out of the
> power of darkness.
> Strengthen them with the grace
> of Christ,
> and watch over them at every
> step in life's journey.

(Page 34)

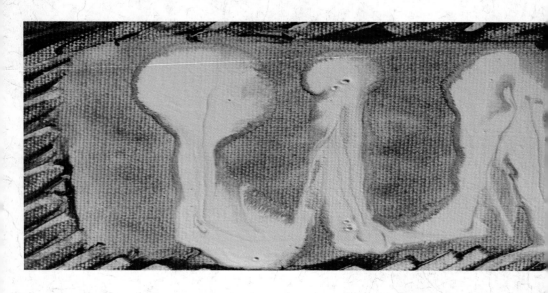

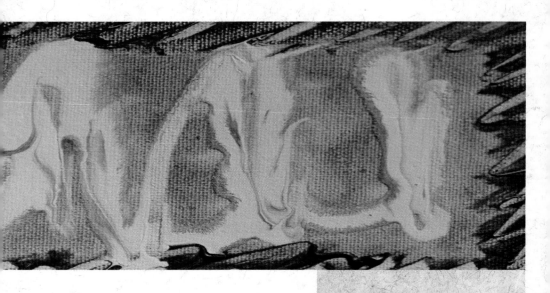

...holic Quick Facts is a mini-encyclopedia of ...ormation on Catholicism. In these pages you ... find the following sections:

Catholic
Quick Facts

Catholic Beliefs and Practices

In using this collection of major Catholic beliefs and practices, be aware of two things:

- Many of the items that are only listed here are more fully defined in the glossary of Catholic terms and definitions. For example, here we list the seven Catholic sacraments; in the glossary of terms, we define each one.
- Behind many of these items, you will see a number in parentheses. That number refers to a paragraph in the *Catechism of the Catholic Church*. The referenced paragraph is often just the beginning of a complete discussion of the item that we can only briefly name here. If you would like more information on any of these beliefs and practices, look to the *Catechism* as a primary reference.

Two Great Commandments

- You shall love the Lord your God with all your heart, with all your soul, and all your mind, and with all your strength.
- You shall love your neighbor as yourself.

(Matthew 22:37–40, Mark 12:29–31, Luke 10:27)

Ten Commandments *(cf. 2084ff)*

1. I am the Lord your God: you shall not have strange gods before me.
2. You shall not take the name of the Lord, your God, in vain.
3. Remember to keep holy the Lord's Day.
4. Honor your father and mother.
5. You shall not kill.
6. You shall not commit adultery.
7. You shall not steal.
8. You shall not bear false witness against your neighbor.
9. You shall not covet your neighbor's wife.
10. You shall not covet your neighbor's goods.

Beatitudes *(cf. 1716)*

- Blessed are the poor in spirit, the kingdom of heaven is theirs.
- Blessed are they who mourn, they will be comforted.
- Blessed are the meek, they will inherit the earth.
- Blessed are they who hunger and thirst for righteousness, they will be satisfied.
- Blessed are the merciful, they will be shown mercy.
- Blessed are the clean of heart, they will see God.
- Blessed are the peacemakers, they will be called children of God.
- Blessed are they who are persecuted for the sake of righteousness, the kingdom of heaven is theirs.

Corporal Works of Mercy *(cf. 2447)*

- Feed the hungry.
- Give drink to the thirsty.
- Shelter the homeless.
- Clothe the naked.
- Care for the sick.
- Help the imprisoned.
- Bury the dead.

Spiritual Works of Mercy *(cf. 2447)*

- Share knowledge.
- Give advice to those who need it.
- Comfort those who suffer.
- Be patient with others.
- Forgive those who hurt you.
- Give correction to those who need it.
- Pray for the living and the dead.

Theological Virtues *(cf. 1813)*

- Faith
- Hope
- Love

Cardinal Virtues *(cf. 1805)*

- Prudence
- Justice
- Fortitude
- Temperance

Seven Gifts of the Holy Spirit *(cf. 1831)*

- *Wisdom.* Through wisdom, the wonders of nature, every event in history, and all the ups and downs of our life take on deeper meaning and purpose. The wise person sees where the Spirit of God is at work and is able to share that insight with others. Wisdom is the fullest expression of the gifts of knowledge and understanding.
- *Understanding.* The gift of understanding is the ability to comprehend how a person must live her or his life as a follower of Jesus. Through the gift of understanding, Christians realize that the Gospel tells them not just who Jesus is; it also tells them who *we* are. The gift of understanding is closely related to the gifts of knowledge and wisdom.
- *Right judgment.* The gift of right judgment is the ability to know the difference between right and wrong and then to choose what is good. It helps us to act on and live out what Jesus has taught. In the exercise of right judgment, many of the other gifts—especially understanding, wisdom, and often courage—come into play in the Christian's daily life.

- *Courage.* The gift of courage enables us to take risks and to overcome fear as we try to live out the Gospel of Jesus. Followers of Jesus confront many challenges and even danger—the risk of being laughed at, the fear of rejection, and, for some believers, the fear of physical harm and even death. The Spirit gives Christians the strength to confront and ultimately overcome such challenges.
- *Knowledge.* The gift of knowledge is the ability to comprehend the basic meaning and message of Jesus. Jesus revealed the will of God, his Father, and taught people what they need to know to achieve fullness of life and, ultimately, salvation. The gift of knowledge is closely related to the gifts of understanding and wisdom.
- *Reverence.* Sometimes called piety, the gift of reverence gives the Christian a deep sense of respect for God. Jesus spoke of his Father, God, as "Abba," a very intimate name similar to "daddy" or "pappa." Through the gift of reverence, we can come before God with the openness and trust of small children, totally dependent on the One who created us.
- *Wonder and awe.* The gift of wonder and awe in the presence of God is sometimes translated as "the fear of the Lord." Though we can approach God with the trust of little children, we are also often aware of God's total majesty, unlimited power, and desire for justice. A child may want to sit on the lap of his loving Father, but sometimes the believer will fall on her knees in the presence of the Creator of the universe.

Fruits of the Holy Spirit *(cf. 1832)*

- Charity
- Joy
- Peace
- Patience
- Goodness
- Kindness
- Long suffering
- Humility
- Faithfulness
- Modesty
- Continence
- Chastity

Four Marks of the Catholic Church *(cf. 750)*

- One
- Holy
- Catholic
- Apostolic

Liturgical Year

- Advent
- Christmas
- Ordinary Time
- Lent
- Easter Triduum
- Easter
- Pentecost
- Ordinary Time

Seven Sacraments *(cf. 1210)*

- Baptism
- Confirmation
- the Eucharist
- Penance and Reconciliation
- Anointing of the Sick
- Matrimony
- Holy Orders

Precepts of the Church *(cf. 2042–2043)*

1. To keep holy the day of the Lord's Resurrection; to worship God by participating in Mass every Sunday and on the holy days of obligation; to avoid those activities that would hinder renewal of the soul and body on the Sabbath (for example, needless work or unnecessary shopping.

2. To lead a sacramental life; to receive Holy Communion frequently and the sacrament of Reconciliation regularly— minimally, to receive the sacrament of Reconciliation at least once a year (annual confession is obligatory only if serious sin is involved); minimally also, to receive Holy

Communion at least once a year between the first Sunday of Lent and Trinity Sunday.

3. To study Catholic teaching in preparation for the sacrament of Confirmation, to be confirmed, and then to continue to study and advance the cause of Christ.
4. To observe the marriage laws of the Church; to give religious training, by example and word, to one's children; to use parish schools and catechetical programs.
5. To strengthen and support the Church—one's own parish community and parish priests, the worldwide Church, and the pope.
6. To do penance, including abstaining from meat and fasting from food on the appointed days.
7. To join in the missionary spirit and apostolate (work) of the Church.

Holy Days of Obligation

- Christmas (December 25)
- Solemnity of the Blessed Virgin Mary, the Mother of God (January 1)
- Ascension of the Lord (the Sunday that follows forty days after Easter)
- Assumption of the Blessed Virgin Mary (August 15)
- All Saints (November 1)
- Immaculate Conception of the Blessed Virgin Mary (December 8)

Regulations on Fasting and Abstinence

The Catholic Church requires its members to observe certain dietary rules—fasting and abstinence—in order to recognize and mark the importance of particular days during its liturgical year, as well as to express penance for personal sin. The regulations apply as follows:

- Generally, the laws of fasting require that on the designated days the person eat just one full meal, two smaller meals, and avoid eating between meals. Abstinence laws require that the person avoid meat altogether.

- The regulations governing abstinence from meat apply to all Catholics age fourteen and older. Adults who have completed their eighteenth year until the beginning of their sixtieth year are bound by the regulations that govern fasting. Pregnant women and sick people are excused from the regulations.
- Ash Wednesday and Good Friday are days of both fasting and abstinence; all the other Fridays of Lent are days of abstinence only.
- In addition, the Church encourages its adult members to observe some form of penance, perhaps including some kind of fast and abstinence, on all Fridays throughout the year.
- The Church also calls for fasting prior to receiving Communion during the Mass. In this case, the fast helps us prepare our mind and heart for the great gift of the Eucharist by doing something physical to help focus our attention. Church law calls for us to avoid all food and drink, with the exception of water and medicine, for one hour before receiving Communion. Again, this regulation does not apply to sick people or others for whom such restrictions would jeopardize health.

Parts of the Mass *(cf. 1346)*

Introductory Rites
- Entrance
- Act of Penitence
- Kyrie
- Gloria
- Collect (opening prayer)

Liturgy of the Word
- First Reading
- Responsorial Psalm
- Second Reading
- Gospel Acclamation
- Gospel Reading
- Homily
- Profession of Faith
- Prayers of the Faithful

Liturgy of the Eucharist
- Preparation of the Altar and the Gifts
- Prayers over the Gifts
- Eucharistic Prayer
- Communion Rite: Lord's Prayer
                   Rite of Peace
                   Breaking of the Bread
                   Communion
                   Silence/Song of Praise
- Prayer After Communion

Concluding Rites
- Greeting and Blessing
- Dismissal

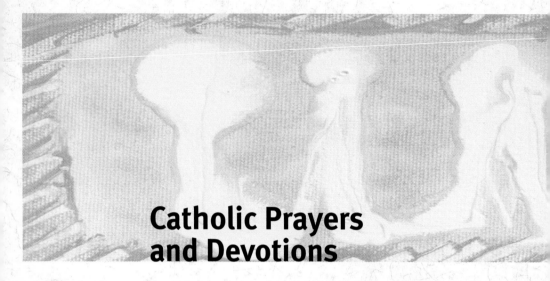

Catholic Prayers and Devotions

As in the section on Catholic beliefs and practices, you will see a number in parentheses behind some of these prayers and devotions. That number refers you to a paragraph in the *Catechism of the Catholic Church* that may offer a more complete explanation of the prayer or devotion.

Act of Contrition *(cf. 1451)*

My God, I am sorry for my sins
with all my heart, and I detest them.
In choosing to do wrong and failing to do good,
I have sinned against you,
whom I should love above all things.
I firmly intend, with your help,
to do penance, to sin no more,
and to avoid whatever leads me to sin.
Our savior Jesus Christ suffered and died for us.
In his name, my God, have mercy.

Act of Faith

My God, I firmly believe you are one God in three Divine
   Persons, Father, Son, and Holy Spirit.

I believe in Jesus Christ, your son, who became man and died
for our sins, and who will come to judge the living and the
dead.
I believe these and all the truths which the Holy Catholic
Church teaches, because you have revealed them, who can
neither deceive nor be deceived.
Amen.

Act of Hope

O my God, trusting in your infinite goodness and promises, I
hope to obtain pardon of my sins, the help of your grace, and
life everlasting, through the merits of Jesus Christ, my Lord
and redeemer. Amen.

Act of Love

My God, I love you above all things, with my whole heart and
soul, because you are all-good and worthy of all my love. I love
my neighbor as myself for love of you. I forgive all who have
injured me, and I ask pardon of all whom I have injured.
Amen.

Angelus

The angel of the Lord declared unto Mary,
And she conceived of the Holy Spirit.
>   Hail Mary . . .
Behold the handmaid of the Lord,
Be it done unto me according to your word.
>   Hail Mary . . .
And the Word was made flesh,
And dwelt among us.
>   Hail Mary . . .
Pray for us, O Holy Mother of God, that we may be made
worthy of the promises of Christ. Let us pray: Pour forth, we
beseech you, O Lord, your grace into our hearts that we to
whom the incarnation of Christ, your Son, was made known
by the message of angel may, by his passion and cross, be
brought to the glory of his resurrection, through Christ our
Lord.

Apostles' Creed *(cf. 194, 197ff)*

I believe in God, the Father Almighty, creator of heaven and earth. I believe in Jesus Christ, his only son, our Lord. He was conceived by the power of the Holy Spirit, and born of the Virgin Mary. He suffered under Pontius Pilate, was crucified, died, and was buried. He descended to the dead. On the third day he rose again. He ascended into heaven and is seated at the right hand of the Father. He will come again to judge the living and the dead.

I believe in the Holy Spirit, the holy catholic Church, the communion of saints, the forgiveness of sins, the resurrection of the body, and life everlasting. Amen.

Confiteor (I Confess)

I confess to almighty God, and to you, my brothers and sisters, that I have sinned through my own fault in my thoughts and in my words, in what I have done and what I have failed to do; and I ask blessed Mary, ever virgin, all the angels and saints, and you, my brothers and sisters, to pray for me to the Lord our God. May almighty God have mercy on us, forgive us our sins, and bring us to everlasting life.

Glory Be

Glory be to the Father, and to the Son, and to the Holy Spirit, as it was in the beginning, is now, and will be forever. Amen.

Grace Before Meals

Bless us, O Lord, and these your gifts,
which we are about to receive
from your bounty,
through Christ our Lord. Amen.

Grace After Meals

We give you thanks, almighty God,
for these and all your gifts
which we have received
through Christ our Lord. Amen.

Hail Mary *(cf. 2676–2677)*

Hail Mary, full of grace,
the Lord is with you;
blessed are you among women,
and blessed is the fruit of your womb, Jesus.

Holy Mary, Mother of God,
pray for us sinners
now and at the hour of our death.
Amen.

The Lord's Prayer (also called the Our Father) *(cf. 2759)*

Our Father who art in heaven,
hallowed be thy name.
Thy kingdom come.
Thy will be done on earth, as it is in heaven.
Give us this day our daily bread,
and forgive us our trespasses,
        as we forgive those who trespass against us,
and lead us not into temptation,
but deliver us from evil. Amen.

Magnificat (Mary's Song) *(cf. Luke 1:46–55)*

My being proclaims the greatness of the Lord,
my spirit finds joy in God my savior.
For he has looked upon his servant
in all her lowliness.
All ages to come shall call me blessed.
God who is mighty
has done great things for me, holy is his name;
his mercy is from age to age
on those who fear him.
He has shown might with his arm;
he has confused the proud
in their inmost thoughts.
He has deposed the mighty from their thrones
and raised the lowly to high places.

The hungry he has given every good thing
while the rich he has sent empty away.
He has upheld Israel his servant,
ever mindful of his mercy,
even as he promised our fathers,
promised Abraham and his descendants
forever.

Memorare

Remember, O most gracious Virgin Mary, that never was it
known that anyone who fled to your protection, implored
your help, or sought your intercession was left unaided.
Inspired by this confidence, we fly unto you, O virgin of
virgins, our mother. To you do we come, before you we stand,
sinful and sorrowful. O mother of the Word Incarnate, despise
not our petitions, but in your mercy, hear and answer us.

Morning Prayer

Almighty God, I thank you for your past blessings. Today I
offer myself—whatever I do, say, or think—to your loving
care. Continue to bless me, Lord. I make this morning offering
in union with the divine intentions of Jesus Christ who offers
himself daily in the holy sacrifice of the Mass, and in union
with Mary, his Virgin Mother and our Mother, who was
always the faithful handmaid of the Lord. Amen.

Prayer of Saint Francis

Lord, make me an instrument of your peace:
    where there is hatred, let me sow love;
    where there is injury, pardon;
    where there is doubt, faith;
    where there is despair, hope;
    where there is darkness, light;
    where there is sadness, joy.
Divine Master,
    grant that I may not so much seek
    to be consoled as to console,
    to be understood as to understand,
        to be loved as to love.

For it is in giving that we receive,
> it is in pardoning that we are pardoned,
> it is in dying that we are born to eternal life.

Prayer to the Holy Spirit *(cf. 2671)*

Come, Holy Spirit, fill the hearts of your faithful. Enkindle in them the fire of your love. Send forth your Spirit, and they will be created. And you will renew the face of the earth.
Let us pray:
Lord, by the light of the Holy Spirit, you have taught the hearts of the faithful. In the same Spirit, help to us relish what is right and always rejoice in your consolation. We ask this through Christ our Lord. Amen.

The Rosary *(cf. 971)*

The rosary is perhaps the most popular devotion to Mary, the Mother of God. The central part of the rosary consists of the recitation of five sets of ten Hail Marys (each set is called a decade). Each new decade begins by saying an Our Father, and each decade concludes with a Glory Be. The prayer keeps track of the prayers said by moving from one bead to the next in order.

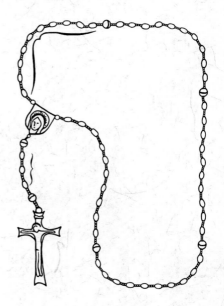

The recitation of the rosary begins with a series of prayers, said in the following order while using as a guide a small chain of beads and a crucifix (see the illustration at right):
1. the sign of the cross
2. the Apostles' Creed
3. one Our Father
4. three Hail Marys
5. one Glory Be
After these introductory prayers, the recitation of the decades, as described above, begins.

The saying of a five-decade rosary is connected with meditation on what are called the mysteries of the life of Jesus. These mysteries too are collected into series of five—five joyful, five sorrowful, five glorious, and five mysteries of light (recently added by Pope John Paul II). The mysteries of the rosary are listed below. The prayer devotes one recitation of the rosary to each set of mysteries. She or he chooses which set of mysteries to meditate on while saying the decades of Hail Marys. Therefore, the *complete* rosary consists of fifteen decades.

With a little practice, the regular praying of the rosary can become a source of great inspiration and consolation for the Christian.

Joyful Mysteries
- The Annunciation
- The Visitation
- The Birth of Our Lord
- The Presentation of Jesus in the Temple
- The Finding of Jesus in the Temple

Sorrowful Mysteries
- The Agony of Jesus in the Garden
- The Scourging at the Pillar
- The Crowning of Thorns
- The Carrying of the Cross
- The Crucifixion

Glorious Mysteries
- The Resurrection of Jesus
- The Ascension of Jesus into Heaven
- The Descent of the Holy Spirit on the Apostles (Pentecost)
- The Assumption of Mary into Heaven
- The Crowning of Mary as Queen of Heaven

Mysteries of Light
- The Baptism of Jesus
- Jesus Reveals Himself in the Miracle at Cana
- Jesus Proclaims the Good News of the Kingdom of God
- The Transfiguration of Jesus
- The Institution of the Eucharist

Sign of the Cross *(cf. 232)*

In the name of the Father, and of the Son, and of the Holy Spirit. Amen.

Stations of the Cross

1. Jesus is condemned to death.
2. Jesus takes up his cross.
3. Jesus falls the first time.
4. Jesus meets his mother.
5. Simon helps Jesus carry the cross.
6. Veronica wipes the face of Jesus.
7. Jesus falls the second time.
8. Jesus meets the women of Jerusalem.
9. Jesus falls the third time.
10. Jesus is stripped of his garments.
11. Jesus is nailed to the cross.
12. Jesus dies on the cross.
13. Jesus is taken down from the cross.
14. Jesus is laid in the tomb.

Patron Saints
and Their Causes

abortion, protection against, Catherine of Sweden [March 24]

accountants, Matthew [September 21]

actors, Genesius [August 25]

addiction, drug, Maximilian Maria Kolbe [August 14]

advertisers, Bernardino of Siena [May 20]

alcoholics, John of God [March 8], Matthew [September 21], Monica [August 27]

altar servers, John Berchmans [November 26]

anesthetists, René Goupil [October 19]

animals, Francis of Assisi [October 4], Nicholas of Tolentino [September 10]

animals, domestic, Anthony of Egypt [January 17]

apprentices, young, John Bosco [January 31]

archaeologists, Damasus I [December 11]

archers, Sebastian [January 20]

architects, Barbara [December 4], Thomas the Apostle [July 3]

art, Catherine of Bologna [May 9]

arthritis, James the Great [July 25]

artillerymen, Barbara [December 4]

artists, Catherine of Bologna [May 9], Fra Angelico (Blessed John of Fiesole) [February 18], Luke [October 18]

astronomers, Dominic [August 8]

athletes, Sebastian [January 20]

aviators, Joseph of Cupertino [September 18], Theresa of the
   Child Jesus ("Little Flower") [October 1]

babies, Nicholas of Tolentino [September 10]

bakers, Elizabeth of Hungary [November 17], Honoratus of
   Arles [January 16], Nicholas of Myra [December 6]

bankers, Matthew [September 21]

banks, savings, Anthony Claret [October 24]

barbers, Cosmas and Damian [September 26], Martin de
   Porres [November 3]

basket weavers, Anthony of Egypt [January 17], Mark [April
   25]

bees, Ambrose [December 7]

beggars, Martin of Tours [November 11]

birds, Gall [October 16]

bishops, Ambrose [December 7], Charles Borromeo
   [November 4]

blind (see *sightless, the*)

blood banks, Januarius [September 19]

bookbinders, Celestine V [May 19], John of God [March 8]

bookkeepers, Matthew [September 21]

booksellers, John of God [March 8], Thomas Aquinas
   [January 28]

Boy Scouts, George [April 23]

boys, young, Dominic Savio [March 9]

breast-feeding, Giles [September 1]

breasts, diseases of the, Agatha [February 5]

brewers, Amand [February 6], Augustine of Hippo [August
   28], Luke [October 18], Nicholas of Myra [December 6],
   Wenceslaus [September 28]

bricklayers, Stephen [December 26]

brides, Nicholas of Myra [December 6]

bridges, John Nepomucen [May 16]

brothers, lay, Gerard Majella [October 16]

builders, Barbara [December 4], Vincent Ferrer [April 5]

bus drivers, Christopher [July 25]

businesspeople, Homobonus [November 13]

butchers, Anthony of Egypt [January 17], Luke [October 18]

cabdrivers, Fiacre [August 30]

cabinetmakers, Anne [July 26]

cake makers, Honoratus of Arles [January 16]

cancer patients, Peregrine of Auxerre [May 16]

candle makers, Bernard of Clairvaux [August 20]

canon lawyers, Raymond of Penafort [January 7]

carpenters, Joseph [March 19], Matthias [May 14], Thomas the Apostle [July 3]

catechists, Charles Borromeo [November 4], Robert Bellarmine [September 17]

Catholic Action, Francis of Assisi [October 4]

Catholic charities, Elizabeth of Hungary [November 17]

Catholic press, Francis de Sales [January 24]

Catholic schools, Joseph Calasanz [August 25], Thomas Aquinas [January 28]

Catholic universities, Thomas Aquinas [January 28]

cattle breeders, Mark [April 25]

cemeteries, Anne [July 26], Michael the Archangel [September 29]

charitable organizations, Vincent de Paul [September 27]

charity, works of, Vincent de Paul [September 27]

chastity, Thomas Aquinas [January 28]

childbirth, Clare of Assisi [August 11], Erasmus (Elmo) [June 2]

children, Nicholas of Myra [December 6]

children, abandoned, Ivo Hélory of Kermartin [May 19], Jerome Emiliani [February 8]

children, convulsive, Scholastica [February 10]

Children of Mary, Agnes [January 21], Maria Goretti [July 6]

choirboys, Dominic Savio [March 9]

Church, the, Joseph [March 19], Peter the Apostle [June 29]

clergy, diocesan, John of Ávila [May 10]

clerics, Gabriel Possenti [February 27]

coin collectors, Eligius [December 1]

comedians, Vitus [June 15]

communications personnel, Bernardino of Siena [May 20]

confectioners, Cosmas and Damian [September 26]

confessors, Alphonsus Liguori [August 1], John Nepomucen [May 16]

construction workers, Thomas the Apostle [July 3]

contagious diseases, victims of, Roch [August 17], Sebastian [January 20]

contemplative life, Mary Magdalene [July 22]

converts, Helen [August 18], Vladimir of Kiev [July 15]

cooks, Lawrence [August 10], Martha [July 29]

coppersmiths, Maurus [January 15]

crops, protector of, Ansovinus [March 13]

Cursillo movement, Paul [June 29]

customs officials, Matthew [September 21]

dairy workers, Brigid of Kildare [February 1]

dancers, Vitus [June 15]

deacons, Stephen [December 26]

deaf (see *hearing impaired*)

dentists, Apollonia [February 9], Cosmas and Damian
 [September 26]

desperate causes, Gregory Thaumaturgus [November 17], Jude
 [October 28], Rita of Cascia [May 22]

dieticians, Martha [July 29]

diplomats, Gabriel the Archangel [September 29]

disabled, the, Giles [September 1]

divorced, Helen [August 18]

dog bites, Vitus [June 15]

domestic workers, Martha [July 29]

drought, Geneviève of Paris [January 3]

drug addicts, Maximilian Maria Kolbe [August 14]

dying, the, James the Less [May 3], Joseph [March 19]

earthquakes, Agatha [February 5]

ecologists (see *environmentalists*)

ecumenists, Cyril and Methodius [February 14]

editors, John Bosco [January 31]

embroiderers, Clare of Assisi [August 11]

endurance, Pantaleon [July 27]

engineers, Ferdinand of Castile [May 30]

environmentalists, Francis of Assisi [October 4]

epileptics, Vitus [June 15], Willibrord [November 7]

Eucharistic confraternities and congresses, Paschal Baylon
 [May 17]

eye diseases, Clare of Assisi [August 11], Lucy [December 13]

falling, Venantius Fortunatus [December 14]

falsely accused, the, Raymond Nonnatus [August 31]

farmers, Isidore the Farmer [May 15]

farmworkers, Benedict of Nursia [July 11]

fathers of families, Joseph [March 19]

fever, Geneviève of Paris [January 3]

firefighters, Agatha [February 5], Barbara [December 4],
 Florian [May 4], Lawrence [August 10]

fire prevention, Bernardino of Siena [May 20]

First Communicants, Tarcisius [August 15]

fishermen, Andrew [November 30], Peter the Apostle [June 29]

flight attendants, Bona of Pisa [May 29]

florists, Theresa of the Child Jesus ("Little Flower") [October 1]

foreign missions, Francis Xavier [December 3], Theresa of the Child Jesus ("Little Flower") [October 1]

friendship, John the Evangelist [December 27]

funeral directors, Dismas [March 25], Joseph of Arimathea [August 31]

garage workers, Eligius [December 1]

gardeners, Dorothy [February 6], Fiacre [August 30], Phocas of Sinope [September 22]

garment workers, Homobonus [November 13]

gas station workers, Eligius [December 1]

girls, teenage, Maria Goretti [July 6]

girls, young, Agnes [January 21]

glassworkers, Luke [October 18], Mark [April 25]

goldsmiths, Anastasius I [December 19], Dunstan [May 19], Eligius [December 1]

good weather, Clare of Assisi [August 11]

governors, Ferdinand of Castile [May 30]

grave diggers, Anthony of Egypt [January 17]

grocers, Michael the Archangel [September 29]

hairdressers, Mary Magdalene [July 22]

harvests, Anthony of Padua [June 13]

headaches, Denis [October 9], Teresa of Ávila [October 15]

health inspectors, Raphael the Archangel [September 29]

hearing impaired, Francis de Sales [January 24]

heart patients, John of God [March 8]

hemorrhoids, Fiacre [August 30]

highways, John the Baptist [June 24]

hoarseness, Bernardino of Siena [May 20]

homeless, Benedict Joseph Labre [April 17], Margaret of Cortona [February 22]

homemakers, Anne [July 26], Martha [July 29]

horse riders, Martin of Tours [November 11]

horses, Eligius [December 1], Giles [September 1], Hippolytus [August 13], Martin of Tours [November 11]

hospital administrators, Basil the Great [January 2], Frances Xavier Cabrini [November 13] *hospitals,* Camillus de Lellis [July 14], John of God [March 8], Jude [October 28], Vincent de Paul [September 27]

house hunters, Joseph [March 19]

hunters, Hubert [November 3]

immigrants, Frances Xavier Cabrini [November 13]

infantrymen, Maurice [September 22]

innkeepers, Amand [February 6], Martha [July 29]

invalids, Roch [August 17]

janitors, Theobald of Provins [June 30]

jewelers, Dunstan [May 19], Eligius [December 1]

journalists, Francis de Sales [January 24]

judges, Ivo Hélory of Kermartin [May 19]

jumping, Venantius Fortunatus [December 14]

jurists, John of Capistrano [October 23]

laborers, Isidore the Farmer [May 15], James the Great [July 25]

lawyers, Fidelis of Sigmaringen [April 24], Genesius [August 25], Ivo Hélory of Kermartin [May 19], Thomas More [June 22]

lay apostolate, Paul [June 29]

leaping, Venantius Fortunatus [December 14]

learning, Ambrose [December 7]

lepers, Giles [September 1]

librarians, Jerome [September 30]

lightning, protection from, Barbara [December 4], Vitus [June 15]

locksmiths, Dunstan [May 19]

lost articles, searchers of, Anthony of Padua [June 13]

lovers, Raphael the Archangel [September 29], Valentine [February 14]

maids, Zita [April 27]

marble workers, Clement of Rome [November 23]

mariners, Michael the Archangel [September 29], Nicholas of Tolentino [September 10]

marriage, Francis Regis [July 2]

medical profession, Pantaleon [July 27]

medical technicians, Albert the Great [November 15]

mentally ill, Dymphna [May 30]

merchants, Francis of Assisi [October 4], Homobonus [November 13], Nicholas of Myra [December 6]

messengers, Gabriel the Archangel [September 29]

metalworkers, Eligius [December 1]

midwives, Raymond Nonnatus [August 31]

military chaplains, John of Capistrano [October 23]

miners, Anne [July 26], Barbara [December 4]

missionary priests, Vincent Pallotti [January 22]

missions, foreign, Francis Xavier [December 3], Theresa of the
    Child Jesus ("Little Flower") [October 1]

monks, Benedict of Nursia [July 11], John the Baptist [June 24]

mothers, Gerard Majella [October 16], Monica [August 27],
    Nicholas of Tolentino [September 10]

mothers, expectant, Anne [July 26], Gerard Majella [October
    16], Raymond Nonnatus [August 31]

mothers, single, Margaret of Cortona [February 22]

motorists, Christopher [July 25], Frances of Rome [March 9]

mountain climbers, Bernard of Montjoux [May 28]

musicians, Cecilia [November 22], Dunstan [May 19], Gregory
    the Great [September 3]

mystics, John of the Cross [December 14]

naval officers, Francis of Paola [April 2]

navigators, Francis of Paola [April 2]

neighborhood watches, Sebastian [January 20]

notaries, Luke [October 18], Mark [April 25]

nuns, Bridget of Sweden [July 23]

nuns, Benedictine, Scholastica [February 10]

nurses, Agatha [February 5], Camillus de Lellis [July 14],
    Catherine of Siena [April 29], Cosmas and Damian
    [September 26], Elizabeth of Hungary [November 17], John
    of God [March 8], Raphael the Archangel [September 29]

nurses' associations, Camillus de Lellis [July 14]

opticians, Mark [April 25]

orators, John Chrysostom [September 13]

orphans, Jerome Emiliani [February 8]

painters, Luke [October 18]

pallbearers, Joseph of Arimathea [August 31]

paratroopers, Michael the Archangel [September 29]

parish missions, Leonard of Port Maurice [November 26]

pawnbrokers, Nicholas of Myra [December 6]

penitents, Mary Magdalene [July 22]

perfumers, Nicholas of Myra [December 6]

pharmacists, Cosmas and Damian [September 26], James the
    Great [July 25]

philosophers, Justin [June 1]

physicians, Cosmas and Damian [September 26], Luke [October 18], Pantaleon [July 27], Raphael the Archangel [September 29], Sebastian [January 20]

pilgrims, Christopher [July 25], James the Great [July 25], Nicholas of Myra [December 6]

plagues, victims of, Gregory the Great [September 3], Roch [August 17], Sebastian [January 20]

plasterers, Bartholomew [August 24]

plumbers, Vincent Ferrer [April 5]

poets, Brigid of Kildare [February 1], Cecilia [November 22], Columba [June 9], David of Wales [March 1], John of the Cross [December 14]

poisoning, victims of, Benedict of Nursia [July 11], John the Evangelist [December 27]

police, local, Sebastian [January 20]

police officers, Michael the Archangel [September 29]

politicians, Thomas More [June 22]

poor, the, Anthony of Padua [June 13], Ferdinand of Castile [May 30], Giles [September 1], Lawrence [August 10]

popes, Gregory the Great [September 3], Peter the Apostle [June 29]

porters, Christopher [July 25]

possessed, the, Bruno [October 6], Denis [October 9]

postal employees, Gabriel the Archangel [September 29]

preachers, John Chrysostom [September 13]

priests, diocesan, John of Ávila [May 10]

priests, missionary, Vincent Pallotti [January 22]

priests, parish, John Vianney [August 4]

printers, Augustine of Hippo [August 28], Genesius [August 25], John of God [March 8]

prisoners, Barbara [December 4], Dismas [March 25], Ferdinand III [May 30], Joseph Cafasso [June 23], Roch [August 17], Vincent de Paul [September 27]

prison guards, Hippolytus [August 13]

prisons, Joseph Cafasso [June 23]

public education, Martin de Porres [November 3]

public health service, Martin de Porres [November 3]

public relations, Bernardino of Siena [May 20]

public speakers, John Chrysostom [September 13]

publishers, John Bosco [January 31], John the Evangelist
    [December 27]
purgatory, souls in, Nicholas of Tolentino [September 10]
rabies, victims of, Hubert [November 3]
race relations, Martin de Porres [November 3]
radiologists, Michael the Archangel [September 29]
radio workers, Gabriel the Archangel [September 29]
rain (excessive), Geneviève of Paris [January 3]
refugees, Alban [June 20]
restaurants, Martha [July 29]
retreats, Ignatius of Loyola [July 31]
sailors, Andrew [November 30], Brendan [May 16],
    Christopher [July 25], Cuthbert [March 20], Erasmus
    (Elmo) [June 2], Nicholas of Myra [December 6], Phocas of
    Sinope [September 22]
scholars, Brigid of Kildare [February 1], Jerome [September
    30], the Venerable Bede [May 25]
schools, Catholic, Joseph Calasanz [August 25], Thomas
    Aquinas [January 28]
scientists, Albert the Great [November 15]
scrupulous, the, Ignatius of Loyola [July 31]
sculptors, Claude La Colombière [February 15], Louis IX
    [August 25], Luke [October 18]
sea pilots, Nicholas of Myra [December 6]
secretaries, Genesius [August 25]
security guards, Matthew [September 21]
seminarians, Charles Borromeo [November 4]
senior citizens, Teresa of Jesus [August 26]
shepherds, Paschal Baylon [May 17]
ships, Matthew [September 21]
shoemakers, Crispin and Crispinian [October 25], Homobonus
    [November 13]
sick, the, Camillus de Lellis [July 14], John of God [March 8],
    Michael the Archangel [September 29]
sightless, the, Cosmas and Damian [September 26], Odilia
    [December 13], Raphael the Archangel [September 29]
silversmiths, Dunstan [May 19]
singers, Cecilia [November 22], Gregory the Great
    [September 3]
skiers, Bernard of Montjoux [May 28]
skin diseases, victims of, Anthony of Egypt [January 17]

slandered, the, John Nepomucen [May 16]

sleepwalkers, Dymphna [May 30]

snakebites, Vitus [June 15]

social justice, Joseph [March 19], Martin de Porres [November 3]

social workers, Francis Regis [July 2], Louise de Marillac [March 15]

soldiers, George [April 23], Ignatius of Loyola [July 31], Joan of Arc [May 30], Martin of Tours [November 11], Sebastian [January 20]

spas, John the Baptist [June 24]

speleologists, Benedict of Nursia [July 11]

stamp collectors, Gabriel the Archangel [September 29]

stenographers, Genesius [August 25], John Cassian [July 23]

stomach and abdominal ailments, Erasmus (Elmo) [June 2]

stonecutters, Clement of Rome [November 23]

stonemasons, Barbara [December 4], Stephen [December 26]

storms, protection against, Vitus [June 15]

stress, those suffering from, Walter of Pontoise [April 8]

students, Thomas Aquinas [January 28]

students in Jesuit colleges and universities, Aloysius Gonzaga [June 21]

surgeons, Cosmas and Damian [September 26], Luke [October 18], Roch [August 17]

surveyors, Thomas the Apostle [July 3]

swimmers, Adjutor [April 30]

Swiss Guard, papal, Maurice [September 22]

swordsmiths, Maurice [September 22]

tailors, Homobonus [November 13]

tanners, Bartholomew [August 24]

tax collectors, Matthew [September 21]

teachers, Gregory the Great [September 3], John Baptist de La Salle [April 7]

telecommunications workers, Gabriel the Archangel [September 29]

television, Clare of Assisi [August 11]

television workers, Gabriel the Archangel [September 29]

tertiaries, Franciscan, Elizabeth of Hungary [November 17]

theologians, Alphonsus Liguori [August 1], Augustine of Hippo [August 28]

thieves, Dismas [March 25]

throat ailments, Blase [February 3]

toothaches, those suffering from, Apollonia [February 9]

toy makers, Claude La Colombière [February 15]

travelers, Anthony of Padua [June 13], Christopher [July 25], Joseph [March 19], Nicholas of Myra [December 6], Raphael the Archangel [September 29]

truck drivers, Christopher [July 25]

universities, Catholic, Thomas Aquinas [January 28]

venereal diseases, Fiacre [August 30]

veterinarians, Blase [February 3], Eligius [December 1]

vine growers, Vincent of Saragossa [January 22]

vocations, religious, Alphonsus Liguori [August 1]

volcanic eruptions, protection against, Agatha [February 5]

waiters, Martha [July 29]

waitresses, Martha [July 29]

watchmen, Peter of Alcántara [October 22]

weavers, Anthony Claret [October 24], Bernardino of Siena [May 20], Maurice [September 22]

whales, Brendan of Clonfert [May 16]

widows, Anne [July 26], Frances of Rome [March 9], Paula [January 26]

wine makers, Vincent of Saragossa [January 22]

wine merchants, Amand [February 6]

women, barren, Anthony of Padua [June 13], Felicity [March 7]

women, childless, Anne [July 26]

women in labor, Anne [July 26], Erasmus (Elmo) [June 2]

women, unhappily married, Rita of Cascia [May 22]

workers, Bonaventure [July 15], Joseph [March 19]

writers, Francis de Sales [January 24], John the Evangelist [December 27], Lucy [December 13]

yachtsmen, Adjutor [April 30]

young boys, Dominic Savio [March 9]

young girls, Agnes [January 21]

youth, Aloysius Gonzaga [June 21], Gabriel Possenti [February 27], John Berchmans [November 26]

youth, African Catholic, Charles Lwanga [June 3]

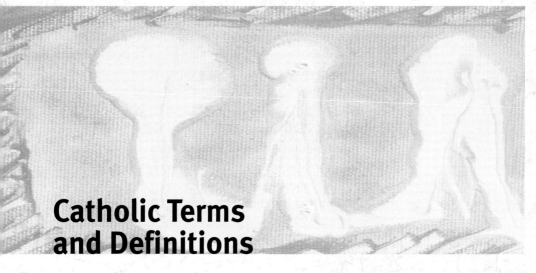

Catholic Terms and Definitions

abortion. The deliberate termination of a pregnancy by killing the unborn child. The Roman Catholic Church considers such direct abortion a grave contradiction of the moral law and a crime against human life.

absolution. An essential part of the sacrament of Penance and Reconciliation in which the priest pardons the sins of the person confessing, in the name of God and the Church.

abstinence. The avoidance of a particular kind of food as an act of penance or spiritual discipline; in Catholicism, the avoidance of meat on certain days.

act of contrition. A prayer of sorrow for one's sins, a promise to make things right, and a commitment to avoid those things that lead to sin. Such a prayer can be said anytime, but is always part of the sacrament of Penance and Reconciliation.

adoration. The prayerful acknowledgment that God is God and Creator of all that is.

adultery. Sexual activity between two persons, at least one of whom is married to another. Prohibited by the sixth commandment.

Advent. The four-week liturgical season during which Christians prepare themselves for the celebration of Christmas.

almsgiving. Freely giving money or material goods to a person who is needy. It may be an act of penance or of Christian charity.

amen. A Hebrew word meaning "let it be so" or "let it be done." As a conclusion to prayer, it represents the agreement by the person praying to what has been said in the prayer.

angel. Based on a word meaning "messenger," a personal and immortal creature, with intelligence and free will, who constantly glorifies God and serves as a messenger of God to humans in order to carry out God's saving plan.

annulment. A declaration by the Church that a marriage is null and void, that is, it never existed. Catholics who divorce must also have the marriage annulled by the Church in order to be free to marry again in the Church.

Annunciation. The biblical event in which the angel Gabriel visits the virgin Mary and announces that she is to be the mother of the Savior.

Anointing of the Sick. One of the seven sacraments, sometimes formerly known as "the sacrament of the dying," in which a gravely ill, aging, or dying person is anointed by the priest and prayed over by him and attending believers. One need not be dying to receive the sacrament.

Apostles. The general term *apostle* means "one who is sent," and can be used in reference to any missionary of the Church during the New Testament period. In reference to the twelve companions chosen by Jesus, also known as "the Twelve," the term refers to those special witnesses of Jesus on whose ministry the early Church was built, and whose successors are the bishops.

apostolic fathers. A group of Greek Christian authors in the late first and early second centuries. They are our chief source of information about the early Church, and may have historical connections to the Apostles.

apostolic succession. The uninterrupted passing on of authority from the Apostles directly to all bishops. It is accomplished through the laying on of hands when a bishop is ordained.

Apostolic Tradition. *See* Tradition.

apparition. An appearance to people on Earth of a heavenly being—Christ, Mary, an angel, or a saint. The New

Testament includes stories of multiple apparitions by Jesus between Easter and his Ascension into heaven.

arms race. The competition between nations to build up stockpiles of weapons of all kinds, including weapons of mass destruction. Many of these stockpiles are large enough to destroy the world several times over.

artificial insemination. The process by which a man's sperm and a woman's egg are united in a manner other than natural sexual intercourse. In the narrowest sense, it means injecting sperm into a woman's cervical canal. The Church considers it morally wrong because it separates intercourse from the act of procreation.

Ascension. The "going up" into heaven of the risen Christ forty days after his Resurrection.

assembly. Also known as a congregation, it is a community of believers gathered for worship as the Body of Christ.

Assumption of Mary. The dogma that recognizes that the body of the Blessed Virgin Mary was taken directly to heaven after her life on Earth had ended.

atheist; atheism. One who denies the existence of God; and the denial of the existence of God.

Baptism. The first of the seven sacraments, by which one becomes a member of the Church and a new creature in Christ; the first of the three sacraments of initiation, the others being Confirmation and the Eucharist.

Baptism of blood. The Catholic Church's firm conviction that someone who dies for the faith without being baptized actually receives Baptism through his or her death.

Beatitudes. The teachings of Jesus during the Sermon on the Mount in which he describes the actions and attitudes that should characterize Christians, and by which one can discover genuine meaning and happiness.

benediction. In general, another name for a blessing prayer. For Catholics, it more often refers to the prayer in which the Blessed Sacrament is used to bless the people.

Bible. The collection of Christian sacred writings, or Scriptures, accepted by the Church as inspired by God, and composed of the Old and New Testaments.

bishop. Based on a word for "overseer," one who has received the fullness of the sacrament of Holy Orders, is a member of the "college" of bishops, and is recognized as a successor of the Apostles. When he serves as head of a diocese, he is often referred to as the ordinary or local bishop.

blasphemy. Speaking, acting, or thinking about God in a way that is irreverent, mocking, or offensive. It is a sin against the second commandment.

Blessed Sacrament. Another name for the Eucharist, especially for the consecrated bread and wine when they are reserved in the tabernacle for adoration or for distribution to the sick.

blessing. A prayer asking that God care for a particular person, place, or activity. A simple blessing is usually made with the sign of the cross.

Body of Christ. A term which when capitalized designates Jesus' body in the Eucharist, or the entire Church, which is also referred to as the Mystical Body of Christ.

breviary. A prayer book that contains the prayers for the Liturgy of the Hours.

brothers. *See* religious life, congregation, order.

calumny. Ruining the reputation of another person by lying or spreading rumors. It is also called slander, and is a sin against the seventh commandment.

canon. This word has a variety of meanings. The canon of the Scriptures refers to the Church's list of books of the Bible. The canon of the Mass is another name for the Eucharistic prayer. Canon law is the official body of laws for Catholics.

canonization. The official proclamation by the Pope that a deceased member of the Church is to be recognized as a saint and may serve as a model of the Christian ideal for all believers; also the name of the process by which one is found worthy of such recognition.

capital punishment. Another name for the death penalty, a sentence sometimes given to people who commit serious crimes. The Church teaches that the necessity for capital punishment in today's world is rare.

cardinal virtues. Based on the Latin word for "pivot," four virtues that are viewed as pivotal or essential for full Christian living: prudence, justice, fortitude, and temperance.

catechesis. Based on a word meaning "to echo," the process of education and formation of Christians of all ages, by which they are taught the essentials of Christian doctrine and are formed as disciples of Jesus. Those who serve as ministers of catechesis are called catechists.

catechism. A popular summary, usually in book form, of Catholic doctrine about faith and morals and commonly intended for use within programs of formal catechesis. The official and most authoritative Catholic catechism is the *Catechism of the Catholic Church.*

catechumen. One who is preparing for full initiation into the Catholic Church by engaging in formal study, reflection, and prayer.

catechumenate. The name of the full process, as well as of one formal stage within the process, by which persons are prepared for full initiation into the Church. The process is commonly reserved for adult converts to Catholicism.

cathedral. Based on a word for "chair," the official Church of the bishop of a diocese, at which he is recognized as the chief pastor. The bishop's "chair" symbolizes his teaching and governing authority within the diocese.

Catholic Church. The name given to the universal group of Christian communities that is in communion with the Pope, the successor of Peter. It was established by Christ on the foundation of his Apostles.

celebrant. The person who oversees any act of public worship. In a Eucharistic liturgy or Mass, the celebrant is always an ordained priest.

celibacy. The state or condition of those who have chosen or taken vows to remain unmarried in order to devote themselves entirely to service of the Church and the Kingdom of God. (*See also* vow(s).)

charism. A special gift or grace of the Holy Spirit given to an individual Christian or a community, commonly for the benefit and building up of the entire Church.

charity. The theological virtue by which we love God above all things and, out of that love of God, love our neighbor as ourselves.

chastity. The virtue by which people are able successfully and healthfully to integrate their sexuality into their total person; recognized as one of the fruits of the Holy Spirit. Also, one of the vows of the religious life.

chief priests. In biblical Judaism, the priests (descendants of the tribe of Levi) were responsible for the proclamation of

God's will, the interpretation of the Law, and worship and ritual sacrifice in the synagogues. Jesus often found himself in conflict with them.

chrism. Perfumed oil, consecrated by the bishop, which is used for special anointings in Baptism, Confirmation, and Holy Orders. It signifies the gift of the Holy Spirit.

Christ. *See* Jesus Christ.

Christmas. The feast day on which Christians celebrate the birth of Jesus; also refers to the liturgical season that immediately follows Christmas Day.

church. In common Christian usage, the term *church* is used in three related ways: (1) the entire people of God throughout the world; (2) the diocese, which is also known as the local church; and (3) the assembly of believers gathered for celebration of the liturgy, especially the Eucharist. In the creed, the Church is recognized as one, holy, catholic, and apostolic—traits which together are referred to as "marks of the Church."

civil authorities. The people in society who are responsible for making and enforcing civil laws. They have a responsibility for safeguarding human freedom and human dignity.

civil disobedience. Deliberate refusal to obey a law prescribed by the state, usually on moral grounds.

civil laws. The laws that govern society. Civil laws should reflect the natural law that God has placed in every human heart.

clergy. In the Catholic Church, the term refers to men who receive the sacrament of Holy Orders as deacons, priests, or bishops. In the broader Church, the term refers to anyone ordained for ministry.

college of bishops. The assembly of bishops, headed by the Pope, that holds the teaching authority and responsibility in the Church.

commandments. In general, a norm or guide for moral behavior; commonly, the Ten Commandments given by God to Moses. Jesus summarized all the commandments within the twofold or Great Commandments to love God and neighbor.

common good. Social conditions that allow for *all* citizens of the earth, individuals and families, to meet basic needs and achieve fulfillment.

communion of saints. The spiritual union of all those who believe in Christ and have been redeemed, including both those who have died and those who are still living.

concupiscence. The tendency of all human beings toward sin, as a result of original sin.

confession, private. Telling one's sins to a priest. It is an essential element of the sacrament of Penance and Reconciliation.

confidentiality. Keeping safe a truth that must not be shared with others because to do so would be immoral or illegal.

confirmand. A candidate for the sacrament of Confirmation.

Confirmation. With Baptism and the Eucharist, one of the three sacraments of Initiation. Through an outpouring of special gifts of the Holy Spirit, Confirmation completes the grace of Baptism by confirming or "sealing" the baptized person's union with Christ and by equipping that person for active participation in the life of the church.

congregation. *See* assembly.

conscience. The "interior voice" of a person, a God-given internal sense of what is morally wrong or right. Conscience leads people to understand themselves as responsible for their actions, and prompts them to do good and avoid evil. To make good judgments, one needs to have a well-formed conscience.

conscientious objection. Refusal to join the military or take part in a war, based on moral or religious grounds. Conscientious objectors must seek official approval of their status from the government.

consecrated life. A state of life recognized by the official Church in which a person publicly professes vows of poverty, chastity, and obedience.

consecration. Making a person (candidate for ordination), place (a new church), or thing (bread and wine) holy. During the Mass, the term refers to that point in the Eucharistic prayer when the priest recites Jesus' words of institution, changing the bread and wine into the body and blood of Christ.

contemplation. A form of wordless prayer in which one is fully focused on the presence of God; sometimes defined as "resting in God," a deep sense of loving adoration of God.

contraception. The deliberate attempt to interfere with the creation of new life as a result of sexual intercourse. It is considered morally wrong by the Church, which teaches that a married couple must remain open to procreation whenever they engage in sexual intercourse.

conversion. A profound change of heart, turning away from sin and toward God.

council of the Church. An official assembly of Church leaders, often for the purpose of discernment and decision-making about particular issues. When represented by and concerned with the entire Church, it is called *ecumenical*, from a word meaning "the whole wide world." Councils can also be regional or local.

covenant. In general, a solemn agreement between human beings or between God and a human being in which mutual commitments are recognized; also called a testament. In the Bible, two covenants are central: (1) the Covenant between God and the ancient people of Israel established in God's Sinai Covenant with Moses; also called the Old Testament or Old Covenant; and (2) the New Covenant established by Jesus through his sacrificial death and Resurrection; also called the New Testament. The term *testament* has come to be associated primarily with the sacred Scriptures that record the history and meaning of the two biblical covenants.

Creation. The beginning of all that exists as a result of an act of God, who made everything from nothing. The story of Creation is told in the Book of Genesis.

Creator. A title given to God to signify that God and only God is the ultimate creator of everything that is and everything that ever will be.

creed. An official profession of faith, usually prepared and presented by a council of the Church and used in the Church's liturgy. Based on the Latin *credo,* meaning "I believe," the two most familiar Catholic creeds are the Apostles' Creed and the Nicene Creed.

deacon; diaconate. The third degree or level of the sacrament of Holy Orders, after that of bishop and priest. Deacons are ordained to assist priests and bishops in a variety of ministries. Some are ordained deacons as one stage of their preparation for eventual priesthood. Others do not seek priesthood but commit to lifelong ministry to the church. The latter are known as permanent deacons.

Decalogue. Another name for the Ten Commandments. Also called the Law or the Law of Moses.

denomination. A group of religious organizations uniting under a single legal and administrative body and subscribing to the same creed and moral code.

detraction. Revealing something about another person that is true, but is harmful to his or her reputation.

devil; demon. A fallen angel, one created naturally good but who sinned against God by refusing to accept God's Reign. The term *devil* refers to Satan, Lucifer, or the Evil One, the chief of the fallen angels; *demon* refers to an agent of the Evil One.

diocesan priest. A man ordained by the bishop for service to the local Church in parish ministry or another diocesan apostolate.

diocese. Also known as a "particular" or "local" Church, the regional community of believers, who commonly gather in parishes, under the leadership of a bishop. At times, a diocese is determined not on the basis of geography but on the basis of language or culture.

discernment. From a Latin word meaning "to separate or to distinguish between," it is the practice of listening for God's call in our life and distinguishing between good and bad choices.

disciple. A follower of Christ. Based on a word for pupil or student, used both to designate those who learned from and followed Jesus in New Testament times (the disciples) as well as those who commit to follow him today.

dismissal rite. The final part of the liturgy, comprising a closing prayer, a blessing, and usually a closing song.

disposition. An inner attitude and readiness to receiving God's gifts (graces), particularly through the sacraments.

doctrine. An official teaching of the Church based on the Revelation of God by and through Christ.

dogma. Those teachings that are recognized as central to Church teaching, defined by the Magisterium, and accorded the fullest weight and authority. (*See also* heresy.)

domestic church. Another name for the first and most fundamental community of faith: the family.

doxology. A prayer of glory and praise to one God in three divine persons. Two examples of doxologies from the Mass are the Glory to God and the words that precede the great Amen.

Easter. The day on which Christians celebrate Jesus' Resurrection from the dead; considered the most holy of all days and the climax of the Church's liturgical year. (*See also* Triduum.)

ecumenical council. A gathering of all Catholic bishops, convened by the Pope and under his authority and guidance. The last ecumenical council was Vatican II, called by Pope John XXIII in 1962.

ecumenism. The movement to restore unity among the Christian Churches and, ultimately, of all humans throughout "the whole wide world" (the literal meaning of the word).

efficacious. The power something holds to cause a desired effect. The sacraments are efficacious in bringing about the spiritual reality that they signify.

embezzlement. The sin of taking funds that are not yours, from a business, an organization, or the government.

encyclical. A letter written by the Pope and sent to the whole Church and, at times, beyond the Church to the whole world; commonly focused on Church teaching regarding a particular issue or currently important matter.

envy. Jealousy, resentment, or sadness because of another person's good fortune. It is one of the capital sins, and contrary to the tenth commandment.

Eucharist, the. Also called the Mass or Lord's Supper, and based on a word for "thanksgiving," the central Christian liturgical celebration; established by Jesus at the Last Supper. In the Eucharist, the sacrificial death and Resurrection of Jesus is both remembered ("Do this in memory of me") and renewed ("This *is* my body, given for you"). The Sunday celebration of the Eucharist is considered the heart of the Church's life and worship, and participation in it is expected of all Catholics of the age and ability to do so.

Eucharistic adoration. A type of prayer in which one meditates before the Blessed Sacrament, either privately or during a communal prayer such as benediction.

Eucharistic prayer. The part of the Mass that includes the consecration of the bread and wine. It begins with the preface and concludes with the great Amen.

euthanasia. A direct action, or a deliberate lack of action, that causes the death of a handicapped, sick, or dying person.

Some attempt to justify it as an act of mercy intended to relieve suffering, but the Catholic Church rejects that position, and considers euthanasia a violation of the fifth commandment against killing.

evangelist. Based on a word for "good news," in general, anyone who actively works to spread the Gospel of Jesus; more commonly and specifically, one of the persons traditionally recognized as authors of the four Gospels: Matthew, Mark, Luke, and John.

evangelization. The proclamation of the Gospel of Jesus through word and witness.

examination of conscience; examen. Prayerful reflection on and assessment of one's own words, attitudes, and actions in light of the Gospel of Jesus; more specifically, the conscious evaluation of one's life in preparation for reception of the sacrament of Penance and Reconciliation.

exorcism. A power given to the Church, in the name of Jesus Christ, to free or protect a person or object from the power of the devil.

exposition. As part of Eucharistic adoration, exposition is the custom of taking the Eucharist from the tabernacle and placing it in a special vessel called a monstrance, designed to hold a host and "expose" it—that is, to make it visible—so that people can pray before it.

faith. In general, the belief in the existence of God. For Christians, the gift of God by which one freely accepts God's full Revelation in Jesus Christ. It is a matter of both the head (acceptance of Church teaching regarding the Revelation of God) and the heart (love of God and neighbor as a response to God's first loving us); also, one of the three theological virtues.

fall, the. Also called the fall from grace, the biblical revelation about the origins of sin and evil in the world, expressed figuratively in the story of Adam and Eve in Genesis. (*See also* original sin.)

fasting. Refraining from food and drink as an act of spiritual discipline or as an expression of sorrow for sin; sometimes required by the Church, especially during the liturgical season of Lent.

Father. The name for God used most commonly by Jesus and, therefore, held in high esteem by the Church. (*See also* Trinity.)

final judgment. The judgment of the human race by Jesus Christ at his Second Coming, as noted in the Nicene Creed. It is also called the last judgment.

first Friday. A particular devotion to the sacred heart of Jesus that involves receiving Eucharist on nine consecutive first Fridays of the month. According to Tradition, those who do so will receive special graces.

fornication. Sexual intercourse between a man and a woman who are not married. It is morally wrong to engage in intercourse before marriage, and it is a sin against the sixth commandment.

fortitude. Also called strength or courage, the virtue that enables one to maintain sound moral judgment and behavior in the face of difficulties and challenges; one of the four cardinal virtues.

forty hours' devotion. A three-day period of worship of the Blessed Sacrament, approximately equaling the time Jesus lay in the tomb. The Blessed Sacrament is exposed in a monstrance during this time.

free will. The gift from God that allows human beings to choose from among various actions, for which we are held accountable. It is the basis for moral responsibility.

fruits of the Holy Spirit. The characteristics and qualities of those who allow themselves to be guided by the Holy Spirit. They are listed in Galatians 5:22–23.

fundamentalism. An interpretation of the Bible and Christian doctrine based on the literal meaning of the words and without regard to the historical setting in which the writings or teachings were first developed; the person who holds such a perspective is called a fundamentalist.

gathering rite. The opening of the liturgy, designed to prepare the assembly for the celebration. It consists of the opening procession, the penitential rite, the Glory to God, and an opening prayer.

genetic engineering. Manipulating the genetic code of plants, animals, or human beings to alter it in some way. Such activity with human DNA is considered a violation of the sanctity of life.

genuflection. Kneeling on one knee as a sign of reverence for the Blessed Sacrament.

gifts of the Holy Spirit. Special graces given to us by the Holy Spirit to help us respond to God's call to holiness. The list of seven gifts is derived from Isaiah 11:1–3.

God. The infinite and divine being recognized as the source and creator of all that exists. (*See also* Trinity.)

Gospel. Most basically, "the good news" (the phrase on which the word *gospel* is based) of the Revelation of God in and through Jesus Christ, proclaimed initially by him, then by the Apostles, and now by the Church; also refers to those four books of the New Testament that focus on the person, life, teachings, death, and Resurrection of Jesus.

grace. The free and undeserved gift of God's loving and active presence in the universe and in our life. (*See also* sanctifying grace.)

healing, sacraments of. The two sacraments that are concerned with healing the mind, body, and spirit: the sacrament of Anointing of the Sick and the sacrament of Penance and Reconciliation.

heaven. Traditionally, the dwelling place of God and the saints, meaning all who are saved; more accurately, not a place but a state of eternal life and union with God, in which one experiences full happiness and the satisfaction of the deepest human longings.

hell. The state of permanent separation from God, reserved for those who freely and consciously choose to reject God to the very end of their life.

heresy. The conscious and deliberate rejection of a dogma of the Church. (*See also* doctrine; dogma.)

hierarchy. In general, the line of authority in the Church; more narrowly, the Pope and bishops, as successors of the Apostles, in their authoritative role as leaders of the Church. (*See also* Magisterium.)

Holy Communion. Another name for the Eucharist, the body and blood of Jesus Christ.

holy days of obligation. Feast days in the liturgical year on which, in addition to Sundays, Catholics are obliged to participate in the Eucharist.

Holy Orders. The sacrament by which members of the Church are ordained for permanent ministry in the Church as bishops, priests, or deacons.

Holy Spirit. The third person of the Blessed Trinity, understood as the perfect love between God the Father and the Son, Jesus Christ, who inspires, guides, and sanctifies the life of believers. (*See also* Trinity.)

holy water. Blessed water used in ritual sprinklings or when making the sign of the cross as a reminder of Baptism.

Holy Week. In the church's liturgical year, the week preceding Easter, beginning with Palm Sunday; it culminates the annual celebration of Christ's Passion, death, and Resurrection.

homosexuality. A sexual attraction to members of one's own gender. The Church teaches that homosexual activity is morally wrong.

hope. The theological virtue by which we trust in the promises of God and expect from God both eternal life and the grace we need to attain it; the conviction that God's grace is at work in the world and that the Kingdom of God established by and through Jesus Christ is becoming realized through the workings of the Holy Spirit among us.

human dignity. The idea that because all people are created in God's image, they have fundamental worth. This notion is the foundation of Catholic social teaching.

human rights. The basic political, social, and economic rights that every human being claims, by virtue of their human dignity as beings created by God. Society cannot grant these rights and must not violate them.

humility. The virtue by which one understands that one is totally dependent on God, and also appreciates and uses properly the gifts she or he has been given by God.

idolatry. Worship of other beings, creatures, or material goods in a way that is fitting for God alone. It is a violation of the first commandment.

Ignatian Gospel contemplation. A prayer form that uses the imagination to immerse a person in a story from the Scriptures, in order to better understand the story's meaning.

Immaculate Conception. The Catholic dogma that the Blessed Virgin Mary was free from sin from the first moment of her conception.

immortality. The quality or state of unending, everlasting life; the Catholic doctrine that the human soul survives the death of the body and remains in existence, to be reunited with the body at the final resurrection; identified in the creed as belief in "the resurrection of the body and life everlasting."

Incarnation. Based on words meaning "in flesh," the mystery and church dogma that the Son of God assumed human nature and "became flesh" in the person of Jesus of Nazareth. The Incarnation means that Jesus, the Son of God and second person of the Trinity, is *both* fully God and fully man.

indissolubility. A property of the sacrament of Marriage that excludes any possibility for breaking the marital bond.

inerrancy. The fact that the books of the Scriptures are free from error regarding the spiritual and religious truth that God wishes to reveal through them for the sake of our salvation. (*See also* inspiration, biblical.)

infallibility; infallible. The gift of the Spirit to the whole Church by which the leaders of the Church—the Pope and the bishops in union with him—are protected from fundamental error when formulating a specific teaching on a matter of faith and morals.

initiation. The process by which a nonbaptized person is prepared to become a full member of the Church. The three sacraments of initiation are Baptism, Confirmation, and the Eucharist.

inspiration, biblical. The guidance of the Holy Spirit in the development of the Scriptures, whereby the Spirit guided the human authors to teach without error those truths of God that are necessary for our salvation. It is on the basis of inspiration that we can call the Bible the word of God.

intercession. A prayer on behalf of another person or group.

in vitro fertilization. The fertilization of a woman's ovum (egg) with a man's sperm outside of her body. The fertilized egg is transferred to the woman's uterus. The process is considered to be a moral violation of the dignity of procreation.

Islam. Founded by the prophet Muhammad, it is one of the three great religions of the Western world, with connections to both Judaism and Christianity. The holy scriptures of the faith are gathered in the Qur'an.

Israelites. The chosen People of God; members of the twelve tribes descended from Jacob who inhabited the land of Israel during biblical times.

Jesus Christ. The Son of God, the second person of the Trinity, who took on flesh in Jesus of Nazareth. Jesus in Hebrew means, "God saves," and was the name given the historical Jesus at the Annunciation. Christ, based on the word for "Messiah," meaning "the anointed one," is a title that was given Jesus by the church after his full identity was revealed.

Judaism. The religious practices, beliefs, perspectives, and philosophies of the Jewish people. The biblical roots are in the Hebrew Scriptures, particularly in the Torah (which is also the first five books of the Bible). The Jews also have a rich wisdom tradition handed down to them from their rabbis (teachers.)

justice. The cardinal virtue concerned with rights and duties within relationships; the commitment, as well as the actions and attitudes that flow from the commitment, to ensure that all persons—particularly the poor and oppressed—receive what is due them.

justification. God's act of bringing a sinful human being into right relationship with him. It involves removal of sin and the gift of God's sanctifying grace to renew holiness.

just war. War involves many evils, no matter the circumstances. For a war to be just, it must be declared by a lawful authority, and there must be just cause, the right intention (such as self-defense), and weapons must be used in a way that protects the life of innocent people.

Kingdom of God. The reign or rule of God over the hearts of people and, as a consequence of that, the development of a new social order based on unconditional love. Also called the Reign of God.

Kyrie Eleison. Greek for "Lord, have mercy." The short prayer, along with its counterpart, Christe Eleison, "Christ, have mercy," is part of the penitential rite at the beginning of a Eucharistic liturgy.

laity. All members of the Church, with the exception of those who are ordained. The laity share in Christ's role as priest, prophet, and king, witnessing to God's love and power in the world.

Last Supper. A supper during the Jewish celebration of Passover that was the last meal Jesus shared with his disciples before being handed over for crucifixion. It is remembered by Catholics as the occasion of the first Eucharist, and is commemorated by believers on Holy Thursday.

Law, the. Another name for the Ten Commandments, it is also called the Law of Moses or the Old Law.

lectio divina. A form of meditative prayer, usually focused on a passage from the Scriptures, that involves repetitive readings and periods of reflection; can serve as either private or communal prayer.

lectionary. The official liturgical book from which the readings selected for the liturgy of the word during Mass are proclaimed. The person who proclaims the word is called a lector.

legitimate defense. The teaching that limited violence is morally acceptable in defending yourself or your nation from an attack.

Lent. The liturgical season of forty days that begins with Ash Wednesday and ends with the celebration of the Paschal mystery in the Easter Triduum, the season during which believers focus on penance for sin.

liturgical celebration. *See* liturgy.

liturgical year. The annual cycle of religious feasts and seasons that forms the context for the Church's worship. (*See also* the section on Catholic beliefs and practices for a list of seasons and a diagram of the Church year.)

liturgist. One who has the training and responsibility for planning and coordinating all aspects of the worship life of a faith community.

liturgy. Based on a word meaning "public work," the official public worship of the Church, the heart and high point—or source and goal—of which is the Eucharist.

liturgy of the Eucharist. The second major part of the Mass, it comprises the preparation of gifts, the Eucharistic prayer, and the rite of Holy Communion.

Liturgy of the Hours. The official, nonsacramental daily prayer of the Catholic Church. The prayer provides standard prayers, Scripture readings, and reflections at regular hours throughout the day. (*See also* breviary.)

liturgy of the word. The first major part of the Mass, it comprises three scriptural readings, a responsorial psalm, a homily, the Nicene Creed, and petitions.

living wage. Also called just wage, it is a fair payment that a worker receives from an employer, which allows the wage earner and his or her family to live a life of dignity and meet basic needs.

Lord. The Old Testament name for God that in speaking or reading aloud was automatically substituted for the name Yahweh, which was considered too sacred to be spoken; in the New Testament, used for both God the Father and, on occasion, for Jesus, to reflect awareness of Jesus' identity as the Son of God.

Lord's Day. Another name for Sunday and holy days of obligation. Catholics are required to attend Mass on these days and refrain from any work that might stand in the way of relaxation and renewal of mind and body.

Lord's Prayer. Another name for the Our Father. (*See also* the section on Catholic prayers and devotions.)

love. The human longing for God and a selfless commitment to supporting the dignity and humanity of all people, simply because they are created in God's image. Also called "charity," it is one of the three theological virtues.

lust. Intense and uncontrolled desire for sexual pleasure. It is one of the seven capital sins.

Magisterium. The name given the official teaching authority of the Church, whose task is to interpret and preserve the truths of the Church revealed in both the Scriptures and Tradition.

Magnificat. Mary's prayer of praise when she visited her cousin Elizabeth. It is recorded in Luke 1:46–55. The name of the prayer is the first word of the prayer in Latin, which means "magnify."

marks of the Church. The four characteristics of the true Church of Jesus Christ: one, holy, catholic (universal), and apostolic. These marks are recited at Mass as part of the Nicene Creed.

marriage; Matrimony. Marriage is an exclusive, permanent, and lifelong contract between a man and a woman in which they commit to care for each other and to procreate and raise children; when the marriage takes place between baptized persons who enter into a covenant modeled on that between Christ and the Church, it is recognized as the sacrament of Matrimony. The two terms are often interchanged.

martyr. A person who voluntarily suffers death because of her or his beliefs. The Church has canonized many martyrs as saints.

Mary. The mother of Jesus, sometimes called the Blessed Virgin Mary. Because Jesus is the Son of God and the second person of the Trinity, Mary is also given the title Mother of God.

Mass. Another name for the Eucharist. Based on the Latin word *missa,* meaning "to be sent," refers to the dismissal, in which worshipers are told to "go in peace to love and serve the Lord."

masturbation. Self-manipulation of one's sexual organs for the purpose of erotic pleasure or to achieve orgasm. The Church considers masturbation to be a sin because the act cannot result in the creation of a new life. It is also wrong because it is self-serving, and God created sex not for self-gratification but to unify a husband and wife in marriage.

meditation. A form of prayer involving a variety of methods and techniques, in which one engages the mind, imagination, and emotions in order to focus on a particular truth, biblical theme, or other spiritual matter.

ministry. Based on a word for service, in a general sense any service offered to help the Church fulfill its mission; more narrowly, particular expressions of such service (e.g., the ministry of catechesis and liturgical ministries).

miracle. A special manifestation, or sign, of the presence and power of God active in human history.

modesty. From the same root word as "moderation," it means keeping one's attitudes, actions, speech, dress, and other behaviors controlled in a way that acknowledges one's own dignity.

monotheism. Belief in one God instead of many.

monstrance. The special vessel designed to hold a host and make it visible for Eucharistic adoration.

morality. Dealing with the goodness or evil of human acts, attitudes, and values; involves matters such as right judgment, decision-making skills, personal freedom and responsibility, and so on.

mortal sin. An action so contrary to the will of God that it results in a complete separation from God and God's grace. As a consequence of that separation, the person is condemned to eternal death. To be a mortal sin requires three conditions:

it must involve grave matter, the person must have full knowledge of the evil of the act, and the person must give his or her full consent in committing the act.

mysticism. An intense experience of the presence and power of God, resulting in a deeper sense of union with God; those who regularly experience such union are called mystics.

natural law. Our God-given instinct to be in right relationship with God, other people, the world, and ourselves. The basis for natural law is our participation in God's wisdom and goodness because we are created in the divine likeness. The fundamental expressions of natural law remain fixed and unchanging, which is why natural law is the foundation for both personal morality and civil norms.

New Law. The law of the Gospel of Jesus Christ, it is a law of love, grace, and freedom. It is distinguished from the Old Law, or the Law of Moses.

New Testament. The twenty-seven books of the Bible written during the early years of the Church in response to the life, mission, death, and Resurrection of Jesus; also, another name for the New Covenant established between God and humanity by Jesus.

Nicene Creed. The formal statement or profession of faith commonly recited during the Eucharist. (*See also* creed.)

novena. From the Latin word for "nine," it is a public or private devotion that extends for a period of nine days. In some cases a novena is offered on a designated day for nine weeks or nine months.

nuns. *See* religious life, congregation, order.

obedience. Based on a word meaning to hear or listen, the willingness and commitment to submit to the will of God, as well as to Church teachings and practices that reflect the will of God. (*See also* vow(s).)

oil of the sick. The oil used in the sacrament of the Anointing of the Sick. It is blessed by the bishop along with other holy oils during the annual chrism Mass.

Old Law. The Law of Moses, the Ten Commandments. It contrasts to the New Law of the Gospel.

Old Testament. The forty-six books of the Bible that record the history of salvation from Creation, through the story of ancient Israel, and up to the time of Jesus; also refers to the

Old Covenant established between God and the people of Israel in God's encounter with Moses on Mount Sinai.

ordained ministers. Those who have received the sacrament of Holy Orders, that is, deacons, priests, and bishops.

Ordinary Time. The time in the liturgical year that is *not* part of a special season like Advent, Christmas, Lent, or Easter.

ordination. *See* Holy Orders.

original sin. The sin by which the first humans disobeyed God, resulting in separation from God; also, the state of human nature that affects every person now born into the world. (*See also* fall, the.)

papacy. The name given the office and authority of the Bishop of Rome, the Pope. As the successor of Saint Peter, the Pope serves as both a symbol and an agent of the unity of all believers.

parable. A story intended to convey a religious truth or particular teaching through the use of metaphors; a central feature of Jesus' teaching ministry.

Paraclete. A name for the Holy Spirit, based on a word for helper or advocate.

parish. A specific community of believers, commonly but not always defined geographically, whose pastoral and spiritual care is guided by a priest or other leader appointed by a bishop.

Parousia, Christ's. The Second Coming of Christ, when his Kingdom will be fully established and his triumph over evil will be complete.

Paschal lamb. A name for Jesus, whose death and Resurrection redeemed humanity. The name is associated with Passover, a commemoration of the deliverance of the Jewish people from Egypt. To avoid the slaughter of firstborn sons by the Egyptian army, the Jews sprinkled the blood of a lamb on their doorposts.

Paschal mystery. The term given the entire process of God's plan of salvation by which God redeemed humanity from sin in and through Jesus' life, death, Resurrection, and Ascension into glory. Christians enter into the Paschal mystery through sacramental initiation, and participate in it by faithfully living out the process of dying and rising that characterizes all life.

Passion, the. The suffering and death of Jesus.

pastoral. Refers to the daily life of the Church, especially as it takes place at parish and diocesan levels. Based on a word for shepherd or shepherding, the person who tends to the pastoral care of a community is commonly called the pastor.

penance. In general, an attitude of the heart in which one experiences regret for past sin and commits to a change in behavior or attitudes; particular acts of penance may include the practice of spiritual disciplines such as prayer or fasting, or participation in the sacrament of Penance and Reconciliation.

penance, communal. The sacrament of Penance and Reconciliation celebrated within a gathering of a faith community. The most common form includes opportunities for individual confession and absolution.

Penance and Reconciliation, sacrament of. One of the seven sacraments of the Church, the liturgical celebration of God's forgiveness of sin, through which the sinner is reconciled with both God and the Church.

Pentecost. The biblical event following the Resurrection and Ascension of Jesus at which the Holy Spirit was poured out on his disciples; the first Pentecost is often identified as the birth of the Church. In the Christian liturgical year, the feast fifty days after Easter on which the biblical event of Pentecost is recalled and celebrated.

People of God. The biblical image for the Church. Those who share in Christ's mission as priest, prophet, and king.

perjury. The sin of lying while under an oath to tell the truth.

permanent deacon. *See* deacon, diaconate.

petition. A prayer form in which one asks God for help and forgiveness.

Pharisees. A Jewish sect during the time of Jesus known for their strict adherence to the Law and their concern with superficial matters.

plagiarism. Using another person's thoughts, creative ideas, writings, music, and so forth without permission, and presenting them as one's own. It is a form of stealing, and a sin against the seventh commandment.

polygamy. Having more than one spouse. It is contrary to the sanctity of marriage.

Pope. Based on a word for "father," the successor of Saint Peter and Bishop of Rome, who holds the office of the papacy. Often called the Holy Father.

pornography. A written description or visual portrayal of a person or action, that is created or viewed with the intention of stimulating sexual feelings.

poverty. As a social reality, indeed, a social sin, a condition of material need experienced by the poor. The Church, in imitation of Jesus, expresses its central concern for the poor through its commitment to justice. As an attitude and value, a spirit of detachment from material things and a commitment to share all that one has with those who have not.

praise. A prayer of acknowledgment that God is God, giving God glory not for what he does, but simply because he is.

prayer. The lifting of mind and heart to God in praise, petition, thanksgiving, and intercession; communication with God in a relationship of love.

precepts of the Church. Sometimes called the commandments of the Church, these are obligations for all Catholics that are dictated by the laws of the Church.

preferential option. A moral obligation for individuals and for the Church that requires special attention to those who are poor, considering their needs first and above all others.

presbyter. A term used for officials in the early Church. Today it is an alternative word for priest.

priest; priesthood. The second of three degrees or "orders" in the sacrament of Holy Orders, along with bishop and deacon. The priest is called to serve the community of faith and its members by representing and assisting the bishop in teaching, governing, and presiding over the community's worship. Priests generally minister within a parish, school, or other setting within a diocese.

priesthood of the faithful. The belief that the Body of Christ is made up of priestly people who share in Christ's royal priesthood.

prostration. A prayer posture in which a person lies stretched out on the ground, face down, as a sign of adoration, submission, and humility. This posture is part of the rite of ordination.

prudence. The virtue by which a person is inclined toward choosing the moral good and avoiding evil; sometimes called the rudder virtue, because it helps steer the person through complex moral situations; related to conscience, and one of the four cardinal virtues.

purgatory. A state of final purification or cleansing which one may need to enter following death and before entry into heaven.

reason. The natural ability human beings have to know and understand truth.

Reconciliation. *See* Penance and Reconciliation, sacrament of.

redemption; Redeemer. The process by which we are "bought back" (the meaning of redeem) from slavery to sin into a right relationship with God. We are redeemed by the grace of God and through the life, death, and Resurrection of Jesus Christ. As the agent of redemption, Jesus is called the Redeemer.

Reign of God. *See* Kingdom of God.

religion. The beliefs and practices followed by those committed to the Gospel of Jesus and full participation in the life of the Church. By virtue of the first commandment, the first duty of a religious person is to worship and serve God alone.

religious life; congregation; order. A permanent state of life and an organized group of Christians, recognized by the Church, who have taken vows to live in community and to observe the disciplines of poverty, chastity, and obedience. Religious men are often called brothers, monks, or friars; religious women, sisters or nuns.

religious priests. Priests who are ordained within a religious community for service to the community and its ministries. With the permission of the local bishop, they may also lead parishes within a diocese.

religious vows. The vows, or promises, made by a person who becomes a full member of a religious community. Traditionally there are three vows: poverty, chastity, and obedience.

reparation. Making amends for something one did wrong that caused harm to another person or led to loss.

repentance. An attitude of sorrow for a sin committed and a resolution not to sin again. It is a response to God's gracious love and forgiveness.

restitution. Making things right with another person or people who have been harmed by an injustice, or returning or replacing what rightfully belongs to another.

Resurrection, the. The passage of Jesus from death to life "on the third day" after his Crucifixion; the heart of the Paschal mystery, and the basis of our hope in the resurrection of the dead.

resurrection of the dead. The Christian dogma that all those deemed righteous by God will be raised and will live forever with God in heaven; the conviction that not only our souls but also our transformed bodies will live on after death ("I believe in the resurrection of the body").

Revelation. God's self-communication and disclosure of the divine plan to humankind through creation, events, persons, and, most fully, in Jesus Christ.

ritual. The established form of the words and actions for a ceremony that is repeated often. The actions often have a symbolic meaning, such as the anointing with chrism at Confirmation.

rosary. A popular devotion to Mary, the Mother of God.

Sabbath. In the Old Testament, the "seventh day" on which God rested after the work of Creation was completed; in Jewish Law, the weekly day of rest to remember God's work through private prayer, communal worship, and spiritual disciplines such as fasting; for Catholics, Sunday, the day on which Jesus was raised, which we are to observe with participation in the Eucharist in fulfillment of the commandment to "keep holy the Sabbath."

sacrament. In Catholic life and worship, the seven efficacious signs of God's grace, instituted by Christ and entrusted to the Church, by which divine life is dispensed to us.

sacramental character. A permanent and indelible spiritual mark on a person's soul, sealed by the Holy Spirit as a result of Baptism, Confirmation, and Holy Orders. For this reason these sacraments cannot be repeated.

sacramentals. Sacred signs (such as holy water and a crucifix) that bear some resemblance to the sacraments, but which do not carry the guarantee of God's grace associated with the seven sacraments.

sacraments at the service of communion. The name given to the two sacraments that are directed toward building up the People of God, namely Holy Orders and Marriage.

sacraments of healing. *See* healing, sacraments of.

sacraments of initiation. *See* initiation.

sacrilege. An offense against God. It is the abuse of a person, place, or thing dedicated to God and the worship of God.

saint. Someone who has been transformed by the grace of Christ and who resides in full union with God in heaven. (*See also* canonization; communion of saints.)

salvation. Liberation from sin and eternal union with God in heaven. Salvation is accomplished by God alone through the Paschal mystery—the dying and rising of Jesus Christ.

salvation history. The pattern of events in human history that exemplify God's presence and saving actions. In Catholic thought, *all* of history is salvation history, even though God's presence may not be recognized.

sanctifying grace. A supernatural gift of God by which our sins are forgiven and we are made holy. It restores our friendship with God.

scandal. An action or attitude—or the failure to act—that leads another person into sin.

scribes. In Jewish history, these were government officials and scholars of the Law of Moses. They enforced the requirements of the Law.

Scripture(s). Generally, the term for any sacred writing. For Christians, the Old and New Testaments that make up the Bible and are recognized as the word of God.

simony. Buying or selling of something spiritual, such as a grace, a sacrament, or a relic. It violates the honor of God.

sin. Any deliberate offense, in thought, word, or deed, against the will of God.

sisters. *See* religious life, congregation, order.

slander. Injuring another person's reputation by telling lies and spreading rumors. It is also called calumny.

social doctrine. The body of teaching by the Church on economic and social matters that includes moral judgments and demands for action in favor of those being harmed.

social encyclical. A letter from the Pope addressed to members of the universal Church regarding topics related to social justice, human rights, and peace.

social justice. The Church's commitment, and mandate to its members, to engage in conscious efforts to fight against, if not overcome, social sin.

social sin. The collective effect of sin over time, which corrupts society and its institutions by creating "structures of sin." Examples of social sin are racism, sexism, and institutionalized poverty.

society. A broad part of the human community that is distinguished by common values, traditions, standards of living, or conduct.

solidarity. Union of one's heart and mind with those who are poor or powerless, or who face an injustice. It is an act of Christian charity.

Son of God. Title frequently applied to Jesus Christ, which recognizes him as the second person of the Blessed Trinity.

soul. The spiritual life principle of human beings that survives after death.

spirituality. In general, the values, actions, attitudes, and behaviors that characterize a person's relationship with God and others. For Christians, a life guided by the Holy Spirit, lived out within the community of believers, and characterized by faith, hope, love, and service.

stewardship. An attitude that we do not own the gifts God has given us, but are trustees of those gifts. We have an obligation to share our time, talent, and material treasures with others.

suicide. Deliberately taking one's own life. It is a serious violation of God's Law and plan. It is usually accomplished as a result of serious mental and emotional anguish, and in such cases is not considered a free and deliberate act.

superstition. Attributing to someone or something else a power that belongs to God alone, and relying on such powers rather than trusting in God. It is a sin against the first commandment.

symbol. An object or action that points us to another reality. It leads us to look beyond our senses to consider the deeper mystery.

tabernacle. The receptacle in a church in which the consecrated bread and wine of the Eucharist is reserved for Communion for the sick and dying; sometimes the focus of private and communal prayer and adoration.

temperance. The cardinal virtue by which one moderates her or his appetites and passions in order to achieve balance in the use of created goods.

temptations. Invitations or enticements to commit an unwise or immoral act that often include a promise of a reward, to make the immoral act seem more appealing.

thanksgiving. A prayer of gratitude for the gift of life and the gifts of life.

theological virtues. The name for the God-given virtues of faith, hope, and love. These virtues enable us to know God as God and lead us to union with God in mind and heart.

theology. Literally, the study of God; the academic discipline and effort to understand, interpret, and order our experience of God and Christian faith; classically defined as "faith seeking understanding."

Theotokos. Greek for "God-bearer." It is the name given to Mary after an ecumenical council in the fifth century to affirm that she is the mother of the human Jesus and the mother of God.

Tradition. Based on a word meaning "to hand on," the central content of Catholic faith contained in both the Scriptures and in Church doctrines and dogmas, as well as the process by which that content is faithfully passed on from generation to generation, under the guidance of the Holy Spirit.

transubstantiation. In the sacrament of the Eucharist, this is the name given to the action of changing the bread and wine into the body and blood of Jesus Christ.

Triduum. The three days of the liturgical year that begins with the Mass of the Lord's Supper on Holy Thursday and ends with evening prayer on Easter Sunday.

Trinity. Often referred to as the Blessed Trinity, the central Christian mystery and dogma that there is one God in three persons: Father, Son, and Holy Spirit.

venerate. An action that shows deep reverence for something sacred. For example, on Good Friday, individuals in the assembly venerate the cross by bowing before or kissing the cross.

venial sin. A less serious offense against the will of God that diminishes one's personal character and weakens but does not rupture one's relationship with God. (*See also* mortal sin.)

vice. A practice or a habit that leads a person to sin.

vigil for the deceased. Another name for a wake service. It is a prayer service the takes place before a funeral, to pray for the repose of the soul of the deceased and for strength for those who grieve the loss.

virginal conception and birth. The dogma that Jesus was conceived in the womb of Mary and born by the power of the Holy Spirit and without the cooperation of a human father. (*Note:* This is not to be confused with the Immaculate Conception of Mary.)

virtue. A good habit, one that creates within us a kind of inner readiness or attraction to move toward or accomplish moral good. The theological virtues are faith, hope, and love.

vocal prayer. A prayer that is spoken aloud or silently, such as the Lord's Prayer. It is one of the three expressions of prayer, the other two being meditation and contemplation.

vocation. A call from God to all members of the Church to embrace a life of holiness. Specifically, it refers to a call to live the holy life as an ordained minister, as a vowed religious (sister or brother), in a Christian marriage, or in single life.

vow(s). A free and conscious commitment made to other persons (as in marriage), to the Church, or to God. Religious vows—those taken by members of religious congregations or orders—commonly include poverty, chastity, and obedience.

wake service. *See* vigil for the deceased.

way of the cross. A religious devotion or exercise modeled on Jesus' Passion—his trial, walk toward his death on the cross, and burial in the tomb. Sometimes called the stations of the cross, the devotion involves meditation on each step in Jesus' journey.

worship. Adoration of God, usually expressed publicly in the Church's official liturgy as well as through other prayers and devotions.

Yahweh. The Old Testament name for God, frequently translated as "I am who I am."

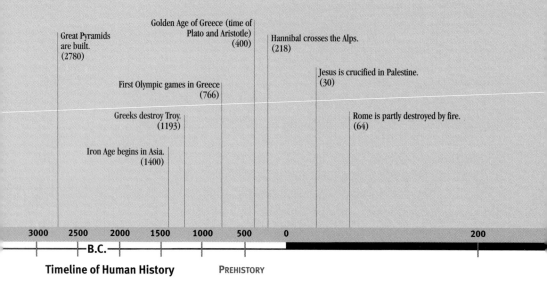

Great Pyramids
are built.
(2780)

Golden Age of Greece (time of
Plato and Aristotle)
(400)

Hannibal crosses the Alps.
(218)

Jesus is crucified in Palestine.
(30)

First Olympic games in Greece
(766)

Rome is partly destroyed by fire.
(64)

Greeks destroy Troy.
(1193)

Iron Age begins in Asia.
(1400)

| 3000 | 2500 | 2000 | 1500 | 1000 | 500 | 0 | | 200 |

B.C.

Timeline of Human History

PREHISTORY

Timeline of Church History

B.C.

| 3000 | 2500 | 2000 | 1500 | 1000 | 500 | 0 | | 200 |

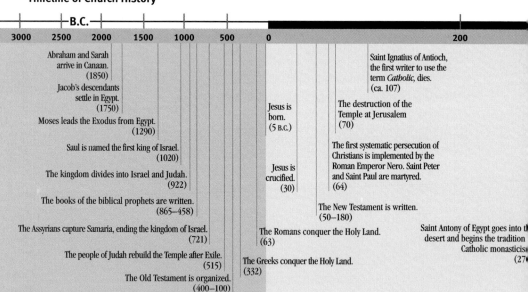

Abraham and Sarah
arrive in Canaan.
(1850)

Jacob's descendants
settle in Egypt.
(1750)

Moses leads the Exodus from Egypt.
(1290)

Saul is named the first king of Israel.
(1020)

The kingdom divides into Israel and Judah.
(922)

The books of the biblical prophets are written.
(865–458)

The Assyrians capture Samaria, ending the kingdom of Israel.
(721)

The people of Judah rebuild the Temple after Exile.
(515)

The Old Testament is organized.
(400–100)

Jesus is
born.
(5 B.C.)

Jesus is
crucified.
(30)

The Romans conquer the Holy Land.
(63)

The Greeks conquer the Holy Land.
(332)

Saint Ignatius of Antioch,
the first writer to use the
term *Catholic*, dies.
(ca. 107)

The destruction of the
Temple at Jerusalem
(70)

The first systematic persecution of
Christians is implemented by the
Roman Emperor Nero. Saint Peter
and Saint Paul are martyred.
(64)

The New Testament is written.
(50–180)

Saint Antony of Egypt goes into th
desert and begins the tradition
Catholic monasticis
(27

BEFORE THE BIRTH OF JESUS CHRIST (B.C.)

LIFE OF JESUS CHRIST AND THE EARLY CHURCH

Important Church Figures

Saint Peter
Saint Paul
Saint Ignatius
Saint Antony

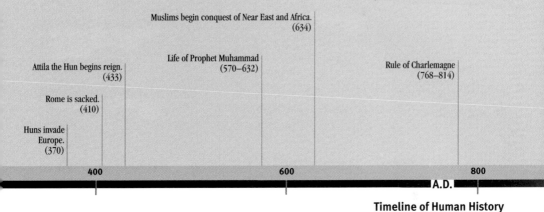

Muslims begin conquest of Near East and Africa.
(634)

Life of Prophet Muhammad
(570–632)

Rule of Charlemagne
(768–814)

Attila the Hun begins reign.
(433)

Rome is sacked.
(410)

Huns invade
Europe.
(370)

| 400 | 600 | 800 |

A.D.

Timeline of Human History

Timeline of Biblical History

A.D.

| 400 | 600 | 800 |

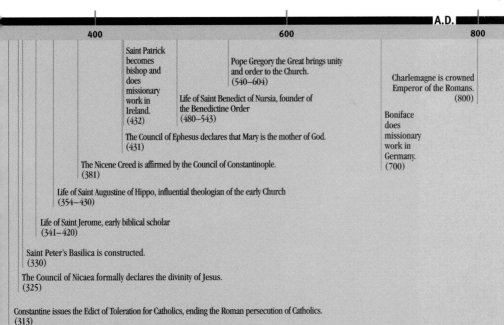

Saint Patrick
becomes
bishop and
does
missionary
work in
Ireland.
(432)

Pope Gregory the Great brings unity
and order to the Church.
(540–604)

Life of Saint Benedict of Nursia, founder of
the Benedictine Order
(480–543)

The Council of Ephesus declares that Mary is the mother of God.
(431)

The Nicene Creed is affirmed by the Council of Constantinople.
(381)

Life of Saint Augustine of Hippo, influential theologian of the early Church
(354–430)

Life of Saint Jerome, early biblical scholar
(341–420)

Saint Peter's Basilica is constructed.
(330)

The Council of Nicaea formally declares the divinity of Jesus.
(325)

Constantine issues the Edict of Toleration for Catholics, ending the Roman persecution of Catholics.
(313)

Charlemagne is crowned
Emperor of the Romans.
(800)

Boniface
does
missionary
work in
Germany.
(700)

THE CHURCH EXPANDS

Important Church Figures

Saint Constantine
Saint Augustine
Saint Jerome
Saint Patrick
Saint Benedict
Saint Gregory the Great
Saint Boniface

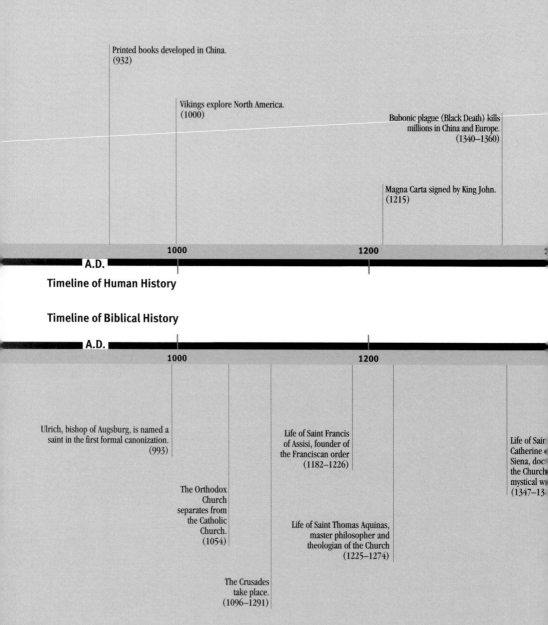

Printed books developed in China.
(932)

Vikings explore North America.
(1000)

Bubonic plague (Black Death) kills
millions in China and Europe.
(1340–1360)

Magna Carta signed by King John.
(1215)

1000

1200

A.D.

Timeline of Human History

Timeline of Biblical History

A.D.

1000

1200

Ulrich, bishop of Augsburg, is named a
saint in the first formal canonization.
(993)

Life of Saint Francis
of Assisi, founder of
the Franciscan order
(1182–1226)

Life of Sair
Catherine o
Siena, doc
the Church
mystical wi
(1347–13

The Orthodox
Church
separates from
the Catholic
Church.
(1054)

Life of Saint Thomas Aquinas,
master philosopher and
theologian of the Church
(1225–1274)

The Crusades
take place.
(1096–1291)

THE CHURCH OF MEDIEVAL EUROPE

Important Church Figures

Charlemagne   Saint Thomas Aquinas
Saint Francis of Assisi   Saint Catherine of Siena
Saint Dominic   Saint Julian of Norwich

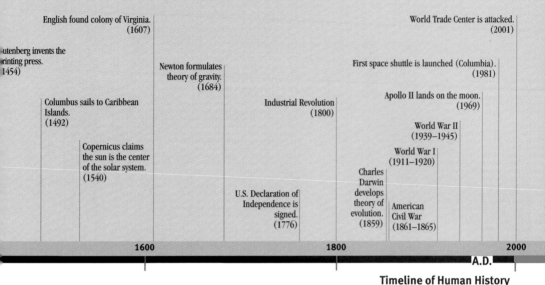

English found colony of Virginia.
(1607)

Gutenberg invents the
printing press.
(1454)

Newton formulates
theory of gravity.
(1684)

Columbus sails to Caribbean
Islands.
(1492)

Industrial Revolution
(1800)

Copernicus claims
the sun is the center
of the solar system.
(1540)

U.S. Declaration of
Independence is
signed.
(1776)

Charles
Darwin
develops
theory of
evolution.
(1859)

World Trade Center is attacked.
(2001)

First space shuttle is launched (Columbia).
(1981)

Apollo II lands on the moon.
(1969)

World War II
(1939–1945)

World War I
(1911–1920)

American
Civil War
(1861–1865)

| 1600 | 1800 | 2000 |

A.D.

Timeline of Human History

Timeline of Biblical History

A.D.

| 1600 | 1800 | 2000 |

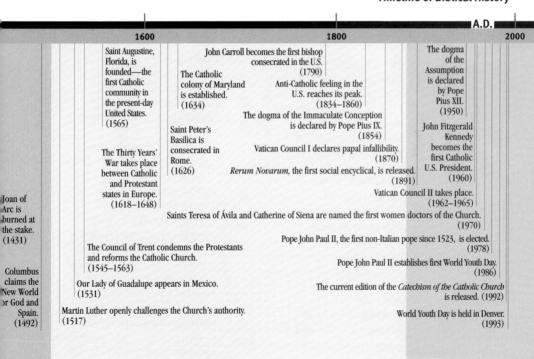

Saint Augustine,
Florida, is
founded—the
first Catholic
community in
the present-day
United States.
(1565)

The Catholic
colony of Maryland
is established.
(1634)

John Carroll becomes the first bishop
consecrated in the U.S.
(1790)

Anti-Catholic feeling in the
U.S. reaches its peak.
(1834–1860)

The dogma of the Immaculate Conception
is declared by Pope Pius IX.
(1854)

The dogma
of the
Assumption
is declared
by Pope
Pius XII.
(1950)

Saint Peter's
Basilica is
consecrated in
Rome.
(1626)

The Thirty Years'
War takes place
between Catholic
and Protestant
states in Europe.
(1618–1648)

Vatican Council I declares papal infallibility.
(1870)

Rerum Novarum, the first social encyclical, is released.
(1891)

Vatican Council II takes place.
(1962–1965)

John Fitzgerald
Kennedy
becomes the
first Catholic
U.S. President.
(1960)

Joan of
Arc is
burned at
the stake.
(1431)

Saints Teresa of Ávila and Catherine of Siena are named the first women doctors of the Church.
(1970)

The Council of Trent condemns the Protestants
and reforms the Catholic Church.
(1545–1563)

Pope John Paul II, the first non-Italian pope since 1523, is elected.
(1978)

Pope John Paul II establishes first World Youth Day.
(1986)

Columbus
claims the
New World
for God and
Spain.
(1492)

Our Lady of Guadalupe appears in Mexico.
(1531)

The current edition of the *Catechism of the Catholic Church*
is released. (1992)

Martin Luther openly challenges the Church's authority.
(1517)

World Youth Day is held in Denver.
(1993)

THE REFORMATION AND COUNTER-REFORMATION

Important Church Figures

Martin Luther
Saint Teresa of Ávila
Saint Thomas More
Saint Ignatius Loyola
Saint Vincent de Paul

THE MODERN CHURCH

Important Church Figures

Pope Pius XII
Mother Teresa
Pope John XXIII
Dorothy Day
Pope John Paul II

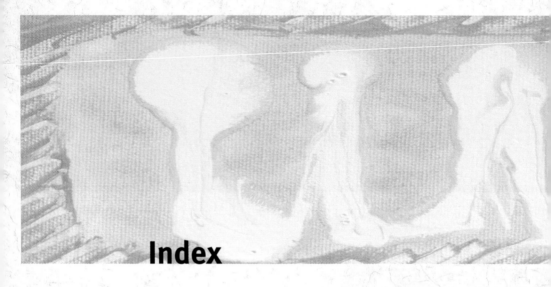

Index

L

M

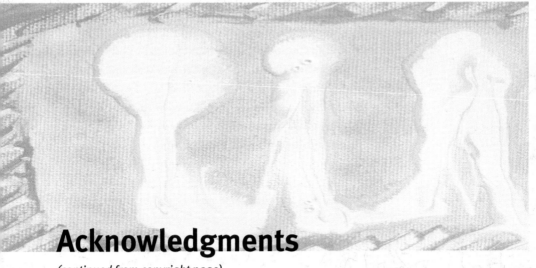

Acknowledgments

(continued from copyright page)

All scriptural quotations in this book are from the New Revised Standard Version of the Bible, Catholic Edition. Copyright © 1993 and 1989 by the Division of Christian Education of the National Council of the Churches of Christ in the United States of America. All rights reserved.

All excerpts marked *CCC,* the Apostles' Creed on page 31, and the excerpts from the Nicene Creed are quoted or adapted from the English translation of the *Catechism of the Catholic Church* for use in the United States of America. Copyright © 1994 by the United States Conference of Catholic Bishops (USCCB)—Libreria Editrice Vaticana.

The information in the Saintly Profiles sections of each chapter and the Patron Saints and Their Causes appendix is adapted and quoted from *Lives of the Saints: From Mary and St. Francis of Assisi to John XXIII and Mother Teresa,* by Richard P. McBrien (San Francisco: HarperSanFrancisco, 2001). Copyright © 2001 by Richard P. McBrien. Reprinted with permission from HarperCollins Publishers, Inc.

The statistics about the number of Catholics in the world in the sidebar on page 14 are taken from the *2002 Catholic Almanac,* from Our Sunday Visitor, edited by Matthew Burnson (Huntington, IN: Our Sunday Visitor Publishing Division, 2001), pages 340 and 450–474.

The information on page 14 about the number of adherents to the Catholic religion as compared to other religions is from the Religious Tolerance.org Web site, *www.religioustolerance.org/worldrel.htm,* accessed July 19, 2002.

The testimonials on page 15 are used with permission of the authors, Tara Okapalaeke-Wood and Laura Marie Gerson.

The excerpts on pages 18, 36, 110, and 141 are from *Dogmatic Constitution on the Church,* number 2, *Declaration on the Relationship of the Church to Non-Christian Religions,* number 2, *Dogmatic Constitution on the Church,* number 8, and *The Constitution on the Sacred Liturgy,* number 14, found in *The Documents of Vatican II,* Walter M. Abbott, general editor; Very Rev. Msgr. Joseph Gallagher, translation editor (New York: America Press, 1966), pages 15–16, 662, 24, and 144, respectively. Copyright © 1966 by the America Press. All rights reserved. Used with permission.

The "Act of Faith" on page 19 and the beliefs and practices on pages 372–379 of the Catholic Quick Facts appendix are taken from *Handing On the Faith: A Unified Content Reference for Teaching the Catholic Faith* (Birmingham, AL: Diocese of Birmingham in Alabama, 1999), pages 112–120. Copyright © 1999 by the Diocese of Birmingham in Alabama. Used with permission.

The quotes by Saint Augustine on pages 21 and 51 are taken from *The Holy Longing: The Search for a Christian Spirituality,* by Ronald Rolheiser (New York: Doubleday, 1999), page 5. Copyright © 1999 by Ronald Rolheiser.

The excerpt by Thomas Merton on page 37 is from *Thoughts in Solitude,* by Thomas Merton (New York: Farrar, Straus and Cudahy, 1958), page 83. Copyright © 1956, 1958 by the Abbey of Our Lady of Gethsemani.

The prayer on page 41, the words from the veneration of the cross on page 82, the words from the Easter proclamation on page 91, the prayer on page 124, and Eucharistic prayer 3 on page 345 are from *The Sacramentary,* English translation prepared by the International Commission on English in the Liturgy (ICEL) (New York: Catholic Book Publishing Co., 1987), pages 346, 156, 182–184, 734, and 552, respectively. Illustrations and arrangement copyright © 1985–1974 by Catholic Book Publishing Co., New York. All rights reserved. Used with permission.

Saint Thomas Aquinas's five proofs for God on page 44 are paraphrased from his *Summa Theologica*, the text of which is from *www.newadvent.org/summa/100203.htm*, accessed August 5, 2002.

The quote by Julian of Norwich on page 47 is taken from her book *Revelations of Divine Love*, found at *elvis.rowan.edu/~kilroy/JEK/05/08.html*, accessed August 5, 2002.

The prayer by Tom Moore on page 52 is from *Dreams Alive: Prayers by Teenagers*, edited by Carl Koch (Winona, MN: Saint Mary's Press, 1991), page 24. Copyright © 1991 by Saint Mary's Press. All rights reserved.

The excerpts from the funeral rites on page 53, the excerpts from the Confirmation Mass on page 170, and the prayer on page 191 are from *The Rites of the Catholic Church*, volume one, prepared by the International Commission on English in the Liturgy, a Joint Commission of Catholic Bishops' Conferences (New York: Pueblo Publishing Co., 1990), pages 1037 and 1040, 490, and 784, respectively. Copyright © 1976, 1990 by Pueblo Publishing Co., Inc. All rights reserved. Used with permission.

The prayer by J. Barrie Shepherd on page 65 is from *Diary of Daily Prayer*, by J. Barrie Shepherd (Minneapolis: Augsburg Publishing House, 1975). Copyright © 1975 by Augsburg Publishing House.

The quotes by John Wooden and by Carrie Mach on pages 67 and 320 are from Carrie Mach's writings, quoted in *Church Women: Probing History with Girls*, by Laurie Delgatto with Marilyn Kielbasa (Winona, MN: Saint Mary's Press, 2002), pages 121 and 124. Copyright © 2002 by Saint Mary's Press. Used with permission of Ricky and Ann Mach.

The excerpt about the miracle at Ribera del Fresno on page 71 is based on a story in *Making Saints: How the Catholic Church Determines Who Becomes a Saint, Who Doesn't, and Why*, by Kenneth L. Woodward (New York: Simon and Schuster, 1990), pages 209–210. Copyright © 1990 by Kenneth L. Woodward.

The quote from Saint Francis of Assisi on page 73 is from *straylight.dhs.org/art,* accessed September 20, 2002.

The story "One Solitary Life," on page 77, attributed to James Allen Francis, is from *www.geocities.com/onesolitarylife _isjesus/Lord-and-Savior.html,* accessed September 6, 2002.

The excerpt by Julian of Norwich on page 79 is from her book *Julian of Norwich: Showings,* long text, chapter 5, as quoted in *Spirituality and Theology: Christian Living and the Doctrine of God,* by Philip Sheldrake (Maryknoll, NY: Orbis Books, 1998), page 109. Copyright © 1998 by Philip Sheldrake.

Lisa Boyer's story on page 85 is used with permission.

The excerpts from Saint Augustine on page 90 and Leo the Great on page 127 are from *The Liturgy of the Hours: According to the Roman Rite,* volume 2, English translation prepared by the International Commission on English in the Liturgy (New York: Catholic Book Publishing Co., 1976), pages 635–637 and 661. Illustrations and arrangement copyright © 1975 by the Catholic Book Publishing Co.

The excerpt on page 94 from *Grace for the New Springtime,* a statement from the U.S. Conference of Catholic Bishops, is from *www.garg.com/ccc/articles/nonattributed/US_Bishops_001 .html,* accessed May 21, 2002.

The quote from Kateri Tekakwitha on page 97 is from *Saint of the Day: Lives, Lessons and Feasts,* edited by Leonard Foley, and Pat McCloskey (Cincinnati: St. Anthony Messenger Press, 2001), page 154. Copyright © 2001 by St. Anthony Messenger Press.

"Prayer to the Holy Spirit" on page 99 and the prayers, devotions, and illustration on pages 380–387 of the Catholic Quick Facts appendix are taken directly or adapted from *Handbook for Today's Catholic,* a Redemptorist Pastoral Publication (Liguori, MO: Liguori Publications, 1994). Copyright © 1994 by Liguori Publications. Used with permission of Liguori Publications, Liguori, MO 63057-9999. No other reproduction of this material is permitted.

The excerpt from Pope John Paul II's 1996 World Youth Day message on page 103 is taken from *Renewing the Vision: A Framework for Catholic Youth Ministry,* by the United States Conference of Catholic Bishops' Department of Education (Washington: USCCB, 1997), page 49. Copyright © 1997 by the USCCB.

The prayer on page 116 is from the World Council of Churches Web site, *www.wcc-coe.org/wcc/what/faith/wop2002.html*, accessed June 27, 2002. Used with permission.

The excerpts from Valeen Schnurr and Cassie Bernall on page 129 are from *She Said Yes: The Unlikely Martyrdom of Cassie Bernall*, by Misty Bernall (New York: Pocket Books, a division of Simon and Schuster, 1999), page ix. Copyright © 1999 by Misty Bernall.

The excerpt from Saint Ignatius on page 131 is from *The Liturgy of the Hours: According to the Roman Rite*, volume 4, English translation prepared by the International Commission on English in the Liturgy (New York: Catholic Book Publishing Co., 1976), pages 1490–1491. Illustrations and arrangement copyright © 1975 by the Catholic Book Publishing Co.

"Saint Patrick's Breastplate," paraphrased by Cecil Frances Alexander, on page 153 is from *www.ccel.org/p/patrick/confession/confession.html*, accessed July 18, 2002.

The excerpt by Helen Keller on pages 154–155 is from *The Story of My Life*, by Helen Keller (New York: Grosset and Dunlap, 1905) n.p.

The blessing prayer on page 159 is from *Rite of Christian Initiation of Adults*, study edition, prepared by the International Commission on English in the Liturgy and Bishops' Committee on the Liturgy (Chicago: Liturgy Training Publications, 1988), page 134. Copyright © 1988 by the Archdiocese of Chicago. All rights reserved. Used with permission of ICEL.

The quote by Saint Teresa of Ávila on page 173 is taken from *The Catholic Family Prayer Book,* edited by Jacquelyn Lindsay (Huntington, IN: Our Sunday Visitor Publishing Division, 2001). Copyright © 2001 by Our Sunday Visitor Publishing Division. This quote was found at the Our Sunday Visitor Web site, *www.osvpublishing.com/whatthechurchteaches/prayingforpeace/prayerssaints.asp,* accessed July 26, 2002.

The quote by Oscar Romero on page 173 is from *A Martyr's Message of Hope: Six Homilies by Archbishop Oscar Romero* (Kansas City: Celebration Books, 1981), page 166, as quoted in *A Eucharist Sourcebook,* compiled by J. Robert Baker and Barbara Budde (Chicago: Liturgy Training Publications, 1999), page 53. Copyright © 1999 by the Archdiocese of Chicago.

The quote by Saint Augustine on page 173 is from *www.artsci.villanova.edu/dsteelman/augustine/days/0610.html,* accessed July 26, 2002.

The excerpt from the U.S. Catholic bishops on page 175 is from *Built of Living Stones: Art, Architecture, and Worship,* numbers 16 and 17, at *www.usccb.org/liturgy/livingstones.htm #preface,* accessed October 18, 2002. Copyright © 2000 by USCCB, Inc., Washington, DC. All rights reserved. Used with permission.

The excerpts from the liturgy of the Eucharist on page 180 are from *Peoples Mass Book,* edited by Nicholas T. Freund, Betty Zins Reiber, and Jeanne H. Schmidt (Schiller Park, IL: World Library Publications, 1984), page 264. Copyright © 1984 by World Library Publications.

The English translation of the prayer on page 185, "Prayer of the Penitent," from *The Rite of Penance;* and the divine praises on page 319 are from *Catholic Household Blessings and Prayers,* pages 250 and 334–335. Copyright © 1974 by the ICEL. All rights reserved. Used with permission.

The excerpt from Pope John Paul II's *Dilecti Amici* on page 209 is reprinted by permission of *L'Osservatore Romano.*

The examination of conscience questions on page 210 are adapted from *The Rites of the Catholic Church,* volume one, prepared by the International Commission on English in the Liturgy, a Joint Commission of Catholic Bishops' Conferences (Collegeville, MN: Liturgical Press, a Pueblo Book, 1990), pages 625–628. Copyright © 1976, 1990 by Pueblo Publishing Co. All rights reserved. Used with permission.

The prayer by Theresa Vonderwell on page 215 is from *More Dreams Alive: Prayers by Teenagers,* edited by Carl Koch (Winona, MN: Saint Mary's Press, 1995), page 28. Copyright © 1995 by Saint Mary's Press.

The excerpt by Dorothy Day on page 219 is from *Dorothy Day Selected Writings: By Little and By Little,* edited by Robert Ellsberg (Maryknoll, NY: Orbis Books, 1992), page 98. Copyright © 1983, 1992 by Robert Ellsberg and Tamar Hennessey.

The excerpt by Cardinal Joseph Bernardin on page 261 is from *A Moral Vision for America,* by Joseph Cardinal Bernardin, edited by John P. Langan, SJ (Washington: Georgetown University Press, 1998), page 157. Copyright © 1998 by Georgetown University Press.

The excerpt by Pope John Paul II on page 267 is from the papal encyclical *Role of the Christian Family,* 1981, number 12, at *www.vatican.va/holy_father/john_paul_ii/apost_exhortations/documents/hf_jp-ii_exh_19811122_familiaris-consortio_en.html,* accessed October 28, 2002.

The excerpt from the Vatican Council II document *Gaudium et Spes,* number 48, on page 267 is from *Vatican Council II: The Conciliar and Postconciliar Documents,* volume 1, new revised edition, Austin Flannery, general editor (Northport, NY: Costello Publishing Co., 1996), page 950.

The prayer on page 271 is from the National Federation for Catholic Youth Ministry (NFCYM) True Love Waits program Web site, *www.nfcym.org/2001/programs/tlw_prayers.html,* accessed July 19, 2002. Copyright © 2001 by the NFCYM. Used with permission.

The statistics about teens' sexual behavior on page 272 are from the article "Youths' Essays Urge Peers to Delay Sex," by Helena Oliviero, in the *Atlanta Journal-Constitution,* July 15, 2002.

Robert Fulghum's simple insights for living on page 276 are paraphrased from his book *All I Really Needed to Know I Learned in Kindergarten: Uncommon Thoughts on Common Things* (New York: Ivy Books, 1988). Copyright © 1986, 1988 by Robert L. Fulghum.

The statistics about hunger on pages 278–279 are from the Bread for the World Web site, *www.bread.org/hungerbasics/index.html,* accessed July 17, 2002.

The statistic about slavery on page 282 is from the Anti-slavery: today's fight for tomorrow's freedom Web site at *www.antislavery.org/archive/press/pressRelease2002-UNmeeting.htm,* accessed July 18, 2002. Used with permission.

The statistics about advertising on page 283 are from *Deadly Persuasion: Why Women and Girls Must Fight the Addictive Power of Advertising,* by Jean Kilbourne (New York: Free Press, 1999), page 58. Copyright © 1999 by Jean Kilbourne.

The excerpt from Madaleva Wolf on page 284 is from *Simpson's Contemporary Quotations,* page 191, as quoted in *Remarkable Women, Remarkable Wisdom: A Daybook of Reflections,* by Sr. Mary Francis Gangloff (Cincinnati: St. Anthony Messenger Press, 2001), page 306. Copyright © 2001 by Sr. Mary Francis Gangloff.

The excerpts from the U.S. Catholic bishops on page 284 are from *Economic Justice for All: Pastoral Letter on Catholic Social Teaching and the U.S. Economy,* by the United States Conference of Catholic Bishops (USCCB) (Washington, DC: USCCB, 1986), numbers 49, 50, 87, and 90, respectively. Copyright © 1986 by the USCCB.

The excerpt from Pope Paul VI's World Day for Peace message on page 284 was found at *www.vatican.va/ holy_father/paul_vi/messages/peace/documents/hf_p-vi_mes_ 19711208_v-world-day-for-peace_en.html,* accessed October 28, 2002.

The quote from the U.S. Catholic bishops on page 287 is from their Web site *www.usccb.org/comm./renewingeng.htm,* accessed July 23, 2002. The suggestions to youth regarding the media are adapted from the information found on their Web site *www.usccb.org/comm/pledge.htm,* accessed July 24, 2002.

The quote by Sir Walter Scott on page 288 is from *www.brainyquote.com/quotes/quotes/s/q118003.html,* accessed July 19, 2002.

The quote from Saint Dominic on page 289 is from *www.op-stjoseph.org/dominic/index.htm,* accessed July 24, 2002.

The excerpt from the Code of Canon Law, number 983, paragraph 1, and the information about Saint John Nepomucene on page 292 are from *The Compass* Web site, *www.thecompassnews.org/compass/2002-03-15/02cn0315f1.htm,* accessed July 24, 2002.

The quote by James A. Garfield on page 292 is from *www.brainyquote.com/quotes/quotes/j/q140609.html,* accessed September 5, 2002.

The excerpt by Pope John Paul II on the occasion of World Youth Day VIII on page 296 is from *www.vatican.va/ holy_father/john_paul_ii/messages/youth/documents/hf_jp-ii_mes_ 15081992_viii-world-youth-day_en.html,* accessed July 26, 2002.

The excerpt from Saint Thérèse of Lisieux on page 315 is from her book *Story of a Soul,* translated by Fr. John Clarke (Washington: ICS Publications, 1976), page 165. Copyright © 1976 by the Washington Province of Discalced Carmelites.

The excerpt from *The Interior Castle,* by Teresa of Ávila, on page 329 is quoted in *A Treasury of Catholic Reading,* edited by John Chapin (New York: Farrar, Straus and Co., 1957), at *www.cin.org/7thmans.html,* accessed July 24, 2002.

The quote from Cardinal Hans Urs von Balthasar on page 332 is from his book *Prayer,* at the *U.S. Catholic* Web site, *www.uscatholic.org/1997/02/cov9702.htm,* accessed September 11, 2002.

The excerpt from the Rule of Benedict, chapter 53, on page 341 is from *www.osb.org/rb/text/rbeaad1.html,* accessed July 24, 2002.

The article "Why Sunday Mass Is Important to Me" on page 343 is used with permission of the author, Kari Heltemes.

The quote by Clare of Assisi on page 349 is from *The Sun and Moon Over Assisi: A Personal Encounter with Francis and Clare,* by Gerard Thomas Straub (Cincinnati: St. Anthony Messenger Press, 2000), page 396. Copyright © 2000 by Gerard Thomas Straub.

The information about the seven traditional hours of the liturgy on page 351 is based on *The Complete Idiot's Guide to Understanding Catholicism,* by Bob O'Gorman, PhD, and Mary Faulkner, MA (Indianapolis: Alpha Books, 2000), pages 193–194. Copyright © 2000 by Bob O'Gorman and Mary Faulkner.

The first quote by Mother Teresa on page 355 is from *Mother Teresa: In My Own Words,* compiled by José Luis González-Balado (New York: Gramercy Books, 1996), page xiii. Copyright © 1996 by José Luis González-Balado.

The second quote by Mother Teresa on page 355 is from *A Simple Path,* compiled by Lucinda Vardey (New York: Ballantine Books, 1995), page 8. Copyright © 1995 by Mother Teresa.

The excerpt from the paraphrase of the Lord's Prayer by Saint Francis of Assisi on page 358 is from *www.cwo.com/ ~pentrack/catholic/francis1.html,* accessed July 5, 2002. The more modern paraphrase of Saint Francis's prayer is taken from *Gathered at Table in Prayer and Song,* by Edward F. Gabriele (Winona, MN: Saint Mary's Press, 2000), page 25. All rights reserved.

The statistics about hunger on page 363 are from the Bread for the World Web site, *www.bread.org/hungerbasics/ international.html,* accessed July 22, 2002.

The excerpt from the prayer of exorcism on page 369 is from the English translation of *The Rite of Baptism for Children,* prepared by the International Commission on English in the Liturgy (New York: Catholic Book Publishing Co., 1969), page 34. Copyright © 1985–1974 by Catholic Book Publishing Co., New York. Used with permission.

To view copyright terms and conditions for Internet materials cited here, log on to the home pages for the referenced Web sites.

Endnotes Cited in Quotations from the *Catechism of the Catholic Church*, Second Edition

Chapter 2

1. Pius XII, *Humani Generis,* 561: Denzinger-Schönmetzer, *Enchiridion Symbolorum, definitionum et declarationum de rebus fidei et morum* (1965) 3875.[13]

Chapter 3

1. *Ad gentes* 7; cf. *Heb* 11:6; *1 Cor* 9:16.[338]

2. *Lumen gentium* 16; cf. Denzinger-Schönmetzer, *Enchiridion Symbolorum, definitionum et declarationum de rebus fidei et morum* (1965) 3866–3872.[337]

Chapter 4

1. Cf. *2 Sam* 7:14; *Ps* 68:6.[62]

Chapter 11

1. St. Augustine, *Sermo* 268, 4: J. P. Migne, ed., Patrologia Latina (Paris: 1841–1855) 38, 1231D.[243]

Chapter 17

1. Cf. *Roman Ritual,* Rite of Confirmation *(Ordo confirmationis),* Introduction 1.[89]

Chapter 19

1. *Ordo paenitentiae* 46: formula of absolution.[48]

Chapter 22

1. Cf. *Gaudium et spes* 26 § 2.[28]

Chapter 23

1. St. Thomas Aquinas, *Dec. praec.* I.[8]

Chapter 24

1. St. John Chrysostom, *De incomprehensibili* 3, 6: J. P. Migne, ed., Patrologia Graeca (Paris, 1857–1866) 48, 725.[116]

Chapter 26

1. John Paul II, *Evangelium vitae* 56.[68]

Chapter 27

1. *Familiaris consortio* 84.[161]

Chapter 30

1. St. Thomas Aquinas, Summa Theologiae II–II, 47, 2.[67]
2. St. Augustine, *De natura et gratia,* 31: J. P. Migne, ed.,
   Patrologia Latina (Paris: 1841–1855) 44, 264.[51]

Chapter 33

1. St. John Chrysostom, *Ecloga de oratione* 2: J. P. Migne,
   ed., Patrologia Graeca (Paris, 1857–1866) 63, 585.[2]

Chapter 34

1. *Dei Verbum* 25; cf. *Phil* 3:8; St. Ambrose, *De officiis
   ministrorum* 1, 20, 88: J. P. Migne, ed., Patrologia Latina
   (Paris: 1841–1855) 16, 50.[4]

Chapter 35

1. St. John Chrysostom, *Ecloga de oratione* 2: J. P. Migne,
   ed., Patrologia Graeca (Paris, 1857–1866) 63, 585.[37]

Chapter 37

1. Attributed to St. Ignatius Loyola, cf. Joseph de Guibert, SJ,
   The Jesuits: Their Spiritual Doctrine and Practice, (Chicago:
   Loyola University Press, 1964), 148, n. 55.[122]
2. Origen, *De orat.* 29: J. P. Migne, ed., Patrologia Graeca
   (Paris, 1857–1866) 11, 544CD.[155]

Endnotes Cited in Quotations from *Built of Living Stones*, Numbers 16–17

Chapter 18

1. *Rite of Dedication of a Church and an Altar,* chapter 2,
   number 1 (*Documents on the Liturgy, 1963–1979: Conciliar,
   Papal, and Curial Texts* 547, number 4369): "Rightly, then,
   from early times 'church' has also been the name given to
   the building in which the Christian community gathers
   to hear the word of God, to pray together, to receive the
   sacraments, and to celebrate the eucharist."[13]
2. Cf. *CCC,* number 2691: The church, the house of God,
   is the proper place for the liturgical prayer of the parish
   community. It is also the privileged place for adoration of
   the real presence of Christ in the Blessed Sacrament. The
   choice of a favorable place is not a matter of indifference for
   true prayer." Cf. *Rite of Dedication of a Church and an Altar,*
   TC, number 6.[14]

Endnotes Cited in Quotations from *The Harvest of Justice Is Sown in Peace*

Chapter 26

1. National Conference of Catholic Bishops, *Human Life in our Day* (Washington, D.C.: USCC Office for Publishing and Promotion Services, 1968), nos. 143–153.
2. Archbishop John Roach, "Letter to Secretary of Defense Richard Cheney," October 23, 1991, Origins 21:22 (November 7, 1991), 352.

Endnotes Cited in Quotations from *Role of the Christian Family*, Number 12

Chapter 27

1. Cf. e.g., Hos. 2:21; Jer. 3:6–13; Is. 54

Endnotes Cited in Quotations from *Gaudium et Spes*, Number 48

Chapter 27

1. Cf. Pius XI, encyclical letter Casti Connubii: *Acta Apostolicae Sedis* 22 (1930), pp. 546–547; Denzinger-Schönmetzer 3706.[2]

Endnotes Cited in Quotations from *Economic Justice for All*, Number 87

Chapter 28

1. On the recent use of this term see: Congregation for the Doctrine of the Faith, *Instruction on Christian Freedom and Liberation*, 46–50, 66–68; *Evangelization in Latin America's Present and Future*, Final Document of the Third General Conference of the Latin American Episcopate (Puebla, Mexico, January 27–February 13, 1979), esp. part VI, ch. 1, "A Preferential Option for the Poor," in J. Eagleson and P. Scharper, eds., *Puebla and Beyond* (Maryknoll: Orbis Books, 1979), 264–267; Donal Dorr, *Option for the Poor: A Hundred Years of Vatican Social Teaching* (Dublin: Gill and Macmillan/Maryknoll, N.Y.: Orbis Books, 1983).

Endnotes Cited in Quotations from *Dei Verbum*, number 25

Chapter 34
1. Second Council of Orange, Canon 7: Denzinger 180 (377);
   First Vatican Council, loc. cit.: Denzinger 1791 (3010).[5]

Photo and Art Credits

Chapter and part opening page images are from PhotoDisc.

AFP/CORBIS: page 364
Haitian painting by Gabriel Alix, courtesy of Galerie
    Macondo, Pittsburgh, PA, *www.artshaitian.com:* page 49
AP/Wide World Photos: pages 8, 112, 221, 256, 354
Archives Charmet/Private Collection/Bridgeman Art Library:
    page 70, 129
Archivo Iconografico, S.A./CORBIS: pages 268, 340
Rudolfo Arellano, Solentiname, Nicaragua, courtesy of
    Hermann Schulz and Father Ernesto Cardenal: page 68
© 2003 Artists Rights Society (ARS), New York/ADAGP,
    Paris. Photo courtesy of Archives Charmet/Private
    Collection/Bridgeman Art Library: page 298
The Barnes Foundation, Merion Station, PA/CORBIS:
    page 279
Dave Bartruff/CORBIS: page 160
"Wise Men from the East," by Agha Behzad, courtesy of Stony
    Point Center, Stony Point, NY: page 60
Bettmann/CORBIS: pages 106, 166, 222, 243, 262
Birmingham Museums and Art Gallery/Bridgeman Art
    Library: page 16
St. Edith Stein © Lu Bro/Bridge Building Images/
    www.BridgeBuilding.com: page 212
Burstein Collection/CORBIS: pages 88, 126
Catholic News Service: page 250
Macduff Everton/CORBIS: page 325
Giraudon/Art Resource, NY: page 282
Hamburg Kunsthalle, Hamburg, Germany/Bridgeman Art
    Library: page 35

With many thanks to Bishop Bernard Harrington and his staff:
   page 338
Hessisches Landesmuseum, Darmstadt, Germany/Bridgeman
   Art Library: page 368
Painting by Jeanne Hollington: page 272
The Jewish Museum of New York/Art Resource, NY: pages 22,
   229
Lauros/Giraudon/Private Collection/Bridgemen Art Library:
   page 287
Lisette Le Bon/SuperStock: page 202
Danny Lehman/CORBIS: page 337
Julian of Norwich © 1995 Robert Lentz/Bridge Building
   Images/*www.BridgeBuilding.com:* page 46
Erich Lessing/Art Resource, NY: pages 77, 214
Araldo de Luca/CORBIS: page 321
LWA-Dann Tardif/CORBIS: page 266
Ben Mangor/SuperStock: cover
Francis G. Mayer/CORBIS: page 230
Musée des Beaux-Arts, Orleans, France/Giraudon/Bridgeman
   Art Library: page 240
Musée du Louvre, Paris/SuperStock: page 54
Museo di San Marco dell'Angelico, Florence, Italy/Bridgeman
   Art Library: pages 26, 288
The Pierpont Morgan Library/Art Resource, NY: page 24
Plaisted, Gene, The Crosiers: pages 80, 93, 96, 152, 188, 195
Private Collection/Bridgeman Art Library: page 79
Réunion des Musées Nationaux/Art Resource, NY: pages 84,
   308, 366
Reuters NewMedia Inc./CORBIS: page 260
Photo by Br. Emile Rousset, printed by Limet, Paris: page 198
Saint Mary's Press: page 9
Santa Maria del Popolo, Rome, Italy/A.K.G.,
   Berlin/SuperStock: page 316
Chuck Savage/CORBIS: page 277
Scala/Art Resource, NY: pages 86, 130, 174, 184, 237, 312,
   328, 348, 356
Courtesy of the Sisters of the Blessed Sacrament, Bensalem,
   PA: page 176
Sistine Chapel, Vatican/Canali Photobank Milan/SuperStock:
   page 43

Courtesy of Smith College Museum of Art, Northampton, MA. Gift of Mr. and Ms. Anthony L. Michel (Sarah Prescott, class of 1930): page 58

Sonia Halliday Photographs: pages 28, 38, 72, 108, 120, 156, 163

Sonia Halliday Photographs and Laura Lushington: pages 66, 101, 142

SuperStock: pages 200, 208, 217, 248, 254

Prat Thierry/CORBIS SYGMA: page 346

W. P. Wittman Limited: pages 103, 118, 119, 136, 137, 148, 158, 169, 178, 180, 190, 305, 307, 334, 344

8/5 (15) 1/13